MEASUREMENT IN TODAY'S SCHOOLS

PRENTICE-HALL, INC., *Englewood Cliffs, N. J.*

FOURTH EDITION

MEASUREMENT

IN TODAY'S SCHOOLS

JULIAN C. STANLEY

Departments of Education and Psychology
The Johns Hopkins University

PRENTICE-HALL INTERNATIONAL, INC., *London*

PRENTICE-HALL OF AUSTRALIA, PTY., LTD., *Sydney*

PRENTICE-HALL OF CANADA, LTD., *Toronto*

PRENTICE-HALL OF INDIA PVT., LTD., *New Delhi*

PRENTICE-HALL OF JAPAN, INC., *Tokyo*

C-56830

Current printing (last digit):
13 12 11 10 9 8 7

TO ROSE AND SUZY

PREFACE

This fourth edition of *Measurement in Today's Schools* comes 23 years after C. C. Ross's first edition, 17 years after his second edition, and 10 years after my third edition. (Dr. Ross, a professor of education at the University of Kentucky, died in 1948.) Like previous editions, the fourth is a basic textbook for measurement and evaluation courses. No specific background in education, psychology, or statistics is required to understand it.

The present edition contains 11 revised and rearranged chapters, six fewer than the third edition, but is not appreciably shorter. Much of it, such as all of Chapters Five, Nine, and Eleven ("Characteristics of a Satisfactory Measuring Instrument," "Self-Reports and Reports by Others," and "Grading, Reporting, and Promoting"), is new. The presentation has been modernized, made less "folksy," and largely freed from dependence on long quotations.

With considerable assistance from Andrew B. Crider, I have incorporated new historical and and theoretical material into Chapter Two, "Historical Development of Measurement," to substitute for the third-edition Chapters One and Two. This treatment is meant to be systematic and concise, and interesting enough to make the student want to read further in the references cited.

By omitting obsolescent "arbitrary-origin" computing methods from Chapter Three, "Analyzing Test Results," it proved possible to simplify the statistical instruction considerably (not a single summation sign appears in that chapter!) and yet to include several new topics, such as stanines and the computation of percentile ranks. Gene V. Glass labored with me to make this key chapter correct, learnable, and teachable.

The new Chapter Four, "Graphical Representation, Norms, and Applications," replaces and updates the former Chapters Nine and Ten. Notice especially the applications of norms in the last part of the chapter.

Concepts of reliability and validity have changed so much since 1941—or even since 1953, when the third edition went to press—that the present Chapter Five, "Characteristics of a Satisfactory Measuring Instrument," differs radically (except for the title) from the former Chapter Four. It is more in the spirit of the APA-AERA-NCME technical recommendations.

Chapters Six and Seven explain in illustrated detail how to construct different types of objective tests. I am especially indebted to Harry D. Berg, William J. McIlrath, and Jason Millman for materials that helped me to expand and revise the item-writing sections considerably.

Chapter Eight, on essay testing, incorporates some recent findings from the perpetual quest to improve the reliability and validity of such tests.

Chapter Nine, "Self-Reports and Reports by Others," had no counterpart in the third edition. It amplifies those parts of Chapter Two that deal with the

history of ratings and observations, as when Thurstone's "Attitude Toward
the Movies" scale is illustrated in the former chapter and the procedure for constructing his "Attitude Toward the Church" scale is studied in the latter. Empirical keying, judgmental keying, sociometric techniques, personality inventories, and similar topics complement the three preceding chapters.

Chapter Ten, "The Testing Program," is a modernized version of the former Chapter Eight.

The title of Chapter Eleven, "Grading, Reporting, and Promoting," sounds
a little like that of the former Chapter Thirteen ("Classification and Promotion"), but there the resemblance ends. This short concluding chapter gives
the teacher practical help with important aspects of school practice and rein-
forces certain principles stated earlier.

The ten appendixes include the former six, revised and reordered, plus four
new ones: a rank-order correlation table that was in the body of the third edition, the classified objectives for a unit in algebra, an illustrative sta-eleven
frequency distribution, and a table for converting the percentile ranks 1, 2, . . . ,
99 into z-scores for a normal distribution.

What, then, was deleted? Reviewers had agreed that Part IV of the third
edition, consisting of Chapters Eleven through Seventeen and called "Measurement in Instruction," was suitable for methods or curriculum courses, but not
essential for a basic measurement text. A number of the points covered in those
seven chapters were incorporated into the present edition, but many were
dropped in order to permit fuller development of measurement and evaluation
principles.

An author incurs many debts for assistance during the course of a revision
such as this. It is not possible to list all the persons who have contributed to it,

but besides those four mentioned above special thanks are due Clinton I. Chase, Elinor Elfner, David Freund, Scarvia Grant, Charlotte Holmes, and John M. Newell for valuable comments. Martin Greene of Prentice-Hall constantly helped improve the clarity of the text; without his insightful suggestions, the writing would have been much less intelligible. A number of publishers and individuals, cited in the text, generously permitted me to reproduce their tabular or graphic material.

To my wife and daughter, who patiently bore my neglect of them while I was preparing the manuscript, I dedicate this book.

Julian C. Stanley

CONTENTS

TABLES

FIGURES

MEASUREMENT IN TODAY'S SCHOOLS

MEASUREMENT AND EVALUATION PERMEATE SCHOOLS

All of us know how widely various "measures"—e.g., tests of achievement, intelligence, and aptitude—are used in our schools. Are we equally aware how greatly schools depend on a related procedure called *evaluation?* Throughout this book, we shall use the word "evaluation" *to designate summing-up processes in which value judgments play a large part,* as in grading and promoting students. We shall consider the administration and scoring of tests as *measurement.* Interpreting such scores, i.e., saying whether they are good or bad for a specific purpose, is evaluation.

A familiar, simple illustration may help clarify the distinction between measurement and evaluation. Miss Roe gives her class a spelling test consisting of 37 words. (Devising, administering, and scoring the spelling test can, for convenience, be considered measurement, by an analogy with physical measurement that we shall discuss in Chapter Two.) She finds that the number of words spelled correctly ranges from 8 to 37, the average number correct being 24.

But will Miss Roe stop here? The mother of one of her pupils may ask, "How *well* is David doing in spelling?" Miss Roe may show her his paper and explain that he spelled 25 words correctly out of 37 on the test last Friday. David's mother may press for—in effect, demand—an evaluation of the measurement (score of 25) by replying: "Twelve words wrong! Is that as terrible as it sounds?"

If Miss Roe answers, "More than half the pupils missed a greater number than he," she is still confining her remarks to the distribution of scores on the test—that is, staying within the area we are calling measurement. If, however, she agrees that 25 is indeed a "poor" score or insists that in view of his limited verbal ability David is spelling about as well as can be expected, Miss Roe is evaluating the score.

We shall consider the assigning to test scores of grades such as A, B, C, D, F, or "Excellent," "Good," "Fair," "Poor," or "High," "Average," "Low" as evaluation rather than measurement, because value judgments are made. But, you say, both measurement and evaluation, as here defined, involve value judgments. Indeed they do, but measurement does to a lesser extent and usually in advance of the scoring of the test. Selecting items, devising a scoring key for them, and setting up norm groups require test constructors to make many choices. The tester, however, may use the scoring key mechanically to obtain scores. Whether a student's score is good or bad for a given purpose cannot be determined solely from the score itself. An interpretation must be made, usually in terms of fixed standards such as 80-89 per cent right equals *B,* or in terms of the student's rank on the test in his class or his rank in relationship to his estimated potential for learning.

This is an elementary level of evaluation. It is simpler than evaluating a curriculum or helping Joe decide on the basis of all available evidence, including test scores and teacher judgments, whether he "should" study to be a dentist.

It may be helpful to note that rather great value judgments often occur in assigning "scores" to themes, rating students, and the like, procedures for which the scorer has no prearranged set of answers, exactly the same for every paper being marked. As we shall see throughout the book, distinctions between measurement and evaluation, though usually clarifying, are not always sharp or meaningful. A little subjectivity occurs in even the most objective measurement, such as that of height, as in deciding how hard to press down on hair. Likewise, it is often both possible and desirable to make more objective essay testing, interviewing, rating, and similar enterprises frequently pursued quite subjectively. In fact, *increasing objectivity of carrying out and interpreting evaluative procedures is one of the chief aims of this book.*

EDUCATIONAL DECISIONS
FOUNDED ON EVALUATION
If one views "tests and measurements" narrowly as the preparing, administering, scoring, and norming[1] of objective tests, he is likely to overlook important ways in which evaluation supports our whole educational system. Why do we have schools at all? Obviously, because society has decided that without them many people would probably not acquire essential knowledge, understanding, skills, and attitudes. Schools are organized the way they are because society has concluded, on the basis of much experience, that current patterns "work best" now. Why is a particular school built where it is, the size it is, and with certain facilities? Why are some teachers hired to staff it, others not? What determines salaries, choice of textbooks and other instructional aids, grades, promotions, reporting to parents, ability grouping, the community's reactions to the school and its products, recommendations for college and for jobs? All involve evaluations. Objective measurement is usually one essential prerequisite for sound evaluation, but by no means sufficient.

Most educators consider that a school's main business is promoting "growth" toward desirable individual and societal objectives; fewer agree as to who should judge the desirability of these objectives. However, since all schools focus on pupil progress as the ultimate criterion, it is important to evaluate status and gains of pupils expertly. How well are Mary and Paul doing? Should they be doing better?

Measurement and evaluation encompass such subjective aspects as the judgments made by teachers and administrators. Let us not fall into the trap of asking which one we should use, teacher judgments *or* test scores. Faced

---

[1] "Norms" are tables of standards, such as percentile ranks or standard scores, for comparing a student's score with the scores of other students.

by complex problems of measurement and evaluation of pupil growth and influences affecting it, one cannot reject any promising resource. Various sorts of
information *supplement* each other.

ESSENTIAL KNOWLEDGE AND SKILLS

What do school personnel have to know about
measurement and evaluation, and what abili-
ties do they need in this area? Of course, the answers depend somewhat on the
position held. Teachers of kindergarten and primary grades differ in this
respect from high-school teachers of physics and chemistry. Principals and
school psychologists need certain competencies not essential for teachers. To
be effective, a college dean must have knowledge and abilities specific to his
duties. Similarly, college teachers will have different orientations with respect
to measurement and evaluation than will their counterparts in the junior high
school.

Fortunately, *certain concepts, principles, and skills prove useful at all levels* and in nearly all positions. Even parents and others not professionally concerned would benefit from a clear understanding of such concepts as "validity"
and "reliability." By concentrating on fundamental ideas and skills, we present
in one basic textbook the *essentials* for most teachers. These fundamentals
are carefully illustrated with materials from various age and grade levels. No
single book can present all specialized phases of measurement and evaluation,
but it should try, as *Measurement in Today's Schools* does, to refer the reader to
good supplemental sources.

Teachers must know how to carry out certain aspects of measurement and
evaluation themselves, such as constructing tests, preparing sociograms, giving
grades, and assessing potentialities.

They should know how to select from among the many available tests, inventories, questionnaires, rating scales, check lists, and the like those most
suitable for a particular purpose. Besides being able to understand directions
for administering, scoring, and interpreting tests, teachers should possess the
higher ability to compare the most promising ones before the choice itself is
made. This requires attaining various concepts necessary to understand test
publishers' literature, reviews, and articles reporting test research. *Measurement in Today's Schools* is designed to help you in the direction of this important objective.

PLAN OF THE BOOK

We hope that this book will contribute to your
thinking and actions. You should finish it
with more *knowledge* about the special concepts and principles of measurement
and evaluation than you may now possess, but not sheer memorization without
comprehension. You will learn to *apply* your knowledge to new problems that

confront you, to *analyze* situations efficiently, to *synthesize* (put ideas together creatively) well, and to *evaluate* soundly on the basis of internal evidence (for example, within a test itself) and outside information (for instance, published standards for tests).[2]

What you do with this book is important only to the extent that it permits the book to *change* you. Your altered thoughts and actions are the sole objectives of instruction. Your continuous increase in measurement competence over the years following the first use of *Measurement in Today's Schools* is the ultimate criterion.

In this chapter you have glimpsed a few of the ways in which measurement and evaluation figure prominently in the educative process. The ideas and operations we have hinted at will get detailed treatment in the following ten chapters.

Measurement in Today's Schools, 4th ed., falls into two main sections: the first five chapters deal with fundamental principles of measurement and evaluation, and the last six chapters are concerned with the construction and use of measuring instruments. In addition, appendixes provide technical material for easy reference during the course and later.

If you use *Measurement in Today's Schools* as a textbook in a course (rather than for private study), your instructor may omit certain chapters, reflecting local needs. The extensive author and subject indexes should help you bridge any discontinuity that might result.

RECOMMENDED READINGS

Ebel, R. L., Improving the competence of teachers in educational measurement, *Clearing House*, 1961, 36, 67–71.

Educational Policies Commission, *The central purpose of American education.* Washington, D.C.: National Education Association, 1961.

Flanagan, J. C., Dailey, J. T., Shaycoft, M. F., Gorham, W. A., Orr, David B., and Goldberg, Isadore, *The talents of American youth. Vol. 1. Design for a study of American youth.* Boston: Houghton Mifflin, 1962.

Gardner, E. F., chairman, Educational and psychological testing, *Review of Educational Research,* 1962, 32, whole February issue, 1–114. There are nine chapters covering general considerations, general mental ability, special aptitude, educational achievement, personality tests and projective techniques, statistical methods applicable to measurement, and creativity.

Harris, C. W., ed., *Encyclopedia of educational research,* 3rd ed. New York: Macmillan, 1960.

---

[2]The six levels, knowledge through evaluation, are explained and illustrated in B.S. Bloom *et al., Taxonomy of educational objectives* (New York: Longmans; Green, 1956). We consider them further in Chapter Six.

Los Angeles County, Calif., *Guiding today's children.*   Los Angeles: California Test Bureau, 1961.

Lyman, H. B., *Test scores and what they mean.* Englewood Cliffs, N. J.: Prentice-Hall, 1963.

HISTORICAL

DEVELOPMENT

OF MEASUREMENT

Measurement and evaluation have played a far more prominent role in human history than is generally recognized. Nor have they been employed only in schools. Actually, some of the earliest records of the use of various testing devices are found in the Bible, although they generally had no reference to education. One illustration will suffice:

"And the Gileadites took the passages of Jordan before the Ephraimites: and it was so, that when those Ephraimites which were escaped said, Let me go over; that the men of Gilead said unto him, Art thou an Ephraimite? If he said, Nay; then said they unto him, Say now **Shibboleth:** and he said **Sibboleth:** for he could not frame to pronounce it right. Then they took him, and slew him at the passages of Jordan: and there fell at that time of the Ephraimites forty and two thousand."[1]

Here indeed is an old "final examination," though in a field other than education. Doubt-

---

[1] *Judges.* Chap. 12, Verses 5-6, King James Version. (Boldface type added.)

less, today's measurement experts would point out that, in spite of its high degree of objectivity, it had certain questionable features: it was oral, it was very short, and the "mortality rate" was excessively high!

The sole test of a man's being a Gileadite was his using the *h* sound in the word *Shibboleth*. Notice that it was a one-question test which yielded for each examinee a score of "right" or "wrong," and that the consequences of failing the exam were rather extreme. It is possible, however, that other paths might have been taken if the Gileadites had different attitudes towards the Ephraimites. This illustrates the fact that measurement is always a means to an end and never an end in itself. The uses made of measurement always depend on the broader contexts of values, goals, and purposes of the measurers. The Gileadites seem to have been satisfied with their examination, although a modern-day tester would have his doubts. Isn't it possible that some true Gileadites failed and some true Ephraimites passed? Isn't it possible that an examiner might have made a wrong judgment on the basis of only one question? These are questions touching on the principles of test validity and reliability.

In education, some form of measurement is inevitable and is, indeed, inherent in the teaching process. Consider the constant evaluative role of the classroom teacher as he goes about determining the degree of scholastic and social growth of pupils in order to make hundreds of major and minor educational decisions each year. And, as we shall see later, measuring devices are also indispensable to the guidance counselor, the school administrator, the curriculum planner, and the professional researcher. In the remainder of this chapter, we will discuss the historical events and practical necessities which determined modern trends in educational measurement, and we will also review the various kinds of tests available and the theoretical concerns involved in their development.

9

FORERUNNERS
OF MODERN MEASUREMENT
IN EDUCATION   *Psychophysics: "Physics of the Mind"*

A turning point in the history of psychology occurred in 1879 when Wilhelm Wundt established the first laboratory for experimental psychology at the University of Leipzig, Germany. The rise of *scientific* psychology, as opposed to the traditional *philosophic* psychology, was intimately related to the use of objective measuring devices. Although Wundt interested himself in questions concerning the physiology of sensory processes, reaction times, and word association, he also inherited and extended the psychological legacy known as "psychophysics."[2] This field had been opened 20 years earlier by another German, Gustav Fechner, who saw in psychophysics "an exact science of the functional relations of the dependency between mind and body."[3] Up to this time, physics had made great progress in measuring such objective attributes as length, weight, time, temperature, and volume. Fechner came to believe that certain purely "mental" or psychological processes, such as sensation, perception, and feeling, could be accurately measured. According to Fechner, scales measuring them would be definitely and mathematically related to the strength of the sensation-producing stimulus under investigation.

For example, a psychophysicist might be interested in developing a scale of brightness as perceived by a person, using units of "just-noticeable-differences" (j.n.d.'s) in the intensity of the source of light the individual sees. Fechner's Law states that the degree of sensation is related to the actual magnitude of the physical stimulus in a certain specific mathematical way.[4] In this case the magnitude of perceived brightness, as measured in j.n.d.'s, should be that mathematical function of the actual intensity of the light, as measured in a physical unit such as candlepower.

Fechner also developed several procedures, now known as "psychophysical methods," for determining units of just-noticeable-differences. His basic law has not gone unscathed over the years, however, and its revision and extension in the light of experimental findings continue to be a lively source of debate among researchers.[5]

---

[2] G. Murphy, *Historical introduction to modern psychology,* rev. ed. (New York: Harcourt, Brace, 1949), pp. 155–156.

[3] As quoted in J. P. Guilford, *Psychometric methods,* 2nd ed. (New York: McGraw-Hill, 1954), p. 3.

[4] E. G. Boring, The beginning and growth of measurement in psychology, *Isis,* 1961, 52 (168), 238–257.

[5] See, for example, Psychophysics: one hundred years after (symposium commemorating the 100th anniversary of the publication of Fechner's *Elemente der Psychophysik*), *Psychometrika,* 1961, 26, 3–63.

In 1927 L. L. Thurstone extended the classical psychophysical measuring operations in his "law of comparative judgment,"[6] which allowed the investigator to "measure" a psychological characteristic such as "attitude toward war" for which no known corresponding physical measure could be obtained. Obviously, you could not weigh an individual's attitude toward war in ounces or measure its length in inches, whereas you could determine how bright the light actually was versus how bright it seemed to the observer.

The new psychophysics asked such questions as "How strong is this man's attitude towards the Negro?" "How good are these essays relative to one another?" "What judgment factors underlie preference for movie stars—beauty? gender? type of role? color of hair?" In order to answer these questions, Thurstone and others abandoned the original physical reference point.

Since the physical intensity aspect of the psychological response was made unnecessary for certain purposes, a new field of *response-response* investigation developed. If responses made on an attitude scale indicated that an individual hated war, what did this suggest about his responses in other areas? Would he have more intensely negative attitudes than a person with neutral feelings toward war? What about his intelligence, his open-mindedness, his needs for love or dominance, his political views? Thus psychology directed some of its efforts away from the development of directional *stimulus-response* laws, where the stimulus produces the response (S → R), in favor of the development of *response-response* relationships (R ↔ R) that do not obviously have directionality.

Galton and the Study
of Human Differences

Coincident with the blossoming of Wundt's experimental psychology laboratory in Leipzig, a slightly different tradition was developing in England under Sir Francis Galton (1822–1911). Although the psychophysicists were interested in determining universal psychological processes and treated the response differences between subjects as so much "experimental error," Galton worked in the intellectual tradition of Darwinian biology, with its emphasis on *variation*, both between and within species. We see in Galton's work the beginnings of a concern for *individual differences*, which have been a keystone in the history of psychological and educational testing. From his "laboratory of anthropometry," established in London in 1882, came studies of topics such as word association, mental imagery, and the genetic basis of genius. To facilitate his research, Galton invented several statistical devices, the most important of which was a graphical method for finding the degree of relationship between two variables (height and weight, for example).[7] As later refined by his colleague, Karl Pearson, this device be-

---

[6]L. L. Thurstone, A law of comparative judgment, *Psychological Review,* 1927, 24, 273–286.
[7]G. Murphy, *op. cit.,* pp. 117–122.

came the now-classic *product-moment coefficient of correlation* (see Chapter Three for a fuller discussion of this technique).

EARLY
SCIENTIFIC MEASUREMENT
IN AMERICAN EDUCATION

Oral questioning dates back to the beginnings of human language. Socrates used it effectively in the fifth century B.C. to "draw out" his students, and until the coming of inexpensive pencils and paper after the middle of the nineteenth century, oral examinations were standard in our schools. Some countries today still require oral final examinations by law.[8] Our own universities harbor vestiges in the form of "thesis orals." From time to time, oral-quiz "giveaway" programs have appeared on radio and television, though the contestants are often chosen in advance by means of written tests. Not until the present century did writing instruments largely replace glib or faltering tongues.

The first important steps toward the scientific use of measurement in education were taken by Horace Mann more than a century ago.[9] This prominent New England educator, famous for his doctrine of free, compulsory, and universal education, had a remarkable understanding both of the importance of examinations and of the limitations of the ones then being used. His penetrating analysis of the weakness of the oral examinations then in vogue and of the superiority of written examinations can hardly be improved by today's specialist in educational measurement. Mann showed clearly where oral examinations were lacking, employing those concepts which have become the cornerstones of today's theories, and which are now known as validity, reliability, and usability. (These concepts are discussed in Chapter Five).

Another American educator who understood both the value and the limitations of examinations was Emerson E. White, educational writer and school administrator. In 1886 he wrote, "It may be stated as a general fact that school instruction and study are never much wider or better than the tests by which they are measured."[10] In the same volume (pages 197–198) he enumerated several "special advantages" of the written test:

> It is more impartial than the oral test, since it gives all the pupils the same tests and an equal opportunity to meet them; its results are more tangible and reliable; it discloses more accurately the comparative progress of the different pupils, information of value to the teacher; it reveals more clearly defects in teaching and study, and thus assists in their correction; it emphasizes more distinctly the im-

---

[8]J. C. Stanley, College studies and college life in Belgium, *College Board Review,* 1960, No. 40, pp. 10–14.

[9]H. Mann, Report of the annual examining committees of the Boston grammar and writing schools, *Common School Journal,* 1845, 7 (21), 326–336.

[10]E. E. White, *The elements of pedagogy* (New York: American Book Company, 1886), p. 148.

portance of accuracy and fullness in the expression of knowledge . . . ; it is at least an equal test of the thought-power or intelligence of pupils. . . .

These views of Mann and White appear surprisingly modern and show how far general practice is apt to fall behind the theory of the pioneer thinker. And even though measurement specialists now tend to shy away from the early enthusiasm for the ordinary written test, pointing out that many of the cited limitations of the oral tests also hold in some degree for written tests, the best thinkers of yesteryear were often far ahead of many persons today.

The actual improvement of existing tests and other measuring instruments has always lagged far behind theory, and school practice has been farthest behind of all. In spite of the marked superiority of written examinations over oral, pointed out by Mann as early as 1845, teachers moved neither to adopt the former nor to improve the latter. It is interesting to note, however, that by 1864 an enterprising English schoolmaster, the Reverend George Fisher, had proposed the widespread use of objective and standardized measures of academic attainment. Reverend Fisher outlined the practice of the new system in his school as follows:[11]

> A book, called the "Scale-Book," has been established, which contains the numbers assigned to each degree of proficiency in the various subjects of examination: for instance, if it be required to determine the numerical equivalent corresponding to any specimen of "writing," a comparison is made with various standard specimens, which are arranged in this book in order of merit; the highest being represented by the number 1, and the lowest by 5, and the intermediate values by affixing to these numbers the fractions 1/4, 1/2, or 3/4. So long as these standard specimens are preserved in the institution, so long will constant numerical values for proficiency in "writing" be maintained. And since facsimiles can be multipled without limit, the same principle might be generally adopted.
>
> The numeral values for "spelling" follow the same order, and are made to depend upon the percentage of mistakes in writing from dictation sentences from works selected for the purpose, examples of which are contained in the "Scale-Book," in order to preserve the same standard of difficulty.
>
> By a similar process, values are assigned for proficiency in mathematics, navigation, Scripture knowledge, grammar, and composition, French, general history, drawing, and practical science, respectively. Questions in each of these subjects are contained in the "Scale-Book," to serve as types, not only of the difficulty, but of the nature of the question, for the sake of future reference . . .

Apparently, Fisher was too far advanced for his times, since his incisive work seems not to have attracted a widespread audience. As Leonard P. Ayres put it, "progress in the scientific study of education was not possible until people could be brought to realize that human behavior was susceptible of

---

[11] From a letter quoted in E. Chadwick, Statistics of educational results, *Museum, A Quarterly Magazine of Education, Literature, and Science,* 1864, 3, 479–484.

quantitative study, and until they had statistical methods with which to carry on their investigations."[12]

Although Ayres felt that Sir Francis Galton's great contributions had largely met these two needs, he credits J. M. Rice with being the "real inventor of the comparative test."[13] A young American ex-physician turned zealous researcher, Rice had studied pedagogy in Germany and had been influenced by experimental psychologists at the Universities of Leipzig and Jena. His great concern for the quality of contemporary education prompted him to conduct two large studies of spelling achievement in various U.S. cities. In each study, he administered his own specially constructed tests to all students under uniform conditions. The volume of his purely personal delving is awesome even in this day of mass research; he secured test results on 13,000 children under his own direction and on 16,000 more by mail, his researches spanning 16 months and 21 cities.[14] Though of course this first approach to test standardization falls somewhat short of modern practice, it promoted Rice's aim of making education more scientific.

The conclusion to his first article on the results of his investigations sets forth the value of what we now call "norms": "Whether or not the spelling in a particular locality is actually below the average can be learned only by comparing the results of an examination conducted *on the same basis* in many localities. By examining children in any one city, on a set of arbitrarily selected words, the question cannot be solved, because the results in other places, on the same list of words, would remain an unknown quantity. A common standard is offered, however, by a ... test such as I have undertaken"[15] (italics added). How obvious to us now, but how radical then!

Far more than just a tester, Rice was a pioneer in what later came to be known as progressive education. He was, during the years 1891–1899, a relentless investigator of American education, publishing a series of 20 articles in the *Forum,* a leading literary magazine. The educational leaders of the time were anything but cordial to him, and for many years little progress was made beyond Rice's own work.

If Ayres credits him with the invention of educational measurement, he awards the title, "father of the educational testing movement," to Edward L. Thorndike. During his distinguished and prolific career at Columbia's Teachers College, Thorndike was concerned with many phases of the measurement movement. In addition to his very influential publications on statistical methods in education and his pioneer work on college entrance intelligence tests,

---

[12]L. P. Ayres, History and present status of educational measurements, *Seventeenth Yearbook of the National Society for the Study of Education, Part II* (Bloomington, Ill.: Public School Publishing Company, 1918), p. 10.

[13]*Ibid.,* p. 11.

[14]J. M. Rice, The futility of the spelling grind: I, *Forum,* 1897, 23, 163–172.

[15]*Ibid.,* p. 172. See also J. M. Rice, The futility of the spelling grind: II, *Forum,* 1897, 23, 409–419.

Thorndike and his students were responsible for nearly all of the early stand-ard achievement tests and scales. The year 1910 saw the publication of the Thorndike Handwriting Scale,[16] the first of its kind. It consisted of formal writing samples of children in grades five through eight, arranged in an equal-unit, 15-category scale of increasing quality (see Figure 2-1). Two years earlier

---

[16] E. L. Thorndike, Handwriting, *Teachers College Record,* 1910, 11 (2), 83–175.

Figure 2-1 *Excellent, average and poor handwriting. (From E. L. Thorndike,* Handwriting. *New York: Teachers College, Columbia University, 1910.)*

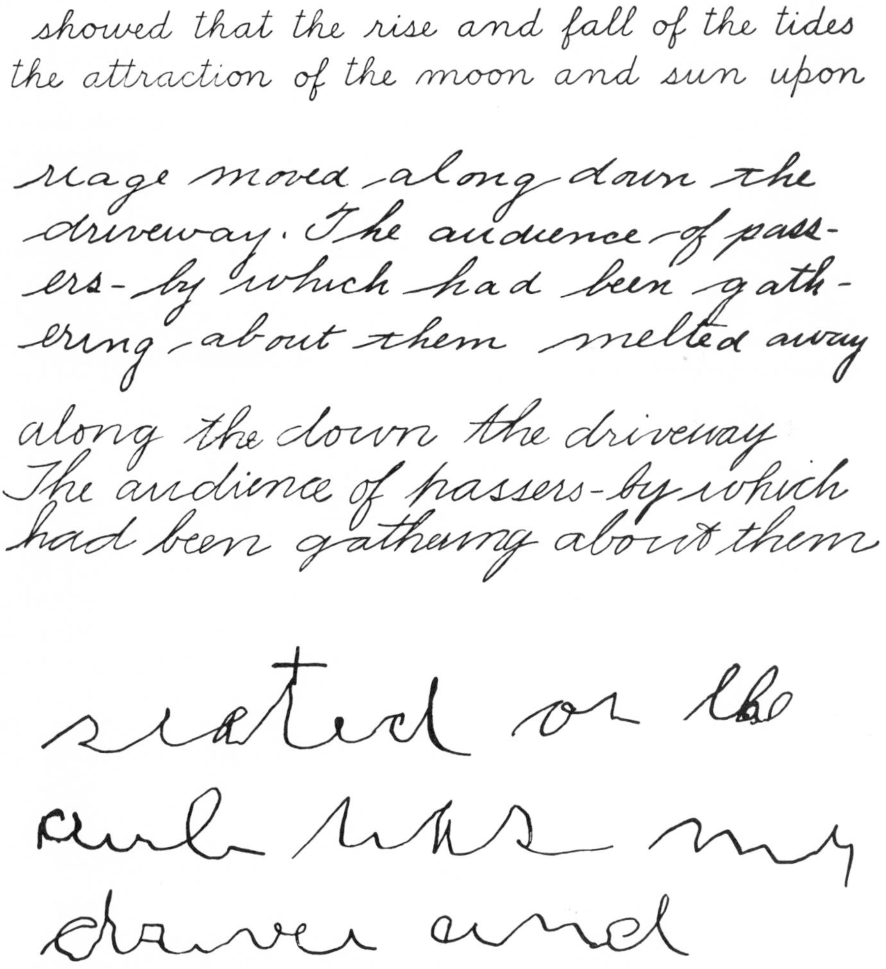

Stone had reported his doctoral research on elementary school arithmetic,[17] in which he employed instruments that became widely known as "Stone's Standard Tests."[18] A section from an early derivative of the Stone test is reproduced in Figure 2-2. The next few years saw the appearance of scales and tests in many other fields.

THE HISTORY OF MODERN ACHIEVEMENT TESTS

Studies of the Unreliability of School Marks and Tests

Tests designed to determine a student's mastery of a given academic area are as old as formal education itself. Only in the last half-century or so, however, have techniques been developed in an effort to insure a maximum of objectivity in the assessment of school achievement. We have already sketched some of the scientific and practical concerns which established the intellectual climate for a tremendous blossoming of educational measurement. But good arguments in favor of new methods do not always assure their adoption because existing methods first must be shown to be inadequate. Certainly a factor that greatly spurred the development and use of standard tests was a series of studies begun after the turn of the century. These clearly documented the questionable status of the forms of educational measurement then in use.

Course marks proceed directly from some forms of measurement by the teacher. Sometimes the measurement procedures are explicit, but a mark may often be the result of some tacit and subjective value scale particular to the teacher or department. The need for reform in college marking was sharply brought to public attention by Professor Max Meyer,[19] an experimental psychologist educated at the University of Berlin who reported on the marks assigned by 40 teachers over a five-year period at the University of Missouri. He found such astonishing variations as 55 per cent of A's in philosophy and only one per cent in Chemistry III, while there were 28 per cent failures in English II and none in Latin I. Franklin Johnson[20] found a similar situation at the University of Chicago High School, where he was the principal; in a two-year period the marks in German showed 17.1 per cent A's and 8.4 per cent F's, whereas the marks in English showed 6.5 per cent A's and 15.5 per cent F's. And even when the ability differences of the various groups were allowed for, much of this inconsistency in marking could be more readily attributed to varying marking severity than to varying subject difficulty. In short, school marks ap-

---

[17]C. W. Stone, *Arithmetical abilities and some factors determining them* (New York: Columbia University, 1908).

[18]J. C. Stone, *The teaching of arithmetic* (New York: Benj. H. Sanborn, 1922).

[19]M. Meyer, The grading of students, *Science,* 21 August 1908, 27, 243–250.

[20]F. W. Johnson, A study of high-school grades, *School Review,* 1911, 19, 13–24.

peared highly subjective and arbitrary, the mark assigned often seeming more a function of the *personality of the instructor* than of the *performance of the student*. Without exception, further studies elsewhere showed similar results. This was certainly disturbing, if not, as Thorndike suggested, actually "scandalous."[21]

---

[21] E. L. Thorndike, Measurement in education, *Twenty-first Yearbook of the National Society for the Study of Education, Part I*, 1922, p. 2.

Figure 2-2. *A speed test of arithmetic, composed of exceedingly homogeneous items and published in 1913. (Courtesy of S. A. Courtis.)*

COURTIS STANDARD RESEARCH TESTS

Arithmetic   Test No. 1   Addition

SCORE

No. Attempted_____

Series B   Form 1   No. Right_____

You will be given eight minutes to find the answers to as many of these addition examples as possible. Write the answers on this paper directly underneath the examples. You are not expected to be able to do them all. You will be marked for both speed and accuracy, but it is more important to have your answers right than to try a great many examples.

927	297	136	486	384	176	277	837
379	925	340	765	477	783	445	882
756	473	988	524	881	697	682	959
837	983	386	140	266	200	594	603
924	315	353	812	679	366	481	118
110	661	904	466	241	851	778	781
854	794	547	355	796	535	849	756
965	177	192	834	850	323	157	222
344	124	439	567	733	229	953	525
537	664	634	572	226	351	428	862
695	278	168	253	880	788	975	159
471	345	717	948	663	705	450	383
913	921	142	529	819	174	194	451
564	787	449	936	779	426	666	938
932	646	453	223	123	649	742	433
559	433	924	358	333	755	295	599
106	464	659	676	996	140	187	172
228	449	432	122	303	246	281	152
677	223	186	275	432	634	547	588
464	878	478	521	876	327	197	256
234	682	927	854	571	327	685	719
718	399	516	939	917	394	678	524
838	904	923	582	749	807	456	969
293	353	553	566	495	169	393	761
423	419	216	936	250	491	525	113
955	756	669	472	833	885	240	449
519	314	409	264	318	403	152	122

But the evidence presented by later studies was to be even more damaging. Although the departmental variations in grading could be partially accounted for by variations in the background, intelligence, and application of the students in those departments, such factors clearly could not be held responsible for differences when several persons were marking the same student's paper and, least of all, when the same person marked the same paper on two different occasions. Many convincing studies revealed great variability of marks under both conditions.

Perhaps the most striking of the early investigations were those of Daniel Starch, a pioneering applied psychologist. In one of these studies[22] he and Edward Elliott analyzed facsimiles of the same geometry paper marked independently by 116 high-school teachers of mathematics. The grades given ranged from a low of 28 per cent to a high of 92. Certainly, if high-school teachers could not agree any more closely in mathematics, supposedly one of the most objective subjects, the situation was poor indeed.

Later studies confirmed the early findings. In one of the most spectacular,[23] 100 English teachers were asked to mark a composition and also to indicate the grade level in which they would expect to find that quality of work. The percentage values (see Table 2-1) varied from 60 to 98, averaging about 87 per cent, and the estimated grade location varied from the fifth grade to the junior year of college, averaging about the beginning of the tenth grade. As a matter of fact, the composition was the best one found by a survey committee at Gary, Indiana, and was written by a high-school senior whose special interest was journalism and who was already a correspondent for some of the Chicago newspapers. It seems reasonable to suppose that many of these English teachers would seldom, if ever, have as good a composition submitted by one of their own pupils. Yet the typical one of these teachers considered it "B" quality for the tenth grade!

Starch[24] also presented the problem in a different and even more unfavorable light. He found that college instructors assigned different marks when they *regraded their own papers* without knowledge of their former marks. Later, Ashbaugh[25] had 49 college seniors and graduate students, the latter with teaching experience, rate a seventh-grade arithmetic paper on a percentage basis three times, at intervals of four weeks between ratings. The lack of consistency in scoring can be appreciated when it is mentioned that only one of the 49 students gave the same total score on all three trials and only seven gave the same total score on any two successive trials. The average variation between pairs of scores on successive trials was 8.1 points between the first and second

[22] D. Starch and E. C. Elliott, Reliability of grading work in mathematics, *School Review*, 1913, 21, 254–259.

[23] J. D. Falls, Research in secondary education, *Kentucky School Journal*, 1928, 6, 42–46.

[24] D. Starch, Reliability and distribution of grades, *Science*, 31 October 1913, 38, 630–636.

[25] E. J. Ashbaugh, Reducing the variability in teachers' marks, *Journal of Educational Research*, 1924, 9, 185–198.

TABLE 2–1

*The Estimated Grade-Value and Percentage Marks Assigned
to an English Composition by 100 Teachers (after Falls)*

Grade-Value	Percentage Mark								
	60–64	65–69	70-74	75–79	80–84	85–89	90–94	95–99	Total
XV								2	2
XIV									0
XIII							1	2	3
XII					1		2	3	6
XI			2			6	5	2	15
X			1	3	8	4	7	1	24
IX	1		1	1	8	4	4	3	22
VIII			2	2	2	3	4	3	16
VII				2	2	2	1		7
VI	1				1	1		1	4
V	1								1
Total	3		6	8	22	20	24	17	100

trials, and 7.3 points between the second and third trials. These are *averages.* Many of the markers had considerably larger discrepancies.

In a similar study, another researcher[26] found that 28 experienced high-school English teachers differed widely, after an interval of two months, in their grading of an English composition which they believed was written by an eighth-grade pupil, but actually was part of a new and still unfamiliar standard composition scale. He found that 15 teachers who gave passing marks the first time failed the paper the second time, and that 11 teachers who gave failing marks the first time passed the paper the second time. Studies involving English composition are especially significant, because an essay examination is a series of compositions; and when English teachers who presumably have more than ordinary skill in this field can find only limited agreement both with others, and with themselves in a second trial, a more refined technique is called for.

A Half-Century of Development

We may conveniently take 1908 and the publication of Stone's arithmetic tests[27] as the advent of the modern achievement testing movement. The next ten years represented a period of slow but sub-

---

[26]C. E. Hulten, The personal element in teachers' marks, *Journal of Educational Research,* 1925, 12, 49–55.
[27]Stone, 1908, *op. cit.*

stantial development of printed, objectively scored, and standardized instruments for achievement testing in a number of subject areas. The major problems facing the early test-makers were not so much in theory and technique as in gaining a more favorable opinion among educators as to the value of standardized measuring instruments. The outlook of those early educational psychologists who championed the use of precise measurement in education was put forth by Thorndike in a now classic paper:[28]

> Whatever exists at all exists in some amount. To know it thoroughly involves knowing its quantity as well as its quality. Education is concerned with changes in human beings; a change is a difference between two conditions; each of these conditions is known to us only by the products produced by it—things made, words spoken, acts performed, and the like. To measure any of these products means to define its amount in some way so that competent persons will know how large it is, better than they would without measurement. To measure a product well means so to define its amount that competent persons will know how large it is, with some precision, and that this knowledge will be conveniently recorded and used.

Large-scale testing was first done in the City of New York Survey, 1911–1913, and then soon after by other large cities.[29] In 1915, the National Educational Research Association was founded. Among its constitutional goals was the "promotion of the practical use of educational measurement in all educational research" and, by 1918, a substantial bibliography of tests and test-oriented research had appeared.[30] Monroe,[31] an effective promoter of educational research, saw 1920 as marking the "beginning of the widespread use of objective tests in American schools." By the end of the decade there were more than 1300 tests available for teachers and researchers.[32] At the same time, investigators became less concerned with stressing scoring objectivity and concentrated more on developing the wider range of item forms needed for tests of higher mental abilities. The true-false item form may have been objective, but usually it required little more than rote memorization on the part of the pupil. For educators interested in measuring abilities such as understanding, comprehension, and critical analysis, new types of items had to be developed and, for the first time, questions were raised as to the reliability

---

[28] E. L. Thorndike, The nature, purposes, and general methods of measurements of educational products, *Seventeenth Yearbook of the National Society for the Study of Education, Part II,* 1918, p. 16.

[29] D. E. Scates, Fifty years of objective measurement and research in education, *Journal of Educational Research,* 1947, 41, 241–264.

[30] E. Bryner, A selected bibliography of certain phases of educational measurement, *Seventeenth Yearbook of the National Society for the Study of Education, Part II,* 1918, 161–190.

[31] W. S. Monroe, Educational measurement in 1920 and 1945, *Journal of Educational Research,* 1945, 38, 334–340.

[32] W. W. Cook, Achievement tests, *Encyclopedia of Educational Research,* rev. ed. (New York: MacMillan, 1952), p. 1461.

and validity of the standard tests: Is this test a consistent measure of a student's knowledge of arithmetic, or will his score fluctuate greatly? Does this test adequately cover the subject matter presented by the teacher? Are the scores obtained in accord with the teacher's own judgments? New statistical methods and research techniques had to be designed to help answer such questions.

In the same decade, a number of textbooks were published which supplemented or replaced E. L. Thorndike's original *Introduction to the theory of mental and social measurements.*[33] At the same time, teachers were urged to construct their own achievement examinations for subject areas not covered by published and standardized tests. McCall[34] was among the first to suggest that classroom teachers employ the so-called "new-type" examination, and, in effect, that they should adopt the objective measurement principles of the professional. These were indeed days of consolidation, extension, and innovation in achievement testing.

With the thirties, educational measurement passed from adolescence into maturity.[35] The number of tests developed, standardized, and published increased tremendously. Organizations such as the Cooperative Test Service were established to supply, administer, and score achievement tests. By 1940, there were over 2600 achievement tests[36] available for all the traditional subject areas—reading, mathematics, science, and language—and such areas as health, commerce, aeronautics, and engineering.[37] Evidence that educational measurement was coming of age is seen in the extensive bibliographies of tests and scales that appeared in this decade; the outstanding volumes are listed in Buros' *Mental Measurements Yearbook* series,[38] which offers timely catalogs of published tests with expert critiques and extensive research bibliographies. It is an invaluable reference.

Educational measurement specialists began to think differently in the thirties. In 1935, Lindquist, later to become one of the country's outstanding leaders in measurement, warned that "it is . . . important that the *limitations* of present measuring instruments be more adequately recognized. Even the best of the tests now being provided fall far short of measuring all of the desirable outcomes of instruction in any field of subject matter."[39] Similarly, reports of the famed Eight Year Study, under the auspices of the Progressive Education

---

[33] New York: Bureau of Publications, Teachers College, Columbia University, 1904.

[34] W. A. McCall, A new kind of school examination, *Journal of Educational Research,* 1920, 1, 33-46.

[35] W. S. Monroe, *op. cit.,* p. 340.

[36] W. W. Cook, *op. cit.,* p. 1461.

[37] A. D. Woodruff and M. W. Pritchard, Some trends in the development of psychological tests, *Educational and Psychological Measurement,* 1949, 9, 105-108.

[38] O. K. Buros, ed., *The mental measurements yearbook series* (Highland Park, N. J.: Gryphon Press, 1936–65).

[39] E. F. Lindquist, Cooperative achievement testing, *Journal of Educational Research,* 1935, 28, p. 519.

Association,[40] declared that educational measurement had overemphasized the testing of limited areas of knowledge and skills, excluding other important educational objectives.   Tyler pointed out that educational objectives must ultimately be conceived of as changes in pupil behavior patterns and that adequate "evaluation" of pupil progress requires devices capable of measuring broad areas of learning. Accordingly, these investigators showed how assessment procedures could be developed to measure the attainment of such objectives as critical thinking, social sensitivity, aesthetic appreciation, and personal and social adjustment.

The so-called "evaluation movement," as exemplified in the work of Lindquist and Tyler, who also became quite prominent, had a profound influence on educational measurement. Not only did it point out that existing testing devices neglected significant realms of student behavior, it also led to more adequate assessment of higher mental processes, such as application and analysis, and broad areas of non-intellectual skills and learnings, such as interests and attitudes.

The Second World War, like the First, stimulated the further development of rigorous measurement practices, not only through the demands of military classification, but also because the war unified many research efforts under the auspices of the government. Construction of all the College Entrance Examination Board examinations, which were inaugurated around the turn of the century, was taken over by the Educational Testing Service in 1947.   ETS was responsible, in 1957, for the development of the Sequential Tests of Educational Progress (STEP), a "battery" of tests designed to measure achievement in several broad areas at various levels from Grade 4 through the sophomore year of college. This followed the tradition of the well-known Stanford Achievement Tests, Metropolitan Achievement Tests, Iowa Every Pupil Tests, and California Achievement Tests, which have, for years, been revised continually.

Since the Second World War, measurement specialists have worked to increase the precision and usefulness of their instruments and to improve educational and psychological measurement theory. The momentum towards rigorously scientific methods was increased by the founding of two quarterly professional journals in the late thirties and early forties: *Psychometrika,* "devoted to the development of psychology as a quantitative rational science," and *Educational and Psychological Measurement,* "devoted to the development and application of measures of individual differences." In the late 1940's and the 1950's, many important books appeared which discussed testing theory and practice. A few of the more noteworthy are F. L. Goodenough's *Mental testing, its history, principles, and applications,*[41] J. P. Guilford's *Psychometric methods,*

---

[40] E. R. Smith and R. W. Tyler, *Appraising and recording student progress* (New York: Harper, 1942).

[41] New York: Rinehart, 1949.

2nd ed.,[42] H. O. Gulliksen's *Theory of mental tests,*[43] E. F. Lindquist's *Educational measurement,*[44] and L. J. Cronbach and G. C. Gleser's *Psychological tests and personnel decisions.*[45] A number of textbooks also appeared which were designed to introduce college students to educational and psychological testing, and to develop teachers' skills in the construction and use of classroom examinations.

The concerns of today's specialist in educational measurement are many. Continued efforts are being made to develop and standardize new and more efficient achievement tests, to carry on research concerned with their reliability and validity, and to develop new statistical procedures for use in test construction and data analysis. A recent review of research publications reveals a variety of endeavor: test development, testing techniques, scoring problems, achievement tests as predictors, evaluative studies, characteristics of achievement testing.[46] The concerns of educational achievement measurement are vast, and we hope that this volume may add to your understanding of the subject.

THE HISTORY
OF INTELLIGENCE TESTING

The Search for an Adequate Measure of Intelligence

Individual differences in mental abilities such as comprehension, problem-solving, analytic ability—qualities which are usually grouped under the heading of "intelligence"—were not discovered by modern psychologists; terms such as idiot, genius, bright, and dull have a long history in our language. Scientific psychology's *real* contribution to the study of intelligence has been that of heightening our understanding of that "archfaculty," to use Sir Charles Spearman's term,[47] and, particularly, in devising accurate measures of the *degree* of intelligence of an individual.

The earliest mental tests were those of Sir Francis Galton, who studied individual performance differences on tests of reaction time, memory, and sensory acuity. This tradition of using rather simple "sensory" and "motor" tasks as indicators of intellectual ability was continued by James McKeen Cattell, one of the earliest and best known of American psychologists, a product of Wundt's experimental psychology laboratory at the University of Leip-

---

[42]New York: McGraw-Hill, 1954.

[43]New York: Wiley, 1950.

[44]Washington: American Council on Education, 1951. Lindquist edited this handbook and wrote one of its chapters.

[45]Urbana: University of Illinois Press, 1957.

[46]J. C. Merwin and E. F. Gardner, Development and application of tests of educational achievement, *Review of Educational Research,* 1962, 32, 40-50.

[47]C. Spearman, *The nature of intelligence and the principles of cognition* (London: Macmillan, 1923), p. 349.

zig. It was Cattell who, in 1890, suggested the term "mental test," describing in detail a series of tests with which he attempted to measure the intelligence of his students at the University of Pennsylvania.[48] Cattell, along with many of his contemporaries, regarded simpler mental and motor processes such as speed of tapping, reaction time, judgment of time intervals, and keenness of vision and hearing as reliable indications of what we now call the "higher" mental processes.[49] But, because he directed his efforts away from tests of more complex mental processes where individual differences are greatest, his efforts were doomed to failure. In 1899, Iowa Psychologist Carl Seashore[50] found only a chance correlation between children's ability to judge time intervals, to judge length of lines, and to discriminate loudness and pitch, and teachers' estimates of general mental ability. A year later Bagley[51] reported that simple motor abilities like hand strength, trilling a telegraph key, and quick reaction times bore no relation to a child's actual class standing or a teacher's judgment of him. When Clark Wissler[52] studied the tests Cattell used with college students (in which study Pearson's correlation technique[53] was applied to test scores for the first time) and found little relationship between the tests *themselves,* the attempt to measure intelligence with such tests was all but abandoned.

Binet's Breakthrough

The scene now shifts to France and the incisive work done by Alfred Binet, the father of modern intelligence testing. As early as 1896, Binet had published a proposal for a series of tests designed to measure children's intellectual capacity. Binet saw that a measure, or test, of intelligence should call for a range of performances normally regarded as intelligent behavior. The test should comprise a series of tasks requiring the ability to reason, make sound judgments, recognize familiar objects, and understand commands; i.e., it should call for a variety of mental skills. A child's intelligence would be represented by a summation of his scores on each separate task. We see then that for Binet, intelligence was a phenomenon requiring many different abilities. Two children might obtain the same total score on his test by scoring quite differently from each other on the subtests.

In 1904 Binet was commissioned by the French Minister of Public Instruction to extend his investigations to determining workable methods of

---

[48] J. McK. Cattell, Mental tests and measurements, *Mind,* 1890, 15, 373-380.

[49] For a review of early work with mental tests, see C. Spearman, "General intelligence," objectively determined and measured, *American Journal of Psychology,* 1904, 15, 206-219.

[50] C. E. Seashore, Some psychological statistics, *University of Iowa Studies in Psychology,* 1899, 2, 1-84.

[51] W. C. Bagley, On the correlation of mental and motor ability in school children, *American Journal of Psychology,* 1900, 12, 193-205.

[52] C. Wissler, The correlation of mental and physical tests, *Psychological Review, Monograph Supplements,* 1901, 8 (16), 62 pp.

[53] This is a method for measuring the association of, say, height with weight in a group of school children. See Chapter Three for a fuller explanation.

identifying mentally retarded school children so that they might be given special instruction. The results appeared in three now-classic papers published in 1905[54] in which Binet discussed a number of tasks he had found useful in approaching the problem. These had been arranged in order of difficulty and then "standardized" on a group of normal children at each age level from three to eleven years. By comparing an individual child's performance with the age of children who typically performed likewise, Binet was able to get an indication of the subject's intellectual development; i.e., a child's mental age was determined by referring his performance to the chronological age at which the average child successfully completed the same tasks. Reports of further investigations and revisions of the original scale appeared in 1908 and 1911.[55]   The last version of the scale included such tasks as the following: to earn mental-age credits at the nine-year level a child must give change for 20 cents, define five words at an abstract level, recognize the value of a piece of money, name the months of the year, and understand simple questions such as "When one has missed the train, what must one do?" Similarly, five task groups were established as norms for each age level from three to 16 years. Figure 2-3 reproduces the seven-year level "unfinished picture" task from Binet's 1908 scale. Compare this with the analogous task of the 1960 revision of the Stanford-Binet Scale, known as "picture completion" and now presented at the five-year level (see Figure 2-4 on page 27).

Later Developments

Binet's method of determining intelligence was met with some criticism but much acclaim. By 1916 it had been translated into seven languages and was used in at least 12 countries.[56]   Henry Goddard was probably the first American psychologist to recognize the practical value of Binet's 1908 and 1911 scales, which he translated and, with minor adaptation, tested at the Vineland Training School for the mentally retarded in New Jersey.[57]   In 1911 and 1912 Kuhlmann published his revision of the 1911 Binet scale, extending it downward to the age of three months, considerably below Binet's three-year limit.[58]

It remained for Lewis M. Terman of Stanford University to provide the first thoroughgoing revision of the Binet scale, carefully adapted to and stand-

---

[54] A. Binet and T. Simon, *The development of intelligence in children*, trans. by Elizabeth S. Kite (Baltimore: Williams and Wilkins, 1916), ch. 1-3.

[55] *Ibid.*, ch. 4-5.

[56] *Ibid.*, Introduction by Goddard.

[57] H. H. Goddard, Four hundred feebleminded children classified by the Binet method, *Pedagogical Seminary*, 1910, 17, 387-397; A measuring scale for intelligence, *The Training School*, 1910, 6, 146-155; Two thousand normal children measured by the Binet measuring scale of intelligence, *Pedagogical Seminary*, 1911, 18, 232-259.

[58] For an excellent historical discussion, see Florence L. Goodenough, *Mental testing* (New York: Rinehart, 1949), ch. 4-5.

Figure 2-3. *Unfinished pictures from Year VII of the 1908 Binet Scale. (From Binet, A. and Simon T., Le développement de l'intelligence chez les enfants, L'Année psychologique, 1908, 14, 1-94.)*

ardized for use with American children, average as well as deviant. Terman's scale, known as the Stanford Revision or Stanford-Binet, appeared in 1916 together with a most complete manual, *The Measurement of Intelligence.*[59] In 1937 and again in 1960 two further revisions of the Stanford-Binet appeared.[60]

---

[59] Boston: Houghton Mifflin, 1916.

[60] L. M. Terman and Maud A. Merrill, *Measuring intelligence* (Boston: Houghton Mifflin, 1937); L. M. Terman and Maud A. Merrill, *Stanford-Binet Intelligence Scale* (Boston: Houghton Mifflin, 1960).

This highly regarded instrument has remained a favorite among individual intelligence scales for school age children.

Two other distinctly American developments, both aiming to make intelligence tests more practical, remain to be discussed. The early tests had two disadvantages which limited their usefulness. They were highly *verbal;* that is, their successful administration required that the subject taking the test understand English. Also, the tests were *individual;* that is, only one person could be examined at a time. Reasonably satisfactory solutions came in the year 1917 when the pioneering applied psychologists Rudolph Pintner and Donald Paterson, finding the Stanford-Binet unsatisfactory for deaf children, met the first difficulty by developing a series of 15 manipulation, or performance, tests such as the form board (an intellectual jigsaw puzzle) already in use by researchers. This combination, which appeared in 1917, is known as the Pintner-Paterson Performance Scale.[61] That same year the United States found itself in the First World War, faced with the necessity of training a large citizen army with too few commissioned and non-commissioned officers. In this emergency, the American Psychological Association of-

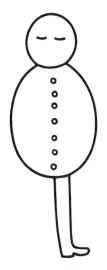

Figure 2-4. *Picture-completion man from Year V of the 1960 Stanford-Binet Intelligence Scale Record Booklet. (Boston: Houghton Mifflin, 1960.)*

fered its services to the War Department. The Binet individual intelligence tests were not only unsuitable for illiterate and foreign-speaking recruits, but were also far too slowly administered and scored to be used with the huge number of literate English-speaking soldiers. To deal with this problem, a committee of psychologists, basing their efforts on the unpublished work of Arthur S. Otis, prepared the Army Alpha, the first of a long series of group tests destined to receive wide use. Thus, the second problem of the early tests, their "one-at-a-time" quality, had been solved; the new group tests could be administered to more than 100 men at a time and could then be routinely scored by clerks.

It should be noted, however, that the Pintner-Paterson Performance Scale and the Army Alpha group tests each solved but one difficulty at a time. In fact, group tests of the Army Alpha type are generally even more verbal than the individual tests had been. (Figure 2-5 shows a sample page from the Army

---

[61] R. Pintner and D. G. Paterson, *A scale of performance tests* (New York: Appleton, 1917).

TEST 7

SAMPLES
{
sky—blue::grass—**table <u>green</u> warm big**
fish—swims::man—**paper time <u>walks</u> girl**
day—night::white—**red <u>black</u> clear pure**
}

In each of the lines below, the first two words are related to each other in some way. What you are to do in each line is to see what the relation is between the first two words, and underline the word in heavy type that is related in the same way to the third word. Begin with No. 1 and mark as many sets as you can before time is called.

1 finger—hand::toe—**box foot doll coat** 1
2 sit—chair::sleep—**book tree bed see** 2
3 skirts—girl::trousers—**boy hat vest coat** 3
4 December—Christmas::November—**month Thanksgiving December early** 4
5 above—top::below—**above bottom sea hang** 5

6 spoon—soup::fork—**knife plate cup meat** 6
7 bird—song::man—**speech woman boy work** 7
8 corn—horse::bread—**daily flour man butter** 8
9 sweet—sugar::sour—**sweet bread man vinegar** 9
10 devil—bad::angel—**Gabriel good face heaven** 10

11 Edison—phonograph::Columbus—**America Washington Spain Ohio** 11
12 cannon—rifle::big—**bullet gun army little** 12
13 engineer—engine::driver—**harness horse passenger man** 13
14 wolf—sheep::cat—**fur kitten dog mouse** 14
15 officer—private::command—**army general obey regiment** 15

16 hunter—gun::fisherman—**fish net bold wet** 16
17 cold—heat::ice—**steam cream frost refrigerator** 17
18 uncle—nephew::aunt—**brother sister niece cousin** 18
19 framework—house::skeleton—**bones skull grace body** 19
20 breeze—cyclone::shower—**bath cloudburst winter spring** 20

21 pitcher—milk::vase—**flowers pitcher table pottery** 21
22 blonde—brunette::light—**house electricity dark girl** 22
23 abundant—cheap::scarce—**costly plentiful common gold** 23
24 polite—impolite::pleasant—**agreeable disagreeable man face** 24
25 mayor—city::general—**private navy army soldier** 25

26 succeed—fail::praise—**lose friend God blame** 26
27 people—house::bees—**thrive sting hive thick** 27
28 peace—happiness::war—**grief fight battle Europe** 28
29 a—b::c—**e b d letter** 29
30 darkness—stillness::light—**moonlight sound sun window** 30

31 complex—simple::hard—**brittle money easy work** 31
32 music—noise::harmonious—**hear accord violin discordant** 32
33 truth—gentleman::lie—**rascal live give falsehood** 33
34 blow—anger::caress—**woman kiss child love** 34
35 square—cube::circle—**line round square sphere** 35

36 mountain—valley::genius—**idiot write think brain** 36
37 clock—time::thermometer—**cold weather temperature mercury** 37
38 fear—anticipation::regret—**vain memory express resist** 38
39 hope—cheer::despair—**grave repair death depression** 39
40 dismal—dark::cheerful—**laugh bright house gloomy** 40

Figure 2-5. *Test 7 from the Army Alpha. (Courtesy National Academy of Sciences.)*

Alpha.) The early performance scales, on the other hand, although nonverbal, could be administered to only one person at a time. The Army Beta, designed for illiterate and foreign-speaking soldiers, was the first test to combine the group and performance ideas; it also appeared in 1917. Figure 2-6 shows the picture completion test of the Army Beta.

Figure 2-6. *Test 6 from the Army Beta. (Courtesy National Academy of Sciences.)*

The Army Alpha and Army Beta proved to be a great boon both to Army administrators and to researchers interested in the patterns of mental ability in our culture and, as was inevitable, a large number of group intelligence tests based on the principle of the Army Alpha were soon made available to educators. Unfortunately, the determination of children's IQ's tended to become little more than a fashionable fetish, without concern for the practical value of such a score, or even the exact meaning of what was being measured. Half a century of experience with such instruments has resulted in a more realistic perspective on the value of group intelligence tests; it is generally agreed, for example, that verbal, numerical, and reasoning abilities are the major determinants of scores. These abilities are certainly dependent upon past learning experiences, though of a more general nature than specific classroom learnings. The value of the tests has been demonstrated by their use in assigning students to "ability groups," in comparing general scholastic ability with specific subject matter achievement, and in predicting scholastic and occupational success. General intelligence group tests have become important working tools for educators; some of the most familiar of these are the California Test of Mental Maturity, the Henmon-Nelson Test of Mental Ability, the Terman-McNemar Test of Mental Ability, the Kuhlmann-Anderson Intelligence Tests, the Otis Quick-Scoring Mental Abilities Tests, and the Lorge-Thorndike Intelligence Tests.

Related to the group intelligence tests, but even more specifically meant to assess school-learned abilities and to predict academic success, are several tests which yield separate scores for verbal and quantitative abilities. Although not achievement tests in the strict sense, they measure students' abilities to recognize, understand, and manipulate verbal and mathematical symbols. The Cooperative School and College Ability Test (SCAT), for example, is composed of four parts. The first contains incomplete sentences, each missing a word which the student must supply; the second consists of arithmetic computation items; the third is a vocabulary test; and the fourth consists of arithmetic reasoning items. A student's scores on the first and third parts are summed (that is, added together) to obtain his verbal score, and his scores on the second and fourth parts are summed to obtain his quantitative score. There is no question that these SCAT abilities are considerably dependent on educational experiences. For this reason they prove useful in the prediction of scholastic success in most subjects. The two score categories can be considered together or separately, depending on the to-be-predicted area of study. We would expect the verbal score to be the better indicator of success in the humanities and social studies, and the quantitative score superior in the fields of mathematics and science. The Scholastic Aptitude Test (SAT), a major segment of the College Entrance Examination Board's widely administered test battery, is an examination of the verbal-quantitative abilities type, as are the aptitude tests of the more advanced Graduate Record Examinations.

THE NATURE
OF INTELLIGENCE   The Binet test and its descendants are perhaps .
the most publicized accomplishments of mod-
ern psychology. The term "IQ," though often misunderstood, has become a
household word. The practical success of the "IQ test" in its ability to place
individuals along a spectrum of intelligence, from dull to bright, and in its relationship to school and occupational success has overshadowed doubts as to
just what the tests were measuring in an exact, psychological sense. Binet himself continually revised his estimations of the nature of intelligence as determined by his test; he finally characterized intelligence as *inventiveness* dependent upon *comprehension* and marked by *purposefulness* and corrective
judgment.[62] He did little, however, to define these abilities more exactly or to
point to the specific test behavior which demonstrated them.

In 1921, the *Journal of Educational Psychology* published a series of articles
by 14 prominent psychologists, each of whom presented his conception of the
nature of "intelligence."[63] Although there was occasional agreement, it was
both startling and undeniable that 14 clearly different conceptions of intelligence emerged. Some of the participants stressed the adaptive nature of intelligence; others saw it as the ability to learn, the ability to think abstractly, or
the degree of past learning. This muddled state prompted later researchers to
propose that since the only intelligence we can discuss objectively is the intelligence which is apparent on a test, we should define intelligence as "that which
an intelligence test measures."[64] This so-called "operational definition" has
been a favorite among psychometricians wary of theoretical disputes, but still
very impressed with the widespread utility of intelligence tests. Indeed, even the
term "intelligence test" has gone out of favor. Most psychologists now refer to
tests of "general mental ability," "scholastic aptitude," or "academic aptitude."

Thorndike also recognized that "intelligence" is given meaning only by its
observable consequences or, as he put it, by its "products."[65] The "products"
of intelligence are simply the tasks an individual is able to complete, the difficulty level of the tasks completed being an indication of the person's intel-

---

[62]A. Binet, *Les idées modernes sur les enfants* (Paris: Flammarion, 1911), pp. 117–118.
(Binet wrote: "Compréhension, invention, direction et censure, l'intelligence tient dans ces
quatre mots.")

[63]Intelligence and its measurement: a symposium, *Journal of Educational Psychology,* 1921,
12, 123–147, 195–216, 271–275.

[64]Helen Peak and E. G. Boring, The factor of speed in intelligence, *Journal of Experimental
Psychology,* 1926, 9, p. 71.

[65]E. L. Thorndike, *The measurement of intelligence* (New York: Teachers College, Columbia
University, 1926).

lectual level. Thorndike therefore saw as many different types of intelligence as there are different types of tasks. For his own purposes, however, Thorndike felt that the best indicators of what we normally mean by intelligence would be the abilities to supply words to make a statement true and sensible (completion test), solve arithmetic problems, understand single words (vocabulary test), and understand connected discourse as in oral directions for paragraph reading (directions test). From this formulation, there developed his well-known CAVD tests of mental ability, which correlated very well with the more traditional intelligence examinations.[66]

Some years later, a clinical psychologist named David Wechsler developed an individual intelligence examination especially for adults, to supplement the Stanford-Binet, which was designed for testing children and adolescents. First published in 1939 and revised in 1955 as the Wechsler Adult Intelligence Scale (WAIS), this test consists of 11 different subtests.[67] Part of the scale is verbal, the tests being Information, Comprehension, Digit Span, Similarities, Arithmetic, and Vocabulary. The other part depends mainly on "performance" or manipulative skills: Picture Arrangement, Picture Completion, Block Design, Object Assembly, and Digit Symbol. Each subtest yields a separate score; this, Wechsler feels, is important for determining an individual's *profile* of abilities. The tester is also able to compute a Verbal IQ, a Performance IQ, and a Full-Scale IQ. In 1949 the test was "scaled down" for use with children, and the Wechsler Intelligence Scale for Children (WISC) has become a serious competitor to the Stanford-Binet for testing at ages 5 to 15.

In a similar vein, leading psychometrist Louis Thurstone characterized intelligence as a series of distinct abilities. His approach was somewhat different from that of Thorndike or Wechsler, however, both of whom *assumed* that their individual subtests were pure measures of the designated ability. According to Thurstone, an ability is isolated by giving mental tests to a great number of persons and then determining, through a sophisticated mathematical process known as "factor analysis," the least number of abilities necessary to explain the correlations among the tests. In his pioneering study,[68] Thurstone isolated six "factors" which accounted for most of the score similarity of 56 different tests given to a group of college students. These were Verbal (V), Number (N), Spatial (S), Word Fluency (W), Memory (M), and Reasoning (R). The verbal factor, for one, was identified by its heavy "loadings" on tests of reading, synonyms, analogies, grammar, and vocabulary. Similarly, Thurstone's number factor was identified by its loadings on such tests as addition, multiplication, and arithmetical reasoning. Out of this research came the first of the "multi-aptitude" test batteries, the Primary Mental Abilities tests. Later

[66]*Ibid.,* pp. 96–101.

[67]D. Wechsler, *The measurement and appraisal of adult intelligence,* 4th ed. (Baltimore: Williams and Wilkins, 1958).

[68]L. L. Thurstone, Primary mental abilities, *Psychometric Monographs,* 1938 (1).

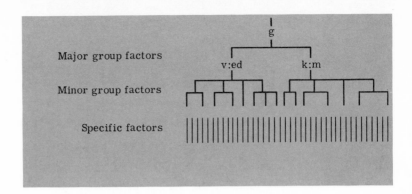

Figure 2-7. *Diagram illustrating hierarchical structure of human abilities. (From P. E. Vernon,* The structure of human abilities. *New York: Wiley, 1950, p. 22.)*

investigations showed, however, that the number of factors isolated depended considerably on the educational and environmental backgrounds of the subjects tested, and the number and types of tests used in the factor analysis. It was even shown that Thurstone's so-called "primary" mental abilities correlated positively with each other, suggesting the presence of a still more basic and general mental factor, as had long been argued by the outstanding British psychologist, Charles Spearman.[69]

More recent thinking among factor analysts about the nature of human intelligence has led to two somewhat different ideas. One is represented by Spearman's British tradition of investigation, exemplified by Philip Vernon's structure of human abilities,[70] in which human mental abilities are arranged in a hierarchy with a broad general factor (*g*) and split into two major "group" factors, one distinguished by verbal and educational abilities (*v:ed*) and the other by practical or performance abilities (*k:m*). Each of these major group factors is then differentiated into more specific factors like Thurstone's Verbal, Number, and Space. These finally break into factors found in specific types of tests. (See Fig. 2-7.) Thus any mental performance can be described as involving percentages of *g, v:ed,* Verbal, and others until all the factors needed to account for the performance have been determined.

A second view of mental organization grows out of the Thurstonian American tradition of investigation. Its chief advocate is J. P. Guilford, who has devised a theoretical "structure of intellect" in which he classifies human mental abilities in three dimensions: The first is defined by the kind of test content confronting the individual—"figural," "symbolic," "semantic," or "behavioral." The second is defined by the types of mental "operations" necessary to deal with the various content forms—"cognition," "memorization," "convergent thinking," "divergent thinking," and "evaluation." The last deals with the outcome or "products" yielded by the various mental operations applied to the various content forms. There are six products: units of information, classes of units, relations between units, systems of information, transformations, and implications. With 4 kinds of content, 5 kinds of operations, and 6 kinds of products involved in mental performances, Guilford suggests 120 (4 × 5 × 6) distinct mental abilities. (See Fig. 2-8.) He reports that about half

[69]C. Spearman, *The abilities of man* (New York: Macmillan, 1927).
[70]P. E. Vernon, *The structure of human abilities* (London: Methuen, 1950).

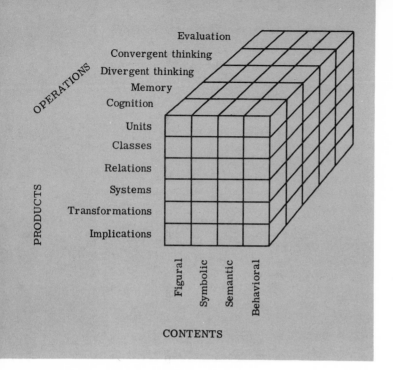

OPERATIONS
Evaluation
Convergent thinking
Divergent thinking
Memory
Cognition

PRODUCTS
Units
Classes
Relations
Systems
Transformations
Implications

CONTENTS
Figural
Symbolic
Semantic
Behavioral

Figure 2-8. *Theoretical model for Guilford's structure of intellect. (From J. P. Guilford,* Personality. *New York: McGraw-Hill, 1959, p. 397.)*

of these have been isolated through factor analytic investigations. This analysis of the "structure of intellect" is rather complex, so the reader is referred to some of Guilford's articles for further explication.[71]

The most important application of factor analytic studies of mental abilities has been the increasing use of "multi-aptitude" test batteries in educational and vocational guidance. These batteries are composed of a series of individual tests built around the findings of factor analysis; to a certain degree, each of the general battery's subtests tests a specific ability. One such battery is the Differential Aptitude Test (DAT), whose form, for use with high school students, contains seven subtests which measure verbal reasoning, numerical ability, abstract reasoning, space relations, mechanical reasoning, clerical speed and accuracy, and language usage. Although the DAT subtests are not intended to be "pure" measures of single "factors," its authors hope that they will provide a profile of an individual's mental strengths and weaknesses which will be more specific, descriptive, and meaningful than an omnibus test of "general mental ability." Besides the greater *descriptive* value of such a test, *prediction* of success or failure in a variety of academic or occupational endeavors can be achieved by isolating the important abilities specifically required. It was found, for example, that a combination of three of the DAT subtests correlated highly with the College Board Scholastic Aptitude Test, and that college graduates are high scorers on the Verbal Reasoning and Numerical Ability subtests, compared with high school graduates. Engineers were found superior on all sub-

---

[71] J. P. Guilford, Three faces of intellect, *American Psychologist,* 1959, 14, 469–479; Factorial angles to psychology, *Psychological Review,* 1961, 68, 1–20; and Factors that aid and hinder creativity, *Teachers College Record,* 1962, 63, 380–392.

tests, and most markedly in numerical ability, abstract reasoning, and mechanical reasoning.[72]

Conceptualizing the Human Personality

Men have always been busy categorizing and evaluating the personalities of their neighbors. The simplest form of personality evaluation is perhaps in the construction of various *typologies* under which individuals can be classified. A personality typology can be as simple as "good person" versus "evil person," a familiar distinction made by religious and ethical theorists. More elaborate are the four temperaments of medieval times —sanguine, melancholy, phlegmatic, and choleric, a classification based on a supposed predominance in an individual of one of the four bodily "humours," or fluids—blood, bile, phlegm, or choler. A still rather popular typology, suggested by the Swiss psychoanalyst C. G. Jung, is introversion-extroversion. But although traces of typological psychology still remain in personality theory,[73] more elaborate methods of assessment have been devised in a growing effort to compass the diversity of human personality. Measurement theory has, of course, followed the development of personality theory. Often, the tests and other evaluative methods used by psychological investigators have been constructed for the sake of a particular research problem. On the other hand there are many fairly standardized "personality tests" (Buros[74] lists 145 published "character and personality" tests) which measurement students should know about.

What do we mean by "personality"? There is, of course, much discussion among psychologists as to the proper meaning of this term; as in the paradoxical case of intelligence tests, we have measuring instruments which apparently have some validity, without ourselves possessing a clear understanding of that which we are measuring. Although there is nothing final about the following, or any other theory, we may, by *adopting* a theory of personality, be more able to discuss those measuring instruments now available to the teacher, counselor, and researcher.

According to Psychologist David McClelland,[75] personality comprises three major dimensions: *traits, schema,* and *motives.* A trait is defined as "the learned

---

[72]For excellent coverage of the DAT and other multi-aptitude tests, see *The use of multi-factor tests in guidance* (Washington, D. C.: American Personnel and Guidance Association, n.d.), 91 pp.

[73]See, for example, W. H. Sheldon and S. S. Stevens, *The varieties of temperament* (New York: Harper, 1942).

[74]O. K. Buros, *op. cit.,* 1959.

[75]D. C. McClelland, *Personality* (New York: Dryden, 1951).

tendency of an individual to react as he has reacted more or less successfully in the past in similar situations when similarly motivated" (p. 216). Personality variables such as "cheerfulness," "emotional control," and "tenacity" are examples of traits. While these and other traits can be inferred from an individual's overt behavior, schema are those internal frames of reference with which an individual confronts the world: his beliefs, interests, ideas, and attitudes. Finally, the concept of motive helps to explain the "push" and the directive aspect of human behavior. As McClelland puts it:

> Trait psychology developed to explain recurrent responses and consistencies in behavior, in order to explain the *how* of behavior. The *schema* or *attitude* concept developed to handle the problem of *what* the person knew, of what the symbolic contents of his mind were. The motive concept has developed in answer to the question *why*. Why do people behave as they do? (p. 383)

Traits Measured by Direct Observation

Here, a sample of real life behavior which manifests the trait in question is observed and analyzed. A widely reported study of this type was the Character Education Inquiry of Yale University researchers Hartshorne and May,[76] in which they assessed such traits as truthfulness, honesty, and persistence in children by subjecting them to situational tests of these traits. Hartshorne and May found that most traits investigated depended strongly on the situation; i.e., a child might cheat on an examination but not steal pennies. Thus they cast doubt on the then-current belief that a child is either wholly honest or wholly dishonest; honesty did not emerge as a single, unitary characteristic of individuals.

Another study of this type was carried out for the war-time Office of Stategic Services (OSS), which was interested in selecting highly qualified men for risky undercover operations.[77] The assessment staff felt that such traits as energy and initiative, effective intelligence, emotional stability, and leadership would be indispensable in this sort of work and so devised a number of situational tests to measure the degree of these and other attributes. In one situation, the subject had to build a five-foot cube of giant Tinkertoys with the aid of two workmen. Unknown to the subject, the two helpers were psychologists who did everything possible to obstruct his progress and to belittle him. His reactions under such conditions were later evaluated in terms of the traits being sought. In another trial called the stress interview, the candidate was given a short time to invent a story to cover the fact that he had been caught going through secret governmental papers. In a subsequent third-degree "grilling," his reactions were again weighed.

---

[76] H. Hartshorne and M. A. May, *Studies in deceit* (New York: Macmillan, 1928).
[77] OSS Assessment Staff, *Assessment of men* (New York: Rinehart, 1948).

Trait Measurement through Self-Report

Today's personality tests are largely of the paper-and-pencil, self-report variety in which the examinee is presented with a series of true-false questions describing typical behavior patterns. His score will then consist of the number of questions answered in a direction supposedly displaying those traits. Sometimes a self-report test measures only one trait dimension, e.g., security-insecurity or high anxiety-low anxiety. Other times, a test can be devised and scored to measure several traits at once; for example, the California Psychological Inventory yields 18 different scores, such as sociability, dominance, sense of well-being, self-control, tolerance, and flexibility.

The grandfather of all such devices is the Woodworth Personal Data Sheet, devised during the First World War to facilitate the psychiatric screening of draftees. It consisted of 116 yes-no questions which described typical symptoms of neurotic behavior (Fig. 2-9). Whereas "normals" averaged about 10 psychoneurotic answers, those with neurotic complications averaged close to 40 such answers.[78] Such high scorers would then be more intensively interviewed.

A number of these presumedly "uni-dimensional" tests were developed in the twenties and thirties to determine the strength of a variety of personality traits. It remained for psychologist Robert Bernreuter to demonstrate that *one* test could measure a number of personality traits simultaneously. To do this he gathered a great number of self-report questions and determined which of them discriminated between high and low scorers on each of four tests which respectively measured "introversion-extroversion," "ascendance-submission," "neurotic tendency," and "self-sufficiency." By this method, he found that a given item might correlate well with more than one of the uni-dimensional tests; and, by judicious selection, he was able to produce a 125-item test the responses to which could be variously combined to produce four separate scores, each of which correlated highly with the uni-dimensional test it was expected to replace.[79]

Further refinement in the development of self-report personality scales was introduced by insightful measurement specialist John C. Flanagan[80] who maintained that since the four Bernreuter scales showed significant intercorrelation (for example, people scoring high on the introversion scale tended similarly on the neuroticism scale), the traits could not be called independent and that, therefore, each separate scale did not necessarily bear a precise

---

[78] S. I. Franz, *Handbook of mental examination methods* (New York: MacMillan, 1919), p. 171.

[79] For an excellent discussion, see L. W. Ferguson, *Personality Measurement* (New York: McGraw-Hill, 1952), pp. 173–182.

[80] J. C. Flanagan, *Factor analysis in the study of personality* (Palo Alto, Calif.: Stanford University Press, 1935).

psychological meaning. Flanagan overcame this difficulty by subjecting the Bernreuter test to a trait, or factor analysis. After examining the item correlations, he proposed that only two separate factors need be supposed to account for the score patterns produced by a great number of individuals. He defined these factors as the self-confident, socially aggressive vs. the self-conscious, emotionally unstable dimension and the sociable vs. the non-sociable dimension. This method of defining personality traits is analogous to the factor analytic method of determining mental abilities and has become a favorite device for producing multi-dimensional personality tests. Two of the more prominent are the Guilford-Zimmerman Temperament Survey,[81] which yields 10

---

[81] Beverly Hills, Calif.: Sheridan Supply Company.

Figure 2-9. *The first 36 items of the Woodworth Personal Data Sheet. (From P. M. Symonds,* Diagnosing personality and conduct. *New York: Century, 1931, p. 175.) The neurotic response to each item is italicized here, but of course not on the inventory itself.*

1. Do you usually feel well and strong?	yes	*no*
2. Do you usually sleep well?	yes	*no*
3. Are you frightened in the middle of the night?	*yes*	no
4. Are you troubled with dreams about your work?	*yes*	no
5. Do you have nightmares?	*yes*	no
6. Do you have too many sexual dreams?	*yes*	no
7. Do you ever walk in your sleep?	*yes*	no
8. Do you ever have the sensation of falling when going to sleep?	*yes*	no
9. Does your heart ever thump in your ears so that you cannot sleep?	*yes*	no
10. Do ideas run through your head so that you cannot sleep?	*yes*	no
11. Do you feel well rested in the morning?	yes	*no*
12. Do your eyes often pain you?	*yes*	no
13. Do things ever seem to swim or get misty before your eyes?	*yes*	no
14. Do you often have the feeling of suffocating?	*yes*	no
15. Do you have continual itching in the face?	*yes*	no
16. Are you bothered much by blushing?	*yes*	no
17. Are you bothered by fluttering of the heart?	*yes*	no
18. Do you feel tired most of the time?	*yes*	no
19. Have you ever had fits of dizziness?	*yes*	no
20. Do you have queer, unpleasant feelings in any part of the body?	*yes*	no
21. Do you ever feel an awful pressure in or about the head?	*yes*	no
22. Do you often have bad pains in any part of the body?	*yes*	no
23. Do you have a great many bad headaches?	*yes*	no
24. Is your head apt to ache on one side?	*yes*	no
25. Have you ever fainted away?	*yes*	no
26. Have you *often* fainted away?	*yes*	no
27. Have you ever been blind, half-blind, deaf, or dumb for a time?	*yes*	no
28. Have you ever had an arm or leg paralyzed?	*yes*	no
29. Have you ever lost your memory for a time?	*yes*	no
30. Did you have a happy childhood?	yes	*no*
31. Were you happy when 14 to 18 years old?	yes	*no*
32. Were you considered a bad boy?	*yes*	no
33. As a child did you like to play alone better than to play with other children?	*yes*	no
34. Did the other children let you play with them?	yes	*no*
35. Were you shy with other boys?	*yes*	no
36. Did you ever run away from home?	*yes*	no

scores including general activity, ascendance, sociability, emotional stability, and friendliness; and Raymond B. Cattell's Sixteen Personality Factor Questionnaire,[82] which can differentiate such trait pairs as aloof and warm, confident and insecure, tough and sensitive, conventional and eccentric, conservative and experimenting.

Measurement of Perceptual Traits

Here we are concerned with tests which draw out a person's typical manner of perceiving, evaluating, and reacting to environmental stimuli; i.e., these tests show how an individual takes in, categorizes, and processes the "information" that comes to him from his surroundings. Although investigators are often content simply to *describe* these perceptual traits, others believe that these traits indicate more dynamic aspects of the personality.

The well-known Rorschach Ink Blot test (Fig. 2-10) is classic in this type. The subject is shown one blot at a time and is asked what he sees in it. The examiner notes not just the content of the responses, but such things as the use of the whole blot instead of the use of details, the injection of movement into the blots, and the use of color and white spaces in making a response. Elaborate systems attempt to relate the various perceptual modes to such personality variables as impulsiveness, sensitivity, and emotional stability. Since its appearance in 1921, much controversial literature has sprouted around the Rorschach technique (Buros[83] lists some 2300 references) and its final standing as a yardstick of personality is yet to be established.

A lively interest has developed in the possibilities of fathoming personality through investigation of individual differences in perception. Clinical researchers Goldstein and Scheerer[84] devised a series of tests to determine whether an individual brings "concrete" or "abstract" attitudes to his perception of the environment, and to relate these attitudes to various personality characteristics as well as to the diagnosis of brain injury and mental illness. Figure 2-11 shows a series of nonsense figures arranged in order of increasing complexity. The examinee is shown one figure at a time and is then asked to reproduce it from memory using matchsticks. An "abstract attitude" is shown by an ability to reproduce the figures in correct spatial location. The absence of this abstracting ability—the "concrete attitude"—is often seen in brain-damaged or schizophrenic subjects who can only reproduce the figures through a series of specific associations; their success depends, for example, on their seeing a roof in number 5, or an inverted "F" in number 15. A figure as simple as Number

---

[82]Champaign, Ill.: Institute for Personality and Ability Testing.
[83]O. K. Buros, *op. cit.,* 1959.
[84]K. Goldstein and M. Scheerer, Abstract and concrete behavior: an experimental study with special tests, *Psychological Monographs,* 1941, 53 (2).

3 in Figure 2-11 is often failed because the abstract idea of "one-line 45° to the horizontal" cannot be conceived.

Psychologist Jerome Bruner[85] has offered a broadly conceived theory of

[85] J. S. Bruner, On perceptual readiness, *Psychological Review,* 1957, 64, 123–152.

Figure 2-10. *Card II and experimental modifications of the Rorschach. (Adapted by permission from E. Earl Baughman; original blot courtesy Hans Huber Publishers.)*

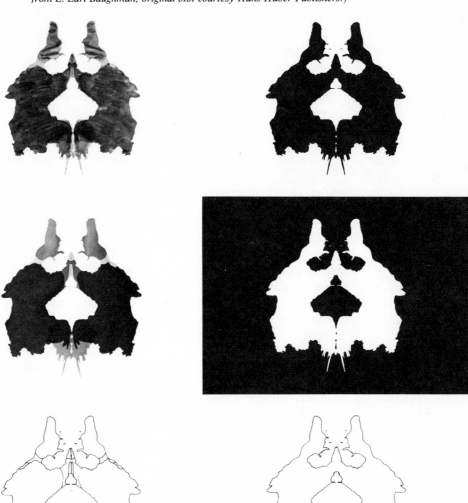

these processes which nicely ties together perception, thinking, learning, and individual differences. In extensive research carried out at the Menninger Foundation, several investigators[86] have isolated what they term "cognitive controls" which describe modes of perceptual mediation between the needs of

[86]R. Gardner, P. S. Holzman, G. S. Klein, Harriet Linton, and D. P. Spence, Cognitive control: a study of individual consistencies in cognitive behavior, *Psychological Issues,* 1959, 1 (4).

Figure 2-11. *Nonsense figures for detecting abstract vs. concrete attitude. (From K. Goldstein and M. Scheerer, Abstract and concrete behavior: an experimental study with special tests,* Psychological Monographs, *1941, 53 (2), p. 132.)*

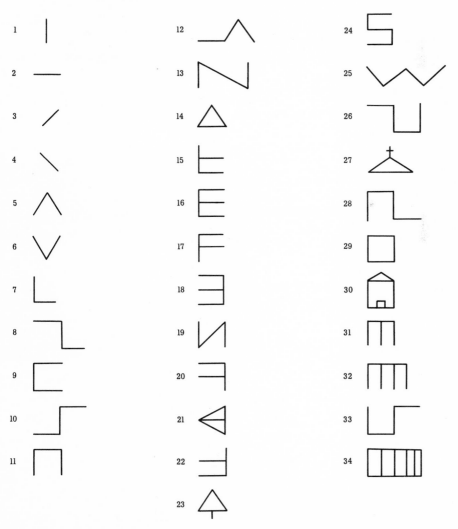

the individual and the demands of the environment. For example, what the authors call "field articulation" refers to an ability to isolate perceptually a simple element from a complex configuration. The Embedded Figures Test (Fig. 2-12) is a good test of this ability. According to Gardner, good "field articulators" are characterized by such traits as self-awareness and high self-esteem. Poor performances are given by people who are passive, have low self-esteem, and lack self-awareness. Although a relatively new area of research, personality through perception promises a better understanding of human functioning.

Measurement of Personality Schema

Under schema, we consider the typical content of a person's thought and ideas. What are his preferences and aversions, his interests, opinions, and values? Ever since the groundbreaking study of Pro-

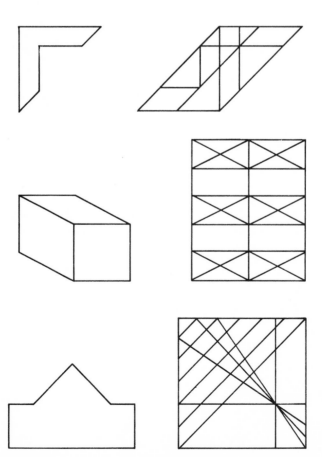

Figure 2-12. *Problems from an embedded figures test. (From L. J. Cronbach,* Essentials of psychological testing, *2nd ed. New York: Harper, 1960, p. 548.)*

fessors Thurstone and Chave at the University of Chicago in 1929,[87] psychologists have been busy devising scales to determine people's attitudes towards a variety of objects and situations, from war to God. As psychologist Leonard Ferguson[88] states:

> Attitude scales developed in accord with the Thurstone equal-appearing-interval procedure have been put to many uses. There are more than 500 references to them in the literature in which they have played an important part. In these studies, Thurstone-type attitude scales have been used to determine the effects of movies on attitudes toward crime and toward nationality groups ... the effects of social science courses upon student attitudes ... the relative effectiveness of written and oral propaganda ... the effect of college attendance upon attitudes ... the degree of employee morale.

Most attitude scales have been developed to answer specific research questions and therefore are not available in fully standardized commercial form. Thurstone, however, had a broader purpose. His great contributions were in showing how scales of attitude expression could be constructed for any specified topic with an eye toward consistency, and in developing items which revealed various strengths of feeling towards a given object or situation. One of his attitude scales is presented in Figure 2-13. The scale value of each statement is shown in the parentheses following its number. Notice the difference between the strongest pro-movie statement (No. 27) and the strongest anti-movie statement (No. 15). For a discussion of his technique, see Chapter Nine.

Interest Assessment through Self-Report

Many high school and college students, anxious to know more about themselves so as to define their academic or vocational futures better, have become familiar with self-report interest inventories. What kind of activities does he find most appealing? Are his scientific interests stronger than his literary interests? Is the pattern of his interests similar to those of school teachers, chemists, or accountants? These questions are the kind answered by the interest inventory.

Of these, perhaps the best known is the Kuder Preference Record—Vocational (KPR-V), which consists of 168 three-choice items of the form:[89]

a) Collect autographs
b) Collect coins
c) Collect butterflies

---

[87]L. L. Thurstone and E. J. Chave, *The measurement of attitude* (Chicago: University of Chicago Press, 1929).

[88]Ferguson, *op. cit.*, p. 102.

[89]Sample KPR-V item courtesy of the publishers, Science Research Associates, Chicago, Ill.

ATTITUDE TOWARD MOVIES

This is a study of attitudes toward the movies. On the following pages you will find a number of statements expressing different attitudes toward the movies.

✓ Put a check mark if you agree with the statement.

✗ Put a cross if you disagree with the statement.

If you simply cannot decide about a statement you may mark it with a question mark.

This is not an examination. There are no right or wrong answers to these statements. This is simply a study of people's attitudes toward the movies. Please indicate your own attitude by a check mark when you agree and by a cross when you disagree.

LIST OF OPINIONS IN THE SCALE

1. (1.5) The movies occupy time that should be spent in more wholesome recreation.
2. (1.3) I am tired of the movies; I have seen too many poor ones.
3. (4.5) The movies are the best civilizing device ever developed.
4. (0.2) Movies are the most important cause of crime.
5. (2.7) Movies are all right but a few of them give the rest a bad name.
6. (2.6) I like to see movies once in a while but they do disappoint you sometimes.
7. (2.9) I think movies are fairly interesting.
8. (2.7) Movies are just a harmless pastime.
9. (1.7) The movies to me are just a way to kill time.
10. (4.0) The influence of the movies is decidedly for good.
11. (3.9) The movies are good, clean entertainment.
12. (3.9) Movies increase one's appreciation of beauty.
13. (1.7) I'd never miss the movies if we didn't have them.
14. (2.4) Sometimes I feel that the movies are desirable and sometimes I doubt it.
15. (0.0) It is a sin to go to the movies.
16. (4.3) There would be very little progress without the movies.
17. (4.3) The movies are the most vital form of art today.
18. (3.6) A movie is the best entertainment that can be obtained cheaply.
19. (3.4) A movie once in a while is a good thing for everybody.
20. (3.4) The movies are one of the few things I can enjoy by myself.
21. (1.3) Going to the movies is a foolish way to spend your money.
22. (1.1) Moving pictures bore me.
23. (0.6) As they now exist movies are wholly bad for children.
24. (0.6) Such a pernicious influence as the movies is bound to weaken the moral fiber of those who attend.
25. (0.3) As a protest against movies we should pledge ourselves never to attend them.
26. (0.1) The movies are the most important single influence for evil.
27. (4.7) The movies are the most powerful influence for good in American life.
28. (2.3) I would go to the movies more often if I were sure of finding something good.
29. (4.1) If I had my choice of anything I wanted to do, I would go to the movies.
30. (2.2) The pleasure people get from the movies just about balances the harm they do.
31. (2.0) I don't find much that is educational in the current films.
32. (1.9) The information that you obtain from the movies is of little value.
33. (1.0) Movies are a bad habit.
34. (3.3) I like the movies as they are because I go to be entertained, not educated.
35. (3.1) On the whole the movies are pretty decent.
36. (0.8) The movies are undermining respect for authority.
37. (2.7) I like to see other people enjoy the movies whether I enjoy them myself or not.
38. (0.3) The movies are to blame for the prevalence of sex offenses.
39. (4.4) The movie is one of the great educational institutions for common people.
40. (0.8) Young people are learning to smoke, drink, and pet from the movies.

In scoring the attitude scale, we cannot say that one score is better or worse than another; we can only say that one person's attitude toward the movies is more or less favorable than another person's. It is purely arbitrary that attitudes unfavorable to the movies have lower scale values than favorable attitudes.

Any individual's attitude is measured by the average or mean scale value of all the statements he checks. The person who has the larger score is more favorably inclined toward the movies than the person with a lower score.

For the purpose of comparing groups, the distributions of attitude in each group can be plotted, and it can then be said whether and how much one group is more favorable to the movies than another group.

Figure 2-13. *An attitude-toward-movies scale. (From L. L. Thurstone,* The measurement of values. *Chicago: University of Chicago Press, 1959, pp. 285–286.)*

The student marks the activity he finds most appealing and also the one he finds least appealing. The item form forces him to choose among what were established in a wide range of people to be equally preferred activities. The 168 items include a great variety of activities, and the scoring system determines his relative preference strength on ten distinct scales: outdoor, mechanical, computational, scientific, persuasive, artistic, literary, musical, social-service, and clerical. (See Fig. 2-14.) These scores are interesting and suggestive, but unfortunately their meaning for vocational guidance purposes is not yet sufficiently precise; still more extensive research must be done towards determining the kind of scores achieved by the specific groups in which the examinee might be interested and the predictive values of these scores. (For a Kuder inventory more recent than the KPR-V, see Chapter Nine.)

A different approach was taken by E. K. Strong when he developed his Vocational Interest Blank. (See Fig. 2-15.) He felt that the interests typical of any one occupational group would differ from a people-in-general group and at least a little from any other occupational group. His method was to collect 400 items in which an individual could indicate his interests and preferences in a wide range of activities, as well as indicate what *he himself* considered his present abilities. Instead of grouping items together in similar-interest clusters and then devising a number of scales as Kuder did, Strong simply gave the test to the members of many different occupational groups. For each group he determined those items chosen, as opposed to those chosen by men or women in general, and, from this information, derived scoring scales for each group.[90] From this point, an individual taking the test can be told whether his interests resemble those of men in Group X, Y, or Z. Scoring scales have been developed for some 47 occupations, from artist to production manager and from minister to real estate salesman. Notice that Strong was not prejudicial in choosing which items would make up each given scale; it was the *actual* interest choices of the different groups which decided the weights of the items for each scale. The success and prestige of the SVIB examinations is due to the extensive research involved in their formulation. They have few competitors. It is interesting that Kuder has adopted a rather similar scoring approach in the development of his second interest test, the Kuder Preference Record—Occupational; see Chapter Nine.

In certain respects similar to the Kuder or Strong interest inventories is the Allport-Vernon-Lindzey Study of Values, an instrument which represents an interesting combination of personality theory and psychometric technique. Drawing from the work of Eduard Spranger, a German philosopher who speculated that people could be typed according to their value orientations, the authors developed a number of self-report-and-opinion statements which they

---

[90]The development of the prototype for the later SVIB is described in K. M. Cowdery, An evaluation of the expressed attitudes of members of three professions (medical, engineering, and legal). Unpublished Ph.D. dissertation. Stanford University, 1925.

felt reflected Spranger's value types. The six value orientations, each represented by an equal number of test statements, are theoretical, economic, aesthetic, social, political, and religious. The test result is an individual score profile which represents the relative strengths of the six value orientations. Evidence cited in the test manual suggests that the various scales stand up in

---

NAME _____ AGE ____ SEX ____ GROUP _____ DATE OF TEST _____
Print   Last   First   Initial   M or F

First Revision, February 1951
REPRODUCTION BY ANY MEANS STRICTLY PROHIBITED

PROFILE SHEET
for the
KUDER PREFERENCE RECORD
VOCATIONAL
Forms CH, CM

MEN and WOMEN

DIRECTIONS FOR PROFILING

1. Copy the V-Score from the back page of your answer pad in the box at the right.

If your V-Score is 37 or less, there is some reason for doubting the value of your answers, and your other scores may not be very accurate. If your V-Score is 45 or more, you may not have understood the directions, since 44 is the highest possible score. If your score is not between 38 and 44, inclusive, you should see your adviser. He will probably recommend that you read the directions again, and then that you fill out the blank a second time, being careful to follow the directions exactly and to give sincere replies.

If your V-Score is between 38 and 44, inclusive, go ahead with the following directions.

2. Copy the scores 0 through 9 in the spaces at the top of the profile chart. Under "OUTDOOR" find the number which is the same as the score at the top. If your score is not shown, draw a line *between* the scores above and below your own. Use the numbers under M if you are a man and the numbers under F if you are a woman. Draw a line through this number from one side to the other of the entire column under OUTDOOR. Do the same thing for the scores at the top of each of the other columns. If a score is larger than any number in the column, draw a line across the top of the column; if it is smaller, draw a line across the bottom.

3. With your pencil blacken the entire space between the lines you have drawn and the bottom of the chart. The result is your profile for the *Kuder Preference Record—Vocational*.

An interpretation of the scores will be found on the other side.

The profile chart consists of columns numbered 0 through 9 with the following scale headings (each divided into M and F subcolumns), flanked by PERCENTILES scales on both sides:

0 OUTDOOR	1 MECHANICAL	2 COMPUTATIONAL	3 SCIENTIFIC	4 PERSUASIVE	5 ARTISTIC	6 LITERARY	7 MUSICAL	8 SOCIAL SERVICE	9 CLERICAL

practical application; e.g., clergymen score high on the religious scale, business administration students high on the economic scale.[91]

[91]H. G. Gough, Review of "Study of Values," in O. K. Buros, ed., *Fourth mental measurements yearbook* (Highland Park, N. J.: Gryphon Press, 1953), p. 156.

Figure 2-14. *Kuder Preference Record—Vocational Profile Sheet by G. Frederic Kuder, published by Science Research Associates. (Reproduced with permission of G. Frederic Kuder.)*

Your INTEREST PROFILE

Your profile on the *Kuder Preference Record—Vocational* shows your interest in the ten important areas listed across the top of the chart. The profile will also help you learn how you compare with other people.

The lines you drew on the chart show whether your interest is high, average, or low. If your score is above the top dotted line in any column, it is a high score and shows that you like activities in that area. If your score is between the two dotted lines, your interest is about average. If your score is below the bottom dotted line, it is a low score and shows that you dislike activities of that type.

Like most people, you are probably high in some areas, low in some, and average in others. Look at your highest score first. This score shows the type of activities you probably like best. If you have more than one score above the top dotted line, you have a combination of high interests.

Look at your low scores, too. They should be considered in any plans you make because they indicate the kinds of activities you probably do not enjoy. Remember that high interests are not better or worse than low, nor are some interests better than others. It is your own *pattern* of interests that counts.

Here is what your scores on the *Preference Record* mean:

OUTDOOR interest means that you prefer work that keeps you outside most of the time and usually deals with animals and growing things. Forest rangers, naturalists, and farmers are among those high in outdoor interests.

MECHANICAL interest means you like to work with machines and tools. Jobs in this area include automobile repairmen, watchmakers, drill press operators, and engineers.

COMPUTATIONAL interest means you like to work with numbers. A high score in this area suggests that you might like such jobs as bookkeeper, accountant, or bank teller.

SCIENTIFIC interest means that you like to discover new facts and solve problems. Doctors, chemists, nurses, engineers, radio repairmen, aviators, and dieticians usually have high scientific interests.

PERSUASIVE interest means that you like to meet and deal with people and to promote projects or things to sell. Most actors, politicians, radio announcers, ministers, salesmen, and store clerks have high persuasive interests.

ARTISTIC interest means you like to do creative work with your hands. It is usually work that has "eye appeal" involving attractive design, color, and materials. Painters, sculptors, architects, dress designers, hairdressers, and interior decorators all do "artistic" work.

LITERARY interest shows that you like to read and write. Literary jobs include novelist, historian, teacher, actor, news reporter, editor, drama critic, and book reviewer.

MUSICAL interest shows you like going to concerts, playing instruments, singing, or reading about music and musicians.

SOCIAL SERVICE interest indicates a preference for helping people. Nurses, Boy or Girl Scout leaders, vocational counselors, tutors, ministers, personnel workers, social workers, and hospital attendants spend much of their time helping other people.

CLERICAL interest means you like office work that requires precision and accuracy. Jobs such as bookkeeper, accountant, file clerk, salesclerk, secretary, statistician, and traffic manager fall in this area.

The occupations listed for each area on this profile are only examples. Your counselor can help you think of many others that are suggested by your pattern of interests. He can also tell you about many books and pamphlets that will help you learn more about these occupations. You may find that many school courses and leisure-time activities fit into your high interest areas.

Another form of the *Preference Record*, the *Personal*, will help you find out more about the types of things you like to do. It will help you discover, for example, how much you like meeting new people, whether you prefer situations you are familiar with, if you would rather work with ideas or things, how much you prefer pleasant social situations, and if you like to direct others. Your scores in these areas, too, will help you plan your career.

What you can do well depends, of course, on many things in addition to interest. Your abilities are particularly important. Many abilities can be measured by tests. Here, again, your counselor is the person to see.

Try to get as much information as you can about your interests, abilities, and the jobs you want to consider. The more you know about yourself, the more opportunity you have to make wise plans for your future.

Report on Vocational Interest Test for Men

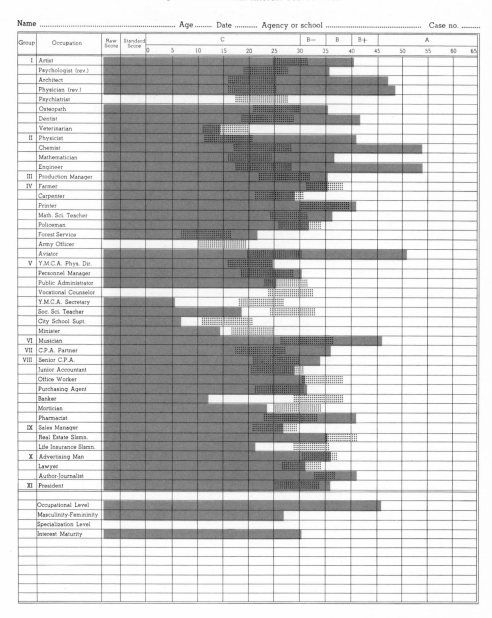

Figure 2-15. *Strong Vocational Interest Blank showing profile of scores made by a college student. The A and B+ scores suggest several possible careers, but the combination of Physician, Chemist, and Engineer, taken with the A on Architect, make Architecture seem the most promising, since it unites artistic and scientific interests. (Reprinted from* Manual for Strong Vocational Interest Blanks for Men and Women *by E. K. Strong, Jr., with the permission of Consulting Psychologists Press, Inc.)*

Measurement of Motivation

Psychologists have had a difficult time making good theoretical sense of our third personality dimension—the "why" or motivational aspect. A motive is a psychological state of the individual which we infer from his behavior. Thus if a person sets out to eat we say his motive is hunger; if he struggles for success, his motive is ambition; if he acts uncharitably, his motive is selfishness. One of the founders of modern social psychology, William McDougal,[92] made a list of primary human motives (he called them instincts) which included such things as curiosity, pugnacity, self-assertion, reproduction, and repulsion. Further thought, however, led theorists to believe that such lists of motives really were nothing but *descriptions* of a wide range of human behavior. Rather than explaining anything, they simply provided another way of categorizing outwardly similar behaviors, and the number of such motives or categories depended solely on the grouping preferences at work. As one critical wag observed, if a person twiddles his thumbs, need we infer a thumb-twiddling motive?

This sort of thinking has led many psychologists to suggest that aside from physiological necessities such as those for food, air, and rest, the motivation concept should be abandoned or reformulated. The minimum assumption to be made in explaining human action is that the individual will set goals whose attainment provides satisfaction, pleasure, or gratification. The particular goals of any one person, however, will depend on his history of rewards and punishments, these in turn probably depending on the value systems of his environment—parents, social groups, and general culture. Thus if a culture values warriorlike behavior, aggression will be rewarded and we will expect many aggressive individuals.

We see that in this formulation, the motive concept differs from the trait concept only in degree of generality. Whereas motives predict behavior in a wide variety of differing environments, traits refer to more specific responses in more highly specified conditions. For our purposes, the important question concerns the measurement of human motives. Building upon the work of Harvard Psychologist Henry Murray,[93] who theorized on the basis of Freud's insights, McClelland and his associates[94] propose that motives are nothing more than a person's "inner concerns" and that if we learn these concerns we may predict much of his behavior. We can get at these by having a person write down spontaneous, imaginative stores in response to picture cues, such as

---

[92]W. McDougal, *An introduction to social psychology,* 15th ed. (Boston: John W. Luce, 1923).

[93]H. A. Murray and others, *Explorations in personality* (New York: Oxford University Press, 1938).

[94]D. C. McClelland and others, *The achievement motive* (New York: Appleton-Century-Crofts, 1953).

Figure 2-16. *One of the T A T cards. (Reprinted by permission of the publishers from Henry Alexander Murray,* Thematic Apperception Test. *Cambridge, Mass.: Harvard University Press. Copyright, 1943, by the President and Fellows of Harvard College.)*

those used in Murray's Thematic Apperception Test (TAT). (See Fig. 2-16.) By analyzing the content of a series of these spontaneous, imaginative stories according to well-defined rules, the investigator can identify the presence or absence, as well as the strength, of one or more "motives."

A motive which McClelland and his associates have found prevalent in our culture is what they term the "achievement" motive. It reflects a person's drive to attain success and is associated with competent and effective behavior in a majority of situations. For example, people so motivated have been found to learn faster, receive better school marks, and make decisions which show an awareness of both their abilities and limitations. As might be expected, this high achievement motivation is characteristic of successful businessmen and, following this lead, it has been shown that the average level of a nation's achievement motivation reflects its degree of economic development.[95]

The use of thematic apperception (or fantasy) techniques for the measurement of human motivation does not, of course, exhaust the possibilities in this

[95] D. C. McClelland, *The achieving society* (New York: Van Nostrand, 1961).

field. The interested reader is encouraged to consult the stimulating papers covering theoretical, experimental, and psychometric approaches to the problems of motivation which appear in the yearly proceedings of the *Nebraska Symposia on Motivation.*[96]

---

[96] Lincoln, Nebraska: University of Nebraska Press. Annually since 1953.

RECOMMENDED READINGS

Boring, E. G., *A history of experimental psychology,* 2nd ed. New York: Appleton-Century-Crofts, 1950.

Buros, O. K., *The mental measurements yearbook series.* Highland Park, N. J.: Gryphon Press, especially the 1965 edition.

Cronbach, L. J., *Essentials of psychological testing,* 2nd ed. New York: Harper, 1960.

Ferguson, L. W., *Personality measurement.* New York: McGraw-Hill, 1952.

Goodenough, Florence L., *Mental testing: its history, principles, and applications.* New York: Rinehart, 1949.

Guilford, J. P., *Personality.* New York: McGraw-Hill, 1959.

Jenkins, J. J. and Paterson, D. G., *Studies in individual differences.* New York: Appleton-Century-Crofts, 1961. A well-edited book of readings.

Layton, W. L., ed., *The Strong Vocational Interest Blank: research and uses.* Minneapolis: University of Minnesota Press, 1960.

Likert, R. A., A technique for the measurement of attitudes, *Archives of Psychology,* 1932, No. 10.

Murphy, G., *Historical introduction to modern psychology,* rev. ed. New York: Harcourt, Brace & World, 1949.

Rabin, A. I. and Haworth, M. R., *Projective techniques with children.* New York: Grune and Stratton, 1961.

Ramul, K., Some early measurements and ratings in psychology, *American Psychologist,* 1963, 18, 653–659.

Scates, D. E., Fifty years of objective measurement and research in education, *Journal of Educational Research,* 1947, 41, 241–264.

Smith, E. R. and Tyler, R. W., *Appraising and recording student progress.* New York: Harper, 1942.

Spearman, C. E., *Psychology down the ages, Vols. I and II.* London: Macmillan, 1937.

Thurstone, L. L., *The measurement of values.* Chicago: University of Chicago Press, 1959.

Vernon, P. E., *The structure of human abilities.* London: Methuen, 1950.

ANALYZING

TEST RESULTS

Measurement and evaluation, which involve the assigning of numbers to observed data and the interpretation of those numbers, are coming more and more to depend on statistical procedures. Nearly all of today's test manuals refer to central tendency, variability, percentiles, percentile ranks, standard scores, reliability, and validity. They usually presume that the reader is at least familiar with the most commonly used statistical terms and concepts. Not only test-publishers' catalogs but also educational literature of all types refer to such concepts, and they are mentioned frequently at professional meetings of educational researchers.

At this point, the reader may be ready to throw up his hands and admit that he's just going to *have* to read this chapter if only to get some idea of what these ever-obscure terms mean. That's certainly one good reason—but not the most important one. Statistical methods are not reserved to bureaus of educational testing and research, and may, when understood, be put to very good use by the individual classroom teacher. Certainly, people in virtually *all* fields of education can expect increased emphasis on and use of statistical techniques.

The view emphasized by a renowned teacher of educational statistics some years ago is even broader:[1]

"The conclusion seems inescapable that some aspects of statistical thinking which were once assumed to belong in rather specialized technical courses must now be considered part of general cultural education."

Nearly all elementary measurement texts and most general psychology books hopefully include a chapter on statistics designed to teach in a week or so material usually covered in a semester or year-long course. Though some of these chapters are very good, they inevitably fail to attain their unrealistic goal, for it is virtually impossible to teach much about statistics in a short period of time. This becomes doubly frustrating when we realize that it is neither practicable nor justifiable to devote a *large* portion of the measurement course to this area.

We have tried to solve this dilemma by omitting the more advanced material, by emphasizing concepts more than computations, by repeating main ideas frequently, and by saving certain techniques for the Appendix. Fifty multiple-choice items are presented in Appendix B, to help you test your grasp of basic principles. A summary of common statistical terms and a selected list of statistics textbooks appear at the end of the chapter.

Despite these aids, you will probably find that you cannot read this chapter quickly and easily. It will require the same sort of careful study you would use

---

[1] Helen M. Walker, Statistical understandings every teacher needs, *High School Journal,* 1950, 33, 30–36.

in preparing a chemistry or physics assignment. This effort, however, should result in a considerable improvement of your ability to understand statistical communication.

CLASSIFICATION AND TABULATION   Before test scores or other quantitative data can be understood and interpreted, it is usually necessary to summarize them.   Table 3–1 shows a class record for a reading readiness test administered at the beginning of the school year.   The scores appear in alphabetical order as they are recorded in the teacher's class roll book.   However, the scores do not mean very much in this form, and we can

TABLE 3-1

A Class Record for a Reading Readiness Test (38 Pupils)

Pupil	Score	Pupil	Score	Pupil	Score	Pupil	Score
David A	90	Robert D	59	Jerome L	75	Paul S	81
Barbara B	66	Don F	95	Mary M	75	Richard S	71
Charles B	106	Larry F	78	Billy N	51	Robert S	68
Robert B	84	Richard G	70	Nancy O	109	William S	112
Mildred C	105	Grover H	47	Carrie P	89	Jean T	62
Robbin C	83	Robert H	95	Ralph R	58	Adolfo W	91
Robert C	104	Sylvia H	100	George S	59	Dolores W	93
Diney D	82	Warren H	69	Gretta S	72	Richard W	84
Jim D	97	Clarence K	44	Jack S	74		
John D	97	Jack K	80	Mary S	75		

tell only with some difficulty whether, for example, David, with a score of 90 points out of a possible 128, is a very superior or just an average pupil, compared with his classmates.

Rank Order

Ordinarily the first step is to arrange the scores in order of size, usually from highest to lowest.   This is called an *ungrouped series*.   In a small class, this is often all that is necessary.   Table 3–2 shows the same 38 scores as Table 3–1, arranged in order of size from 112 to 44.   This table also shows the *rank order* of the pupils (1st, 2nd, . . . , 38th) and the scores tabulated without further grouping.   It is now easy to see that David A's score of 90 gives him a rank of 13 in a class of 38, or about one-third of the way from the top.   Similarly, it is easy to interpret each of the other scores in terms of rank.   But ties are likely to occur, especially in classes of 20 or more pupils.   Notice, for example, that two pupils made a score of 97.   Since it is not correct to say that one ranks higher than the other, we must assign them the same rank.   Since there are six pupils who rank higher (1, 2, 3, 4, 5, 6), the next

TABLE 3-2

Reading Readiness Scores from Table 3-1
Arranged in Order of Size and Rank Order and Tabulated

Order of Size	Rank Order	Score	Frequency (f)	
		Tabulated without Further Grouping		
112	1	112	1	
109	2	109	1	
106	3	106	1	
105	4	105	1	
104	5	104	1	
100	6	100	1	
97	7.5	97	2	
97	7.5	95	2	
95	9.5	93	1	Sum = 19
95	9.5	91	1	
93	11	90	1	
91	12	89	1	
90	13	84	2	
89	14	83	1	
84	15.5	82	1	
84	15.5	81	1	Midpoint of
83	17	80	1	frequencies
82	18	78	1	
81	19	75	3	
80	20	74	1	
78	21	72	1	
75	23	71	1	
75	23	70	1	
75	23	69	1	Sum = 19
74	25	68	1	
72	26	66	1	
71	27	62	1	
70	28	59	2	
69	29	58	1	
68	30	51	1	
66	31	47	1	
62	32	44	1	
59	33.5		N = 38 = 19 + 19	
59	33.5			
58	35			
51	36			
47	37			
44	38			

two ranks, 7 and 8, are averaged, giving 7.5. In like manner the average of ranks 9 and 10 is 9.5, and so on for the other pupils with tied scores. There are *three* pupils with scores of 75, and there are 21 pupils who rank above this score; the average of the next three ranks (22, 23, and 24) is 23, which is the rank assigned to each of the scores of 75. In addition to the time and trouble required to determine these ranks, the list is long, unwieldy, and inadequate for making comparisons with other classes that are much larger or much smaller; ranking 19th in a class of 38 pupils is poorer than ranking 19th in an equally capable class of 70.

The Frequency Table or Distribution

We can make the list of scores shorter by arranging the scores in a *frequency distribution,* sometimes simply called a *distribution.* The third and fourth columns of Table 3-2 show the simplest form of a distribution. The various scores are arranged in order of size, here from 112 to 44, and to the right of each score is recorded the number of times it occurs. Each entry to the right of a score is called a *frequency,* abbreviated *f,* and the total of the frequencies is represented by *N.*

Of the 38 frequencies in Table 3-2, half (19) are for scores of 112 through 81; the other half are for scores of 80 through 44, as shown. Thus, the midpoint of the frequencies lies between 81 and 80, or at 80.5. This is the same point we would arrive at by arranging the 38 test papers in decreasing order by score (112, 109, . . . , 47, 44) and then counting down half way in the pile. The average of the score on the 19th test paper (81) and the score on the 20th paper (80) is 80.5, the point in the test-score distribution above and below which half of the scores lie. This point is called the *median.* Clearly, the median is much easier to obtain than is the arithmetic mean, which is found by adding together all 38 scores and dividing by 38. For most of the classroom teacher's purposes, the median, a counting measure, provides a sufficiently good indication of the *central tendency* of the test scores.

A simple measure of the *variability* (scatter, dispersion, heterogeneity, spread) of test scores can be obtained by discarding the highest 10 per cent and the lowest 10 per cent of the scores and locating the highest and lowest remaining scores. For Table 3-2, 10 per cent of 38 = 0.1 × 38 = 3.8, closer to the whole number 4 than to 3. Eliminate the 4 highest scores: 112, 109, 106, and 105. Eliminate the 4 lowest scores: 44, 47, 51, 58. This leaves a distribution of 30 scores [38 − 4 − 4] going from 104 to 59; 45 test-score points [104 − 59] is a serviceable rough measure of variability that represents the spread of approximately the middle 80 per cent [100% − 10% − 10%] of the tested group. Dividing 45 by the number of items on the test (that is, by the highest possible score), 128, yields 35.2 per cent, with which a similar measure of variability from other tests can be compared.

A test discriminates well among all students if their scores lie along most of the possible range, from almost the chance-level score to almost a perfect score, with the median score about half-way between the chance and perfect scores. The test on which the scores in Figure 3-2 are based contained 128 4-option items. Students were encouraged to try every item and were given time to do so. Thus, the student who knew nothing at all but guessed blindly at all 128 items should, on the average, have marked 128 ÷ 4 = 32 of them correctly. Therefore, the effective possible range of the test is from about 32 to 128, the midpoint of which is $(32 + 128) \div 2 = 160/2 = 80$. The scores obtained ranged from 44 to 112, with the actual median at 80.5. Thus the median difficulty of the test was almost exactly 50 per cent for these 38 pupils.

Grouped Frequency Distribution

For a large number of scores—say, 100 or more—it may be desirable to carry the process one step further. As a rule, there is so wide a range of scores that it is economical to group them according to size, such as a group including all scores from 105 to 109, inclusive, from 110 to 114, inclusive, and so on. Each group is called a *score class*. The complete grouping arrangement is usually referred to as a *grouped frequency distribution*. Although there is no fixed rule for the number of score classes, it is usually best to *make not fewer than 12 classes nor more than about 15*. To have fewer than 12 classes is to run the risk of distorting the results, whereas more than 15 classes produce a table that is inconvenient to handle.

Constructing
the Grouped Frequency Table

There are four steps in making the ordinary grouped frequency distribution. These are shown in Table 3-3, using the scores given in Table 3-1.

1. *Determine the range,* which is one more than the difference between the highest score and the lowest. Of these scores, the highest is 112 and the lowest is 44, which gives a range of $(112 - 44) + 1 = 69$.

Actually, 112 is considered to cover the one-point score interval 112.5-111.5, and 44 the interval 44.5-43.5. Notice, therefore, that the range is 69 $[(112 - 44) + 1$, or $112.5 - 43.5]$. The real score limits are not always fractional, however. If age is reckoned at the last (most recent) birthday, then persons who report themselves as being 44 years old (that is, not yet 45) lie within the interval 44.00-44.99...(almost, but not quite 45.00), whose midpoint is 44.5. If they report age to nearest birthday, the interval is 43.5-44.5, with a midpoint of 44. Similarly, if they report themselves "going on 44," the interval is 43.00-43.99 ...,with midpoint 43.5. There will be a difference of almost two years between the youngest possible "going on 44" person, who has just reached the age of 43, and the oldest possible "44 last birthday" respondent, who is almost 45. When we ask merely for "Age____," without specifying the reckoning system, we will not be able to interpret our results precisely.

2. *Select the score-class grouping interval,* which is the width of the groups into which the scores are to be classified, so that there will be not fewer than 12 score classes nor more than 15. To do this, divide the range by 12 to find the largest group, or score-class interval to be used. Divide the range by 15 to find the smallest class interval to be used. In this case, $69 \div 12 = 5.75$, and

TABLE 3-3

An Illustration of the Process of Making a Grouped Frequency Distribution

Original Scores (from Table 3-1)	Steps in Making the Distribution
90	**Step 1.** Determining the range.
66	Highest score 112
106	Lowest score 44
84	Range = Difference + 1 = 68 + 1 = 112.5 − 43.5 = 69
105	
83	
104	**Step 2.** Selecting the class interval.
82	69 ÷ 12 = 5.75, largest class interval desirable.
97	Round *down* to 5.
97	69 ÷ 15 = 4.60, smallest class interval desirable.
59	Round *up* to 5.
95	
78	
70	**Steps 3 and 4.** Determining the limits of the classes and making the tabulation.
47	

	Whole-Number Limits of the 15 Classes	Tabulation	Frequency (f)
95			
100			
69			
44	110–114	/	1
80	105–109	///	3
75	100–104	//	2
75	95–99	////	4
51	90–94	///	3
109	85–89	/	1
89	80–84	ᵗᴴᴴ /	6
58	75–79	////	4
59	70–74	////	4
72	65–69	///	3
74	60–64	/	1
75	55–59	///	3
81	50–54	/	1
71	45–49	/	1
68	40–44	/	1
112			N = 38
62			
91	Range = 114.5 − 39.5 = 75, larger than the 69, above.		
93	Why?		
84			

$69 \div 15 = 4.60$. Since it is impractical to use any class interval except a whole number, the larger number, 5.75, is "rounded *down*" to 5 and the 4.60 "rounded *up*" to 5, even though a class interval of 6 would yield 12 score classes for *these* 38 scores. Odd-numbered interval widths such as 5, which have whole-number midpoints when the score-class limits are fractional (end in .5), are usually preferred to even-numbered interval widths, which have fractional midpoints when the class limits are fractional. The midpoint of the score-class 110-114, which contains the 5 scores 110, 111, 112, 113, and 114, is 112 (that is, $110 + [(114 - 110) \div 2] = 110 + 4/2 = 110 + 2 = 112$). If a class size of 6 were used, with score limits of 108-113, for example, the midpoint of this even-numbered group would be 110.5, which might result in more complex computations.[2] Hence, a class interval of 5 is preferable to 6 when the class limits are fractional.

3. *Determine the limits of the classes.* There must, of course, be enough classes to include the highest score and the lowest score. To facilitate tabulation, start each class with a multiple of the class interval. If the lowest class starts with 40, which is a multiple of 5, it will accommodate the lowest score, 44, whereas a class beginning with 45 will not. Each succeeding whole-number class limit will be 5 points above the one just below it. The next class will start at 45, the next at 50, and so on, until the highest score, 112, is included in the class 110-114.

4. *Make the tabulation.* A short vertical line (tally) is drawn for each score opposite the class in which it falls. To make a tabulation it is not necessary to have the scores arranged in order, for this process may require more time than the tabulation itself. In the original alphabetical list, the first score is 90. In the tabulation column opposite the class which begins with 90, a tally line is drawn to indicate the score. The next score is 66. This falls in the class which begins at 65, so a tally is made there. In the same way, a tally is placed in the column opposite the appropriate class for each of the other scores. To indicate the fifth score, a diagonal line is drawn across the other four tallies. This makes it easier to count the tallies in each class.

The finished table omits the steps by which it was made. Only two columns occur in the simplest form of a frequency distribution. The first shows the various classes, usually arranged in descending order from top to bottom, and the second shows the frequencies— the number of scores in each class.

To be sure that you understand Rules 3 and 4, above, stop at this point and construct a grouped frequency distribution of the 38 scores, using a class (grouping) interval of 6. *Does the number of classes that results meet the 12-15 requirement of Rule 2?*

When two or more schools or grades are to be compared, it is usually best to include all the data in the same table. In that case there will be a column for the classes into which the scores are grouped and one for each of the schools or grades being compared. Table 3-4 shows a frequency table which combines the

---

[2]There are at least four ways to determine the midpoint of the score-class interval that includes the scores 110, 111, 112, 113, and 114, whose integral (whole-number) limits are 110 and 114: $(110 + 114) \div 2 = 224/2 = 112$; $(109.5 + 114.5) \div 2 = 224.0/2 = 112$; $109.5 + [(114.5 - 109.5) \div 2] = 109.5 + 2.5 = 114.5 - [(114.5 - 109.5) \div 2] = 114.5 - 2.5 = 112$; and $110 + [(114 - 110) \div 2] = 114 - [(114 - 110) \div 2] = 112$. Try applying these four methods to finding the midpoint of the class interval 108-113, whose real class limits are fractional.

TABLE 3-4

Distribution of Reading Readiness Scores for Six Schools in a Certain City

Score	School A	School B	School C	School D	School E	School F	All Six Schools
120–124				1			1
115–119							
110–114			1				1
105–109			3		2	2	7
100–104		3	2	2	5	3	15
95–99		6	4	4	4	5	23
90–94	5	2	3	5	6	10	31
85–89	4	4	1	4	4	1	18
80–84	2	3	6	6	4	8	29
75–79	10	5	4	4	1	2	26
70–74	6	2	4	7	6	4	29
65–69	9	4	3		4	1	21
60–64	4	5	1	2	1		13
55–59	1		3		1		5
50–54	1		1				2
45–49	1		1				2
40–44			1	2	2		5
35–39	1	1					2
30–34		2					2
25–29		1					1
20–24							
15–19							
10–14	1						1
N	45	38	38	37	40	36	234

record of six schools on a certain test. The number of grouping intervals varies from 9 for School F to 17 for Schools A and D, although some intervals have no tallies.

The Form of the Table

A few words may be said about the mechanical makeup of the table as it often occurs in typed form. (One format for printed tables is *used in this book*.) Each table bears a number. Although either Roman or Arabic numerals may be used, the Arabic seem to be increasingly favored. The table number may be centered above the title of the table, or it may be given at the beginning of the title. The table usually starts with two horizontal lines and ends with a single horizontal line. Another horizontal line separates the column headings from the body of the table, and other horizontal lines separate any summarizing measures that are given under the table proper. Vertical lines may be used to separate the columns, but usually no lines are drawn along the margins of the page. It is considered good form to avoid abbreviations in the table whenever possible, and to make the title and headings full enough to indicate the contents of the table clearly.

Two-Way Table,

Scattergram, or Scatter Diagram

Table 3-5 shows the chronological, educational, and mental ages of the 20 students in a certain eighth-grade class. It is sometimes helpful to compare pupils' scores on two measures. A two-way table, called a *scattergram* or *scatter diagram,* makes this easier. Table 3-6 contains a two-way distribution of mental and educational ages from Table 3-5.

TABLE 3-5

Chronological, Educational, and Mental Ages
of the 20 Pupils in an Eighth-Grade Class

Pupil	Ages Expressed in Months		
	Chronological (CA)	Educational (EA)	Mental (MA)
A	150	188	208
B	147	186	218
C	155	185	201
D	160	183	185
E	141	183	165
F	160	182	191
G	154	181	185
H	164	180	193
I	165	179	181
J	157	176	165
K	167	176	187
L	157	176	176
M	161	176	180
N	157	175	166
O	158	174	197
P	161	173	154
Q	179	171	180
R	152	167	165
S	160	167	177
T	156	165	164

Mental ages, grouped into class intervals of six months, make up the column headings; educational ages, grouped into class intervals of two months, constitute the rows. For example, Pupil A, with a MA of 208 months and an EA of 188 months, falls in the third column from the right, or 204-209 class, and in the top row, or 188-189 class. Similarly, the horizontal position of each pupil in the distribution shows his MA, and the vertical position shows his EA. You may observe that the scores tend to arrange themselves in a diagonal pattern from lower left to upper right. In general, this means that pupils who are low in MA are low in EA, and pupils who are high in MA are high in EA. How-

TABLE 3-6

A Two-way Distribution of Mental Age and Educational Age for the 20 Pupils in an Eighth-Grade Class (Data from Table 3-5)

($r = .66$)

Educational Age (EA) In Months	Mental Age (MA) in Months												EA Frequency
	150–155	156–161	162–167	168–173	174–179	180–185	186–191	192–197	198–203	204–209	210–215	216–221	
188–189										A			1
186–187												B	1
184–185									C				1
182–183		D				E	F						3
180–181						G		H					2
178–179						I							1
176–177		J			K	L	M						4
174–175		N						O					2
172–173	P												1
170–171						Q							1
168–169													0
166–167		R		S									2
164–165		T											1
MA Frequency	1	0	5	0	2	5	2	2	1	1	0	1	20

ever, a few exceptions stand out. Pupil P, for example, who is lowest in MA, is in the fifth row from the bottom in EA. Below him on EA are Pupils Q, R, S, and T.

When the identification of individual pupils in the scattergram is unimportant, the total frequencies only are entered in the appropriate cells (the squares). For Table 3-6 all such entries would be 1's, though for many scatter diagrams the number of tallies in a given cell will exceed 1.

SOME BASIC NOTIONS CONCERNING QUANTITATIVE DATA   Two of the most important concepts that apply to various kinds of test data are *central tendency* and *variability*. These abstract notions are useful in summarizing the main features of a bewildering mass of figures, and it is possible to understand them fairly well without being an expert computer.

In order to read and understand test manuals and other measurement literature, we must have a good understanding of these concepts; and if we expect to analyze test scores, we must acquire certain basic skills in computing several statistics. The following is designed to provide you with a knowledge of the basic elements of computation.

FINDING THE MODE, MEDIAN, AND MEAN

Central Tendency

A tendency for the scores to concentrate somewhere near the center is characteristic of most frequency distributions. An important statistic is, therefore, the point on the scale around which the scores tend to group. This is a measure of *central tendency;* it is that value which typifies, or best represents, the whole distribution.

We might want to know which of several schools made the "best" record on a certain test, and which the "poorest." To determine this, we would compute an average for each school, and then note which one has the highest average and which one the lowest.[3]

Statisticians use three different "averages." These are the crude mode, or inspectional average; the median, or counting average; and the mean, or computed average. We will now consider the meaning of each of these.

The Mode

The most frequent score is called the *mode.* It is determined by inspection. In Table 3-2, the mode of the scores is 75 because more pupils (3) made that score than any other. The crude mode is not a very trustworthy average, however, especially with small groups. In this case the changing of two scores could shift the mode considerably. If one of the pupils who made 75 had made 76, and if the one who made 58 had made 59, the mode would drop to 59, since more pupils (3) would then have made that score than any other. Largely because of its fickleness, the crude mode is not highly regarded as a measure of central tendency for small groups.

The Median and Other Percentiles

Perhaps the most widely used average in educational measurement is the *median. The median is the score point that divides the distribution into halves.* In an ungrouped series, the *midscore* is sometimes used instead of the median. Strictly speaking, when N is an even number, there is no midscore. In that case, it is customary to average the middle pair of scores. For example, in Table 3-2 there are 38 pupils; 19 made scores of 80 or less, and 19 made scores of 81 or more. The midscore is then considered to be

---

[3]Obviously, in order to be statistically and educationally significant, the difference between high and low schools should be fairly large.

80.5 (the average of 80 and 81, the middle pair of scores), as we noted earlier. For the distribution in Table 3-2, the median also happens to be 80.5. The terms *median* and *midscore* are often used interchangeably, but the latter should be used only for ungrouped scores arranged in order of size rather than in a grouped frequency distribution.

Table 3-7 illustrates the process of locating the median in a frequency distribution. The median is often described as the counting average, and you

TABLE 3-7

The Process of Locating the Median (Scores from Table 3-3)

Frequency Distribution			Steps in the Process
	f		**Step 1.** Obtaining N/2:
110–114	1	⎫	N/2 = 38/2 = 19.
105–109	3	⎪	
100–104	2	⎬ 14	**Step 2.** Locating the lower real class limit of the score class that contains the median: Count *up* $1 + 1 + 1 + 3 + 4 + 4 = 18$. This takes us up to 79.5, which is the lower real limit of the 80–84 class in which the median lies.
95–99	4	⎪	
90–94	3	⎪	
85–89	1	⎭	
80–84	6		
75–79	4	⎫	**Step 3.** Interpolating in the class:
70–74	4	⎪	$$\frac{19 - 18}{6} \times (84.5 - 79.5) = \frac{1}{6} \times 5 = \frac{5}{6} = 0.8,$$
65–69	3	⎪	
60–64	1	⎬ 18	the correction.
55–59	3	⎪	
50–54	1	⎪	**Step 4.** Obtaining the median: $79.5 + 0.8 = 80.3$, the median. That is, the median is the Step 2 result plus the correction.
45–49	1	⎪	
40–44	1	⎭	
	N = 38		**Step 5.** Check by counting down:
			$$84.5 - \left(\frac{19 - 14}{6}\right)(84.5 - 79.5) = 84.5 - \left(\frac{5}{6} \times 5\right) = 80.3,$$
			which agrees with the answer in Step 4.

will notice that counting is rather important in locating it. The steps may be summarized as follows:

1. *Obtain N/2.* That is, divide the total of the frequencies by 2. Here N/2 = 38/2 = 19.

2. *Find the lower real class limit of the score class in which the median lies.* Beginning at the low end of the distribution, count *up* the frequency column as far as possible without passing N/2, obtained in Step 1. In this case the frequencies $1 + 1 + 1 + 3 + 1 + 3 + 4 + 4$ give a total of 18. This is as far as we can go, for to include the next frequency, 6, would carry us too far, or beyond N/2, which is 19. The lower real class limit of the class 80-84 is 79.5, halfway between the classes that include scores of 75-79 and 80-84.[4]

3. *Interpolate in the class.* From N/2 subtract the total obtained in Step 2.

In this case, $19 - 18 = 1$. This shows that one more score or unit is needed to obtain the required $N/2$ scores. This score must come out of the next class, the 80-84 class, where there is a frequency of 6. That is, we must go 1/6th of the distance into the next class. Since the class interval is 5, this means 1/6 of 5, or 0.8. Thus the correction is 0.8.

4. *Obtain the median.* This is done by adding the correction to the lower real class limit: $79.5 + 0.8 = 80.3$, the median.

5. *Check by counting down.* $84.5 - \dfrac{19 - 14}{6} \times 5 = 84.5 - \dfrac{5 \times 5}{6} = 84.5$

$- 4.2 = 80.3$. Notice that when we count *down* from higher to lower numbers, we *subtract* the new correction from the *upper* real limit of the class in which the median lies.

The median is often used as a reference point for describing the location of individual pupils in a distribution. A pupil in the higher half is said to be "above the median," and one in the lower half "below the median." Other points in the distribution are used in a similar manner. For example, three quartiles divide the distribution into fourths, and nine deciles divide it into tenths. A pupil in the highest fourth is said to be "above Q_3," and one in the lowest fourth "below Q_1."[5]

Quartiles should not be confused with the four quarters (fourths) of the distribution. Persons scoring above Q_3 are in the highest fourth (highest quarter) of the group but *not* in the "highest quartile," since this expression is meaningless. Likewise, pupils scoring below Q_1 are in the lowest fourth (lowest quarter) but *not* in the "lowest quartile." There are only three quartiles, all of which are points rather than ranges. Q_2 is the median; Q_0 and Q_4 do not exist.

Similarly, there are 9 deciles, going from 1 through 9. A person may score *at* the 2nd decile (the 20th percentile) or between the 2nd and 3rd deciles, but not *in* the 2nd decile. Rather, we would say that he scored in the third tenth of the group, counting from the bottom. There are no 0th and 10th deciles.

The position of a certain pupil may be described still more precisely by indicating the percentage of pupils whose scores fall below his score. The 99 points that divide a distribution into 100 divisions, each of which contains 1 per cent of the total number of frequencies, N, are called *percentiles,* or simply *centiles.*

---

[4]Each class in this frequency table has fractional (.5) lower and upper limits, even though only whole-number scores are shown. The class 75-79 actually runs from 74.5-79.5, and 80-84 means 79.5-84.5. *If* a score of 79.49 had existed in Table 7-1, it would have gone into the 75-79 class, whereas a score of 79.51 would have appeared in the 80-84 class. Also, the 6 frequencies in the 80-84 class are considered to be distributed evenly over the 5-unit interval extending from 79.5-84.5. (A score of precisely 79.500... would, by arbitrary rule, be rounded *up* to 80 because its last non-decimal integer is an odd number, 9, and hence it would be put into the 80-84 class. A score of 84.500... would be rounded *down* to 84 because 4 is an even number, and hence it would be put into the 80-84 class, also.)

[5]Table 3-9 illustrates computation of Q_1 and Q_3.

Computation of Percentiles

The median, Q_2, is the 50th percentile because 50 per cent of all the frequencies lie below that point and 50 per cent lie above it. A percentile is a score point in the score distribution below which the stated percentage of all measures lies. Thus an individual who scores at the 30th percentile of his class has done better than 30 per cent of the students and poorer than 70 per cent. Percentiles are computed in much the same manner as the median, the only difference being that the number of frequencies to be counted up (or down) varies with the percentile desired.

The 30th percentile of the distribution in Table 3-7 is obtained as follows:

1. 30% of N = 0.30 × 38 = 0.3 × 38 = 11.4. Counting frequencies upward, we secure 1 + 1 + 1 + 3 + 1 + 3 = 10, which carries us to the real class limit 69.5. (Including the next 4 frequencies would yield 14, more than the 11.4 that we need.)

2. 11.4 − 10 = 1.4, the number of frequencies to be gone up into the class that extends from 69.5 to 74.5 and has a total frequency of 4.

3. $\dfrac{1.4}{4} \times (74.5 - 69.5) = \dfrac{1.4 \times 5}{4} = \dfrac{7.0}{4} = 1.75.$

4. 69.50 + 1.75 = 71.25, the 30th percentile.

5. Check by counting down 100% − 30% = 70% of the way:

   a. 0.70 × 38 = 26.6. 1 + 3 + 2 + 4 + 3 + 1 + 6 + 4 = 24.

   b. $74.5 - \dfrac{26.6 - 24}{4} \times 5 = 74.5 - \dfrac{2.6 \times 5}{4} = 74.5 - \dfrac{13}{4} = 74.5 - 3.25$

   = 71.25, which agrees with the result of Step 4.

The 30th percentile in this distribution is 71.25, a point above which 26.6 (70 per cent) of the scores lie and below which 11.4 (30 per cent) lie.

At first it may be difficult for you to think of the 50th percentile as "average" because of the minimum passing percentage mark of 70 or 75 that is used in many high schools. Of course, there is no such thing as a "failing" percentile. The decision to pass or fail a given student is an arbitrary one. For roughly descriptive purposes, however, the 25th and 75th percentiles are sometimes used as boundary lines; arbitrarily, scores in the lowest fourth of a group are said to be "low," and those in the highest fourth are called "high." Other common boundary points for low-average-high are the 17th and 83rd percentiles, which separate approximately the lowest one-sixth, middle two-thirds, and upper one-sixth.

Percentile Ranks

We found that the 30th *percentile* of the scores in Table 3-7 is a *score* of 71.25. The *percentile rank* of a score of 71.25 is, therefore, 30. Percentiles are scores; percentile ranks are percentages. What is the percentile rank of a score of 59 in **Table 3-2 on page 55?** It is the percentage of scores that lie below 59.0 in that distribution. We notice that 4 scores [1 + 1 + 1 + 1] lie below 58.5, which is the lower real limit of the score class 58.5-59.5, whose midpoint is 59.0 and within which 2 frequencies lie. How many frequencies lie within the score interval 58.5-59.0? Half of those in the interval 58.5-59.5, or $1/2 \times 2 = 1$. Thus if one frequency is considered to lie between 59.0 and 58.5, and 4 more frequencies lie below 58.5, then 5 frequencies lie below 59.0. This is 5/38, or 13 per cent of all 38 frequencies, so the percentile rank of a score of 59.0 in this distribution is 13. Thirteen per cent of the 38 students scored below 59.0, and $100\% - 13\% = 87\%$ scored above 59.0. (What per cent of the 38 students scored *exactly* 59.0?) The 13th percentile is a score of 59, and the percentile rank of a score of 59 is 13. Table 3-8 illustrates this relationship.

TABLE 3-8

Computing the Percentile Rank of a Score of 59 from Table 3-2

Fractional Endpoints	Class Midpoint	Frequency (f)	Computation
59.5-112.5		32	Below the score of 59.0 lie 1/2 of 2 = 1 frequency in the
59.0-59.5⎫	59.0	1	interval 59.0-58.5 and 1 + 1 + 1 + 1 = 4 frequencies in the
58.5-59.0⎭			interval 58.5-43.5, a total of 5 frequencies lying below 59.0.
43.5-58.5		1⎫5 / 4⎭	Five is 100(5/38) = 13% of the entire number of frequencies, 38, in the distribution. That is, the 13th percentile in this distri-
		N = 38	bution is (a score of) 59.0.

$$PR_{59.0} = 100 \left[\frac{\left(\dfrac{59.0 - 58.5}{59.5 - 58.5} \right)(2) + 4}{38} \right]$$

$$= 13.2 = 13.$$

What is the percentile rank of a score of 75 (the crude mode) in Table 3-2? (Hint: Half of the 3 frequencies in the score interval 74.5-75.5 lie above 75.0, in the interval 75.0-75.5)

What is the percentile rank of a score of 47 in Table 3-2?

If you *really* feel sharp, what is the percentile rank of a hypothetical score of 59.3? No new rules are required to find it.

If you *still* feel sharp, what is the 5.1th percentile in Table 3-2?

Use of Counting Statistics
in Test Interpretation

Figure 3-1 shows how centile ranks are used to construct a profile for a student. The test scorer need not compute any percentiles or percentile ranks there. He simply circles, in the appropriate columns, the scores that the student earned. In Figure 3-1, a male student (use the *M* columns) scored 60 points on the *theoretical* scale, 28 on *economic,* 41 on *aesthetic,* etc. Thus his scores are, relative to each other, high on *theoretical,* low on *economic,* low on *political,* somewhat but not markedly high on *social,* a little above the median on *aesthetic,* and average on *religious.* One can see the pattern at a glance.

	Centile	Theoretical		Economic		Aesthetic		Social		Political		Religious		Centile
		M	F	M	F	M	F	M	F	M	F	M	F	
	99	(60-62)	52-54	60-63	54-56	54-56	61-64	53-55	58-60	58-60	52-53	59-62	65-68	99
	98	59	50-51	59	53	52-53	60	51-52	56-57	56-57	51	57-58	63-64	98
H	97	58	49	58	52	51	58-59	50	55	55	50	56	61-62	97
I	96	57	48	57	51	50	57		54		49	55	60	96
	94-95	55-56	47	55-56	49-50	48-49	56	48-49	53	53-54	48	53-54	59	94-95
G	93						55				47	52	58	93
	92	54	46	54	48	47		47	52			51	57	92
H	90-91	53	45	53		46	54	46	51	52	46	50	56	90-91
	88-89			52	47	45	53			51		49	55	88-89
	86-87	52	44		46		52	(45)	50	50	45		54	86-87
	83-85	51	43	51	45	44	51	44	49		44	47-48	53	83-85
	81-82		42	50		43	50				49		52	81-82
	78-80	50		49	44	42	49	43	48	48	43	46	51	78-80
	75-77	49	41	48	43	(41)		42	47		42	45		75-77
A	71-74	48	40		42	40	48	41	46	47		44	49-50	71-74
	68-70			47		39	47			46	41	43		68-70
V	64-67	47	39	46	41		46	40	45		40	42	48	64-67
	60-63	46	38	45	40	38	45	39	44	45		41	47	60-63
E	56-59	45	37	44	39	37	44			44	39	40	46	56-59
	52-55					36		38	43			39	45	52-55
R	49-51	44	36	43	38	35		37	42	43	38	38	44	49-51
	45-48	43	35	42	37	34	42				37	37	43	45-48
A	41-44	42		41			41	36	41	42		(36)	42	41-44
	37-40		34		36		40	35	40	41	36	35	41	37-40
G	33-36	41	33	40	35	32	39	34	39	40		34	40	33-36
	30-32	40	32	39	34	31					35		39	30-32
E	26-29	39		38		30	38	33	38	39	34	33	38	26-29
	23-25		31	37	33	29	37	32	37	38		32	37	23-25
	20-22	38	30	36	32	28	36		36		33	31	36	20-22
	18-19	37					35	31		37		30		18-19
	15-17	36	29	35	31	27	34	30	35	36	32	29	34-35	15-17
	13-14		28	34	30	26			34		31	28	33	13-14
	11-12		27	33	29	25	33	29		35		27		11-12
L	9-10	34	26	32	28	24	32	28	33	34	30	26	31-32	9-10
	8					23	31	27	32		29	25		8
O	7	33	25	31	27					33			30	7
	5-6	32	24		26	21-22	29-30	26	31	32	28	23-24	28-29	5-6
W	4	31	23	29	25	20	28	25	30	31	27	22	27	4
	3	30	22	(28)	24	19	27	24	29	(30)	26	20-21	26	3
	2	28-29	21	26-27	23	17-18	25-26	22-23	27-28	29	25	18-19	24-25	2
	1	25-27	18-20	23-25	20-22	14-16	22-24	19-21	24-26	26-28	22-24	15-17	20-23	1

Figure 3-1. *Centile sheet for college men and women in Allport, Vernon, and Lindzey.* A Study of Values, *based upon the norms (2,489 men, 1,289 women) in the Manual of directions (Boston: Houghton Mifflin Company, 1960). The six scores of John Doe are plotted. The centiles were computed by William L. Goodwin. See his article in the* Journal of Educational Measurement, 1964, Vol. 1.

Percentile ranks, based on a 99-point scale, are one kind of norm. If the user does not need 99 categories, he may use fewer, such as the 11 (1— through 9+, or 0—10) shown in Figure 3-2 alongside the percentile ranks. This shorter scale is called a "sta-eleven" scale because it is a *sta*ndard system having 11 categories. It, too, may involve counting, as we shall see later in this chapter. The student depicted, Richard Roe, scored in the "high" portion of the table, above the 82nd percentile (that is, above a percentile rank of 82) on 7 of the 11 tests. He was highest on G (grammar), with a percentile rank of 98, and a sta-eleven score of 9. Even with a percentile rank of 96, he would have obtained 9 because 9 represents any one of the three percentile ranks 96, 97, and 98. He was lowest on H (history), 18th or 19th percentile and sta-eleven 3, which represents all percentile ranks from 11 through 22.

Some students will probably have noticed that Figure 3-2 does not even list the "raw" (original) scores that Richard Roe earned. Everything there is expressed only in normative form, relative to the scores of all the students who were tested along with Richard. For that matter, we could omit the percentile ranks and sta-elevens and still have a pretty good idea of how well he did, simply by seeing on the graph how high or how low the dots representing his scores are. The numbers serve merely to "quantify" this highness or lowness. A ruler would do just as well, wouldn't it? Try expressing Richard's scores as distance in inches (or centimeters) from the bottom of the figure.

Alert readers may also have noticed that the percentile ranks of Figures 3-1 and 3-2 are not spaced equally, while the sta-elevens of Figure 3-2 are. Why? Think about this a little now; we will explain the reason for it later in this chapter, on pages 78-85.

In Figures 3-1 and 3-2 the median, which is the 50th percentile, lies in the interval 49—51, right in the middle of the "Average" range and, of course, in the middle of the entire percentile range. In Figure 3-2, this is exactly where the sta-eleven score of 5 is listed, too; 5 is actually the 5.0 that lies at the center of the interval 4.5-5.5, which contains the percentile ranks 41 through 59.

The Mean

The most familiar average is the arithmetic *mean*. In fact, this measure is in such common use that most people regard it as *the* average because it is the only average they know anything about. When the term "average" comes up in ordinary conversation or in a newspaper in such statements as "average temperature," "average rainfall," "average yield of corn and wheat," and "average price," it is likely that the mean is meant. (The "batting average" in baseball is an exception, however, being 10 times the percentage of hits a player obtains.) The mean can be computed by simply obtaining the sum of the measures and dividing by their number. The measure so obtained is then the value that each individual would have if all shared equally.

Statisticians say that the arithmetic mean is a simple linear function of all the scores in the distribution: $1/N$ times the first score plus $1/N$ times the sec-

Figure 3-2. *A profile based on local norms.*

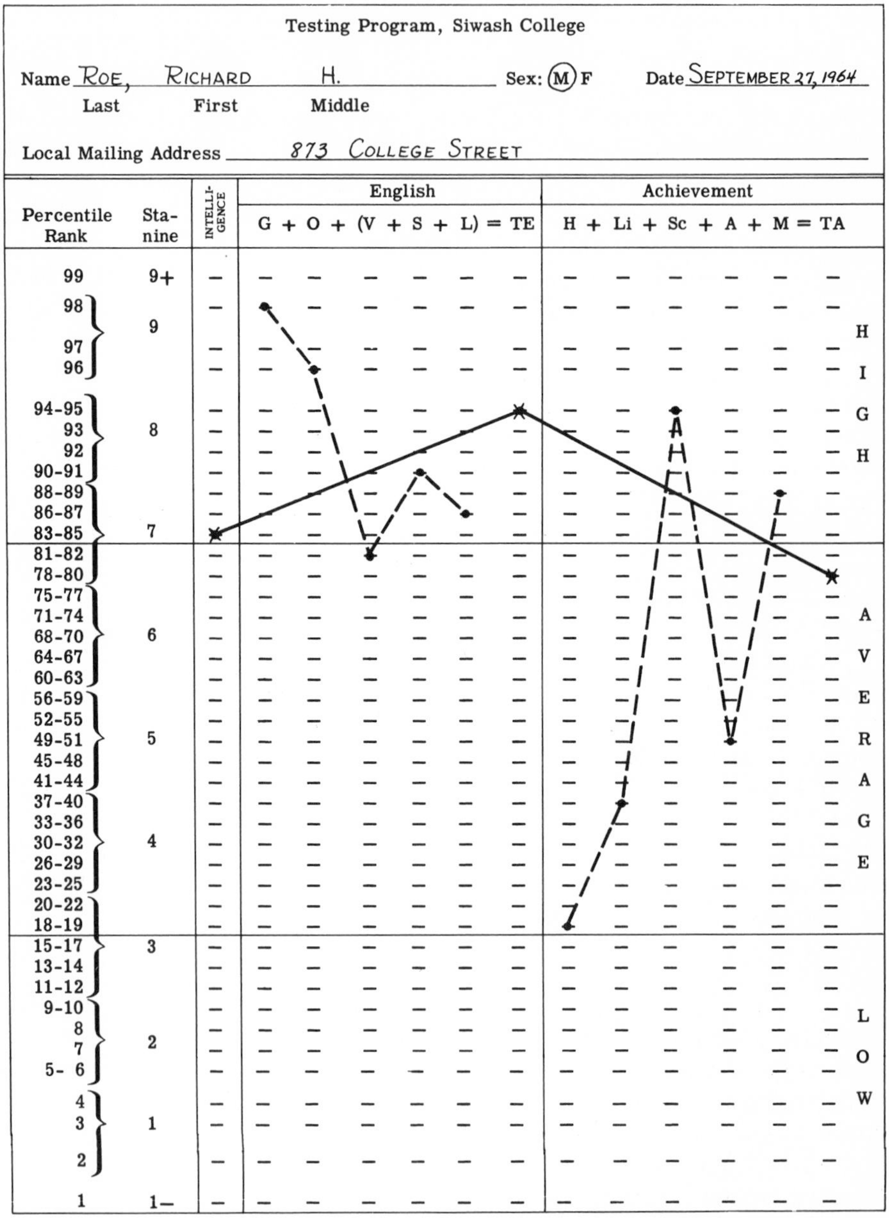

Testing Program, Siwash College

Name ROE, RICHARD H.   Sex: (M) F   Date SEPTEMBER 27, 1964

Last   First   Middle

Local Mailing Address _873 COLLEGE STREET_

Percentile Rank	Sta-nine	INTELLI-GENCE	English G + O + (V + S + L) = TE	Achievement H + Li + Sc + A + M = TA
99	9+			
98	9			
97				H
96				I
94-95	8			G
93				
92				H
90-91				
88-89				
86-87				
83-85	7			
81-82				
78-80				
75-77				
71-74	6			A
68-70				
64-67				V
60-63				
56-59				E
52-55	5			
49-51				R
45-48				
41-44				A
37-40				
33-36	4			G
30-32				
26-29				E
23-25				
20-22				
18-19				
15-17	3			
13-14				
11-12				
9-10	2			L
8				
7				O
5- 6				
4	1			W
3				
2				
1	1−			

ond score plus . . . plus 1/N times the last score, where N is the total number of scores. Unlike the median, the mean is affected by the magnitude of every score in the distribution. Increase any single score by P points and you increase the mean by P/N points. Decrease any single score by P points and you lower the mean by P/N points. Increase the highest score (112) in Table 3-2 and decrease the lowest score (44) all you please and not only will the median remain unchanged, but also so will all percentile ranks and all percentiles except those involving the top and bottom category.

The sum of the deviations of all measures from their arithmetic mean is *always* precisely zero, provided that one uses both plus and minus signs, whereas the sum of the deviations of all measures from their median is minimal if negative signs are treated as positive. This can be shown clearly with an example provided by Eells,[6] which we illustrate in Figure 3-3. Suppose that

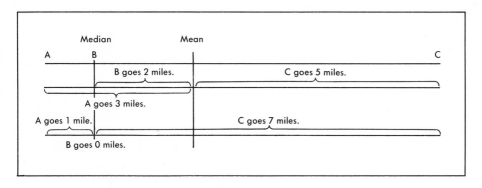

Figure 3-3. *Travel distance less to median than to mean*

three men (*A, B,* and *C*) live along an eight-mile-long straight road at distance 0, 1, and 8 miles from its origin—that is, *A* at the beginning, *B* 1 mile from the beginning, and *C* at the end. The mean of 0, 1, and 8 is 9/3 = 3, whereas the median (here also the midscore) is 1. If these men desire to meet at some one point along the road, where should it be? If they meet at the mean point, 3 miles, then *A* will walk +3 miles, *B* +2 miles, and *C* −5 miles, a total of 3 + 2 + 5 = 10 miles (though 3, 2, and *minus* 5 sum to 0). If they meet at the median, which is *B*'s house, *A* will walk +1 mile, *B* 0 miles, and *C* −7 miles, 8 miles in all (1, 0, and −7 do not sum to 0, we note). Thus they walk 10 − 8 = 2 miles less to the median than to the mean, though *C* may point out that only *A* and *B* benefited, because *he* has to walk two miles further to reach the median than the mean. *A* and *B* each save 2 miles if the median is used, while *C* loses 2, resulting in the net saving of 2 + 2 − 2 = 2 miles.

---

[6]W. C. Eells, Population center, *Science,* 22 September 1961, 134, p. 797.

If we took an 8-inch ruler and put equal weights at 0, 1, and 8 inches, it would balance if a fulcrum were placed at 3. "Weight" on one side of the mean is equal to that on the other side. If we think of frequencies as being weights, we see immediately that any score distribution balances at its mean ("center of gravity"), but not at its median unless mean and median happen to be the same.

We have already recommended use of the midscore for most practical work with the test scores of less than 100 or so students. If a mean is desired, it can be readily computed from an ungrouped or grouped distribution with an electric desk calculator that multiplies, adds, and divides—or even by using an adding machine. The main office of most school systems, even small ones, usually has such equipment. For example, the mean of the 38 ungrouped scores in Table 3-1 on page 54 is found in the following way: $(90 + 66 + \ldots + 84)$ $/38 = 3050/38 = 80.26$. The mean of the 38 scores in Table 3-2 grouped with a score-class interval of 1, would be obtained as follows: $[(112 \times 1) + (109 \times 1) + (106 \times 1) + (105 \times 1) + (104 \times 1) + (100 \times 1) + (97 \times 2) + \ldots + (44 \times 1)]/38 = 3050/38 = 80.26$. On a Friden, Marchant, Monroe, or similar calculator this process can be carried out quickly without copying down *anything* but the answer.

The mean of a grouped frequency distribution with a class interval greater than 1 proceeds similarly; midpoints of the score classes are used as scores. For the grouped distribution in Table 3-3, the mean is computed as follows: $[1(110 + 114)/2 + 3(105 + 109)/2 + \ldots + 1(40 + 44)/2]38 = 3051/38 = 80.29$. In simpler form this is $[1(110 + 114) + 3(105 + 109) + \ldots + 1(40 + 44)]$ $/2(38) = 6102/76 = 80.29$. It is even easier to use the midpoints directly: $[(1 \times 112) + (3 \times 107) + \ldots + (1 \times 42)]/38 = 80.29$. Grouping may change the mean somewhat, but usually not much unless the number of score classes is appreciably less than 12. The difference here is only $80.29 - 80.26 = 0.03$, a mere four-hundredths of one per cent.

When the scores are few in number or in an ungrouped series, the simplest way to compute the mean is the one described above for Table 3-1; that is, the scores are first added, and then this sum is divided by the number of scores.

What average is best? As a rule, *the mean is regarded as the best measure of central tendency,* and the crude mode as the poorest. The mean, however, is greatly influenced by extreme scores, and whenever we wish to avoid this influence, the median is best. Since such situations often arise in educational measurement, the median is widely used. For example, if a test is too difficult, there may be several zero or chance scores; if a test is too easy, there may be several perfect scores. But in neither case are the pupils at the extremes correctly measured. In such situations, the median is usually the best average to use. And, unless an electric calculator or electronic computer is available, the median is also easier to find than the mean.

An illustration may help to indicate appropriate uses of these measures of central tendency.

If a factory has 100 employees, all of whom except for five executives earn between $3000 and $8000 per year, these five each earning more than $15,000, the *mean* salary for the factory is likely to be misleadingly high; it does not adequately characterize the 95 non-executives. However, the *median* will not be sensitive to the few high salaries. In fact, we can determine the median without even knowing the actual salaries of the executives by just having a top category of "more than $8000" whose frequency is 5. In such instances, it may be desirable to use the median instead of the mean. Sometimes, the best way is just to exclude the five executives from the distribution and to report their salaries separately. Then the 95 workers represent a more homogeneous group for which the mean may be used.

An improbable anecdote should make this problem of heterogeneity plain. Five men once sat near each other on a park bench. Two were vagrants, each with total worldly assets of 25 cents. The third was a workman whose bank account and other assets totaled $2000. The fourth man had $15,000 in various forms. The fifth was a multimillionaire with a net worth of $5,000,000. Therefore, the modal assets of the group were 25 cents. This figure describes two of the persons perfectly, but is grossly inaccurate for the other three. The median figure of $2000 does little justice to anyone except the workman. The mean, $1,003,400.10, is not very satisfactory even for the multimillionaire. If we *had* to choose one measure of central tendency, perhaps it would be the mode, which describes 40 per cent of this group accurately. But if told that "the modal assets of five persons sitting on a park bench are 25 cents," we would be likely to conclude that the total assets of the group are approximately $1.25, which is more than five million dollars lower than the correct figure. Obviously, no measure of central tendency whatsoever is adequate for these "strange bench-fellows," who simply do not "tend centrally."

MEASURES OF VARIABILITY OR SCATTER

Meaning of Variability

No distribution is described completely by a measure of central tendency. The mean intelligence in two classes may be the same, and yet the classes may be very unlike. Whereas the members of one class, assigned randomly, may vary all the way from feeble-mindedness to the genius level, the members of the other class (homogeneously arranged) may differ little from each other intellectually. Obviously, these two classes present contrasting instructional problems because they differ in *variability*. Variability is the extent to which the scores of a group tend to scatter (disperse, spread) above and below a central point in the distribution. Clearly, it is important to have some convenient method for determining the variability of a group. Three common measures of variability are the *range,* the *quartile deviation,* and the *standard deviation.* All these measures represent distances rather than points, and the larger they are the greater the variability (scatter, spread, heterogeneity, dispersion) of the scores.

The Range

The *range* has already been referred to as the distance between the highest and the lowest scores plus one,[7] which some measurement specialists call the "inclusive range" in order to distinguish it from the largest score − smallest score. It is a very untrustworthy measure of variability for small groups.[8] The shift in a single score may alter the range greatly and thereby materially increase or reduce the apparent variability of the group. School A and School D in Table 3-4 illustrate this possibility. If, for example, the lowest score in School A had been 35 instead of 10-14, the range would have been 94.5 − 34.5 = 60, instead of 94.5 − 9.5 = 85.

The Quartile Deviation

A measure of variability that avoids being unduly influenced by extreme scores is the *quartile deviation,* denoted by Q. Q is defined as one-half the distance between the first and third quartiles. It is often referred to as the semi-interquartile range (that is, half the range of the extreme quartiles).

The formula used for obtaining Q is

$$Q = \frac{Q_3 - Q_1}{2} = \frac{75\text{th percentile} - 25\text{th percentile}}{2}.$$

Since 25 per cent of the scores fall below the first quartile, Q_1, and 25 per cent of the scores lie above the third quartile, Q_3, the interquartile range is the range of the middle 50 per cent of the scores. The whole interquartile range might be used to express the variability of the group, but it is customary to take half this distance and to set up a new middle-half range extending from Q below the median to Q above the median: $\text{Mdn} \pm Q = Q_2 \pm \frac{Q_3 - Q_1}{2}$. As already noted, the middle of the interquartile range will usually not be exactly the median, whereas the middle of this new range will always be. On the other hand, exactly half of all the frequencies lie within the interquartile range and exactly half outside it, but this does not hold precisely for $\text{Mdn} \pm Q$.

Table 3-9 illustrates the computation of Q. Notice that the process of locating quartiles is like that of locating any other percentile. In the first step, the

---

[7]More precisely, the range is the difference between the lower real limit of the lowest class and the higher real limit of the highest class.

[8]When there are only two measures (N = 2), however, the range gives all the information concerning variability that the distribution can yield.

TABLE 3-9

The Process of Computing the Quartile Deviation, Q (Distributio,. from Table 3-3)

Frequency Distribution f		Steps in Process
110–114	1	1. Computing Q_1, the 25th percentile.
105–109	3	$\dfrac{1}{4}N = \dfrac{1}{4}$ of 38 = 9.5.
100–104	2	
95–99	4	Counting up: $1 + 1 + 1 + 3 + 1 = 7$, therefore Q_1 lies in the class 65–69.
	28	
90–94	3	$9.5 - 7 = 2.5;\; 2.5/3 \times (69.5 - 64.5) = \dfrac{2.5 \times 5}{3} = 4.17,$ correction.
85–89	1	
80–84	6	$64.5 + 4.17 = 68.67, Q_1$.
75–79	4	Check by counting down 75% of frequencies:
70–74	4	$69.5 - \dfrac{28.5 - 28}{3}(69.5 - 64.5) = 69.5 - \dfrac{0.5 \times 5}{3} = 69.5 - \dfrac{2.5}{3} =$
65–69	3	
	7	$69.50 - 0.83 = 68.67.$
60–64	1	
55–59	3	2. Computing Q_3, the 75th percentile.
50–54	1	$\dfrac{3}{4}N = 3/4$ of 38 = 114/4 = 28.5.
45–49	1	
40–44	1	Counting up: $7 + 3 + 4 + 4 + 6 + 1 + 3 = 28;$ therefore Q_3 lies in the class 95–99.
N	38	$28.5 - 28 = 0.5;\; 0.5/4 \times (99.5 - 94.5) = 2.5/4 = 0.62,$ correction.
		$94.5 + 0.62 = 95.12, Q_3$.
		Check by counting down 25% of frequencies:
		$99.5 - \dfrac{9.5 - (1 + 3 + 2)}{4}(99.5 - 94.5)$
		$= 99.5 - \dfrac{3.5 \times 5}{4} = 95.12.$
		3. Substituting in the formula $Q = \dfrac{Q_3 - Q_1}{2}$:
		$Q = \dfrac{95.12 - 68.67}{2} = \dfrac{26.45}{2} = 13.2.$

fractional part of N indicates the proportion of the distribution which falls below the desired point; that is, for Q_1 it is $\tfrac{1}{4}$N and for Q_3 it is $\tfrac{3}{4}$N. There are three steps, as follows:

1. *Compute Q_1*, the 25th percentile. To begin with, 1/4 of 38 is 9.5. The next three steps in locating this point are exactly the same as those in locating any percentile. *Check your work* by counting downward $3/4 \times 38 = 28.5$ frequencies.

2. *Compute Q_3*, the 75th percentile. Here the first step is to take $\tfrac{3}{4}$N; .3/4 of 38 is 28.5. The other three steps are identical with those in locating any percentile. *Check your work* by counting downward $1/4 \times 38 = 9.5$ frequencies.

3. *Substitute in the formula.* Q_3 is 95.12 and Q_1 is 68.67. The difference between them is 26.45. Half of this difference is 13.2, the value of Q.

A much simpler and faster *approximate* way to obtain Q is to arrange the 38 papers in order from highest to lowest score, as at the left of Table 3-2 on page 55, and count down to the 10th paper (that is, beyond 38/4 = 9.5) and up to the 10th paper. The score on the 10th paper from the top is 95. The score on the 10th paper from the bottom is 69. (95 − 69)/2 = 26/2 = 13, which is pretty close to the value of 13.2 shown in Table 3-9.

An even easier-to-compute statistic of variability is D = P_{90} − P_{10}, the distance from the 90th percentile to the 10th percentile. Its approximate value can be found rapidly by counting down past 38/10 = 3.8 to the 4th paper from the top and up to the 4th paper from the bottom: 105 − 58 = 47. (From Table 3-2, the exact P_{90} − P_{10} = 104.7 − 58.3 = 46.4, doesn't it?) D is analogous to P_{75} − P_{25} but indicates the range of the middle 80% of the scores, instead of just the middle 50%. D is less affected by changes in extreme scores than is the range, but more likely to be affected than Q.

Although Q is used much more frequently than D, D is a better percentile measure of variability because it is based on a larger range of scores than Q, but not too large a range; it is considerably easier to compute than Q, also. The interpretation of D, Q, and other measures of variability is a relative matter. Whether a D of 46.4 is to be considered large or small depends on the magnitude of D for other groups using the same test.

The Standard Deviation

A third measure of variability, which has many uses in educational measurement, is the *standard deviation*. It is customarily represented by the letter *s* for samples and σ (the Greek letter "sigma") for populations and is defined as the square root of the mean of the squares of the deviations of the scores from their mean. σ may also be defined in terms of the range above and below the mean (M ± 1σ) that in a normal distribution[9] includes 68.26 per cent, or approximately two thirds, of the scores.

We can, of course, compute the standard deviation of a set of test scores directly, following the above root-mean-square definition. For the 38 ungrouped scores of Table 3-1, whose mean we already know to be 80.26, the standard deviation is

$$s = \sqrt{\frac{(90 - 80.26)^2 + (66 - 80.26)^2 + \ldots + (84 - 80.26)^2}{38}}$$

$$= \sqrt{\frac{11,421.3688}{38}} = \sqrt{300.5623} = 17.34.$$

---

[9]This particular type of frequency distribution is discussed on page 78.

(Refer to Appendix C if you do not remember how to compute square roots.)

You can use an electric calculator and save time by working with "raw" scores instead of means:

$$s = \sqrt{\frac{38(90^2 + 66^2 + \ldots + 84^2) - (90 + 66 + \ldots + 84)^2}{38}}$$

$$= \frac{\sqrt{434,012}}{38} = \frac{658.79}{38} = 17.34.$$

(Will s computed by these two methods always be identical? Yes, except possibly for a slight difference due to rounding-off errors. The two formulas are algebraically equivalent.)

There are many short-cut procedures for computing s, but we will not consider any of them. Persons who really need to compute standard deviations will usually be able to find an electric calculator. For most teachers, bothering with such things as square roots and "arbitrary-origin" computational procedures involving negative deviations is probably a waste of time. In a "normal" distribution the mean plus and minus 1 standard deviation extends from a percentile rank of 15.87 to a percentile rank of 84.13, so you can estimate the standard deviation s from the formula $s' = \dfrac{P_{84.13} - P_{15.87}}{2}$. Count down from the top of the test papers 15.87% of the way and up from the bottom 15.87% of the way. For the 38 papers grouped with an interval of 1 in Table 3-2, this means counting down and up $38(0.1587) = 6.0306$ papers. Thus we just barely enter the 96.5-97.5 score class from the top, so we find the 84.13th percentile to be $97.5 - \dfrac{6.0306 - 6}{2} \times (97.5 - 96.5) = 97.5000 - 0.0153 = 97.4847$. Similarly, we just barely enter the 61.5-62.5 score class from the bottom, so the 15.87th percentile is $61.5 + \dfrac{6.0306 - 6}{1} \times (62.5 - 61.5) = 61.5000 + 0.0306 = 61.5306$. Then the estimated standard deviation, s', is $\dfrac{97.4847 - 61.5306}{2} = 18.0$, fairly close to the actual figure of 17.3.

This percentile method for approximating s is straightforward but likely to be tedious, even if we round off some of the above figures, such as 6.0306 to 6.03; 15.87 is not a very convenient percentile rank to work with. A simpler "rough and ready" approximation of s is 0.4D which, for the value of D that we found above (46.4), yields 18.6. The 0.4D estimate of s may be adequate for your purposes. If it isn't, work out the raw-score-formula computations for s on a machine. Get someone who is familiar with the machine to show you how to square scores and sum them efficiently and accurately at the same time. If you have forgotten how to compute square roots, see Appendix C for refresher material. Be sure, however, that you actually need the standard deviation. If you are working with the scores of only a few students—less than 100— you probably don't. Even when obtaining standard scores (discussed below) for an entire school, you may be wiser to use percentile or percentage methods, rather than means and standard deviations directly.

The standard deviation is the most important measure of the variability of test scores. A small standard deviation means that the group has small variability, or is relatively homogeneous, whereas a large standard deviation means the opposite condition, heterogeneity.

The standard deviation also has certain other important uses, besides being a measure of dispersion of scores within a group. For example, the position of a pupil in a distribution is often expressed in terms of standard-deviation units. In the distribution used in Table 3-2, where the mean is approximately 80 and the standard deviation is approximately 17, a pupil whose score is 97 is said to be one standard deviation above the mean, and his sigma score is written $+1s$. In like manner, a pupil with a score of 63 would be approximately one standard deviation below the mean, and his sigma score is written $-1s$. Such scores are called *standard scores* or *z-scores*, which we discuss below.

Which measure of variability is best? As a rule, s is considered the best measure of variability, the range undoubtedly the poorest. The range is subject to all the limitations that the mode has as a measure of central tendency. Just as the mean is greatly influenced by extreme scores, so is s. Whenever it is desirable, therefore, to avoid the influence of extreme scores, the median is employed as a measure of central tendency, and with it a percentile measure of variability such as D or Q. Similarly, when the mean is used, s is the appropriate measure of variability because like the mean it is a function of all the scores in the distribution.

The standard deviation is of interest to most of you chiefly because it is used a great deal by test publishers and educational researchers. You need to understand what it means far more than how to compute it. Part of the next chapter is devoted to a study of test manuals in order to discover what statistics are mentioned there and how such statistics help you understand the tests better. Before that, however, we will discuss standard scores and several other topics.

STANDARD SCORES   *The "Normal Curve"*

If a test is neither too easy nor too hard for the group tested, scores will often be distributed approximately "normally," i.e. somewhat in the bell-shaped pattern of Figure 3-4. Notice that the curve is symmetrical (the left half is the mirror image of the right half) and unimodal (just one mode). In any symmetrical unimodal distribution, mean = median = mode. The "normal curve" is a special kind of symmetrical unimodal distribution whose relationship of height to width at every score is mathematically specified. (You can find the mathematical formula in statistics books, if you are curious.[10]) As stated above, in a normally distributed set of scores the 15.87th percentile lies one standard deviation below the mean, and the 84.13th percentile lies one standard deviation above the mean. You can readily see this in Figure 3-4. Similarly, a score two standard deviations below the mean has a percentile rank of 2.28, and a score two standard deviations above the mean has a percentile rank of 97.72. The corresponding PR's for -3σ and $+3\sigma$ are 0.13 and 99.87, respectively. The entire "unit" normal distribution has been tabled

---

[10]See G. A. Ferguson, *Statistical analysis in psychology and education* (New York: McGraw-Hill, 1959), p. 79.

Figure 3-4. *The normal curve. (Adapted from Test Service Bulletin No. 48, The Psychological Corporation.)*

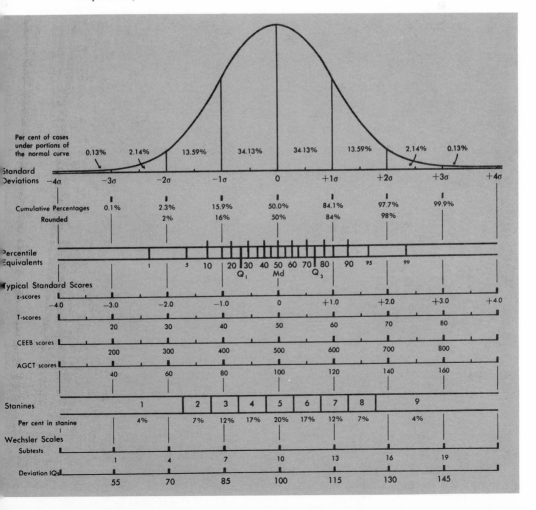

by Kelley[11] and others, so that we can readily ascertain the standard deviation distance from the mean that corresponds to any percentile rank, from 0 s.d. corresponding to a PR of 50 at the mean to -3.719 and $+3.719$ s.d. at the 0.01th and 99.99th PR's, respectively.

We have already wrestled with the problem of giving meaning to a student's raw test-score, relative to his peers. One way is to express his score as a deviation from the mean of the group tested, such as -12 points if his score is 12 points below the mean. How low is his score? Twelve points below the mean might be the lowest score among 1000 persons tested, if the standard deviation were small (3 or 4) and the scores distributed approximately normally. On the other hand, it would be the 16th percentile if the standard deviation were 12 and the scores normally distributed. Sixteen per cent of the students would score more than 12 points below the mean. Therefore, it seems desirable to divide the deviation of a student's raw score from the mean by the standard deviation of the group to secure a "standard score" that indicates how many standard deviations below or above the mean he scored. This basic standard score is defined as

$$z = \frac{\text{Raw score} - \text{Mean}}{\text{Standard Deviation}}$$

and called a z score. (See Figure 3-4 on page 79.) The mean of a full set of z scores (one for each person from whose raw scores the mean and standard deviation are calculated) is 0, because the sum of the (raw scores $-$ mean) is 0. The standard deviation of a full set of z scores is 1. If we plot the distribution of z scores, we find that it has exactly the same shape as the original raw

[11]T. L. Kelley, *The Kelley statistical tables,* rev. ed. (Cambridge: Harvard University Press, 1948).

Figure 3-5. *Negative and positive skewness.*

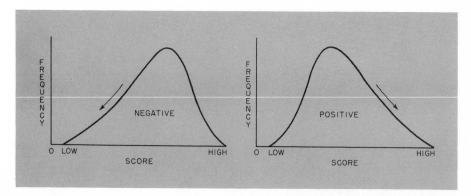

scores. Computing z scores does *not* change the shape of the distribution. Skewed distributions—tailing off in one direction or the other, as in Figure 3-5 —remain skewed; symmetrical distributions remain symmetrical. We consider this point further in Chapter Four.

Of course, z scores below the mean are negative, and in order to get enough precision we must use at least one decimal place for z scores that are not exactly integers. This makes for such hard-to-handle z's as −2.3—negative and fractional. We can avoid minuses and decimals by simply setting up a distribution of standard scores with a mean sufficiently greater than 0 to avoid minuses, and a standard deviation sufficiently greater than 1 to make decimals unnecessary. One such system, called "stanines" (*sta*ndard scores with *nine* categories), was used considerably during World War II. The mean of a full set of stanines is 5 and its standard deviation 2. The formula for computing a student's stanine from his raw score is

$$\text{Stanine} = 5 + 2\left(\frac{\text{Raw Score} - \text{Mean}}{\text{Standard Deviation}}\right) = 5 + 2z.$$

The nine stanines are 1, 2, 3, 4, 5, 6, 7, 8, and 9. The lowest stanine, 1, is 2 standard deviations *below* the mean because $(1 - 5)/2 = -4/2 = -2$, just as the highest stanine, 9, is 2 standard deviations *above* the mean because $(9 - 5)/2 = 2$. Other equivalences of z's and stanines are $z = (2 - 5)/2 = -1.5$ for a stanine of 2, and $z = (8 - 5)/2 = 1.5$ for a stanine of 8. What are the z equivalents for stanines 3, 4, 5, 6 and 7?

If you wanted to stretch the stanine scale to make it a sta-eleven scale, you could do this by simply putting 0 at the low end and 10 at the top without changing the mean of 5 and standard deviation of 2. The z equivalents of 0 and 10 are $(0 - 5)/2 = -2.5$, and $(10 - 5)/2 = 2.5$. The sta-eleven top score, 10, represents the range of computed sta-eleven scores from 9.5 up, which means from a z of $(9.5 - 5)/2 = 2.25$ up. By looking up a z of +2.25 in a table of the unit normal distribution, you can determine that the area from this point up to plus infinity (as *far* as you could possibly go) is 1.22 per cent. Thus, *if* the raw scores are distributed normally, exactly 1.22 per cent of the students will be assigned a sta-eleven score of 10. Also, 1.22 per cent will be assigned a sta-eleven score of 0, representing all sta-eleven scores of 0.5 and lower. Table 3-10 shows the percentages of students who will be assigned each sta-eleven score *if* the raw scores are distributed according to the "normal curve."

You may have suspected by now that we have no intention of actually computing the mean and standard deviation of raw scores in order to compute the sta-eleven scores one by one with the formula 5 + 2z. That procedure could be speeded up quite a bit, but we can get excellent results merely by counting, so why compute? We have only to arrange our test papers in order from highest to lowest score, pick the top 1.22 per cent and call their score 10, the next 2.79 per cent and call their score 9, the next 6.55 per cent and call their score 8, the next

TABLE 3-10

*The Percentages of Scores Assigned to Each Sta-eleven Score
if the Raw Scores are Distributed According to the "Normal Curve"*

Sta-eleven Score	Per Cent of Raw Scores	
10	1.22 ⎫	
9	2.79 ⎭	4.01 for stanine scale 9
8	6.55	
7	12.10	
6	17.47	
5	19.74	
4	17.47	
3	12.10	
2	6.55	
1	2.79 ⎫	
0	1.22 ⎭	4.01 for stanine scale 1
Total	100.00	

12.10 per cent and call their score 7, and the next 17.47 per cent and call their score 6. Then we shall go to the bottom of the pile of test papers, calling the lowest 1.22 per cent 0 (or, if seeming nothingness frightens your viewers, call it 1−), the next lowest 2.79 per cent 1, the next 6.55 per cent 2, the next 12.10 per cent 3, and the next 17.47 per cent 4. We then label all remaining papers 5. Sound simple? With a little practice, it is. Any conscientious clerk can standardize scores this way, and at the same time the scores are being both standardized and *normalized*. The standardization occurs because we set the mean of sta-eleven scores at 5 and their standard deviation at 2. Normalizing (perhaps not complete) occurs because we squeeze the raw scores into an approximately bell-shaped form, as specified by the normal distribution and illustrated in Figure 3-4. This makes it easier to compare scores in, say, arithmetic and English, for the same group of students where the arithmetic test was too difficult for some of the class, producing positively skewed raw scores, and the English test was too easy for some, producing negatively skewed scores; the sta-eleven scores for arithmetic will have more nearly the same shape as the sta-eleven scores for English than the raw scores for arithmetic and English did. (This does not excuse careless or inept choosing of tests. Try to select tests with enough "floor" —easy enough so that few, if any, of the poorest students will make zero or pure chance scores—and enough "ceiling"—hard enough so that few, if any, of the ablest students will make perfect scores.)

National norms for a test can be reported as sta-elevens (or stanines), of course. Also, local norms can be reported as sta-elevens in a school system to supplement the "national norms" offered in test manuals. Let us see how sta-eleven scores are found. (A more extensive illustration appears in Appendix H.)

We start with the right-hand frequency distribution in Table 3-2, where the score-class interval is 1. Our first task is to set up a list of the frequencies desired for the sta-eleven of 10, 9, and so on down. For 10 (and 0) we see in Table 3-10 that we need 1.22 per cent, or 0.0122, of 38, shown as 0.46 at top and bottom of the second column of Table 3-11. The raw score of 112 has a frequency of 1,

TABLE 3-11

Converting the 38 Raw Scores of Table 3-2 to Sta-elevens

Sta-elevens	Theoretical Frequency		Actual Frequency	Equivalent Raw Scores
10	0.46	1.52	0	
9	1.06		2	112, 109
8	2.49		2	106, 105
7	4.60		4	104, 100, 97
6	6.64		6	95, 93, 91, 90, 89
5	7.51		10	84, 83, 82, 81, 80, 78, 75
4	6.64		6	74, 72, 71, 70, 69, 68
3	4.60		4	66, 62, 59
2	2.49		2	58, 51
1	1.06	1.52	2	47, 44
0	0.46		0	
	38.00		38	

which is further from 0.46 than 0.46 is from 0. Thus there is no sta-eleven score of 10. Stating it another way, the frequency for the sta-eleven score of 10 in this distribution is 0, the same as the frequency of sta-eleven scores of 11, 12, 13 etc. (The same thing is true of the sta-eleven score of 0, which also has a frequency of 0. *Unless N is at least 41, not more than 9 sta-categories determined in this way can ever be used.*)

Obviously, then, the highest actual sta-eleven for this distribution is less than 10. Let's try 9. For category 9 we need 2.79 per cent, or 0.0279, of 38 frequencies (see Table 3-10), which is 1.0602. But 9 now represents "8.5 and up," so it must accommodate its own theoretical frequency, 1.0602, plus the theoretical frequency for 10, which is 0.4636; 1.0602 + 0.4636 = 1.5238, which we can shorten to 1.52. This is slightly closer to 2 than it is to 1, so we assign a sta-eleven of 9 to raw scores of 112 (frequency 1) and 109 (frequency 1). We also assign a sta-eleven of 1 to raw scores of 44 (frequency 1) and 47 (frequency 1). Having done that, we go on to sta-elevens of 8 and 2 (working down from the top and up from the bottom.

We need 6.55 per cent of 38 for 8 and for 2; 0.0655 × 38 = 2.4890, which we abbreviate to 2.49. Noticing that the frequencies for raw scores of 106, 105, and 104 are 1 each, and that 2.49 is a bit closer to 2 than to 3, we assign sta-eleven 8 to raw scores of 106 and 105. Similarly, we see that raw scores of 51,

58, and 59 have frequencies of 1, 1, and 2, respectively, so we assign sta-eleven 2 to raw scores of 51 and 58.

Now for sta-elevens of 7 and 3, each of which requires 12.10% of the 38 frequencies: $0.121 \times 38 = 4.598$, which may be shortened to 4.6. 104, 100, and 97 have $1 + 1 + 2 = 4$ frequencies, which is closer to 4.6 than the 6 that would be obtained by including 95 and its 2 frequencies, so we assign the sta-eleven 7 to 104, 100, and 97. Similarly, sta-eleven 3 is assigned to 59, 62, and 66.

Sta-elevens 6 and 4 each need 17.47 per cent of the 38 frequencies, or 6.6. The raw scores 95, 93, 91, 90, and 89 have a total of 6 frequencies, which is closer to 6.6 than the 8 that would be obtained if 84 were included, so sta-eleven 6 is assigned to 95, 93, 91, 90, and 89. Sta-eleven 4 is assigned to 68, 69, 70, 71, 72, and 74, which have 6 frequencies. Obviously, 6.6 is closer to 6 than it is to the 9 frequencies that would result if the score of 75 were included.

Which raw scores remain for the middle sta-eleven category, 5? 84, 83, 82, 81, 80, 78, and 75, with 10 frequencies, contrasted with the 7.5 $[0.1974 \times 38 = 7.5012]$ theoretically needed, over-fill it by one-third. Because it has the highest theoretical frequency, however, the middle category (5) of the stanine or sta-eleven scale can tolerate a larger discrepancy between actual and theoretical frequency than most of the other categories, which is why we assign it the remaining scores rather than trying to meet the 19.47 per cent specification more closely.

The stanine distribution shown in Table 3-11 is perfectly symmetrical: 9 and 1 have the same frequency (2), 8 and 2 have the same frequency (2), 7 and 3 have the same frequency (4), and 6 and 4 have the same frequency (6), leaving 5 in the middle with a frequency of 10. *Perfect* symmetry like this is accidental, but the stanine and sta-eleven method does tend to "unskew" skewed distributions.

How does the stanine distribution differ from the distribution secured with these 38 raw scores by simply setting up 9 score classes according to the rules given on pages 57-60? We would need to use a grouping interval 8 raw scores wide, because $(112.5 - 43.5)/9 = 7.7$. The lowest score class could be 41-48, which would make the highest score class 105-112. It could also be 42-49, 43-50, or 44-51, with the corresponding highest score classes 106-113, 107-114, and 108-115. Any of these will accommodate the lowest raw score, 44, and the highest raw score, 112. (No one of the four agrees with our rule that the lowest integral value in each score class be evenly divisible by the class interval, for with a lowest class 40-47 the highest class of nine would have to be 104-111, which could not accommodate the highest raw score, 112; 10 classes would be required.) Which system would be best? The classes 42-49, 50-57, ..., 106-113 extend from 2 points under the lowest raw score to 1 point above the highest, whereas 43-50, 51-58, ..., 107-114 go 1 under the lowest raw score and 2 over the highest, so either set seems equally suitable and better than the other two possibilities.

Table 3-12 compares frequencies for both of these with frequencies for the stanines from Table 3-11. The two simple groupings yield frequencies that differ little (not more than 1) for any of the 9 categories, but these frequencies differ appreciably (as much as 3) from the stanine frequencies. The simple grouping method does not normalize the distribution of raw scores. If raw scores

TABLE 3-12

Stanines Versus Simple Grouping into Nine Classes
(Data from Table 3-2)

Class	Stanine Frequency	106–113, . . . , 42–49 Frequency	107–114, . . . , 43–50 Frequency
9	2	3	2
8	2	3	4
7	4	7	6
6	6	5	5
5	10	7	7
4	6	6	6
3	4	4	4
2	2	1	2
1	2	2	2
	38	38	38

are not badly skewed, however, it will tend to yield results roughly similar to the stanine or sta-eleven approach. A teacher might always record his test scores as 1, 2,...,9 from a simple grouping into 9 score classes of equal width and thereby make scores from one test to another more comparable than percentage-right scores would be, for percentage right is a function of the difficulty of a particular test for an entire group, while categorical scores are not.

Teachers who have access to a machine that will multiply can readily use stanines for single classes and, for larger groups, sta-elevens. Once the technique is mastered, the counting problem is no greater than that met in the simple grouping into 9 score classes. With such standard scores you can determine whether Johnny is better in arithmetic than in English, relative to his test-mates, or even whether Mary is prettier than she is tall, relative to her female classmates!

Let us leave counting measures (median, percentiles, percentile ranks, D, Q, stanines, and sta-elevens) now in order to supplement our concepts of central tendency and variability with the important concept of co-relationship, also called association or concomitant variation. We hinted at this back in Tables 3-5 and 3-6, at which you may want to glance before going on to the topic of correlation.

MEASURES
OF RELATIONSHIP   *The Concept of Co-Relationship
or Concomitant Variation*

During the latter part of the nineteenth cen-
tury, Sir Francis Galton and the pioneer English statistician Karl Pearson
succeeded in developing the theory and mathematical basis for what is now
known as *correlation.*[12] They were concerned with relationships between two
variables, for example, height and weight. It is easy to see that tall people
usually weigh more than short ones, suggesting that above-average height tends
to go with above-average weight. Height and weight vary together (i. e., correlate positively), though certainly not perfectly; there are "beanpoles" and
"five by fives" to upset the relationship. It would be possible to select a group in
such a way that the taller a person in the group is the less he weighs, but this
negative correlation between height and weight would not be expected for individuals picked at *random* from the general population.

Let us examine some other factors that usually vary together. There is a
substantial, but again by no means perfect, positive correlation between intelligence test scores at the end of high school and grades earned during the freshman year of college. The higher the score obtained by an entering freshman, the
higher his later grades are *likely* to be. The lower his score is, the poorer a student he will *probably* make. This relationship has been found with all sorts of
intelligence tests used in a great number of different type colleges ever since
such tests first became available commercially shortly after the close of World
War I.[13]

Husbands and wives *tend* to be more like each other with respect to age,
amount of education, and many other factors, than they are like people in
general. The sons of tall fathers tend to be taller than average, and the sons
of short fathers tend to be short. Likewise, the fathers of tall sons tend to be
above average height. Children resemble their own parents in intelligence more
closely than they resemble other adults. Positive correlation between members
of families is usually found for almost any characteristic from algebra ability to
knowledge of zoology.

To quantify Galton's concept of co-relationships among traits, Pearson
devised as a measure of relationship the *product-moment coefficient of correla-*

---

[12]A fascinating account is contained in Helen M. Walker, *Studies in the history of statistical method,* Ch. 5 (Baltimore: Williams & Wilkins, 1929). The concepts of correlation and regression are treated together in most statistics texts, but, for the sake of simplicity, we have
omitted regression analysis from the present discussion.

[13]One of the most complete summaries is by H. F. Garrett, A review and interpretation of
investigations of factors related to scholastic success in colleges of arts and sciences and
teachers colleges, *Journal of Experimental Education,* 1949, 18, 91-138.

tion, r. Since about 1900 this has been a widely employed statistic, almost indispensable in the testing field. Virtually all test manuals are sprinkled plenti-
fully with *r*'s, as is most educational literature.

Pearson's original *r* and several other related measures of correlation summarize the magnitude and direction of the relationship between two sets of
measurements, such as height and weight based on the *same* persons, or between the same measurement on *pairs* of persons, like the fathers and sons
mentioned above. It makes no difference whether the measures correlated are
history grades and geography grades, speed of running the hundred-yard dash
and skill in playing the violin, or speed of tapping and age. In each such situation, *r* can have values that range from −1 for a perfect inverse relationship
through 0 for no systematic correlation to +1 for perfect direct relationship;
the *r*'s between radically different kinds of variables are wholly comparable.
For example, it is meaningful to say that for the pupils of a certain group,
reading ability and intelligence are more closely related than height and weight.

The chief purpose of a two-way scatterplot (scatter diagram, bivariate plot)
of dots or tallies, each of which represents the two scores of one student or pair
(such as father-son), is not—as many discussions might lead you to believe—to
simplify computation of *r*. With electric calculators and electronic computers,
we no longer need use the tedious hand-computational methods of the past.
The scatter diagram, however, enables us to study the relationship in all regions,
particularly the four quadrants (fourths): low, low; low, high; high, low; and
high, high. It also enables us to surmise whether or not a computed *r* will accurately summarize the relationship between the two variables. For *linear* correlation it will. (The relationship between two variables is linear if a straight
line more closely fits the dots of the scatterplot than any curved line does.) A
perfect positive linear relationship (*r* = 1.00) is shown in Figure 3-6, where the

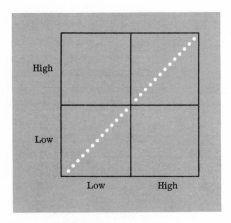

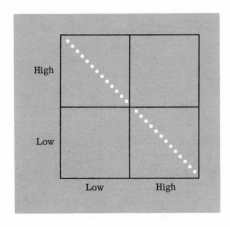

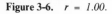

Figure 3-6.   *r = 1.00.*   **Figure 3-7.**   *r = −1.00.*

dots move in a straight line from low-low to high-high, with no dots in the low-high and high-low quadrants. A perfect negative relationship ($r = -1.00$) occurs in Figure 3-7, where the low-low and high-high quadrants are vacant.

A perfect curvilinear relationship ($r = 0$) is shown in Figure 3-8. Knowing one score of an individual, it is possible to predict his other score perfectly, despite the r of 0. For scatterplots of this sort, r is not the appropriate summarizing statistic.[14]

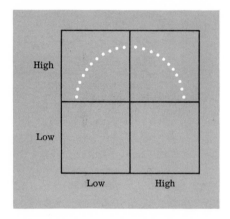

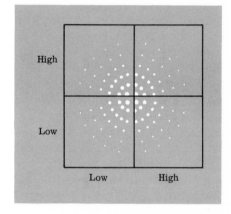

Figure 3-8. *Curvilinear relationship, r = 0.*   **Figure 3-9.** *No curvilinearity, r = 0.*

Figure 3-9 depicts a random relationship between two variables, resulting in an r of zero. No prediction of a student's score on one test from his score on the other test can be made at better than the chance level. No matter how he scored on one test, we would predict that he would score at the mean of the group on the other test.

Actually obtained relationships rarely yield r's of exactly -1, 0, or 1. They are more likely to resemble the positive, moderately large .66 for Table 3-6 on page 62 or the negative, rather low $-.35$ of Table 3-13. The negative r between chronological age and educational age (secured from average score on several achievement tests) may be puzzling at first, until we recall that the youngest students in a school grade are usually high-achieving accelerates, whereas the oldest tend to be low-achieving "holdovers." If we excluded these two atypical groups, the correlation would probably become positive (although low). In other words, the correlation between CA and EA within a school grade is not likely to be negative for the age-in-grade pupils *only*. In support of this position,

---

[14]A statistic labeled "eta" that is useful for such situations is discussed by Q. McNemar in *Psychological statistics,* 3rd ed. (New York: Wiley, 1962), pp. 202-203, 270-271, and 280-281.

TABLE 3-13

*A Scatter Diagram Illustrating Negative Correlation ($r = -.35$)
between Chronological Age and Educational Age for 20 Eighth Graders
(Data from Table 3-5 on Page 61)*

Educational Age (EA) in Months	| Chronological Age (CA) in Months													EA Frequency
	141–143	144–146	147–149	150–152	153–155	156–158	159–161	162–164	165–167	168–170	171–173	174–176	177–179	
188–189			1											1
186–187		1												1
184–185				1										1
182–183	1				2									3
180–181				1			1							2
178–179									1					1
176–177					2	1		1						4
174–175					2									2
172–173						1								1
170–171												1		1
168–169														
166–167			1			1								2
164–165					1									1
CA Frequency	1		1	2	2	5	5	1	2				1	20

we note in Table 3-5 that the oldest pupil ranks 17th out of 20 pupils on EA, while the youngest pupil ranks 4.5th. Similarly, the highest EA was obtained by a young pupil ranking 18th on CA. The lowest EA was obtained by a pupil whose CA ranked 14th. Unfortunately, 20 scores are too few to permit our eliminating the under- and over-age pupils and recomputing a meaningful r.

Two cautions are imperative. First, r is a "pure number" and *cannot be interpreted directly as a percentage.* An r of 0 represents no linear relationship at all, but an r of .66 does *not* directly mean 66 per cent relationship. In one sense, the difference in degree of relationship represented by r's of .91 and .98 is as great as the difference between r's of 0 and .66. As r's get larger, a small gain indicates a considerable increase in the degree of correlation. Therefore, an r of .66 indicates more than twice the relationship shown by an r of .33. These relative magnitudes are depicted graphically in Figure 3-10,[15] where the curve for negative r's is symmetrical with the one for positive r's. Thus, a given r indicates

---

[15] Based on R. A. Fisher, *Statistical methods for research workers,* 11th ed. (London: Oliver and Boyd, 1950), Table V.B., p. 210. The vertical (ordinate) figures, ranging from 0 to 3.0, are Fisher's z-transformation values of the r scale. They are *not* the same as the z scores we mentioned on pp. 78-85.

a high degree of relationship if its magnitude, regardless of sign, is large. An r of $-.72$ denotes just as strong an inverse relationship as an r of $.72$ indicates ·direct covariation, and *both have equal predictive value.* Note that the two curves of Figure 3-10 are approximately straight lines through about the first fourth of the r scale, after which they become increasingly positively accelerated. An r of $.24$ corresponds to a z of $.24$, whereas an r of $.995$ corresponds to a z of 3.00.

The second warning is that correlation does not necessarily mean causation. Often variables other than the two under consideration are responsible for the association. Furthermore, problems in the social sciences, the field in which correlation is most often employed, are usually too complex to be explained in terms of a single cause.

Let us take several examples. It is probably true that in the United States there is some positive correlation between the average salaries of teachers in various high schools and the percentages of the schools' graduates who go on to college, but to say that these students attend college *because* their teachers are well paid is as inaccurate as to say that their teachers are well paid *because* many of the graduates attend college. The relationship is not simple, but one prominent factor is the financial condition of the community which, to a considerable extent, determines its ability to pay *both* teachers' salaries and college tuitions and fees.

Figure 3-10. *Transforming r's to Fisher's z scale.*

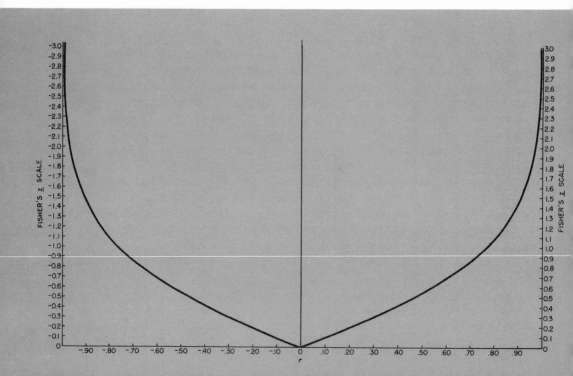

It has been found that the percentage of pupil "dropouts" occurring in high schools varies inversely with the number of books per pupil in the libraries of those schools.[16] But common sense tells us that merely piling more books into the library will no more affect the dropout rate than hiring a better attendance officer will bring about a magical increase in the number of books.

Many investigators make a two-stage assumption.   They assume both causation and direction of causality. Suppose, for instance, that among a large group of pupils the linear relationship between a measure of anxiety while taking an intelligence test and scores on the intelligence tests yields an r of $-.53$. What does this mean? We might surmise that underlying characteristics of pupils besides these two response variables tend to make some anxious and unintelligent, others calm and intelligent. We would then say, loosely, that some other variables "cause" the negative relationship between anxiety and intelligence. Or we might reject this and assume that there is a causative relationship between anxiety and intelligence: pupils are anxious *because* they are unintelligent, or pupils appear unintelligent *because* they are anxious (i.e., low intelligence makes them anxious while taking intelligence tests, but does not actually interfere seriously with their performance, versus the interpretation that their intelligence-test scores are greatly lowered by high anxiety). There is no simple answer to this response-response situation. "Causation" is a treacherous concept, as David Hume forcefully showed long ago.[17] Suffice it to say here that studies of association alone, without experimental substantiation, are most difficult to interpret convincingly. The measurement of anxiety should be supplemented by the study of experimentally created anxiety states.   For example, when students are experimentally made anxious in a testing situation, do their intelligence-test scores suffer?[18]

Failure to recognize that correlation may not mean causation is, in its broadest sense, a widespread logical error, for the fundamental notions of co-relationship affect our lives at many points. Going to Sunday school is generally believed to be valuable from many standpoints, but a positive relationship between the rate of attendance and a characteristic such as honesty does not *necessarily* imply that children are honest because they attend Sunday school. Underlying and causing both attendance and honesty may be home training, for example. A really crucial test of the hypothesis that attending Sunday school makes children more honest would have to be experimental rather than correlational.

---

[16]For several such potentially misleading relationships, see G. V. Ferrell, *High school holding power—an analysis of certain internal factors,* unpublished Ph.D. dissertation, George Peabody College for Teachers, 1951.

[17]D. Hume, *An enquiry concerning human understanding.* Various editions.

[18]For an extensive series of investigations in this area, see S. B. Sarason, K. S. Davidson, F. F. Lighthall, R. R. Waite, and B. R. Ruebush, *Anxiety in elementary school children* (New York: Wiley, 1960). D. R. Stucki, Elinor Wine, and J. C. Stanley reviewed this book in *Educational and Psychological Measurement,* 1963, 23, 403-405.

If honest children tend to go to Sunday school and less honest ones tend not to go, would it follow logically that children attend Sunday school *because* they are honest? (This is the reverse of the contention that they are honest because they attend.) Note several possible interpretations: H $\rightarrow$ SS, SS $\rightarrow$ H, and H $\leftarrow$ HT $\rightarrow$ SS, where H stands for "honesty," SS for "Sunday school," HT for "home training," and $\rightarrow$ for "leads to." H $\leftarrow$ HT $\rightarrow$ SS means that a third variable, home training, leads to both honesty and Sunday-school attendance.

Note carefully that while correlation does not directly establish a "causal" relationship, it may furnish *clues* to causes—and these clues can be formalized as hypotheses in planning controlled experimentation. Therefore, *r* is useful primarily for exploratory purposes. Hence, it is used much more widely in the newer sciences such as sociology, psychology, and education than in physics and chemistry.

Just what is *r*? Thus far we have talked about correlation and the statistic *r* without defining it or exhibiting computational formulas—intentionally so, because knowing technical details is far less important than appreciating the pitfalls you may encounter in test manuals and professional articles. Perhaps the simplest definition of *r* is that it is the mean *z*-score product, merely the arithmetic mean of the N products of the two sets of computed *z* scores. One can actually obtain *r* by means of that definitional formula, though it requires far more tedious computation than less direct methods do. Let's go through the process, however, for in this way you may come to appreciate some of the mathematical aspects of *r* relatively painlessly, and at the same time review computation of the arithmetic mean, standard deviation, and *z* scores.

We begin with "real" data in Table 3-14 for pretest scores (X) and midterm examination scores (Y) of 43 graduate students. We find that the mean of the X's, denoted by the symbol $\overline{X}$, equals $(62 + 55 + \ldots + 49)/43 = 2184/43 =$ 50.79070, and the mean of the Y's, $\overline{Y}$, equals $(51 + 66 + \ldots + 41)/43 =$ $2026/43 = 47.11628$. Then:

$$s_x = \sqrt{43(62^2 + 55^2 + \ldots + 49^2) - (62 + 55 + \ldots + 49)^2/43}$$
$$= \sqrt{156,654}/43 = 395.79540/43 = 9.20454.$$

Also $s_y = \sqrt{43(51^2 + 66^2 + \ldots + 41^2) - (51 + 66 + \ldots + 41)^2/43}$
$$= \sqrt{186,208}/43 = 431.51825/43 = 10.03530.$$

Now that we have the two means and the two standard deviations, we can compute two *z*-scores for each student, one for his pretest score and the other for his midterm score. For the pretest scores, the *z*-score on the pretest (X) is $z_x = \dfrac{X_s - \overline{X}}{s_x}$, meaning simply that from the student's raw pretest score we subtract the mean of the pretest scores and then divide this "raw" deviation from the mean by the standard deviation of the pretest scores. We could do

TABLE 3-14

Pretest and Midterm Scores of 43 Graduate Students
on Two Teacher-Made Objective Tests in Intermediate Statistics

Student	Pretest Score (X)	Midterm Examination Score (Y)	Student	Pretest Score (X)	Midterm Examination Score (Y)
a	62	51	v	62	65
b	55	66	w	53	56
c	55	40	x	62	56
d	49	38	y	49	54
e	46	51	z	52	56
f	67	57	aa	44	39
g	32	42	bb	60	49
h	42	35	cc	47	55
i	67	61	dd	44	45
j	55	46	ee	49	39
k	44	33	ff	36	38
l	46	58	gg	40	15
m	37	48	hh	53	50
n	57	44	ii	44	47
o	34	55	jj	49	41
p	57	44	kk	49	35
q	58	59	ll	44	43
r	58	45	mm	53	60
s	49	51	nn	53	52
t	40	32	oo	42	35
u	73	54	pp	57	45
			qq	49	41

just this for each of the 43 students, but fortunately there is an easier way to compute z-scores. Consider the highest pretest score in Table 3.14, which is 73. Compute z_{73}, the z-score corresponding to this raw score of 73:

$$z_{73} = \frac{73 - \overline{X}}{s_x} = \frac{73 - 50.79070}{9.20454} = \frac{22.20930}{9.20454} = 2.4129.$$

What would the z-equivalent of a raw pretest score of 72 be? Let us write 72 as $(73 - 1)$ and look at the formula for computing it.

$$z_{72} = \frac{(73 - 1) - \overline{X}}{s_x} = \frac{73 - \overline{X} - 1}{s_x} = \frac{73 - \overline{X}}{s_x} - \frac{1}{s_x} = z_{73} - \frac{1}{s_x} = 2.4129 -$$

$$\frac{1}{9.20454} = 2.4129 - 0.1086 = 2.3043.$$

Thus, to get z_{72} we merely subtract $1/s_x$ from z_{73}. It is easy to show in the same way that $z_{71} = z_{72} - 1/s_x$, $z_{70} = z_{71} - 1/s_x, \ldots, z_{32} = z_{33} - 1/s_x$. In general, then, $z_{(X-1)} = z_X - 1/s_x$.[19]

You will have computed the z-equivalent for some raw scores that did not occur, but no matter. Alongside the 43 actually obtained pretest raw scores, write their z-score equivalents. A good way to check the accuracy of all your computations is to compute the sum of these 43 z-scores and their standard deviation. You have already been told that the sum (or the mean) of *any* (correctly computed) full set of z-scores is 0, and the standard deviation is 1. (Save yourself bother by computing the squared standard deviation, called the *variance,* which means that you drop the square root sign from the numerator of the s formula on page 92 and square the denominator, making it 43^2.) We'll permit you a rounding-off discrepancy of 1 or 2 in the second decimal place, so your check should produce a z-sum of 0.00, -0.01, 0.01, or at worst -0.02 or 0.02. Likewise, the variance of the z's should be 1.00, 0.99, 1.01, or at worst 0.98 or 1.02. Only perfect accuracy of statistical computations is tolerable.

We repeat the above operations for Y, where the raw scores range from 66 to 15. If there is an electric calculator available to you, obtain the z_y's in the manner described above for z_x's, checking them by computing the sum and the standard deviation of the z_y's.

In Table 3-15 appear the 43 pairs of z's for students a through qq. We have arranged them in order according to pretest z's from student u with the highest pretest z, 2.4129, to student g with the lowest pretest z, -2.0397. Then in Figure 3-11 we show the paired z's graphically. If correlation were perfect ($r_{xy} = 1$), each student would have the same z_x as z_y, meaning that he did equally well on the pretest and midterm tests. Then all 43 lines connecting z_x and z_y would be parallel. A glance at Figure 3-11 reveals that they are not. A considerable amount of change occurred, most for student o, who went from -1.8225 to 0.7861, and least for student hh, who went from 0.2409 to 0.2881.

Let us now multiply each student's z_x by his z_y, paying attention to plus and minus signs. ($+ \times + = +$, $+ \times - = -$, $- \times - = +$.) Add these 43 products and divide their sum by 43. Thus

$$r_{xy} = \frac{(2.4129)(0.6865) + (1.7613)(1.3837) + \ldots + (-2.0397)(-0.5087)}{43}$$

$$= 22.5662/43 = 0.5248.$$

---

[19]Computation goes rapidly and accurately on an electric calculator. We enter z_{73}, carried out to the nearest four decimal places, into the minuend dial of the calculator. We lock $1/s_x$, also expressed to the nearest four decimal places, in the subtrahend position (usually the keyboard). Then by pushing the "subtract" key repeatedly we find in succession, and copy down to the nearest two decimal places, z_{72}, z_{71}, $\ldots$, until the figures in the dial dip below 0. We add to those figures (such as 99999999999999996428) a number (such as 3572) that will cause the dial to read 00000000000000000000 again (for the example, $z = -0.36$). With a little practice, you can do this "in your head."

Various Ways to Obtain r

There are many devices for computing *r*. One of the simplest methods requires an electric calculator and utilizes the "raw" scores themselves, without any frequency distributions or scattergrams. It is seldom feasible unless a calculator is available, because the arithmetical opera-

TABLE 3-15

z-Scores for Each of 43 Students for Pretest and Midterm Examination Scores from Table 3-14

Student	z-Score on Pretest (X)	z-Score on Midterm Examination (Y)
u	2.4129	0.6865
i	1.7613	1.3837
f	1.7613	0.9853
v	1.2183	1.7821
x, z	1.2183	0.8857
a	1.2183	0.3877
bb	1.0011	0.1885
q	0.7839	1.1845
r	0.7839	−0.2009
pp	0.6753	−0.2009
n, p	0.6753	−0.3095
b	0.4581	1.8817
j	0.4581	−0.1103
c	0.4581	−0.7079
mm	0.2409	1.2841
w	0.2409	0.8857
nn	0.2409	0.4873
hh	0.2409	0.2881
y	−0.1935	0.6865
s	−0.1935	0.3877
jj, qq	−0.1935	−0.6083
ee	−0.1935	−0.8075
d	−0.1935	−0.9071
kk	−0.1935	−1.2059
cc	−0.4107	0.7861
l	−0.5193	1.0849
e	−0.5193	0.3877
ii	−0.7365	−0.0107
dd	−0.7365	−0.2099
ll	−0.7365	−0.4091
aa	−0.7365	−0.8075
k	−0.7365	−1.4051
h, oo	−0.9537	−1.2059
t	−1.1709	−1.5047
gg	−1.1709	−3.1979
m	−1.4967	0.0889
ff	−1.6053	−0.9071
o	−1.8225	0.7861
g	−2.0397	−0.5087

Figure 3-11. *z-Scores from Table 3-15, plotted (r = .52).*

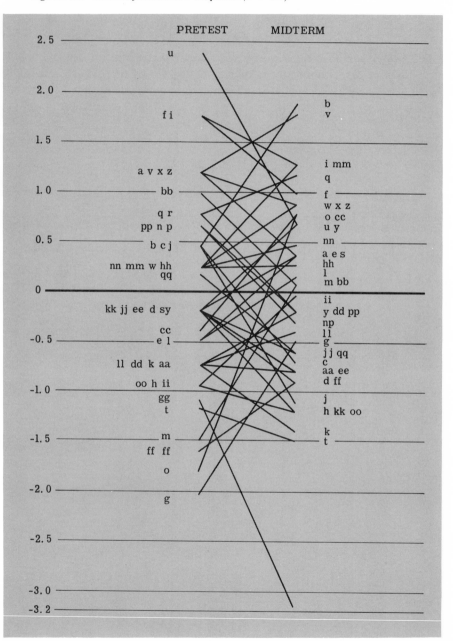

tions involve large numbers and therefore become quite tedious. Almost all other computational procedures require a scattergram. Many routinized "correlation charts" are available commercially, and nearly every statistics book and teacher have their own pet versions, usually to some extent original.

This diversity of computing aids is probably indicative of basic difficulties inherent in the process of computing r "by hand." There is no really simple way to do it. The chief difficulty is that r indicates a relationship between paired scores, so in order to obtain r by hand without undue labor we must find the sum of the products of the paired scores by some *indirect* method.

One complication in the attempt to simplify the computation of r without a calculator is that in order to make the numbers involved as small as possible, most chart designers set up procedures that result in many negative numbers. Whereas negative numbers are likely to confuse most students, large positive ones are tedious to handle, and both invite sizable errors. We think that it is better for persons who are getting their introduction to r in this book to refrain from computing r at all unless they have compelling reasons for doing so and understand how to interpret and use the value computed.

If you do need to compute an r, first set up a scatter diagram of the bivariate frequencies as in Table 3-6. Study this scatterplot for strong nonlinear trends (not likely to result with test scores, but possible). In Table 3-16 we show a scatter diagram for the 43 pairs of test scores from Table 3-14. It appears that a straight line would fit the trend of the bivariate frequencies better than a curved line, though with sizable deviations from the line because the correlation

TABLE 3-16

Scatterplot of Scores from Table 3-14

Score on Midterm Examination	Score on Pretest															Midterm Frequency
	30–32	33–35	36–38	39–41	42–44	45–47	48–50	51–53	54–56	57–59	60–62	63–65	66–68	69–71	72–74	
64–67							1				1					2
60–63							1						1			2
56–59					1		1		1	2			1			6
52–55		1			1	1	1								1	5
48–51			1		1	1	1				2					6
44–47				2				1	4							7
40–43	1			1		2		1								5
36–39			1	1		2										4
32–35				1	3		1									5
28–31																0
24–27																0
20–23																0
16–19																0
12–15				1												1
Pretest Frequency	1	1	2	2	7	3	7	4	3	5	5	0	2	0	1	43

is far from perfect. To compute r, we go back to the raw scores in Table 3-14 and proceed in the following manner:

$$r_{xy} = \frac{43[(62)(51) + (55)(66) + \ldots + (49)(41)] - (62 + 55 + \ldots + 49)(51 + 66 + \ldots + 41)}{\sqrt{43(62^2 + 55^2 + \ldots + 49^2) - (62 + 55 + \ldots + 49)^2} \ \sqrt{43(51^2 + 66^2 + \ldots + 41^2) - (51 + 66 + \ldots + 41)^2}}$$

$$= \frac{43(104,987) - (2184)(2026)}{\sqrt{43(114,570) - (2184)^2} \ \sqrt{43(99,788) - (2026)^2}} = \frac{89,657}{\sqrt{156,654} \ \sqrt{186,208}}$$

$$= \frac{89,657}{\sqrt{29,170,228,032}} = \frac{89,657}{170,793} = .5249.$$

The figure obtained is the same, to three decimal places, as the r secured by averaging the products of z scores, above. Rounding-off "error" caused the .0001 discrepancy; .52 is moderately large but not extremely high, since a considerable number of students shifted position substantially from the pretest to the midterm. We saw this clearly with plotted z's in Figure 3-11. We can also tell from the z's of Table 3-15 that the student (g) who scored lowest on the pretest ranked 30th on the midterm examination, whereas the student (u) who scored highest on the pretest ranked 12.5th at midterm.

Ranks may be expressed as ratio to total number, such as 30/43. A frequently used predictor of college grades is rank in high-school graduating class, such as 3rd out of 122, usually expressed as $1.0000 - 3/122 = .9754$, which is *roughly* a percentile rank of 97.54 and corresponds in a table of area under the unit normal curve to a z of 1.97 or a sta-eleven of $5 + 2(1.97) = 5 + 3.94 = 9$. If no one tied for 3rd place, the PR computed by the method we used earlier in the chapter is really $100[1.0000 - (1 + 1 + 1/2)/122] = 97.95$, for which $z = 2.04$. Why do we have the discrepancy between 97.54 and 97.95, and therefore between 1.97 and 2.04? Because the PR is determined from the middle of the score class, whereas the class rank is determined from the bottom of the score class. The person with the highest grades in a graduating class of N students has a PR of $100 \left(1 - \dfrac{0.5}{N}\right)$ but a class rank of $100 \left(1 - \dfrac{1}{N}\right)$. The sta-eleven score in the above illustration is 9, because either way we compute z the student ranked approximately 2 standard deviations above the mean of his class.

Rank Correlation

If the measures to be correlated are the consecutive, *untied* ranks 1, 2, 3, and so on through N, the r formula reduces to $1 - \dfrac{6[\text{sum of the N } (R_x - R_y)^2\text{'s}]}{N(N^2 - 1)}$, where R_x and R_y represent the paired ranks and N is the number of pairs.[20] $(R_x - R_y)^2$ is the squared discrepancy, D^2, between the two paired ranks of a student. An illustration will show how simple the computational procedure is.

A certain test question requires that six historical events be ranked in chronological order, 1 representing the earliest and 6 the most recent, without ties. Table 3-17 shows the events, the ranks assigned by Richard and by John, and the correct ranks. Note that each boy has 6 "errors," because each one "missed" all six questions. You can see readily that John's rank order was closer to the correct ranks than was Richard's, however.

TABLE 3-17

The Computation of the r_{ranks} for Each of Two Students Who Arranged Six Historical Events in Chronological Order

Events to Be Ranked (1 = earliest)	Richard's Ranks	Correct Ranks	D	D^2	John's Ranks	Correct Ranks	D	D^2
French Revolution	2	6	4	16	5	6	1	1
Magna Charta	4	3	1	1	4	3	1	1
Pompeii Destroyed by Vesuvius	3	1	2	4	2	1	1	1
Columbus Discovers America	1	4	3	9	3	4	1	1
Fall of Roman Empire	5	2	3	9	1	2	1	1
Spanish Armada Destroyed	6	5	1	1	6	5	1	1

Sum of numbers in D^2 column = 40

$$r_{ranks} = 1 - \frac{6(\text{Sum of } D^2)}{N(N^2 - 1)} = 1 - \frac{\cancel{6} \times 40}{\cancel{6} \times [(6 \times 6) - 1]}$$

$$= 1 - \frac{40}{35} = 1 - 1.14 = -.14.$$

Sum of D^2 = 6

$$r_{ranks} = 1 - \frac{\cancel{6} \times 6}{\cancel{6} \times 35}$$

$$= 1 - \frac{6}{35}$$

$$= 1 - .17$$

$$= .83 .$$

The first correlation coefficient is secured by summing the squared differences between Richard's ranks and the correct ranks and substituting in the formula. This r_{Ranks}, abbreviated r_R, equals $-.14$. Like r_{xy}, the correlation between two quantitative variates, r_R can vary (by jumps) from -1 to $+1$. The negative r_R found for Richard probably indicates a chance departure from 0, rather than actual misinformation. Notice that John, with an r_R of .83, seems to have had a fairly good general knowledge of the correct chronology, even though he did not rank any one of the six events precisely. Many teachers would give him no credit at all, despite his superiority to Richard on this ranking item. He deserves 4 or 5 points out of the possible 6. Richard, of course, deserves none.

---

[20]This simplification occurs because the mean of N such ranks is always $(N + 1)/2$ and the variance is always $(N^2 - 1)/12$.

The worst possible ranking, exactly opposite to the key (say, 5, 4, 3, 2, 1 instead of 1, 2, 3, 4, 5 for 5 events), actually yields one "correct" ranking if the number of ranks is odd; here the student's 3 matches the key's 3. Yet in the overall ranking sense misinformation is perfect ($r_R = -1$), and the student deserves a score of *minus* 5. Scores on 5 things ranked can range from -5 to $+5$. A simplified scoring procedure for "sequence" (chronology, rearrangement) items is described in Appendix E for as many as 7 things ranked. We think that such a correlational procedure, instead of a right-wrong method (no credit at all for being close), should be used for scoring ranking items.[21]

It is possible to have answers to ranking items recorded on A, B, ... option answer sheets by using A for 1, B for 2, C for 3, and so on, through the number of option spaces for a single item on that sheet. This may be as few as 4 or 5 on printed sheets. Electronic scoring devices should be able to utilize a correlational formula for scoring ranking items. Otherwise, they can be scored readily by hand with the aid of the table in Appendix E.

Appendix D contains a long table from which every possible r_R for as many as 10 things ranked can be read immediately by entering the table with the sum of squared deviations, making the actual computation of r_R unneccessary.

Strictly speaking, the r_R formula is not appropriate when any ties occur. It is sometimes used as a short-cut procedure for estimating the r between scores by first changing the two sets of scores to ranks. If only an approximate measure of relationship is desired, this method may yield satisfactory results, despite ties. It will usually be inadvisable when N is as great as 25 or 30, however, for the ranking process will be time-consuming and the fractional ranks will be tedious to square. In such a case, it is better to seek an electric calculator and compute r directly from the raw scores by the method shown on page 98.

Interpreting the Coefficient of Correlation

In interpreting a coefficient of correlation, two things must be considered. The first is the *sign* of the coefficient, and the second is the *magnitude* or *size* of the coefficient. The sign indicates the *direction* of the relationship. Positive coefficients indicate direct relationship, that is, tendency for two series of values to vary in the same direction. High values in one column are associated with high values in the other column, low values in one column are associated with low values in the other column, and so on. On the other hand, negative coefficients indicate inverse relationship, which is a tendency for the two series of values to vary in opposite directions, with high values in one column associated with low values in the other column, and high values in that column associated with low values in the first column.

The second aspect, equally important but far more difficult to interpret, is the *size* of the coefficient, which indicates the *degree* or closeness of the re-

---

[21]If you are interested in a possibility other than r_R, you may read about Kendall's *tau* in Ferguson, *op. cit.*, pp. 183-186.

lationship, just as the *sign* of the coefficient indicates the *direction* of the relationship. The minimum coefficient is .00, which indicates no consistent relationship whatsoever. From this minimum value, the coefficients increase in both directions until −1.00 is reached for one limit and 1.00 for the other. It should be noted that both −1.00 and 1.00 indicate equally close relationship, for both are perfect. Their one important difference is in direction, the former being inverse and the latter being direct. Similarly, all other values of the same size, such as − .50 and .50, indicate equally close relationship. The size, not the sign, of the coefficient indicates the closeness or degree of relationship.

The problem, then, is to know how close a relationship is indicated by a coefficient of correlation of a given magnitude, regardless of sign. For example, how close a relationship is indicated by a coefficient of .60? Unfortunately, there is no simple way of answering such a question. Attempts to indicate this relationship by some descriptive adjective, such as "high" or "marked," are vague and often misleading, to say the least. As a matter of fact, a coefficient of .60 might be regarded as high for one type of situation and low for another. For example, a coefficient of .60 between a general intelligence test administered at the beginning of the year and school marks recorded at the end of the year might be regarded as high, because the correlation between that particular predictor and criterion usually falls below that. But a coefficient of .60 between scores on two forms of this intelligence test administered the same day to a typical school class would be unusually low. In other words, "high" and "low" have only *relative* meaning; before an interpretation can be made of a coefficient on this basis, the reader must at least know what the *central tendency* of such coefficients for similar data is. He needs to have "antecedent expectations."

Expectancy Tables

A helpful way to interpret the degree of relationship between two variables is to construct an *expectancy table* from the scatter diagram and inspect it carefully. This may be done with the Table 3-16 data by considering scores of 51 or more on the pretest and scores of 48 or more on the midterm exam as "high"; these cutting points give as near a 50 per cent split of the scores as possible. See Table 3-18. Twenty-three students scored 50 or less on the pretest, and 20 scored 51 or more. Twenty-two students scored 47 or less on the midterm examination, and 21 scored 48 or more.

Of those students who were low on the pretest, 70 per cent [(16 ÷ 23) (100)] were also low on the midterm examination, so the odds are 7:3 that a person scoring low initially will six weeks later again score low. The same 7:3 odds hold in this illustration for those who score above high on the pretest.

The 7 individuals who went from low on the pretest to high at midterm might be called "false negatives," since at first they were classified too low, whereas the 6 who went from high on the pretest to low on the midterm might be labeled "false positives." Only 3 of the 7 "false negatives" changed greatly; the other 4 were not very low on the pretest or very high at midterm. Similarly, none of the 6 "false positives" were very high on the pretest or very low

TABLE 3-18

Simple Expectancy Table Based on Frequencies from Table 3-16

	Scored 50 or Less on Pretest	Scored 51 or More on Pretest	Midterm Sums
Scored 48 or More on Midterm Examination	7	14	21
Scored 47 or Less on Midterm Examination	16	6	22
Pretest Sums	23	20	43

at midterm. Obviously, though the four-cell expectancy table provides a useful summary, it yields much less data than the 210-cell scattergram of Table 3-16.[22]

Validity and Reliability Coefficients

One of the most important uses of the co-efficient of correlation is in determining the validity of a test, as we shall see in Chapter Five. *Predictive validity* is determined by setting up a criterion to be predicted and then computing the coefficient of correlation between the predictor scores and the scores on the criterion—e.g., rank in high-school graduating class correlated with college freshman gradepoint average. The *r* so obtained is called a predictive *validity coefficient* and is interpreted in the same way as other coefficients of correlation.

A second use of the coefficient of correlation is in determining the comparable-forms or the test-retest "reliability" of a test. *Reliability is the degree of consistency with which a test measures.* Three types of reliability coefficients are obtained by computing the *r* between two forms of the same test, two comparable halves of a test, or two administrations of the same test. Such *r*'s usually vary between 0 and 1. For further discussion, see Chapter Five.

Other Coefficients of Correlation

The *r* discussed in this section, called the zero-order coefficient of correlation, is only one of many different types of correlation coefficients. Either distribution of test scores, or both, can be expressed in various ways, such as the scores themselves, as ranks, or as a dichotomy (a division into two categories, such as dead vs. alive, female vs. male, incorrect vs. correct, or below the median vs. above the median). We could have a "natural" dichotomy such as male vs. female sex, or one representing an underlying normally distributed attribute, such as height in inches dichotomized at the

[22]A clear discussion of various types of expectancy tables, of which the one above is the simplest, is contained in A. G. Wesman, Expectancy tables—a way of interpreting test validity, *Test Service Bulletin* No. 38, 1–5, December 1949. Copies may be obtained free from the Psychological Corporation, 522 Fifth Avenue, New York 18, New York.

median. If both distributions are in score form, their correlation is represented by r_{xy}, the standard Pearsonian coefficient of correlation. If both distributions are natural dichotomies such as sex and albinism, or are treated as such, scores on the x distribution may be called 0 and 1 (say, arbitrarily, 0 = female and 1 = male), and scores on the y distribution also 0 and 1 (say, 0 = non-albinism, 1 = albinism). Then the correlation between the two distributions is simply an r_{xy}, usually called a *phi* coefficient and designated ϕ. Fortunately, it is easier to compute *phi* from a special formula than by means of the usual correlational procedure, as Ferguson explains.[23]

If we consider both dichotomous distributions as representing underlying normal distributions of attributes, we would compute a tetrachoric coefficient of correlation, r_{tet}. Such a coefficient might be found for the correlation between the scores of N students on two dichotomously scored (wrong, right) test items, on the assumption that if we measured the ability underlying each item more finely than just 0 and 1, we would discover that the ability is distributed normally for the group tested. For example, instead of scoring a test question merely 0 = wrong and 1 = right, we might have given partial credits of 1, 2, 3, ... points.

Another use for tetrachoric r's in the days before electronic computers was to reduce the considerable computational labor involved in computing the $k(k-1)/2$ r's among k distributions of test scores, particularly for factor analysis. If we intercorrelate 50 tests administered to the same N students, for example, we compute $50(49)/2 = 1225$ r's! With an adequate electronic computer, this is easy, but during the first two decades of factor analysis it was so time-consuming and inaccurate on desk calculators that the founder of modern factor analysis himself chose to dichotomize each of his test variables at the median and compute tetrachoric r's via graphic methods instead of computing r's directly.[24]

The coefficient of correlation most used in item analysis is probably r_{bis}, the *biserial r* between total scores on the test and dichotomous scores on a test item (wrong, right), the 0, 1 scores being treated as if they were simplified scoring of an item that measures a normally distributed ability. The term "*bi*serial" is used because, in this illustration, there are two series of total scores, one for those who answered the item correctly and another for those who did not. If we do not assume that the ability measured by the item is distributed normally, we compute an ordinary Pearson r between the test scores and the 0, 1 item scores; this is called *point* (i.e., two discrete points 0 and 1) biserial r, abbreviated $r_{p\ bis}$. Under certain circumstances $r_{p\ bis}$ may be preferable to r_{bis}, but we shall not enter that controversy in this book.[25]

---

[23] Ferguson, *op. cit.*, pp. 196-199.

[24] If you want to know more about tetrachoric correlation, see Ferguson, *op. cit.*, pp. 204-206.

[25] For this and related points, see F. B. Davis, Item selection techniques, Ch. 9 in E. F. Lindquist, ed., *Educational measurement* (Washington, D. C.: American Council on Education, 1951), esp. pp. 287–301.

Thus far we have dealt with only two variables (x and y) at a time. Suppose, for instance, that there are two predictors—rank in high-school graduating class and score on a vocabulary test—and one criterion—grade-point average (GPA) during the freshman year of college. Label these variables 1, 2, and 3, respectively. We can compute three r's: r_{12}, r_{13}, and r_{23}. The relationship between the predictors is expressed by r_{12}, whereas the other two r's show how well each of the predictors predicts the criterion, freshman-year GPA. How well do the two predictors *together* predict the criterion? A simple way to answer this question would be to convert each rank in high-school graduating class into a z-score and each vocabulary-test score into a z-score, average the two z-scores for each student, and correlate this average z-score with the GPA's. In this way you give equal "weight" to high-school achievement and vocabulary, because your averaging formula is $(1z_1 + 1z_2)/2$. That procedure works well if the two predictors are equally useful for predicting the criterion, but of course they may not be. Usually, high-school achievement correlates better with college grades than do scores on a general vocabulary test (which, incidentally, is a pretty good verbal "intelligence" test), though both correlate appreciably with GPA.

We'll not go into the technical details of *multiple correlation,* but it may be that those equal, 1 and 1, weights for the two predictor z-scores aren't optimal for predicting college grades. Perhaps 4 and 1 would be better—that is, computing for each student $(4z_1 + 1z_2)/5$ would yield new predictor scores that correlate higher with college grades than the $(1z_1 + 1z_2)/2$'s do. The best possible z-score weighting of this sort for predicting the criterion scores (college grades in this case) produces the multiple coefficient of correlation, symbolized by $R_{3.12}$, where the subscript 3 represents the criterion. How does one find the optimal weights for two or more predictors? Most statistics textbooks give procedures.[26]

Suppose, finally, that you have more than one predictor variable *and* more than one criterion, for example GPA in science courses and GPA in non-science courses. Even for such situations (multiple predictors and multiple criteria), there is a method, called *canonical correlation,* for determining the correlation between an optimally weighted composite predictor and the most predictable composite of the criteria.[27] Multiple correlation is the special case of canonical correlation when there is just one criterion. Canonical correlation is of theoretical interest, but its practical applications to measurement in schools seem limited.

---

[26] See, for example, McNemar, *op. cit.*

[27] See W. W. Cooley and P. R. Lohnes, *Multivariate procedures for the behavioral sciences* (New York: Wiley, 1962).

MEASURES OF ERROR

Many types of error prevent obtained scores from being "true" scores. (See Chapter Five for the concepts of obtained score, true score, and error of measurement.) The various errors in educational measurement may be grouped conveniently into three types, according to their source:

1. Errors in technique
    a. Errors in computation
    b. Use of inappropriate measures
    c. Use of approximation techniques
2. Errors in measurement
    a. Imperfect measuring instruments
    b. Unskilled testers
    c. Fluctuations in the persons measured
3. Errors in sampling
    a. Selection or bias in sampling
    b. Chance fluctuations in random sampling

Errors in Technique

Obvious types of errors are mistakes in adding scores and various computational errors in statistical analysis. The only protection against such errors is the exercise of great care. Likely to be more serious are errors due to the use of measures inappropriate for the data in hand. It is poor technique to introduce more refined measures than the data warrant or the purpose requires. All statistical formulas are based on certain assumptions which often are not fully met in actual practice. The following are common examples: Computations based on data in a grouped frequency distribution depend for complete accuracy on the assumption that the scores are uniformly distributed within the several intervals and that, therefore, the midpoint of each interval may be used to represent the average value of all scores in the interval. The Pearson r technique assumes linear correlation between the two variables or, in other words, constancy of the relationship throughout the range of scores. Many formulas are based on the assumption of a normal distribution of the measures. Whenever data fail to conform to these assumptions, errors are introduced. Fortunately, in actual practice, these errors are often not great enough to introduce serious errors of interpretation. But gross errors due to the use of inappropriate techniques are sufficiently numerous to warrant caution. Errors arising from the utilization of approximation procedures, such as 0.4D to estimate the standard deviation, may be large or small depending on how accurate the approximation is.

Errors in Measurement

There are many possible sources of errors in measurement, even when there are no computational errors and when the most appropriate statistical analysis has been employed. First, no measuring instrument is perfectly reliable. Second, the tester himself must be considered a possible source of error. Inexperienced examiners may allow too much or too little time in administering the test, or may otherwise depart from standardized procedure in administering the test or in scoring the papers. Third, there is likely to be great variability in the responses of the subjects taking the test. Accidental occurrences, such as the breaking of a pencil point on timed tests, fluctuations in motivation, fatigue, and other physical and mental factors may seriously affect the test results.

There are errors that affect all individuals approximately alike. Allowing too much or too little time on a test of reading speed is an example. On the other hand, there are many errors of a variable character which affect individuals unequally or even in different directions. Sensory defects, health conditions, and motivation are examples of conditions that produce variable errors in measurement. The effects of these errors are presented briefly in Table 3-19.

TABLE 3-19

Effects of Constant and Variable Errors on Certain Types of Statistics

Measure	Constant Errors	Variable Errors
Central Tendency	Increased or decreased by amount of the error	Usually tend to offset or balance each other
Variability	Little or no effect	Usually made too large
Relationship	Little or no effect	Usually made too small

Notice that constant errors affect measures of central tendency most seriously, and often there are no methods for correcting them. For instance, if a tester allows 35 minutes for a 30-minute test, how can we know how much increase in scores the extra five minutes produced?

We shall not go into the theory of errors of measurement, set down in systematic form by the Princeton psychometrician Harold Gulliksen[28] and revised more recently by his former student Frederic M. Lord.[29] Briefly, however, we can consider an individual's test score to be composed of two independent parts: the individual's "true" score and a random error of measure-

---

[28] H. Gulliksen, *Theory of mental tests* (New York: Wiley, 1950).
[29] See, for example, Lord's The measurement of growth, and Further problems in the measurement of growth, *Educational and Psychological Measurement,* 1956, 16, 421-437, and 1958, 18, 437-451.

ment. We use the obtained score in some way, usually directly, to estimate the true score. Problems arise, though, because obtained scores correlate positively with the errors of measurement that they contain, so that an obtained score which is high or low in the obtained-score distribution tends to have a larger error of measurement than do test scores near the center of the distribution. This leads to a phenomenon called "regression toward the mean," which occurs when the group is retested with a comparable form of the same test. The very highest scorers on the first form will tend on the average not to be quite as high (though still high) on the retest, because their errors of measurement will tend to be smaller the second time; the initially low scorers will tend to "improve" their scores by sheer chance on the retest, because their errors of measurement the first time were too large negatively and will tend to be smaller the second time, making their obtained scores larger. (These changes occur because errors of measurement on the first test are uncorrelated with errors of measurement on the second test.) Therefore, although obtained scores are unbiased estimators of true scores (i.e., have no systematic tendency to be too high or too low) for persons scoring in the middle of the distribution, they tend to underestimate at the bottom of the distribution and overestimate at the top of the distribution. By how much? That depends on the reliability coefficient of the test. Perfectly reliable scores do not regress toward the mean at all on retest, whereas perfectly unreliable ones would be expected to regress all the way to the mean on retest. Somewhat unreliable scores regress that fraction of the way to the mean that the reliability coefficient represents, such as 0.75 or 0.50.

Two illustrations may be clarifying. Ascertain the correct ("true") chronological age "score" of each of your classmates to the nearest month. Repeat this 3 months later. Each person is exactly 3 months older, so his two z-scores are

$$\frac{\text{Age } - \text{ Mean Age}}{s_{\text{age}}} \text{ and } \frac{(\text{Age } + 3) - (\text{Mean Age } + 3)}{s_{(\text{age } + 3)}} = \frac{\text{Age } - \text{ Mean Age}}{s_{\text{age}}}[30],$$

precisely the same, and hence the correlation between age initially and age 3 months later is 1.00. No regression occurs; there were no measurement errors.

Now let each member of the class flip the same type of coin 50 times in random fashion. Then each student must have an obtained number-of-heads score somewhere from 0 to 50, probably averaging about 25 for the class as a whole. Let each of them flip his coin 50 times again, thereby obtaining a second score for each person. How highly will the two sets of scores correlate? Zero, on the average, because each person's true score is the same as every other person's true score, merely the class mean of about 25. By definition of the process of coin-flipping, number-of-heads scores vary from person to person, or from one time to the next for a given person, in purely chance fashion. No matter what number of heads an individual flips the first time, we predict 25

[30]Because $s_{(\text{age } + 3)} = \sqrt{s_{(\text{age})}^2 + s_3^2 + 2r_{(\text{age, 3})} s_{(\text{age})} s_3} = \sqrt{s_{\text{age}}^2 + 0 + 2(0)} = \sqrt{s_{\text{age}}^2} = s_{\text{age}}.$

for him the second time. Reliability of "measurement" is nil, and regression toward the mean is expected to be total.

Regression toward the mean because of errors of measurement has strong implications for measurement and experimentation. For discussion of these consequences, see the excellent articles by Rulon and Thorndike.[31]

Errors in Sampling

It is usually impractical to measure all the cases of a given type. For example, it would be a formidable task to obtain the mean IQ of all high-school freshmen in a state, or the difficulty of each word in a series of textbooks. Fortunately, it is not necessary to do so. It has been found possible to estimate the range within which the true measure probably lies. But to do so, a representative sampling of the total population is necessary. There is no statistical protection against errors in a selected or "hand-picked" sampling. In order for statistics computed from the sample to be unbiased estimators of population values (called *parameters*) with known error, the sample must be chosen in some random way.[32] The larger the sample the more stable the estimates will be, although increasing the number of cases does not in itself eliminate the possibility of bias. The sampling *method* determines whether or not a biased (non-representative) sample will be obtained.

Decision-Making

Cronbach and Gleser[33] have explored the implications for measurement of the recently developed theory of decision making. According to their view, a test should enable a teacher to make better decisions than he could make without the test. This does not mean just better than chance alone, since rarely do we make decisions by sheer chance. Teachers are concerned with acquiring as much information as they can on which to base their many decisions. Does Mary need extra help with reading? Should Jean take chemistry? Should I try to help Joe adjust better to the group?

A crucial aspect of accurate decision making centers in the amount of information one already has, and how much more one or several tests can contribute. For instance, should you administer an intelligence test to your class? Hubbard and Flesher[34] found the average correlation between teachers' esti-

---

[31] P. J. Rulon, Problems of regression, *Harvard Educational Review,* 1941, 11, 213-223; and R. L. Thorndike, Regression fallacies in the matched group experiment, *Psychometrika,* 1942, 7, 85-102.

[32] The way may be to use stratified random samples or randomly drawn clusters, of course. We do not mean that only simple random sampling is permissible.

[33] L. J. Cronbach and Goldine C. Gleser, *Psychological tests and personnel decisions* (Urbana, Ill.: University of Illinois Press, 1957).

[34] R. E. Hubbard and W. R. Flesher, Intelligent teachers and intelligence tests—Do they agree? *Educational Research Bulletin,* 1953, 32, 113-122 and 139-140.

mates of pupils' intelligence and the pupils' intelligence-test scores to be .72. Hanna's[35] interview estimates of intelligence correlated .71 with scores on the ACE Psychological Examination and .66 with the Ohio State University Psychological Test, while the ACEPE and the OSUPT correlated .77. Thus, if you have plenty of testing time available, you can, by using an intelligence test, expect to gain some information concerning your pupils' intelligence that you do not already have, but the amount of extra information may not be great. If, on the other hand, test time is limited (as it usually is), you may want to administer a test of some other significant characteristic, even though it may be less reliable and less "valid" than an intelligence test.

Suppose, for example, that the correlation between your estimates of your pupils' mental health and the best available criterion of mental health (say, careful assessment by a competent child psychiatrist) is only .05, whereas a readily-administered mental-health test correlates .30 with this criterion. Then, even though the test has what is usually interpreted as low validity, it predicts the criterion considerably better than does your assessment of the mental health of your students. Therefore, you might do better to give a mental-health test in place of an intelligence test if both compete for the same time, particularly when you must make important decisions having to do with the mental health of your pupils. This approach stresses the accuracy of the judgment that can be made without the test, and the importance of the area tested.

Thus, the effective value of a test is a function not only of the test itself, but also of the decisions you must make with it. A test is just one step toward the goal of efficient decision making. In the classroom situation, decisions can be changed as further information is acquired. Viewed from this standpoint, deciding tentatively—on the basis of classroom behavior and a low score on a mental health test—that Bill is having adjustment difficulties does not definitely classify him as maladjusted. With its validity coefficient of only .30, the test will yield quite a few "false negatives," that is, persons who score low on it but are not poorly adjusted. These will be discovered by an alert teacher during further screening, when he works with all low scorers more closely than before.

It is important to measure a variety of characteristics, even though somewhat inaccurately, to be aware of the risks involved, and to follow through with subsequent checks. Interviews, essay tests, and projective tests do not have the accuracy of rifles; they are more like shotguns, often spraying rather wildly but frequently hitting the mark, at the same time nicking some bystanders.

We cannot yet determine how much this promising-appearing application of decision theory will contribute to educational measurement. If you are interested, you may follow developments in the journal literature by means of subject and author indexes in a bimonthly journal, *Psychological Abstracts*.

---

[35] J. V. Hanna, Estimating intelligence by interviews, *Educational and Psychological Measurement*, 1950, 10, 420-430.

Further Reading

In a stimulating article entitled "Errors, estimates, and samples—the indispensable concepts," Charles R. Langmuir gives full development to many points that have been only touched upon in this chapter.[36] Three other sources of valuable supplementary information are "Making test scores meaningful,"[37] "The three-legged coefficient,"[38] and "Reliability and confidence."[39] They will do much to help statistically untrained teachers and administrators understand important aspects of measurement theory that might otherwise remain vague.

SUMMARY

The following is an outline summary of three important concepts and some statistics useful in connection with test scores and other quantitative data:

1. *Central tendency*

a. The arithmetic *mean,* usually called the "average" in everyday life, is obtained by adding all the scores and dividing the sum by the number of scores. For many purposes it is the "best" measure of central tendency.

b. The *median* is the point above which half of the scores lie and below which the other half lie. Thus, it is the 50th percentile, also called Q_2.

c. The *mode* is the most frequent score, a rather crude measure.

2. *Variability*

a. The *standard deviation, s,* involves every measure in the distribution. Approximately two thirds of all scores in a "normal" distribution lie within plus or minus one standard deviation from the mean.

b. *D,* a percentile measure of dispersion, is the distance between the 90th and 10th percentiles. Four-tenths of D (0.4D) provides a fairly good estimate of the standard deviation of a normal distribution.

c. *Q,* the quartile deviation or semi-interquartile range, is half of the distance between Q_3 (the 75th percentile) and Q_1 (the 25th percentile). Though widely used, Q is usually a poorer measure of variability than D, which in turn is somewhat inferior to *s.* For use by classroom teachers, D is usually the preferable statistic of variability.

d. The *range* is the distance from the lower real class limit of the lowest class to the higher real class limit of the highest class. For most purposes it is a very inadequate measure of variability.

---

[36] Pp. 68-81 in A. E. Traxler, ed., Measurement and evaluation in the improvement of education, *American Council on Education Studies,* 15, Series I, No. 46, April 1951.

[37] W. B. Schrader, *College Board Review,* May 1951, No. 14, 202-208.

[38] A. G. Wesman, *Test Service Bulletin* No. 40, December 1950, pp. 1-3. Psychological Corporation, 522 Fifth Ave., New York 36, New York. Free.

[39] A. G. Wesman, *Test Service Bulletin* No. 44, May 1952, pp. 1-6. Psychological Corporation. Free.

3. *Correlation, covariation,* or *concomitant variation.* There are numerous ways of expressing co-relationship. The most common statistic is Pearson's *r.* A simplification of *r,* applicable chiefly to data originally secured in the form of untied ranks, is r_R. Both *r* and r_R have values of -1 for perfect inverse relationship, 0 for sheer chance association, and $+1$ for perfect direct relationship.

Most reliability and validity coefficients are *r*'s secured under certain special conditions.

Instructional Test Items

Appendix B contains 50 five-option multiple-choice items covering the material in this chapter. *After* you have gone through the present chapter carefully, turn to them and test your knowledge. Refer back to this chapter as much as you please.

RECOMMENDED READINGS

Blommers, P. and Lindquist, E. F., *Study manual for elementary statistical methods in psychology and education.* Boston: Houghton Mifflin, 1960.

Campbell, D. T. and Stanley, J. C., Experimental and quasi-experimental designs for research on teaching, Ch. 5 (pp. 171-246) in Gage, N. L., ed., *Handbook of research on teaching.* Chicago: Rand McNally, 1963.

Cornell, F. G., *The essentials of educational statistics.* New York: Wiley, 1956.

Cox, D. R., *Planning of experiments.* New York: Wiley, 1958.

Edwards, A. L., *Statistical analysis,* rev. ed. New York: Holt, Rinehart & Winston, 1958.

Ferguson, G. A., *Statistical analysis in psychology and education.* New York: McGraw-Hill, 1959.

Freund, J. E., Livermore, P. E., and Miller, I., *Manual of experimental statistics.* Englewood Cliffs, N. J.: Prentice-Hall, 1960.

Garrett, H. E., *Statistics in psychology and education,* 5th ed. New York: Longmans, Green, 1958.

Hays, W. L., *Statistics for psychologists.* New York: Holt, Rinehart and Winston, 1963.

Hoel, P. G., *Elementary statistics.* New York: Wiley, 1960.

Levinson, H. C., *Chance, luck and statistics.* New York: Dover, 1963.

Moroney, M. J., *Facts from figures.* London: Penguin Books. (Buy the latest paperbound edition.)

Tatsuoka, M. M. and Tiedeman, D. V., Statistics as an aspect of scientific method in research on teaching, Ch. 4 (pp. 142-170) in Gage, N. L., ed., *Handbook of research on teaching.* Chicago: Rand McNally, 1963.

Walker, Helen M. and Lev, J., *Elementary statistical methods,* rev. ed. New York: Holt, Rinehart & Winston, 1958.

Wallis, W. A. and Roberts, H. V., *Statistics, a new approach.* Glencoe, Ill.: Free Press, 1956.

GRAPHICAL REPRESENTATION, NORMS, AND APPLICATIONS

In this chapter we consider graphs and norms together because one of the primary uses of graphs in educational measurement is to show normative data clearly. For example, we may use a graph to compare a student's standardized score on an intelligence test with his standardized scores on various other tests. It would be misleading to graph his *raw* scores on these tests.

"One picture is worth ten thousand words." So runs an old Chinese proverb. And according to a later writer,[1] "There is a magic in graphs." He describes the dynamic role of the graphical representation of numerical data as follows:

"Words have wings, but graphs interpret. Graphs are pure quantity stripped of verbal sham, reduced to dimension, vivid, unescapable.... Wherever there are data to record, inferences to draw, or facts to tell, graphs furnish the unrivaled means whose power we are just beginning to realize and to apply."

---

[1] H. D. Hubbard, quoted by W. C. Brinton, *Graphic presentation* (New York: Brinton Associates, 1939), p. 2.

There can be little doubt that the graphical representation of educational data is a valuable supplement to statistical analysis and summarization. The psychological value of graphs in the testing program may be considered under two headings: they attract attention, and they clarify the meaning of quantitative material.

Graphs Attract Attention

A graph or chart tends to attract the reader's attention. Advertisers employ a wide variety of pictures, charts, and diagrams, for they realize that the first step in making a sale is to attract the prospective customer's attention. They have learned that pictures will do this where numerical data and printed material will not. The average reader is likely to give scant attention to the ordinary printed matter in a school report and be unimpressed by the mass of tabular data often piled up at the end, but his eye is likely to be arrested by any picture or chart that may happen to be included. And this may lead him to read the entire discussion.

Graphs Clarify Points

A graph is often an effective method of clarifying a point. One small chart will often make a point clearer than a dozen tables or paragraphs. It is sometimes said that the facts speak for themselves. In reality, statistics often stand speechless and silent, tables are tongue-tied, and only the chart cries aloud its message to all the world. Ordinary numerical data are quite abstract; they convey their meaning vaguely and with effort to the average mind. The picture or graph is a more concrete representation.

Educational data, such as projected enrollment figures over a 20-year period, may be presented effectively by graphical means, as shown in Figure 4-1. There both line and bar graphs are used to compare the high predicted enrollment of 75.1 million pupils by 1980 with the low predicted enrollment of 62.2 million. The two dotted lines show the predicted figures by five-year periods, while the four bar graphs show the actual 1960 and the projected 1980 enrollments, subdivided by college, high school, and elementary and kindergarten.

A wide variety of charts is shown in Figure 4-2. The basic information concerning "Motor Buses in Operation in the United States" is given first in tabular form, followed by 15 different black-and-white charts.

GRAPHICAL
REPRESENTATION
OF TEST SCORES   The suggestions given by Spear, a specialist in visual presentation, should be kept constantly in mind when constructing graphs.[2]

> In the present day, when visual education in all aspects has become, not only an aid to, but also a vital basis of learning, our attention is called more than ever before to the almost limitless possibilities in this field. The eye absorbs written statistics, but only slowly does the brain receive the message hidden behind written words and numbers. The correct graph, however, reveals that message briefly and simply. Its purposes, which follow, are clear from its context:
> 1. Better comprehension of data than is possible with textual matter alone
> 2. More penetrating analysis of subject than is possible in written text
> 3. A check of accuracy
>
> This triple purpose of the chart can be carried out through careful planning and familiarity with the functions of all types of graphs and media. The following six steps are fundamental to the development of graphic presentation that will describe statistical data with clarity and dramatic impact:
> 1. Determine the significant message in the data.
> 2. Be familiar with all types of charts and make the correct selection.
> 3. Meet the audience on its own level; know and use all appropriate visual aids.
> 4. Give detailed and intelligible instructions to the drafting room.
> 5. Know the equipment and skills of the drafting room.
> 6. Recognize effective results.

Even when no technical assistance is available, teachers and administrators can make excellent use of graphs in attaining educational objectives.

Profiles for a Single Subject
There is no more striking way of representing the test record of an individual pupil than by means of a graph. Such a graphi-

---

[2]Quoted by permission from pp. 3–4 of Mary E. Spear, *Charting statistics* (New York: McGraw-Hill, 1952).

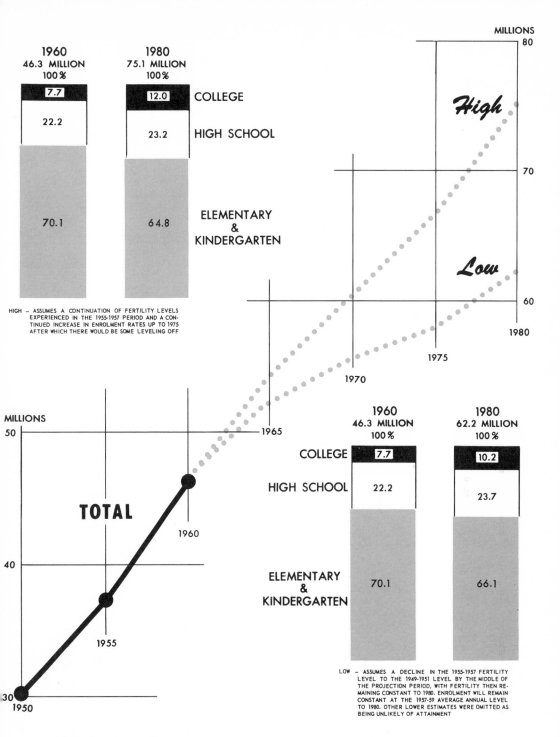

Figure 4-1. *Projected school enrolments, 1965-1980. Data refer to the civilian non-institutional population 5 to 34 years old. (Copyrighted; reproduced with permission of the Conference Board, 845 Third Avenue, New York 22, New York.)*

115

WHICH CHART TO USE?

THE DATA

Motor Buses in Operation in United States

Year	Intercity Buses	Local Buses[1]	Charter and Sightseeing	School Buses[2]	Total Buses
1941	18,420	37,855	2,383	87,400	146,058
1942	22,710	44,101	2,400	79,000	148,211
1943	28,504	45,610	2,000	77,850	153,964
1944	28,000	48,525	3,300	75,500	155,325
1945	29,000	45,955	1,033	83,228	159,216
1946	30,260	47,760	1,475	82,500	161,995
1947	31,900	54,100	3,000	85,900	174,900
1948	31,775	57,175	3,200	90,400	182,550
1949	30,200	57,800	3,500	97,600	189,100

[1]Omits trolley buses. [2]Exclusive of common carrier buses doing schoolwork.
SOURCE: "Bus Transportation" as of December 31st.

THE GROUPED COLUMN

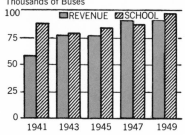

THE CUMULATIVE CURVE

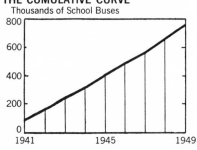

THE SLIDING BAR

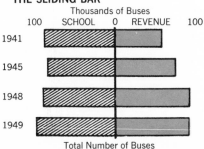

THE CURVE CHART

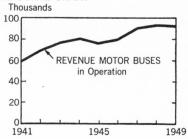

THE BAR CHART

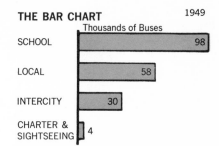

THE SUBDIVIDED SURFACE

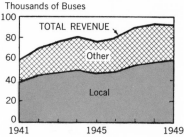

THE PICTOGRAM

Figure 4-2. *Fifteen ways to graph a set of data concerning motor buses in operation in the United States, 1941–1949.* (From Mary E. Spear, *Charting Statistics*, McGraw-Hill, 1952, reproduced with permission of the McGraw-Hill Book Company, New York.)

Figure 4-2 *(continued)*.

THE INDEX CHART

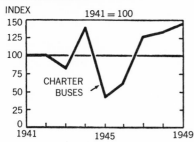

THE LOGARITHMIC CHART

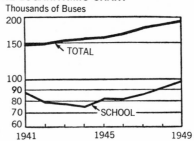

THE SUBDIVIDED COLUMN

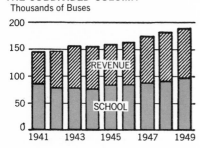

THE PAIRED BAR

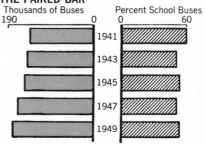

THE BAR and SYMBOL

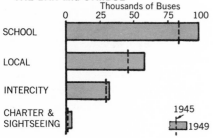

THE COLUMN and CURVE

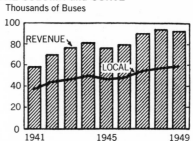

THE PICTORIAL SURFACE

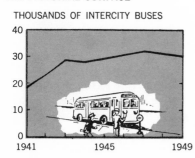

THE PIE CHART

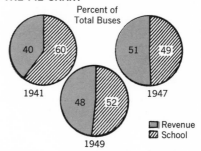

cal picture of the strong and weak points of a single person is called a *profile,* or occasionally a *psychograph.* Many publishers of standard tests provide blank forms for showing these profiles. Sometimes they appear on the first page of the test, where they can be detached easily for filing.

Figure 4-3 shows the profile of a sixth-grade pupil on the Iowa Silent Reading Tests. The broken-line profile for his class, based on medians, is also shown. With a median standard score of 150, corresponding to a percentile rank of 49 for the eighth month of the sixth grade, John is an average reader. The median score of his class is 151, which has a percentile rank of 52. John scored highest on Tests 4 (Paragraph Comprehension) and 6A (Alphabetizing), poorest on Test 6B (Use of Index). He exceeded the class average considerably on Tests 1R (Rate) and 6A (Alphabetizing). Small differences, such as that between 1R and 1C, or even 1C and 2, are probably due to errors of measurement, rather than to "true" within-student variation.

Profiles for a Series of Subjects

Profiles are especially useful for representing a pupil's scores on achievement-test batteries. Most test publishers provide a convenient form for such a profile. Figure 4-4 shows the profile for a tenth-grade pupil on the California Achievement Tests, Advanced Battery.

This student scored highest on Addition (Grade Placement = 13.2) and lowest on Division (GP = 8.0). His worst *area* is Test 3, Mathematical Reasoning (GP = 9.1). On the complete battery he had a dead-center average percentile rank of 50 and a grade placement of 10.2.

After a period of remedial instruction, the purpose of which is to strengthen the weak points of individual pupils, it is a good practice to give a second form of the same test. A second profile drawn in a different color upon the same sheet is one of the best ways of revealing the progress made, *if changes are interpreted cautiously;* practice-effect gains and regression upward toward the class mean because of errors of measurement becloud such interpretations. (See pages 158-159.)

REPRESENTING A FREQUENCY DISTRIBUTION GRAPHICALLY

The ordinary frequency distribution does not give a very clear picture of the situation. There are three common methods of representing a distribution of scores graphically: the *histogram* or *column diagram,* the *frequency polygon,* and the *smooth curve.*

The Histogram or Column Diagram

The *histogram* is a series of columns, each having as its base one class interval and as its height the number of cases, or frequency, in that class. Figure 4-5 represents a histogram showing the distribution of percentage values assigned to an arithmetic paper by 42 scorers. Since the greatest frequency is 9, in the 59.5-64.5 class, it is not necessary to extend the vertical or frequency scale at the left above 9. And since the score range

Figure 4-3. *Profile of a pupil and the sixth-grade class of which he is a member. (Reproduced by permission of World Book Company.)*

IOWA SILENT READING TESTS
NEW EDITION

By H. A. GREENE
Director, Bureau of Educational Research and Service, University of Iowa

and V. H. KELLEY
University Appointment Office, University of Arizona, Tucson, Arizona

Median Score	150
Grade Percentile	49
Grade Equiv.	6.8
Age Equiv.	12-0

Elem.

AM

(Revised)
New Edition

ELEMENTARY TEST : FORM AM
(Revised)

Name... DOE, JOHN .... Age.. 11 .... 11 .. Grade. 6 ..
                                                                          Years   Months

Sex.. ✓ ...... Date .... MAY 8, ...19 64.. Teacher.. MISS SMITH ......
     Boy   Girl

School.. CENTRAL .... City and state.. METROPOLIS, WIS. .....

PROFILE CHART

No.	TEST	STAND. SCORE
1	Rate: A + B	152
1	Comprehension: A + B	148
2	Directed Reading	162
3	Word Meaning	144
4	Paragraph Comprehension	171
5	Sentence Meaning	131
6	Location of Information A. Alphabetizing	172
6	B. Use of Index	121

————— JOHN DOE
- - - - - CLASS

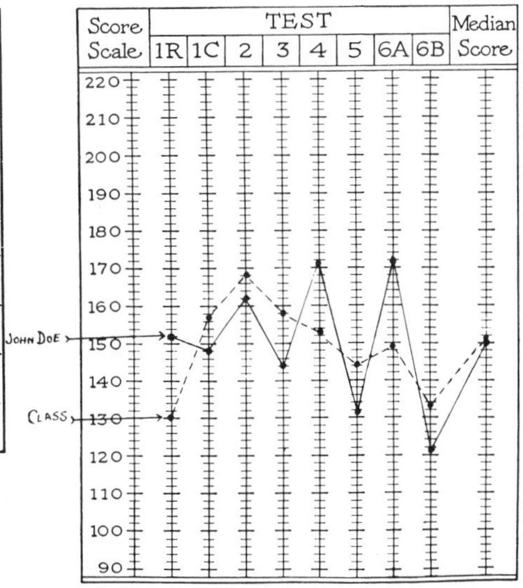

——— JOHN DOE
- - - - - - CLASS

Sex (M)/F

Grade or Occupation L-10

Name Stover, Donald D.
    Last   First   Middle

School or Organization Humbolt   City

Teacher or Examiner Mrs. Fry (Room 11) Student's Age 15

Date of Test Jan. 19, 1964
    Month Day Year

Date of Birth May 21, 1948
    Month Day Year

California Achievement Tests
Advanced • GRADES 9 to 14 • Form W

DEVISED BY ERNEST W. TIEGS AND WILLIS W. CLARK

See MANUAL for instructions.

DIAGNOSTIC PROFILE* (Chart Student's Scores Here)
Grade Placement

TEST	SECTION	POSSIBLE SCORE	STUDENT'S SCORE		
1. READING VOCABULARY	A. Mathematics	15	5		
	B. Science	15	8		
	C. Social Science	15	8		
	D. General	15	7		
	TOTAL (A+B+C+D)	60	28	10.2	50
2. READING COMPREHENSION	E. Following Directions	15	7		
	F. Reference Skills	27	12		
	G. Interpretations	45	24		
	TOTAL (E+F+G)	87	43	10.6	60
	READING GRADE PLACEMENT			10.4	50
3. MATHEMATICS REASONING	A. Meanings	20	9		
	B. Symbols, Rules, and Equations	25	12		
	C. Problems	15	7		
	TOTAL (A+B+C)	60	28	9.1	30
4. MATHEMATICS FUNDAMENTALS	D. Addition	20	16		
	E. Subtraction	20	14		
	F. Multiplication	20	14		
	G. Division	20	10		
	TOTAL (D+E+F+G)	80	54	10.4	50
	MATHEMATICS GRADE PLACEMENT			9.8	40
5. MECHANICS OF ENGLISH	A. Capitalization	40	33		
	B. Punctuation	40	25		
	C. Word Usage	60	40		
	TOTAL (A+B+C)	140	98	10.2	50
6. SPELLING	TOTAL SPELLING	30	15	10.4	60
	LANGUAGE GRADE PLACEMENT			10.3	50
	Handwriting			10.0	
	BATTERY GRADE PLACEMENT			10.2	50
	CHRONOLOGICAL AGE GR. PL.			10.3	
	ACTUAL GRADE PLACEMENT			10.4	
	INTELL. (M.A.) GRADE PLACE.			10.6	

Grade Placement

Percentile Rank

Grade Placement

Grade Placement: 7.0 8.0 9.0 10.0 11.0 12.0 13.0 14.0 15.0 †

*For an interpretation of green area within Profile, see discussion on Articulation in Part 4 of Manual.

†Column designed for recording Expected Grade Placements, Anticipated Grade Placements, School or Class Averages, etc. See Part 2 of Manual.

PUBLISHED BY CALIFORNIA TEST BUREAU – DEL MONTE RESEARCH PARK, MONTEREY, CALIFORNIA – BRANCH OFFICES: NEW CUMBERLAND, PA.; MADISON, WIS.; DALLAS, TEXAS – COPYRIGHT © 1934, 1937, 1943, 1950, 1957 BY CALIFORNIA TEST BUREAU – COPYRIGHT UNDER INTERNATIONAL COPYRIGHT UNION – ALL RIGHTS RESERVED UNDER PAN-AMERICAN COPYRIGHT UNION – PRINTED IN U.S.A.

Figure 4-4. *At left, the profile of a tenth-grade pupil on Form W of the California Achievement Tests. (Reproduced by permission of the California Test Bureau.)*

from the 29.5-34.5 class to the 74.5-79.5 class, it is necessary to represent the horizontal scale only through that distance. For clarity, however, it is customary to extend the scale one class interval above and below that range. In order to avoid having the figure too flat or too steep, it is usually well to arrange the scales so that the width of the histogram itself is about one-and-two-thirds times its height—that is, the ratio of height to width should be approximately 3:5. In actual practice it is customary to represent the histogram in outline form, rather than to show the full length of the columns. Figure 4-6 illustrates the shaded outline form of the histogram.

The Frequency Polygon

The process of constructing a *frequency polygon* is very much like that of constructing the histogram. In the histogram, the top of each column is indicated by a horizontal line the length of one class interval, placed at the proper height to represent the frequency in that class. But in the polygon a point is located above the mid-point of each class interval and at the proper height to represent the frequency in that class. These points are then joined by straight lines. As the frequency is zero at the classes above and below those in the distribution, the polygon is completed by connecting the points that represent the highest and lowest classes with the base line at the mid-points of the class intervals next above and below. Figure 4-7 shows a polygon for the same data represented by a histogram in Figure 4-5.

The Smooth Curve

Sometimes a *smooth curve* is drawn instead of a histogram or frequency polygon. The only difference is that for the former, a

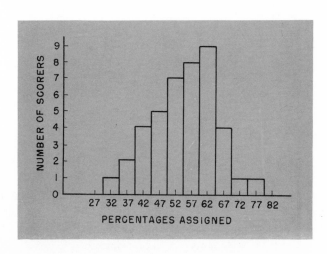

Figure 4-5. *A histogram, or column diagram, representing the percentage values assigned to an arithmetic paper by 42 scorers.*

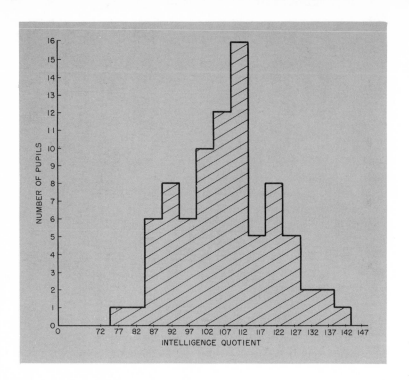

Figure 4-6. *A histogram, or column diagram, representing the distribution of the 83 IQ's in a small junior high school.*

smooth line is drawn as close as possible to the points, and for the latter two figures, an angular or jagged line is used. The most common use of a smooth curve in educational measurement is in the so-called *normal curve.* Figure 4-8 shows such a curve superimposed on a histogram representing the actual distribution of scores obtained by ninth-grade pupils on eleven intelligence tests. (Also see Fig. 3-4.)

Another smooth curve is widely used in representing test scores. This is the *percentile* curve or *ogive.* Figure 4-9 shows a percentile curve used to represent the percentage data already used to illustrate the histogram and the polygon. The points that determine the percentile curve are located on the hori-

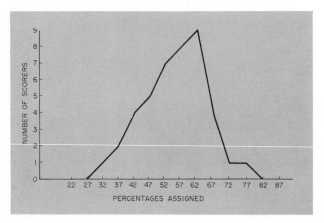

Figure 4-7. *A frequency polygon representing the percentage values assigned to an arithmetic paper by 42 scorers.*

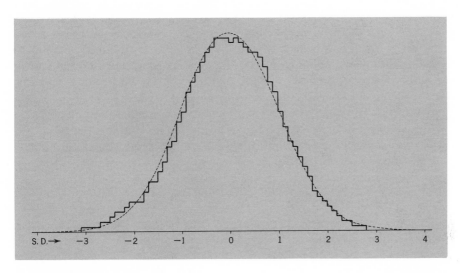

Figure 4-8. *An actual curve compared with the theoretical curve of probability. Actual curve is a histogram based on curves for 11 well-known group intelligence tests administered to the ninth grade. The dotted line represents the theoretical (normal) curve. (From E. L. Thorndike's* The Measurement of Intelligence, *Bureau of Publications, Teachers College, Columbia University, p. 529.)*

Figure 4-9. *A percentile curve representing the percentage values assigned to an arithmetic paper by 42 scorers.*

Score Given	f	Cum f	Cum %
75-79	1	42	100
70-74	1	41	98
65-69	4	40	90
60-64	9	36	86
55-59	8	27	64
50-54	7	19	45
45-49	5	12	29
40-44	4	7	17
35-39	2	3	7
30-34	1	1	2

zontal line at the upper limit of each class, at the position that indicates on the horizontal scale the percentage of scores up to and including that class. Notice, also, that two columns have been added to the ordinary frequency table. The cumulative frequency column indicates the number of scores up to and including each class. For example, there is one score in the 30-34 class, and there are two in the 35-39 class, making a cumulative frequency of 3 in the two lowest classes. The cumulative per cent column shows what percentage each of these cumulative frequencies is of the total. In the illustration, the total, N, is 42. The first entry in this column is, of course, 100; the second is 98, because 41 is 98 per cent of 42; the third is 95, because 40 is 95 per cent of 42; and so on for the others. Each value in the cumulative per cent column is represented as a point on the upper limit of that class interval (the horizontal line separating that class from the class above it), since it includes the percentage of scores up through that class. These points determine the curve. As a rule, especially in small groups where irregularities are most likely to occur, it is best to miss some of the points in order to obtain a smooth and regular curve; but care should be taken in order to leave about as many points on one side of the line as on the other. In this way the ogive will fit the trend of the points as closely as possible.

Figure 4-10 shows another ogive. Such a smoothed curve, although it does not exactly represent the actual sampling, probably indicates rather closely what is to be expected "in the long run."

Typewriter Graphs

A satisfactory *bar graph* can be made on the typewriter. Figures 4-11, 4-12, and 4-13 illustrate this type of graph. Other graphs, such as the *circle,* or *pie graph,* and various *picture graphs,* or *picto-*

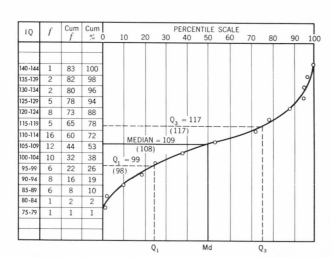

Figure 4-10. *A percentile curve representing the distribution of 83 IQ's in a small junior high school (see Figure 4-6). The values of Q_1, Median (Q_2), and Q_3 read from the curve are shown with the computed values (in parentheses).*

```
IQ                f

145-149           1            X
140-144           2            XX
135-139           2            XX
130-134           5            XXXXX
125-129           8            XXXXXXXX
120-124           5            XXXXX
115-119          16            XXXXXXXXXXXXXXXX
110-114          12            XXXXXXXXXXXX
105-109          10            XXXXXXXXXX
100-104           8            XXXXXXXX
 95- 99           6            XXXXXX
 90- 94           8            XXXXXXXX
 85- 89           6            XXXXXX
 80- 84           1            X
 75- 79           1            X
```

Figure 4-11. *Bar graph made on the typewriter, showing the distribution of 91 IQ's in a junior high school.*

Figure 4-12. *Bar graph made on the typewriter, showing the percentage of pupils of each age group who were graduated from high school and the percentage who entered high school but did not graduate.*

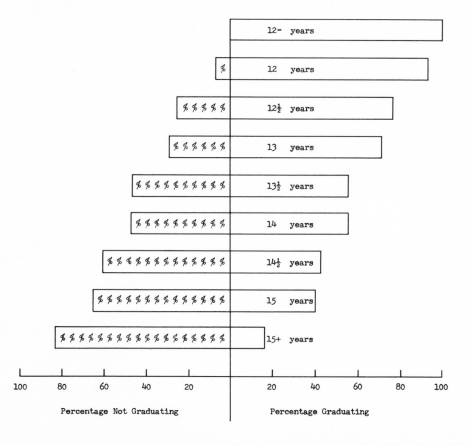

graphs, are occasionally used in educational measurement; these are discussed especially by Spear.[3]

Which Graph Is Best?

As we might expect, no one type of graph is equally good for all purposes. The histogram is the easiest of all to understand and therefore is usually best if no more than one distribution is being represented. But if two or more distributions are to be compared, polygons are usually better, since so many lines coincide when histograms are superimposed that the picture is likely to be confusing. The percentile curves have many advantages not possessed by other curves. The first of these is that it is possible to estimate with a high degree of accuracy the quartiles, medians, and other similar points. This means that one can read directly from the curve percentile measures like those illustrated in Figure 4-10. As we will see in the next section, by means of percentile curves several groups can be presented, for convenient comparison, on a single sheet. The main value of bar graphs, circle graphs, and picture graphs lies probably in school publicity and in the motivation of learning. "A successful graph," as the prominent educationist Douglas Scates pointed out long ago, "depends far more on careful thought and judgment than on techniques."[4]

---

[3] Mary E. Spear, *op. cit.*
[4] D. E. Scates, Reporting, summarizing, and supplementing educational research, *Review of Educational Research,* 1942, 12, 558–574.

Figure 4-13. *Graph made on the typewriter, showing the overlapping of grades seven, eight, and nine in reading comprehension.*

Score	Frequency for Grade			Bar Graph for School Grade		
	7	8	9	Seventh	Eighth	Ninth
200-219			3			999
180-199	1	4	5	7	8888	99999
160-179	3	3	7	777	888	9999999
140-159	4	9	7	7777	888888888	9999999
120-139	11	7	11	77777777777	8888888	99999999999
100-119	4	7	2	7777	8888888	99
80- 99	4	2	1	7777	88	9
60- 79	1	3		7	888	
40- 59		1			8	
20- 39		1			8	

It is often desirable to compare two or more distributions. For example, school administrators may wish to compare the verbal ability of the pupils in one school with that of pupils in other schools. Also, the overlapping of scores among the various grades within a single building is a striking way to present the need for individualized instruction and varied materials.

Representing Entire Distributions

When it is important to compare two or more entire distributions, as would be the case in a study of the status of a school or school system, the choice will usually be between the frequency polygon and the percentile curve. We have already pointed out the difficulty of superimposing two or more histograms. A series of polygons may be drawn on the same sheet one above the other, or alongside each other. Figure 4-13 illustrates a method of showing overlapping by bar graphs made on the typewriter. (Perhaps the scores there are grouped too coarsely. According to the rule on page 57, it would be better to have 12-15 score classes, instead of the 7, 9, and 7 actually used in Figure 4-13.)

The Use of Polygons

The distinct advantage of polygons over histograms for representing a series of distributions is that polygons can be superimposed on each other with less crossing of lines. In this form, comparisons among distributions are more easily made. Figure 4-14 illustrates this possibility with the distribution of reading comprehension scores for the seventh, eighth, and ninth grades of a certain school. One fact stands out clearly: the great overlapping of the three grades in reading ability. But even with only three distributions, the lines cross and recross so many times that it becomes difficult to make any accurate comparison of one grade with another. More than three classes can hardly be represented in the same graph by frequency polygons without considerable confusion. It is also difficult to compare distributions accurately where the numbers of cases vary greatly, unless each frequency is represented as a per cent of its total.

The Use of Percentile Curves

For the graphic comparison of two or more distributions the percentile curve has some distinct advantages. Since the frequencies are reduced to per cents, it is readily possible to compare groups of unequal size. Another important advantage is that several distributions can be represented in a single graph without difficulty or confusion. Figure 4-15 shows the distribution of reading comprehension scores for the same grades as in Figures 4-13 and 4-14 in the form of percentile curves.

From these percentile curves we may observe several relationships that were not apparent in the polygons. It is clear that although the seventh and eighth grades have almost exactly the same average scores, the eighth grade has greater variability. This is evident from the fact that the upper half of the eighth grade exceeds the upper half of the seventh grade, but that the lower half of the eighth grade falls behind the lower half of the seventh.

Furthermore, although the ninth grade runs consistently above the other two grades, about 15 per cent of the ninth-grade pupils fall below the median of the seventh and eighth grades.

Figure 4-16 shows the profiles for the seventh, eighth, and ninth grades of a certain junior high school made by connecting the median scores on each part of the Stanford Achievement Test. This figure shows clearly that the school is weak in arithmetic computation, spelling, and study skills, and particularly strong in the social studies. It seems likely that this school is stressing the content subjects at the expense of some of the more formal "tool" subjects.

Figure 4-14. *Frequency polygons representing the distribution of reading comprehension scores on a reading test for the seventh, eighth, and ninth grades of a certain school. (Data from Figure 4-13.)*

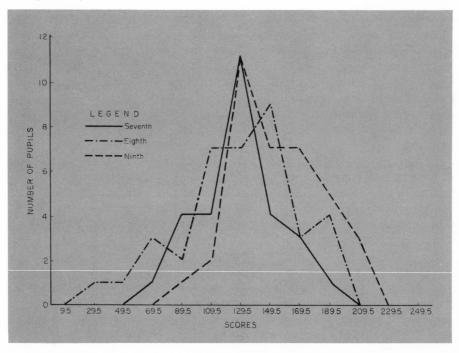

Whether this is a desirable emphasis depends on one's philosophy of education. (Note that grade equivalents are plotted on the base line of Fig. 4-16. GE's are discussed critically later in this chapter. Compare Fig. 4-16 with Fig. 11-5, the stanine-percentile "report card.")

GENERAL SUGGESTIONS
FOR CONSTRUCTING
GRAPHS   *Varied Practice*

A wide diversity of practice will be found in the construction of graphs as used in psychology and education. The title is sometimes placed above the graph, though usually it is placed below. In nearly all books and periodicals the graph title is placed below, but in unpublished charts such as wall charts the title is often more effective when lettered above. The figures are numbered consecutively with Arabic numerals placed at the beginning of the title. Sometimes the title is written in capital letters, as in tables; sometimes the initial letters of all important *words* are capitals; and again, only the first word in the title is capitalized, unless there are proper names, in which case the usual rules for capitalization apply. The second of these three methods is perhaps most common.

Figure 4-15. *Total comprehension scores on a reading test for the seventh, eighth, and ninth grades.*

Test Score	Seventh f	Seventh Cum f	Seventh Cum %	Eighth f	Eighth Cum f	Eighth Cum %	Ninth f	Ninth Cum f	Ninth Cum %	Percentile Scale
200-							3	36	100	
180-	1	28	100	4	37	100	5	33	92	
160-	3	27	96	3	33	89	7	28	78	
140-	4	24	86	9	30	81	7	21	59	
120-	11	20	71	7	21	57	11	14	39	
100-	4	9	32	7	14	38	2	3	8	
80-	4	5	18	2	7	19	1	1	3	
60-	1	1	4	3	5	14				
40-				1	2	5				
20-				1	1	3				

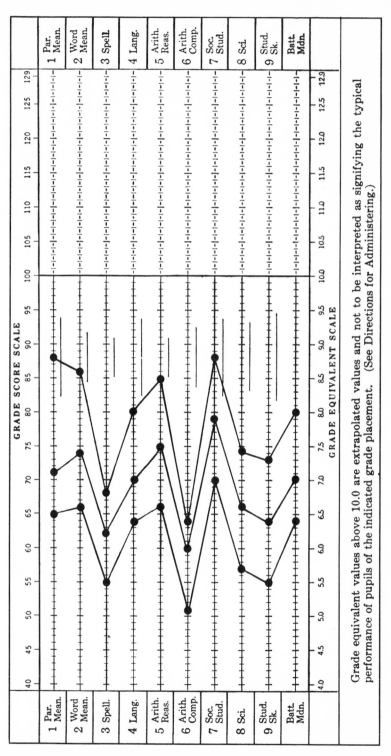

Figure 4-16. Grade profiles for the seventh, eighth, and ninth grades of a certain junior high school made by connecting the median scores on each part of the Stanford Achievement Test, Advanced Battery Complete, Form J. copyright 1953. (Reproduced by permission of Harcourt, Brace & World.)

Suggested Standards

Years ago a committee composed of representatives of the various groups interested in graphical methods prepared a report[5] recommending certain standards for constructing graphs. This report still covers most of the points required for the proper representation of educational data. The following rules are taken from it:

1. The general arrangement of a diagram should proceed from left to right.
2. Where possible represent quantities by linear magnitudes, as areas or volumes are more likely to be misinterpreted.
3. For a curve, the vertical scale, whenever practicable, should be so selected that the zero line will appear on the diagram.
4. If the zero line of the vertical scale will not normally appear on the curve diagram, the zero line should be shown by the use of a horizontal break in the diagram.
5. The zero lines of the scales for a curve should be sharply distinguished from the other coordinate lines.
6. For curves having a scale representing percentages, it is usually desirable to emphasize in some distinctive way the 100 per cent line or other line used as a basis of comparison.
7. When the scale of a diagram refers to dates, and the period represented is not a complete unit, it is better not to emphasize the first and last ordinates, since such a diagram does not represent the beginning or end of time.
8. When curves are drawn on logarithmic coordinates, the limiting lines of the diagram should each be at some power of ten on the logarithmic scales.
9. It is advisable not to show any more coordinate lines than necessary to guide the eye in reading the diagram.
10. The curve lines of a diagram should be sharply distinguished from the ruling.
11. In curves representing a series of observations, it is advisable, whenever possible, to indicate clearly on the diagram all the curves representing the separate observations.
12. The horizontal scale for curves should usually read from left to right and the vertical scale from bottom to top.
13. Figures for the scales of a diagram should be placed at the left and at the bottom or along the respective axes.
14. It is often desirable to include in the diagram the numerical data or formulae represented.
15. If numerical data are not included in the diagram, it is desirable to give the data in tabular form accompanying the diagram.
16. All lettering and all figures on a diagram should be placed so as to be easily read from the base as the bottom, or from the right-hand edge of the diagram as the bottom.
17. The title of a diagram should be made as clear and complete as possible. Subtitles or descriptions should be added if necessary to insure clearness.

---

[5]W. C. Brinton, chairman, Preliminary report, joint committee on standards of graphic representation, *Quarterly Publications of the American Statistical Association,* 1915, 14, 790–797.

NORMS   "Test scores are meaningful and valuable to the extent that they can be interpreted in terms of capacities, abilities, and accomplishments of educational significance."[6] It is self-evident that the value of test scores will depend largely on how well they are understood. In the first part of this chapter, we considered the summarization of scores by graphical methods as an aid to their interpretation. Now let us consider some closely related problems of interpreting scores by the aid of norms.

Standardized and Nonstandardized Tests

To begin with, it is important for us to distinguish clearly between a *norm* and a *standard*,[7] especially because the terms are frequently used interchangeably. The confusion doubtless arises from the fact that norms are used with standard tests and that the derivation of norms is a part of the process of standardization.

Many standard tests began as informal objective tests made by classroom teachers. When an informal test has gone through the process of standardization, it then differs from the original class test in four essential aspects. First, the content has been standardized. This means that each item has survived careful scrutiny by at least one presumably competent person, and that its difficulty and discriminating value have been determined by statistical processes that have eliminated its weaker fellows. Second, its method of administration has been standardized. This means that definite directions have been worked out, usually with appropriate time limits and the like. Third, the method of scoring has been standardized. This means that scoring keys have been prepared and that definite rules have been formulated for marking the papers and for determining the scores on each part and on the whole test. Finally, the process of interpretation has been standardized, at least in part. This means that tables of norms are now available for interpreting the various scores made on the test. These norms are usually merely scores that have been made by large numbers of pupils distributed over wide geographical areas and representing various types of schools, and that have been grouped, as a rule, according to age or school grade.

Norms versus Standards

The word *standard* implies a *goal* or *objective to be reached.* It should be clear, then, that a *norm* is not a measure of *what*

---

[6]J. C. Flanagan, Units, scores, and norms, p. 695 in E. F. Lindquist, ed., *Educational measurement* (Washington, D. C.: American Council on Education, 1951).

[7]Flanagan, *ibid.,* emphasized this distinction on p. 698 and elsewhere. Also, at greater length, did Robert Dion in Norms are not goals, *Newsletter of the Elementary School Principals Association of Connecticut,* October 1958, pp. 1–5.

ought to be—i.e., *a goal*—but merely a measure of *what is,* the *status quo.* When a grade or class is up to the national median on a test, it is just an average or typical group. Of course, this score may in some sense represent a satisfactory performance for the group under the circumstances, but that fact cannot be determined from the norms themselves. The mere fact that the grade attains the norm does not of itself establish anything other than that the performance is that of a typical group. Clearly, a group of students having superior opportunities and capacities ought to make better than a typical record, whereas a group of low ability and opportunity might find it virtually impossible to do that well. Unfortunately, many tests at the present time have only one set of norms for each grade or age group, all types of pupils and schools being lumped together.[8] What is needed is a norm for at least each major type of school organization and type of pupil. Even then such norms could hardly be regarded as reasonable standards of attainment. For one thing, the norms of achievement tests are never more than tentative. They must be continually changing with increases in length of school term and with improvement in training of teachers, in textbooks, in school equipment, and the like. It is also not unreasonable to assume, human nature being what it is, that average achievement with the facilities now available could be considerably better than it is now. Truly, the only valid norm for the individual pupil is his own past record, and the only valid standard is his maximum capacity for growth.

Reasonable standards, or goals of attainment, are almost altogether lacking. It is conceivable that such standards might be worked out and expressed in numerical units on existing tests, or on others to be devised. But such a process is inherently difficult, whereas the process of building norms is time-consuming and laborious but perfectly simple and straightforward. In fact, an adequate technique for establishing standards has yet to be worked out. Ideally, a standard would have to be provided for each individual. At any rate, no one standard could be established that would be equally appropriate for everyone, or even for any considerable number. Certainly an understanding of the way norms are determined would make it obvious that they lay no claims to being goals of performance, unless perhaps one is willing to accept mediocrity as a goal.

RAW SCORES
AND DERIVED SCORES   *What a Score Means*

To take a simple case, let us suppose that a pupil has made a score of 40 on a spelling test of 50 words. What does this score of 40 mean? To say that the score represents an achievement of 80 per cent is

---

[8]This seems most characteristic of achievement tests, least characteristic of "aptitude" tests. Many new types of norms are being tried, however. On this, see W. M. Shanner, New concepts in norms, pp. 64–74 in *The positive values in the American educational system* (Washington, D. C.: American Council on Education, 1959).

true as far as it goes, but this obvious interpretation leaves much to be desired. How were the 50 words for the test chosen? Were they the 50 most frequently misspelled words for the grade in which the test was administered? Or were they a random sample from a certain dictionary, so that we can estimate the pupil's vocabulary as being 80 per cent of the words in that dictionary? How were they presented? How scored? How well did the average pupil do? How variable were the scores on the test? What is the percentile rank of a score of 40 in his school class? The z-score? The stanine or sta-eleven?[9]

What is the "grade equivalent" (GE) of a score of 40 on this test? That is, at what month of which typical school grade is the average score 40? It might, for instance, be listed in the test manual as 3.7, meaning the seventh month of the third grade. If the pupil who earned the 40 has an actual grade placement of, say, 5.2 (second month of the fifth grade), then he is a poor speller compared with the group on which the GE's are based, being 5.2 − 3.7 = one year and five months shy of the GE, 5.2, "expected" for his class.

Grade equivalents have serious disadvantages. They look like standard scores but aren't, because the variability of GE's from one test may be quite different from that for another. Let us consider a fictitious example. Suppose that David is a student in the fourth month of the sixth grade, grade placement 6.4. He takes a battery of achievement tests issued by a certain publisher and normed on a large national sample of pupils. His GE on both reading and arithmetic computation is 7.4, a year ahead of his grade placement on the national norms provided. Quite likely, however, reading-test GE's are much more variable than arithmetic-test GE's; some sixth grade students are virtually non-readers, whereas others have GE's of 12.4 or more, but it is rare to find sixth graders who score that low or that high on arithmetic. Thus, although David's GE deviation on each of the two tests is 7.4 − 6.4 = 1.0, his z-score on reading will be considerably less than his z-score on arithmetic (though both will be positive, because he is above the national median for Grade 6.4 on both tests).

One could, of course, express every raw score on the reading test as a GE and then give David a z-score in the GE distribution for the national sample of Grade 6.4 students, or a z-score in his own class. If David's class is typical of the national norm group used by the publisher of this test, its mean GE will be 6.4, with a standard deviation dependent on the variability of reading achievement among sixth graders. In a similar fashion, David's z-score based on GE's could be found for the arithmetic test.

Would this procedure be worthwhile? Because z-scores are "pure" numbers, independent of the metric of the scores from which they were obtained, it would seem more sensible to determine them directly from the original raw scores, rather than detouring via GE's. Likewise, one would compute percentile ranks directly from raw scores, rather than from GE's. Grade equivalents

---

[9]These statistics were discussed in Chapter Three on pages 66, 79, and 81.

were designed originally to make test scores immediately meaningful, but they seem more likely to confuse than to enlighten.

To make matters worse, national norms often are not comparable from one test company to another, or even from one test to another within a given company. David's class, Grade 6.4, might have an average GE of 7.2 on one reading test and, say, 6.5 on another that appears to be testing the same type of ability. Which GE is "correct"? One must study the test manual and technical reports to see how the norm groups differed and which norm group seems more relevant for David's class. Better still, it may be desirable to set up local norms for a school, district, state, or region so that David's scores on various tests from different publishers may be rendered comparable.

Figure 3-2 on page 70 contains the score profile of a sophomore who took various tests, all of which were normed on his college class via both percentile ranks and sta-eleven scores. He was administered an intelligence test; an English battery consisting of grammar (G), organization (O), and reading tests, the latter having vocabulary (V), reading speed (S), and reading level (L) subtests; and a five-test achievement battery: history (H), literature (Li), science (Sc), art (A), and mathematics (M). The norms are shown both as percentile ranks and as "sta-elevens" (standard scores on the basis of 11 categories— that is, running from 1– through 9+). TE means "total English score," and TA means "total achievement score." The intelligence, TE, and TA points are connected with a solid line, whereas the battery tests and subtests are joined by dotted lines.

In consultation with his adviser, Richard can see at a glance that he scores above his sophomore class average in general, but that his history, literature, and art scores fall considerably below the other eight points. Richard and his adviser can use this information to good advantage in planning his last two years of college courses.

Richard's average sta-eleven score for the three main points on his solid-line profile is $(7 + 8 + 7)/3 = 22/3 = 7$, which is *not* itself a sta-eleven score. It tends to *under*-estimate his overall superiority. If we took his total sta-eleven score, 22, and determined its sta-eleven value among the totals for all sophomores tested at his college, it might be 8 instead of 7.[10]

OTHER NORMING
STATISTICS

For most norms, we recommend sta-eleven scores obtained by the counting-down-and-up method discussed in Chapter Three on pages 81-85, instead of the many norming statistics employed during the infancy and adolescence of the measure-

---

[10]If you are curious as to why the average of sta-elevens is not itself a sta-eleven (mean = 5, but standard deviation is usually less than 2), study the principle involved in J. C. Stanley's Why Wechsler-Bellevue full-scale IQ's are more variable than averages of verbal and performance IQ's, *Journal of Consulting Psychology*, 1953, 17, 419-420.

ment movement. Because you will run across a number of these in test manuals, however, we shall discuss some of them briefly.

MA

By analogy with chronological age (CA), the great French psychologist Alfred Binet in 1908 devised the term *mental age* (MA).[11] Each task (i.e., item) on his scale was scored directly in months of mental age, so that an individual's total score was his MA. More generally, a person's mental age on any "intelligence" test is the CA of the age group that has the same average score that he earned on the test. Paul, for example, may obtain a raw score of 57 points, which on that test happens to be the mean score for persons 11 years 3 months old, so his MA is $11(12) + 3 = 132 + 3 = 135$ months, no matter what his CA happens to be. (Note that MA is analogous to the GE discussed earlier in this chapter.)

IQ

Four years after Binet introduced the MA, the German psychologist William Stern suggested using a mental quotient, MA/CA.[12] Four years later, Stanford University psychologist Lewis Terman multiplied Stern's mental quotient by 100 to remove the decimal, and thereby gave the world something to complain about besides the weather.[13] His *intelligence quotient* (IQ) "standardizes" the derived score, MA, by taking into account the actual age of the individual. If Paul (above), with an MA of 135 months, is 11 years 3 months (= 135 months) old at the time of testing, we say that he has an IQ of $100(135/135) = 100(1) = 100$, strictly normal (that is to say average) for his age. However, if he is only 6 years 2 months (= 74 months) old, his IQ is a phenomenal $100(135/74) = 182$. Why do we call an IQ of 182 "phenomenal"? Because only an extremely small percentage of persons with CA's of 74 months have IQ's of 182 on the 1960 Terman-Merrill scale.[14] Roughly, IQ's of children on Terman's scale range from nearly 0 to slightly over 200, being distributed approximately normally around a mean of 100 with a standard deviation of about 16. (See page 80.) Thus an IQ of 182 is about $\frac{182-100}{16}$, or 5.125 standard deviations above the mean, so it has a *z*-score of $+5.125$ and a standard score of $5 + 2(5.125) = 15$ on the scale whose mean is 5 and standard deviation 2. Only about one person in eight million would score 5.125 standard deviations or more beyond the mean, 100, of a normal distribution whose standard deviation is 16.

Getting IQ means to come out exactly 100 at every CA and causing the variability of IQ's at every CA to be the same as everywhere else by cut-and-try

---

[11] See Florence M. Goodenough, *Mental testing* (New York: Rinehart, 1949), pp. 49–51.

[12] *Ibid.,* p. 63.

[13] L. M. Terman, *The measurement of intelligence* (Boston: Houghton Mifflin, 1916).

[14] L. M. Terman and Maud A. Merrill, *Stanford-Binet Intelligence Scale* (Boston: Houghton Mifflin, 1960).

methods finally proved impossible.   Bellevue Hospital psychologist David Wechsler in 1939[15] abandoned mental-age units in favor of point scores (number right) changed to standard scores at each CA, with the mean set arbitrarily at 100 and the standard deviation at 15.   Terman and Merrill changed in 1960 to standard-score ("deviation") IQ's with mean 100 and standard deviation 16 at every age level.[16]

Thus measurement specialists have abandoned the 100 (MA/CA) ratio IQ in favor of standard scores, so they might as well drop the intelligence quotient nomenclature, which is no longer meaningful because the ratio method that led to a quotient is not involved in standard scores. (Why not? Aren't z scores quotients? They are, but the denominator, the standard deviation of all scores for the group tested, does not vary from student to student, whereas CA, the denominator of the IQ formula, does.) It took a long while to get educators and other citizens to accept IQ's, and it will probably take as long or longer to get them to replace IQ's with standard scores. Perhaps we need some such designation for the student's record as "standard score on the 1960 revision of the Stanford-Binet Intelligence Scale, with mean 100 and standard deviation 16," abbreviated SS, SBIS (100, 16), but surely that would be too cumbersome for all but pedants. As long as we keep clearly in mind its changed nature, IQ may continue to represent age-standardized attainment on an intelligence test.

In Table 4-1, we show how greatly "IQ's" from paper-and-pencil group tests differ from one test to another administered to the *same* students. The five test *means* ranged from 96.4 to 118.2, a span of 21.8 "IQ" points! Study the table to assure yourself that *an individual may have as many "IQ's" as there are different intelligence tests,* regardless of whether they be ratio or deviation IQ's. For more recently normed tests the differences may be somewhat less, because better sampling procedures are usually used nowadays, but caution is still needed.

Doubtless the fundamental solution is for all test makers to standardize their tests, whether they aim to measure intelligence or achievement, on a national population so chosen as to conform fully to the mathematical theory of sampling. If tests are standardized on samples chosen primarily on the basis of convenience, even when they involve large numbers and wide geographical areas, there is no assurance that the samples are truly representative and thus comparable with each other.

EA and EQ

MA and IQ refer solely to performance on "intelligence" tests. Analogous to them for achievement tests are educational age (EA) and educational quotient (EQ), 100 (EA/CA). EA may be subdivided

---

[15] D. Wechsler, *The measurement of adult intelligence* (Baltimore: Williams and Wilkins, 1939).

[16] Terman and Merrill, *op. cit.,* p. 28.

TABLE 4-1

Table for Equating IQ Values (Use only with students like these seniors who are at least 16 years old when tested.)*

Corrected IQ Value	IQ on Otis Higher, Form A	IQ on CTMM[†]			IQ on Terman-McNemar	IQ on SRA PMA	IQ on SRA Non-Verbal	Corrected IQ Value
		Total	Non-Language	Language				
90	88	96	87–88	96	87	75	97	90
91	89	97	89–90	97	88	76	98	91
92	90	98	91–92		89	77	99	92
93	91	99	93–94	98	90	78	100	93
94		100	95–96		91	79	101	94
95	92	101	97–98	99	92	80	102	95
96	93	102	99–101		93	81	103	96
97	94	103	102–105	100	94	82–83	104	97
98	95	104	106–108		95	84	105	98
99	96	105	109–110	101–102	96	85–87	106–107	99
100	97	106	111–112	103–104	97	88	108–109	100
101	98	107	113	105	98	89	110–111	101
102	99	108	114–116	106	99	90	112	102
103	100	109	117–118	107	100	91	113	103
104	101	110–111	119		101	92		104
105	102	112	120	108	102	93	114	105
106	103	113	121–122	109	103	94	115	106
107		114	123		104	95	116	107
108	104	115	124	110				108
109	105	116	125–126	111	105	96	117	109
110	106	117	127–128	112–113	106–107	97	118–119	110
111	107	118	129–130	114	108	98	120	111
112	108	119	131–133	115	109	99	121–122	112
113	109	120	134–136	116–117	110	100–101	123–124	113
114	110	121	137–139	118	111	102–103	125–126	114
115	111	122	140–141	119	112	104	127	115
116	112	123	142–143	120	113–114	105–106	128	116
117	113	124	144	121	115	107	129	117
118	114	125	145		116	108	130	118
119	115	126	146	122	117	109	131	119
120	116	127–128	147	123–124	118	110–111	132–133	120
121	117	129	148	125–126	119	112–113	134–135	121
122	118	130	149	127–128	120	114	136–137	122
123		131		129	121	115	138–139	123
124	119	132	150	130	122	116	140	124
125	120	133	151	131	123	117	141–142	125

*These figures were obtained from a report by W. G. Heil and Alice Horn, "A Comparative Study of the Data for Five Different Intelligence Tests Administered to 284 Twelfth Grade Students at South Gate High School—Los Angeles." Los Angeles: Curriculum Division, Los Angeles City School Districts, February 1950. (Mimeographed.)

[†]These values apply only to the California Test of Mental Maturity, Short Form, 1942 edition.

into reading age, arithmetic age, spelling age, etc., but usually it is based on the composite score from a battery of achievement tests. If Bill's score is the mean for pupils 10 years 2 months old, then Bill has an EA of 10-2, or 122 months. If his CA is 12 years 2 months (= 146 months), his EQ is 100(122/146) = 84. We must, however, be concerned about the (usually unlisted) variability of EA's and of EQ's in the norm group, especially if Bill has taken two different achievement-test batteries and therefore has two EA's and hence two EQ's. Objections to EA and EQ are similar to those for GE, MA, and IQ. Standard scores or percentile ranks serve much better.

AQ

An especially fallible and difficult-to-interpret ratio that has all but vanished under the onslaught of criticism is the accomplishment quotient, $AQ = 100\left(\dfrac{EQ}{IQ}\right) = 100\left(\dfrac{EA \div CA}{MA \div CA}\right) = 100\left(\dfrac{EA}{MA}\right)$. Because it is essentially the ratio of EA to MA, norming considerations for the tests on which they are based become crucial. The deeper we bury the AQ, the better.

MA, IQ, EA, EQ, and AQ all have other objectionable features that need not concern us here. The problems of central tendency and variability are by themselves sufficient to make standard scores or percentile ranks more useful in most situations.

MORE ABOUT STANDARD SCORES

Percentile ranks are easy to understand, but their units are not equal, in the sense that for normally distributed raw scores the difference between PR's of 10 and 20 is further, in standard-deviation units, than is the distance between PR's of 50 and 60, even though $20 - 10 = 60 - 50 = 10$. (The "normal curve" is symmetrical, however, so the distance from PR_{10} to PR_{20} is the same in standard-deviation units as the distance from PR_{80} to PR_{90}. Likewise, the distance from PR_{50} to PR_{60} is the same as that from PR_{40} to PR_{50}.) Because equal percentile-rank ranges do not usually produce equal z-score ranges, it is usually desirable to employ standard scores rather than percentile ranks, particularly if a profile of several points is to be plotted.

The general formula for any computed standard score—that is, one not obtained merely by counting off the required percentage of frequencies—is:

$$Z = M + S(z) = M + S\left(\frac{\text{Raw score} - \text{Mean of raw scores}}{\text{Standard deviation of raw scores}}\right),$$

where Z is the standard score of an individual, M the arbitrary new mean, and S the arbitrary new standard deviation.

You are already familiar with several z-score scales. The first one we considered was the stanine or sta-eleven scale, for which M = 5 and S = 2, so that each sta-eleven unit represents half a standard deviation. The formula for the sta-eleven scale is simply Z = 5 + 2z.

Wechsler's Adult Intelligence Scale (WAIS)[17] has the standardizing formula 100 + 15z. The 1960 Stanford-Binet Intelligence Scale[18] has the standardizing "IQ" formula 100 + 16z. (Should a score of 145 on the WAIS be as rare as a score of 145 on the S-B? It should be rarer, because $\dfrac{145 - 100}{15} = 3$ is greater than $\dfrac{145 - 100}{16} = 2.81$. If scores are normally distributed, 0.135 per cent lie 3 or more standard deviations above the mean, whereas 0.248 per cent lie above 2.81 standard deviations. The percentages themselves are small, but the ratio of 135 to 248 shows that only 54 per cent as many IQ's of 145 or higher should occur on the WAIS as on the 1960 S-B.)

In the formula, M and S may have any values that we desire. For most purposes, the 11-category sta-eleven scale 0, 1, . . . , 10, with M = 5 and S = 2, is ample. If even finer gradation at the extremes is desired, use 13 categories and a mean of 6 instead of 5, thereby producing the standard scores 0, 1, . . . , 12. The tail percentages would then be: for 0 and 12, 0.3 per cent = 0.0030; for 1 and 11, 0.92 per cent = 0.0092; for 2 and 10, 2.79 per cent = 0.0279; for 3 and 9, 0.0655; for 4 and 8, 0.1210; for 5 and 7, 0.1747; and for 6, 0.1974. Thus we have a sta-thirteen scale with mean 6 and standard deviation 2.

If you want each standard-score unit to represent one-third instead of one-half of a standard deviation, use a mean sufficiently high so that scores can go as low as three standard deviations below the mean without becoming negative. A convenient M would be 9 or 10 for S = 3. If 9, the "sta-nineteen" scores would run 0, 1,..., 9,..., 17, 18. The 9 category would extend from 8.5 to 9.5, or 0.5 units below the mean and 0.5 unit above the mean; 0.5 units are 0.5/3 = 0.1667 standard deviations, so in a table of the normal curve we find that 0.4338 of the total area under the curve (1.0000) lies below −0.16670, and 0.5662 lies below +0.16670, so we figure that the interval called "9" should contain 0.5662 − 0.4338 = 0.1324 of the frequencies, contrasted with 0.1974 for the middle ("5") of the sta-eleven scale whose S is 2. We proceed in this way with *The Kelley statistical tables*[19] of the unit normal distribution to construct Figure 4-17. Note that the histogram is symmetrical and unimodal, and that less than one raw score in 400 would be given a sta-nineteen score of 0 (or of 18).

For each of his *sub*tests, Wechsler chose an M of 10 and an S of 3, terminat-

---

[17]D. Wechsler, *Manual for the Wechsler Adult Intelligence Scale* (New York: Psychological Corporation, 1955).

[18]Terman and Merrill, *op cit.,* p. 28.

[19]T. L. Kelley, *The Kelley statistical tables,* rev. ed. (Cambridge: Harvard University Press, 1948).

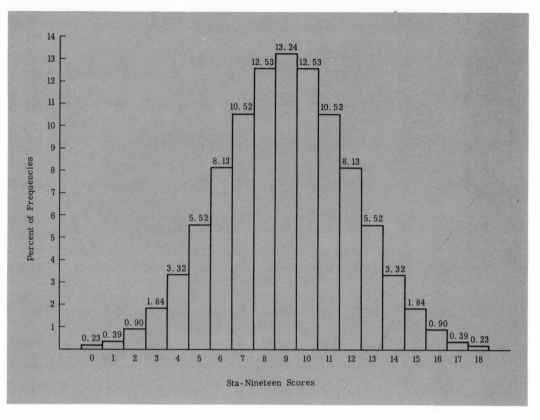

Figure 4-17. *The normal distribution of 19-category standard scores (mean = 9, standard deviation = 3).*

ing his scores at 0 and 20 to produce a sta-21 scale. He actually computed 10 + 3z, however, rather than counting, so his sta-21's have whatever shape the raw scores had, while our sta-elevens and sta-nineteens are a normalized transformation of the raw scores and therefore more interpretable in normal-curve terms than Wechsler's if the raw scores departed considerably from normality. (Are all symmetrical unimodal distributions "normal"? No. The relationship of height to width must conform to a certain mathematical formula, also.)

A commonly used standard scale has a mean of 50 and a standard deviation of 10, with the 61 scores 20 through 80 reported. Thus 20 represents "20.5 and under," and 80 represents "79.5 and over." This, then, is a sta-61 scale. Each unit represents one-tenth of a standard deviation. How, if at all, is this scale superior to a sta-61 scale with M = 30 and S = 10 that runs from 0 through 60? It isn't. The 20 units of "padding" at the lower end of the 20 through 80 scale serve no useful purpose. Some users of the 0–60 scale might, however, misinterpret the 0 as "nothing at all," whereas it merely designates all raw scores at least $\frac{0.5 - 30}{10} = -2.95$ standard deviations below the mean.

It might seem that 61 standard-score categories would suffice for any purpose, but certain test results are reported on a M = 500, S = 100 scale, with scores usually terminated at 200 and 800. (Again, there is "padding"—200 points in this instance.) Sometimes only the first two digits are actually being used, for then all scores end in zero. At other times, however, the third digit is not always zero. Three-digit results, to one-hundredth of a 'standard deviation, are reported for the College Entrance Examination Board's Scholastic Aptitude Tests (SAT) and achievement tests, for instance.[20] Do 601 possible score categories provide enough score differentiation to suit you? The extreme 200 of those units, 200-299 and 701-800, aren't used as much as the scores in the 300–700 range, of course. Most students admitted by highly selective colleges, such as Radcliffe and Swarthmore, however, will score over 600 on the verbal part of the SAT.[21]

There are two important things to keep in mind: (1) M and S, the mean and standard deviation of the standard-score scale, may have any value you choose, without any resemblance to the mean and standard deviation of the raw scores themselves; and (2) computed standard scores are no more or less normally distributed than are the raw scores from which they were obtained, while "counted" standard scores squeezed to fit the normal distribution will tend to approach it more closely. The chief reason for counting instead of computing, though, is that counting methods do not require computing the mean and the standard deviation of the raw scores, thereby simplifying the statistical task enough so that an intelligent, conscientious school clerk can routinely change raw scores to sta-elevens, sta-nineteens, or the like after she has had some training and practice.

There is much more that we could say about norms, but here is a good place to stop and illustrate the concepts and techniques of this chapter by reference to manuals for a recent test. Before doing that, however, let us caution testers to report and record both the raw scores and the derived scores for each individual tested, clearly indicating just how each score was obtained. Also, list the name, level, form, and edition of the tests administered. Perhaps better still, maintain a cumulative-record folder for each active student to contain his test booklets and answer sheets so that they may be readily available for study by teachers, counselors, and administrators. Probably this folder should go along with the elementary-school student to high school, in order to be most useful. When supplemented by national norms and sta-eleven local-norm scores, carefully recorded on the cumulative record, these materials make it easy to employ test data correctly and well. All too many test records still consist solely of entries such as "Otis 72," however, with no date, form, level, time allowance, or norm type indicated; 72 might be the student's percentile rank (in what grade and on what norms?), or his deviation IQ, or his raw

---

[20]Information about these tests can be secured from the Educational Testing Service of Princeton, N.J.
[21]The mean SAT score of high-school juniors and seniors currently taking that test is not 500, because norms are "anchored" to an earlier group.

score. *If tests are worth administering, they are worth recording properly so that results will be used effectively and will not be misinterpreted.*

APPLICATIONS Now that we have discussed statistical procedures, graphical representations, and norms, let's look into some recent test manuals issued by a major publisher to be used in connection with one of its tests and see what statistics, tables, and norms are used there. We shall not try to evaluate the test itself as a measuring instrument (test evaluation is discussed in other parts of the book).

STEP Science

The Sequential Tests of Educational Progress (STEP) were first published by the Educational Testing Service (ETS) of Princeton, New Jersey, in 1957. Page 2 of *A Prospectus: Cooperative Sequential Tests of Educational Progress* (1957) informs us that:

> In each of seven learning fields, the STEP series offers four levels of tests—extending on a single scale from Grade 4 through the sophomore year of college. Each test but one is 70 minutes in length (divided into two 35-minute units) so that individual students are measured reliably on the depth and power of their skill. Except for the essay tests (4 forms), there are two forms of every test at every level in each field: Essay Writing (35 minute test), Listening Comprehension, Reading Comprehension, Writing, Science, Mathematics, Social Studies. The four levels of tests, designed to be appropriate in difficulty for most students in these classes, are: Level 4, Grades 4–6; Level 3, Grades 7–9; Level 2, Grades 10–12; Level 1, Freshman and Sophomore years of college.

Thus implicitly we are promised norms whereby all the tests in a given learning field can extend "on a single scale from Grade 4 through the sophomore year of college." Over on page 23 of the *Prospectus* we are told that:

> In defining the scales for the STEP series, there was no attempt to have the scale score reflect normative information. The primary purpose was to arrive at a reporting system that would make it possible to compare scores obtained on all forms and levels of the *same* test. Norming was considered a separate step in the total standardization program.
> In each field measured by STEP, then, there is a single score scale—extending from the lowest score earned by a fourth-grader to the highest score earned by a college sophomore. All forms and all levels of the tests in the field are equated to that one score scale. *The scale itself is a series of 3-digit numbers, starting at about 150* (so it will not be confused with the IQ) *and running up to about 350* (so it will not be confused with the College Board scale). The scale expresses no normative meaning but, since the scale ties together all tests in each field, the score may be easily related to the tables of norms. [Italics added.]

Notice that the scale of about 200 points is arbitrary and that the scale for one field, such as science, is not the same as the scale for another field, such as

social studies. The scale is not a Z-score scale of the kinds we discussed, because its mean and standard deviation are not set. We leave the *Prospectus* and
go on to the *Manual for Interpreting Scores: Science* to see how the scale works
in practice. Suppose that John, a beginning fifth grader, gets a raw score of 27
"right" out of 60 items on Form 4A (that is, Level 4A for Grades 4-6) of
the STEP Science. From the scoring key we find that 27 right on 4A corresponds to a scaled score of 246. (On Form 4A, 0 right "earns" a scaled score
of 223, while a perfect score—60 right—receives 311. On Form 4B the range is
225-324. The ranges for Forms 1A and 1B are 254-349 and 255-360, respectively. Which form, A or B, contains the easier questions? Form A does, because a perfect score on it does not put one as high on the scale as a perfect
score on Form B does. What is the scaled-score range, from 0 right on 4A to
60 right on 1B? It is 223-360.)

On page 22 of the *STEP Science Manual* we find the "Converted Score"
column and locate the 246-247 row, which includes John's score of 246. His
percentile-rank band on fifth-grade national norms is 22-43, meaning that he
scored better than 22 to 43 percent of fifth graders and worse than 57 to 78
per cent of them. The percentile-rank range is an attempt to reflect the error of
measurement inherent in a fallible score. John, we conclude, is not quite up to
the median fifth grader throughout the nation with respect to knowledge of
science, as measured by this test, but he is not greatly below the median. His
z-score range, corresponding to PR_{22} and PR_{43}, is -0.77 to -0.18. In sta-
eleven form this range is $5 + 2(-0.77) = 3$, to $5 + 2(-0.18) = 5$.

On fourth-grade norms John's PR band for the scaled score of 246 is 51-69,
and on sixth-grade norms it is 18-30. He is a little above average for the grade
lower than his, and in the lowest third of the next higher grade.

Suppose that we had given John Form 4B instead of 4A. What raw score
do we suspect that he would have received? Probably, if Forms A and B were
perfectly reliable, he would have obtained a raw score that would correspond
to a scaled score of about the 246 that he obtained on 4A, which is also 27.
If he had taken Form 3A, designed for Grades 7-9, what raw score would we
guess for him? A glance at the conversion table, from raw score to scaled score,
on the back of the 3A scoring key shows 16 right corresponding to scaled score
of 246. We were right to have John take 4A instead of 3A, because 3A is almost
too difficult for him.

A test of "ideal" difficulty for comparing John with his classmates is one on
which he earns a score halfway between the chance score and a perfect score. *If*
John marked all 60 of the four-option multiple-choice items in 4A randomly,
one-fourth of his answers, 15, would on the average correspond with the scoring key (i.e., be "right") by sheer chance. Half-way between 15 and 60 is $(15 +
60)/2 = 37\frac{1}{2}$, contrasted with John's actual raw score of 27. The "ideal" score,
$37\frac{1}{2}$, corresponds for Form 4A to a scaled score of $255\frac{1}{2}$, close to the fifth-
grade median of 254 reported in the *Manual*. Probably not all fifth graders attempted all 60 items, however, although they are encouraged to do so, but we

seem safe in concluding that 4A is of appropriate difficulty for the average fifth grader.

With STEP scaled scoring, it is feasible and desirable to use two or even three levels for testing a single class. Those fifth graders whom the teacher believes will be especially good answerers of STEP Science items should be given Form 3A or 3B, while the rest of the class takes 4A or 4B. An eighth-grade teacher may want to hand the poorest science students 4A or 4B, the average ones 3A or 3B, and the ablest ones 2A or 2B. The common scaled scores and common format for all eight STEP Science tests (4 levels, 2 comparable forms at each level) make it easy to refer all scores to percentile norms for the grade in which the students are enrolled.

Why did the publishers of the STEP series not use standard-score band norms instead of percentile-rank bands? Probably because percentile ranks are easier for teachers to interpret than are standard scores. You can quickly get standard-score norms for any test that has percentile-rank norms merely by looking up the percentile ranks in a table of the normal curve, such as the brief one in Appendix I.

Other STEP Science Statistics

Raw scores, scaled scores, and percentile ranks form the bulk of the discussion in the *STEP Science Manual,* but a few other statistics are used. On page 11 teachers are told how to count down to the middle converted (scaled) score in their class, having first arranged all papers in rank order according to scaled scores. They are also told that "the mean or average Science score for the class...is obtained by summing the converted scores and dividing the sum by the number of students in the class. (Of course, percentile ranks cannot be averaged.)" We find little about variability or correlation in the *Manual,* however, because that was saved for the *STEP Technical Report,* to which we now turn.

On page 5 of this *Technical Report* the authors assert that "Performance on the [STEP] tests should correlate with appropriate aspects of academic performance." Later, on pages 13–18, they give six tables chock full of statistics, including r's. We reproduce their Table 7, page 17, as our Table 4-2. The SCAT tests are the School and College Ability Tests, which are standardized by the Educational Testing Service along with the STEP series. SCAT-V is the verbal part, SCAT-Q the quantitative part, and SCAT-T the total SCAT. Remember that comparisons of converted-score means within tests are meaningful, but that converted scores are not norms, so between-tests comparisons would have to be made via percentile ranks not shown in the table. Note that the SCAT-V means do rise regularly from grade to grade, from a low of 237.85 for SCAT Form 5B in Grade 4 to a high of 281.72 for SCAT 2B in Grade 12. The standard deviations of converted SCAT-V scores also rise, from 9.39 in Grade 4 to 15.80 in Grade 12 (but note that the 15.76 in Grade 10 is almost as high).

TABLE 4-2

Correlations of STEP Science with SCAT Verbal,
Quantitative, and Total in Grades 4–12

Grade	SCAT Form	STEP Form	Means*				Standard Deviations*				Correlations of STEP Science with		
			SCAT-V	SCAT-Q	SCAT-T	STEP Science	SCAT-V	SCAT-Q	SCAT-T	STEP Science	SCAT-V	SCAT-Q	SCAT-T
4	5A	4A	238.30	243.86	246.84	242.53	9.39	5.22	4.56	12.57	.83	.58	.81
	5B	4A	237.85	244.15	246.81	243.61	9.46	5.71	4.76	12.81	.72	.59	.73
5	5A	4A	246.78	253.53	253.75	252.06	12.32	7.58	7.28	13.75	.81	.72	.81
	5B	4A	245.71	251.94	252.52	251.89	10.73	6.67	5.90	12.69	.80	.62	.81
6	5A	4A	249.79	260.24	257.95	256.67	13.78	10.40	9.28	16.85	.79	.70	.80
	5B	4A	253.70	260.79	259.87	257.05	13.60	11.37	9.68	14.55	.70	.65	.74
	4A	4A	252.13	260.80	259.33	257.02	13.65	9.86	9.28	14.23	.81	.71	.83
	4B	4A	251.56	261.35	259.18	256.35	13.26	8.81	8.48	14.40	.76	.57	.77
7	4A	3A	258.17	270.50	266.01	261.44	13.18	12.86	10.33	11.77	.77	.63	.76
	4B	3A	257.65	270.21	265.56	262.94	13.48	11.85	10.30	11.71	.80	.65	.79
8	4A	3A	263.66	279.56	272.10	266.74	13.72	14.12	11.06	12.08	.80	.69	.82
	4B	3A	264.87	281.05	273.16	267.16	14.58	15.69	12.10	12.03	.75	.66	.77
	3A	3A	262.58	279.12	271.54	266.65	12.45	13.52	10.46	12.42	.69	.57	.70
	3B	3A	262.44	280.76	272.31	266.01	14.50	16.20	12.56	12.54	.77	.62	.77
9	3A	3A	269.62	286.26	278.01	271.24	15.22	15.74	12.83	12.78	.75	.67	.77
	3B	3A	269.62	287.08	278.50	270.92	14.13	16.25	12.29	13.63	.65	.60	.70
10	3A	2A	274.16	288.62	281.37	274.95	14.95	16.82	12.77	12.25	.70	.53	.69
	3B	2A	274.61	290.15	282.40	275.91	15.21	16.67	12.91	11.30	.64	.50	.65
	2A	2A	274.00	287.42	280.68	274.06	15.76	17.73	14.43	13.75	.72	.69	.76
	2B	2A	272.27	285.45	278.95	274.17	14.06	16.15	12.58	11.62	.69	.59	.72
11	2A	2A	281.22	294.72	287.50	280.48	15.06	16.57	12.92	12.98	.60	.58	.67
	2B	2A	280.75	291.87	286.26	280.65	14.54	16.11	13.18	13.18	.67	.59	.70
12	2A	2A	280.73	292.21	286.28	279.32	14.60	15.96	12.71	12.11	.52	.55	.60
	2B	2A	281.72	290.52	286.22	279.68	14.54	16.97	13.23	12.24	.69	.57	.71
	1A	2A	279.77	290.95	285.84	280.81	15.80	17.82	14.11	13.37	.67	.65	.71
	1B	2A	281.13	290.66	285.84	281.51	14.58	17.75	13.79	11.94	.61	.56	.64

*In converted-score units.

The STEP Science means rise rather regularly, from 242.53 to 281.51, but the standard deviations do not seem to change systematically from Grades 4 to 12; note the 12.81 for Grade 4 and the 11.94 for Grade 12.

If the STEP Science converted scores for a given form in a given grade are distributed normally, approximately two-thirds of them (68.26 per cent) will lie within one standard deviation of the mean. Can we infer whether or not the converted scores are normally distributed? Not from Table 4-2 alone, but from it in conjunction with the norms tables in the *Manual for Interpreting Scores: Science*. Let us look at the Grade 5 figures in Table 4-2, where the average STEP 4A Science mean is $(252.06 + 251.89)/2 = 251.98$, and the average standard deviation is $(13.75 + 12.69)/2 = 13.22$. In Table 1 on page 22 of the

STEP Science Manual we estimate that the median STEP Science converted score for the fifth grade is 254, 2 points higher than the above mean. The upper quartile (that is, the 75th percentile) is 261, and the lower quartile (25th percentile) is 244, so the range of the middle 50 per cent of the converted scores is 17 points. In a normal distribution the standard deviation is approximately 3/4 of this range, so here the standard deviation estimated from P_{75} − P_{25} is 3/4 × 17 = 12.75, about 13. Compare this figure with the actual average standard deviation of 13.22 determined from Table 4-2.

We know, then, that the fifth-grade distribution of STEP Science scores is a bit skewed negatively, because the median, 254, is slightly higher than the mean, 252, and the distance from the 50th percentile, 254, to the 75th percentile, 261 (7 points), is less than the distance from the median to the 25th percentile, 244 (10 points). The low scores tend to be a little lower than the high scores are high.

Also, we infer that the actual converted-score distribution is flatter than normally distributed scores would be. There is nothing magical about a distribution that is perfectly symmetrical (i.e., has zero skewness) and that possesses exactly the kurtosis (flatness or steepness) of the normal distribution. Purely chance phenomena have this distribution, and most test scores approach it if the test is not too easy or too difficult for the group tested, because errors of measurement in obtained scores are chance phenomena and therefore conceal the shape of the distribution of "true" scores.[22] Of the two characteristics, skewness and kurtosis, the former seems much more important for test constructors than the latter. A test that yielded error-free scores would discriminate best among all the individuals tested if the scores were distributed rectangularly (every score earned by the same number of individuals as every other score), according to psychometrician George Ferguson.[23] Usually, for actual scores zero skewness and *platykurtosis* (flatter than the normal distribution) are desirable.

Correlations

Coefficients of correlation are almost always difficult to interpret. They harbor many pitfalls. The last three columns of Table 4-2 contain *r*'s for the relationships between STEP Science and SCAT-V, SCAT-Q, and SCAT-T, where T = V + Q. What can we learn from these? In 25 of the 26 instances, STEP science correlated higher with SCAT-V, a test primarily involving words, than with SCAT-Q, which involves arithmetical computations and reasoning problems. This seems conclusive proof that STEP science is measuring something more verbal than quantitative, doesn't it? We must not jump to that conclusion without further study, however. The reliabil-

---

[22] For investigations of this technical point, see F. M. Lord, Elementary models for measuring change, in C. W. Harris, ed., *Problems in measuring change* (Madison: University of Wisconsin Press, 1963).

[23] G. A. Ferguson, On the theory of test discrimination, *Psychometrika*, 1949, 14, 61–68.

ity of a test—the consistency with which it measures, determined by the magnitude of errors of measurement from one administration to another relative to true-score variability—affects its correlation with another variable. If SCAT-Q is less reliable than SCAT-V, then it will tend to correlate more poorly with other tests than SCAT-V will, even though they measure the "same thing," for then they do not measure it equally well.

In Table 5 on page 11 of the original *SCAT Technical Report* (no date), one can find that only at the highest level (Form 1A in Grade 13) does the SCAT-Q reliability coefficient equal or exceed the SCAT-V reliability coefficient, .93 vs. .92. The difference is greatest for Form 5A, Grade 5: .88 for Q, .94 for V. Allowance for these discrepancies in reliability reduces the difference between the SCAT-V and SCAT-Q correlations with STEP Science, but they still favor SCAT-V slightly. As Stanley and Mann[24] commented in their review, STEP Science items require considerable reading of words. We have no logical basis, however, for saying that STEP Science *should* correlate as highly with SCAT-Q as with SCAT-V, do we?

The median correlation of STEP Science with SCAT-V, figured from Table 4-2, is .72, whereas the median reliability coefficients for STEP Science and SCAT-V are, from the respective technical reports, about .86 and .93. If STEP Science and SCAT-V measured exactly the same thing, but with such reliabilities (that is, not without errors of measurement), we would expect them to correlate approximately $\sqrt{(.86)(.93)}$ = .89, considerably more than the .72 that they actually correlate, so we conclude that they do not measure exactly the same characteristics. Not all of a student's STEP Science score can be attributed to his verbal ability as measured by SCAT-V.

SCAT-T scores are somewhat more reliable than either SCAT-V or SCAT-Q scores, for reliability coefficients tend to increase as the number of test items rises. The correlations of STEP Science scores with SCAT-T scores are not much higher than their correlations with SCAT-V scores, however, implying that adding STEP-Q to STEP-V does not improve the correlation much. There is some improvement—probably because of the heightened reliability—in 20 of the 26 comparisons of r's for STEP Science and SCAT-V with r's for STEP Science and SCAT-T, the median r for STEP Science with SCAT-T being .75.

We may conclude that the STEP Science test measures *something* besides intellectual ability as represented by the SCAT-V, SCAT-Q, and SCAT-T scores, and *hope* that this something is "knowledge and understanding of general science." It seems at least as likely as most other general-science tests to do this.

---

[24] J. C. Stanley and Sister M. Jacinta Mann, Review of the Sequential Tests of Educational Progress: Science, pp. 716–717 in Oscar K. Buros, ed., *The fifth mental measurements yearbook* (Highland Park, N. J.: Gryphon Press, 1959). They conclude the review as follows: "Overall, the STEP science tests meet excellently the need for a well planned, coordinated survey series stressing applications of common curricular material to familiar situations."

The *STEP Technical Report* contains much more statistical information concerning six of the seven STEP tests, all but Essay Writing. Having illustrated its contents, however, we leave further study of the *Report* to you as a class or outside activity. Be sure to consider SCAT-STEP supplements, the first of which appeared in 1958.

In concluding this chapter, remember that suitable graphical techniques applied to appropriate normative data can produce useful aids for teaching and counseling.

RECOMMENDED READINGS

Durost, W. N., How to tell parents about standardized test results, *Test Service Notebook* No. 26, Harcourt, Brace & World, n.d. Free.

Ebel, R. L., How to explain standardized test scores to your parents, *School Management,* 1961, 5, 61-64.

Flanagan, J. C., Units, scores, and norms, Ch. 17 in E. F. Lindquist, ed., *Educational measurement.* Washington, D. C.: American Council on Education, 1951.

Hart, Irene, Using stanines to obtain composite scores based on test data and teachers' ranks, *Test Service Bulletin* No. 86, Harcourt, Brace & World, 1957. Free.

Hills, J. R., *Freshman norms for the Georgia University System,* 1962–63. Atlanta 3: The System, 1964.

Lord, F. M., Test norms and sampling theory, *Journal of Experimental Education,* 1959, 27, 247-263.

Peterson, L. V. and Schramm, W., How accurately are different kinds of graphs read? *Audio-Visual Communications Review,* 1954, 2, 178-189.

Rulon, P. J., Problems of regression, *Harvard Educational Review,* 1941, 11, 213-223.

Rulon, P. J., On the concepts of growth and ability, *Harvard Educational Review,* 1947, 17, 1-9.

Seashore, H. G. and Ricks, J. H., Jr., Norms must be relevant, *Test Service Bulletin No. 39,* pp. 1-4. New York: The Psychological Corporation, 1950.

Spear, Mary E., *Charting statistics.* New York: McGraw-Hill, 1952.

Symposium: standard scores for aptitude and achievement tests, *Educational and Psychological Measurement,* 1962, 22, 5–39:
Wesman, A. G., Introduction, pp. 5–6.
Gardner, E. F., Normative standard scores, pp. 7–14.
Ebel, R. L., Content standard test scores, pp. 15–25.
Angoff, W. H., Scales with nonmeaningful origins and units of measurement, pp. 27–34.
Flanagan, J. C., Discussion, pp. 35–39.

Tiedeman, D. V., Has he grown? *Test Service Notebook* No. 12. New York: Harcourt, Brace, and World, 1952. 4 pp.

CHARACTERISTICS OF A SATISFACTORY MEASURING INSTRUMENT

A test should yield consistent results, pertinent for a specific purpose the tester has in mind, without too much trouble and cost. In other words, test scores must be *reliable* and *valid* enough for the tasks at hand, and they must be *usable*—i.e., obtained fairly readily without undue upset to the curriculum and budget. Reliability is consistency or stability of measurement. Validity is usefulness for a given purpose, especially for predicting an outcome. Usability is practicality.

A test cannot be of much value if it doesn't yield roughly the same score for Bill today that it would have yielded under comparable conditions yesterday, or will yield tomorrow without intervening learning. On the other hand, a test might yield highly consistent results from day to day without having any other known value. We can state this more formally as follows: *Reliability is a necessary but not sufficient condition for validity*. A highly reliable test such as speed of tapping may or may not be useful for some purpose such as predicting the quickness with which

C   H   A   P   T   E   R   F   I   V   E

one can apply an automobile brake, but a wholly unreliable test certainly has
no validity.

The concepts of reliability and validity are, in their various forms, central
to the theory and practice of educational and psychological testing. Most basic
concepts are not especially simple, and these aren't exceptions. There are at
least three kinds of reliability, and even more kinds of validity. Specialists in
educational and psychological measurement do not agree fully about test
theory, so we shall merely give you a glimpse of current ways of thinking about
the consistency and meaning of test scores.

RELIABILITY   Let us start with a simple questionnaire study
                designed to estimate the mean age of female
teachers in the United States. If we had a list of all women teaching in the
U.S., we could take a *random* sample and send each woman in that sample a
double postal card asking her month, day, and year of birth. Suppose that each
woman returned the postal card stating her birthday. We could average the
ages and thereby estimate the mean age of all the female teachers in the U.S.
We might wonder, however, how reliable and how valid the reported ages are.
If we had written each woman's name and address on the return card, we would
know to whom each reported date of birth belonged. Now suppose that we
send a *second* double postal card to each, pretending that the first cards were
destroyed in a fire and asking the same question as before. If each and every
woman responds again, we shall have for each woman two birthdates that
should agree perfectly. If the two dates for each woman *do* agree exactly, then
we have perfect reliability of birthdate "scores."

Continue to stretch your imagination and suppose that we have been able to obtain an absolutely correct birth certificate for each woman. How reliable is the date of birth on it? Perfectly reliable, of course, because no matter when we look at a given certificate or photographic copy of it, we see the very same birthdate. Now compare the two birthdates each woman reports on the postal cards with her birthdate on the birth certificate. One woman reported "June 5, 1929" both times (perfect consistency), but her birth certificate shows "June 5, 1919" (imperfect predictive validity). She's shaved 10 years off her age. The agreement of her reliably reported birthdate with her actual birthdate is poor. A teacher reported "January 30, 1942" both times (reliable), and her birth certificate showed the same date (valid). A third woman put "December 12, 1922" on the first card and "December 12, 1927" on the second; her birth certificate showed "December 12, 1922." She is inconsistent by 5 years, but the first report agrees exactly with the certificate. Evidently she tells the truth about her age sometimes but not others. Her reported birthdate is unreliable and hence sometimes invalid—that is, sometimes the reported date does not agree with the correct date.

A coefficient of reliability of the birthdates would be the r between the two sets of birthdates reported—first card vs. second card. It would probably be somewhere between 0 and 1, depending on the way the inquiry was conducted and by whom it was carried out. One might expect the figure to be closer to 1 than to 0 in a well-conducted study, especially if results were to be strictly confidential. A crucial point to remember, however, is that even if each woman reported the same birthdate one time as the other, we would still not be sure this was her *true* birthdate. The coefficient of reliability would be 1, but the coefficient of validity might be less than 1. The coefficient of validity for the first set of birthdates reported would be their r with the birth-certificate dates, and the coefficient of validity for the second set of birthdates reported would be their r with the birth-certificate dates. Each of these two r's could range from -1 to $+1$. If the reported birthdates and the birth-certificate dates are identical, the validity coefficient is 1. Validity coefficients could be small (near zero) or negative, even if the reliability coefficient were perfect, $+1$.

In a study of this sort the older women might falsify their birthdates much more than the younger ones, or perhaps the middle-aged ones would have the largest discrepancies between reports and certificates. Anonymous replies might be much more correct than signed or well-identified ones. The point we are making is that reliability is necessary for validity but not sufficient; it is impossible to know a woman's true age solely from her assertions if she never uses the same figure twice, but it is possible to be deceived systematically even if she always reports the same birthdate. We work for reliability of measurement as an essential prerequisite, but we check further to ascertain validity. We want to know how old each female teacher really is as shown on a correct birth certificate. This is our wholly reliable *criterion*. The reported birthdates are our two predictors, neither perfectly reliable nor wholly valid. (Usually we have just one reported birthdate per woman, and we must keep in mind its probable deficiencies.)

Zero Reliability

Let us now consider another "test." (In what sense is asking a woman her birthdate a test?) Your instructor lends each of you a new quarter, coined at the same mint the same year, and says: "Today we shall have a coin-flipping test. Please go to an uncrowded room and bounce your quarter against the ceiling. Do this 80 times, and each time observe whether or not you obtain a head. If the coin lands on end in a crack, flip it again. Record the number of heads you obtain. This may be anywhere from 0 to 80, of course, but will almost always be between 27 and 53."

You come back into the room with your scores, and the instructor computes their mean, which happens to be 39.88. He then asks you to estimate the number of heads you will obtain the next time you flip your coin against the ceiling 80 times. Suppose that your score the first time is 47, quite high in the group of coin-flippers. Would you consider yourself prone to flipping heads and so estimate that your score the next time will again he 47? Not if you know much about the laws of chance. All deviations from 40 (39.88 rounded off) may be considered random. Your "true score" and the true score of each of your classmates is approximately 40, regardless of your "obtained score" (number of heads secured). Your $(47 - 40) = +7$ luck the first time is called, technically, a 7-point "error of measurement." Generally, an individual's error of measurement is the discrepancy between his *obtained* (i.e., actual) score and his *true* (i.e., "real-ability") score. Such errors of measurement are distributed randomly and independently with a mean of 0, so your best bet is that your error of measurement the second time you make 80 tosses will be 0, and hence that your obtained score the second time will be 40.

The correlation between the number of heads obtained by you and your classmates the first and the second time will, for a fairly large class, be very nearly 0, indicating that a coin-flipping test of this sort yields scores whose reliability coefficient is 0. Can you use the coin-tossing scores of your class to predict your ages? Your IQ's? Your knowledge of English grammar? Anything whatsoever? Most assuredly not. If tosses one time won't predict tosses another time, how can they predict anything external to the coin-tossing itself? If a test won't predict a strictly comparable form of itself, how can it predict anything else? Test scores whose reliability is nil cannot predict anything a bit better than sheer guessing will do.

Thus we have defined the two ends of the reliability continuum: 0 for the coin-tossing "test" and 1 for the same birth certificates examined twice (with perfect accuracy, of course). In between these two points, usually closer to 1 than to 0, lie the reliability coefficients for most test scores. A speed-of-tapping test, for example, can be made quite reliable if the recording apparatus is accurate and if the test is continued long enough, with appropriate rest intervals. Tapping scores may not correlate significantly, however, with things we desire to predict, such as college grades or high-jumping ability. A tapping test may be fine for predicting one's tapping ability at some other time under similar circumstances, but it may not be useful for predicting other criteria. Thus we may say that a certain tapping test has high reliability, perhaps .94, but low predictive validity (perhaps essentially 0) for the criteria of interest to us. Reliability is necessary, but validity of some sort (predictive validity is just one kind) is essential. Reliability does not guarantee validity, although validity does guarantee reliability. A test adequately valid for predictive purposes is sure to be adequately reliable.

Three Reliability Coefficients

The coin-tossing reliability coefficient is a *coefficient of stability,* as is the birth-certificate coefficient, whereas the tapping-test reliability coefficient is a *coefficient of equivalence and stability.* By "stability" we mean that an individual's score may change from one time to the next, not because of a change in the test (which remains constant—the same coin both times, the same birth certificate) but because of fluctuations in the measurement of a "true" characteristic—coin-flipping "ability" or birthdate. True coin-flipping ability does not vary from flipper to flipper, so variation within a given tosser from one set of tosses to another is as great as variation among tossers. Conversely, variation within individuals with respect to true birthdate is nil, while variation among individuals may be great. Once we introduce the possibility of errors of measurement in ascertaining birthdates, as by asking each person his birthdate at two different times, we may discover that within-individual variability exists. The same correct birth certificate has no error of measurement from one time to the next unless it is misread, for it is the same "test" both times, but each time we ask a woman her age we are to some extent giving her another test, for the situation may change from the first questioning to the next.

"Equivalence" refers to the extent to which one form of a test is equivalent in content and difficulty to another form of that same test. Wholly equivalent forms would be interchangeable; it would not matter which form was used on a given occasion. To what extent is a tapping test on one day equivalent to a tapping test with the same equipment another day? A tapper may be well-practiced, but this does not mean that the recording apparatus will function in a strictly equivalent manner the two times. To this lack of strict equivalence must be added the fluctuations in the tapping ability of an individual (lack of stability) from one time to another, which is why we say that the reliability coefficient for speed of tapping is a coefficient of equivalence *and* stability—though much more of the latter than the former if the apparatus and procedure are kept under good control.

With other tests of ability the equivalent-forms problem may become much more serious. Are the two "comparable" Forms A and B of a certain vocabulary test actually interchangeable? Are they even measuring precisely the "same thing"? Is one form easier than the other? How do r_{AA}, r_{BB}, r_{AB}, and r_{BA} determined from four large similar groups of examinees differ from each other? r_{AA}, the correlation between scores from the same Form A administered twice to a group of examinees, is a coefficient of stability (a test-retest reliability coefficient), as is r_{BB} · r_{AB} and r_{BA}, the correlation coefficients for scores from comparable Forms A and B, are coefficients of equivalence and stability (comparable-form reliability coefficients). r_{AA} and r_{BB} may be undesirably high because examinees remembered some of their answers (whether or not correct) from the first time the form was administered to the second time, or learned some of them during the interim, while r_{AB} and r_{BA} may be too low because Forms A and B aren't equivalent. In order to increase equivalence, test constructors sometimes match for content and difficulty each item in one form with the same-numbered item in the other.

Historically, since 1910, the $r_{AB} = r_{BA}$ coefficient of equivalence and stability has been defined as the reliability coefficient of a test: r_{AB} is the reliability coefficient of Form A or of Form B, the reliabilities of the two forms being considered equal because they were constructed carefully to be equivalent (frequently the word "comparable" is used instead of "equivalent"). This meant that in order to determine the reliability coefficient of one form of a test, it was necessary to have two or more forms of that test. For many tests this was impracticable. The user needed just one form, or had financial resources for only one, or was using "insight" questions that did not have comparable analogues.

This dilemma led to splitting a test longitudinally (such as putting the odd items numbered 1, 3, 5,... into one half and the even items 2, 4, 6,...into the other), securing for each examinee a total score for each half, and correlating the half-scores to secure a coefficient of equivalence that we might label r_{ab} for a test half as long as Form A or Form B. From r_{ab} one estimates r_{AB} with the formula $2r_{ab}/(1 + r_{ab})$, which in test manuals is usually referred to as one version of the Spearman-Brown step-up or prophecy formula. The halving procedure is called the split-half method, and the stepped-up r_{ab} is usually referred to as a "corrected" split-half reliability coefficient. (The odd-even splitting procedure will be undesirable if it throws one type of item into one half and another type of item into the other half, in which event other splitting methods are used.)

Note that the stepped-up r_{ab} is a coefficient of equivalence only, for the two half-forms a and b are composed of items interlaced through Form A (or Form B). Thus, Forms a and b are taken almost simultaneously, so no question of stability arises. We need be concerned only with the extent to which Form a scores are equivalent to Form b scores, not with how stable the ability being measured is over time.

There are 126 different ways to split a 10-item test into two 5-item halves, and 63,205,303,218,876 different ways to split a 50-item test into two 25-item halves! Just one of these is the odd-numbered-items, even-numbered-items split mentioned above, so it is small wonder that long ago measurement specialists began to argue about how to split-halve tests. Some splits gave larger stepped-up r_{ab}'s than others. Which stepped-up r_{ab} was to be considered *the* coefficient of equivalence of the test?

Internal Consistency

In 1937 two measurement specialists at the University of Chicago[1] devised a procedure for estimating the *internal consistency* of a test (i.e., the extent to which all items in the test measure the same abilities) without the necessity of splitting it into halves. Their most commonly used procedure, which they called Formula 20, is roughly equivalent to securing the mean intercorrelation of the k items in the test, considering this as the reliability coefficient of the typical *item* in the test, and stepping this average r up with the general Spearman-Brown formula[2] to estimate the coefficient of equivalence of a test consisting of k items. There are 45 item intercorrelations for a 10-item test and 1,225 for a 50-item test, so it is fortunate that we do not actually have to compute all 45 or 1,225 r's, but can instead estimate the coefficient of equivalence fairly easily. It can vary from 0 to 1.

In a test which is perfect in its internal consistency, each item measures exactly the same thing as every other item, and measures it without error, so every item correlates +1 with every other item. In actual practice, item intercorrelations near 1 are rarely obtained, for three reasons:

   1. One item does not measure precisely the same "thing" as another.

   2. Errors of measurement in items are usually appreciable.

   3. When the responses to two dichotomously scored items are correlated, r will not be able to reach 1 if the items are of different difficulty.

Even if the average intercorrelation of items is rather small, however, the internal consistency of the test in the split-half or the Kuder-Richardson sense (which is essentially the average of all possible split-half r's) will be much higher than this $\bar{r}$ if the test is composed of a fairly large number of items. If the average intercorrelation of the 20 items in a test is .10, the coefficient of equivalence for the test will be approximately $20(.10)/[1 + 19(.10)] = .69$. For 50 items that intercorrelate .10 it would be .85. The more items of a given quality, the higher the coefficient of internal consistency. We may state that, other things being equal, *long tests are more reliable than short tests.*

---

[1]G. F. Kuder and M. W. Richardson, The theory of the estimation of test reliability, *Psychometrika,* 1937, 2, 151–160.

[2]If $\bar{r}$ is the average intercorrelation of the k items, then the general Spearman-Brown formula is $k\bar{r}/[1 + (k - 1)\bar{r}]$.

Speeded Tests

Split-half and Kuder-Richardson procedures are appropriate only for *power tests,* where each student has enough time to show what he knows (though he may not mark all items), and not for *speed tests,* where he does not have time to respond to some questions for which he knows the correct answer. If a test begins with items so easy that nearly everyone marks them correctly and ends with items so difficult that nearly everyone misses them, it may not be a "speed" test even if few students actually have time to try all the items. Presumably, the typical student runs out of ability long before he completes the test and thereafter guesses.

The "reliability coefficient" of a pure speed test that has an even number of items is 1, because all items are marked correctly up to the point where time is called. George marks the first 40 of 90 items correctly during the short time limit. His split-half score is 20 on one half and 20 on the other half. Jill marks 72, so her half-scores are 36 and 36. For all even-number total scores, the half scores on odd-numbered items are identical with those on even-numbered items, because by definition we are considering a test where no items are marked incorrectly. If within-individual variation is 0, then the correlation between halves will be perfect. Most ability tests probably lie nearer the power than the speed end of the continuum if the time limit is not severe. Rarely is an educational test strictly a "power" test or only a "speed" test. Educational tests usually contain elements of both. Many students fail to answer or even to read some items; but at the same time, few respond correctly to all items they attempt.

The moral is clear: *Speeded tests usually yield spuriously high coefficients of equivalence.* To assess their reliability, administer separately timed comparable halves *a* and *b* with little or no intervening time, correlate the half-scores, and step up r_{ab} with the Spearman-Brown formula $2r_{ab}/(1 + r_{ab})$. This procedure will yield a coefficient of equivalence and stability, with the stability aspect minimized. The coefficient of equivalence has no useful meaning in situations, such as the measurement of height, where the items (say, the inches) making up the score are not subject to errors. Inches on a ruler are internally consistent. A 71.9-inch-tall man today may be measured as 71.8 or 72.0 tomorrow, but if he got Inch No. 71 "right," he also got Inches No. 1, 2, . . . , 70 right. The ruler is a perfect scale. We merely need read off the last fraction of an inch of height to know that all items below it were "correct." To find the error of measurement at the top of his head we need a second, *independent* measurement of his height. Physical measurement is often more reliable than psychological measurement, particularly because the units of psychological measurement—the items themselves—are subject to substantial errors of measurement.

Let us review the types of reliability:

1. *Coefficient of stability.* This is the test-retest coefficient, r_{AA} (or r_{BB}), which may be made spuriously high by memory carry-over from one adminis-

tration of the form to the next. Obviously, Form A is essentially identical to Form A (and Form B to Form B), so no question of equivalence arises. It may be desirable to rearrange the items in the form for the second administration to minimize memory carry-over and practice effects, but this must be done carefully, particularly if the items vary considerably in difficulty. It may also be desirable to rearrange the order of options within items in order to reduce the effect of memory.

2. *Coefficient of equivalence.* This is the single-form coefficient, $2r_{ab}/(1 + r_{ab})$ for split-halves *a* and *b*, or Kuder-Richardson Formula 20.[3] It may be spuriously high for speeded tests. The two halves are answered "simultaneously," so no question of stability of scores from one time to another arises.

3. *Coefficient of equivalence and stability.* This is the comparable-forms coefficient, r_{AB} (or r_{BA}). It usually becomes smaller with increasing time interval between A and B. Forms A and B must be equivalent, comparable, or parallel in some defined sense. They need not yield the same means and standard deviations in order to correlate perfectly with each other.

A test can have zero internal consistency (that is, a 0 coefficient of equivalence) and yet a high test-retest or comparable-forms coefficient, r_{AA} or r_{AB}. This would occur when the average intercorrelation of items within a form is 0 because the items are measuring as many different "things" as there are items, but measuring them reliably in the test-retest or comparable-forms sense.

The Standard Error
of Measurement

When we administer a test to a student, we secure his *obtained score*—that is, the score he obtains on the test. If we had tested him on some other occasion instead, probably he would not have earned exactly the same obtained score. The score that he would have earned, on the average, if he had been tested at various times under exactly the same testing conditions is called his *true score.* We can never actually know his true score, of course, for testing him at one time would tend to change his score the next time he was tested, because of familiarity with the type of test and the procedures for taking it (which we lump together and call *practice effect*). Nevertheless, we can be aware of the discrepancy between his obtained score, which we know, and his true score, which we do not know. This difference, obtained score minus true score, is called *error of measurement.*

The obtained score of each student in the group tested contains an error of measurement. It will be small or even zero for some students and large (either positively or negatively) for others, small errors being more probable than large ones.

In measurement theory, *the variance of the obtained scores of a huge group of students equals the variance of the true scores of those students plus the variance*

---

[3]Kuder and Richardson, *op. cit.* For short-cut ways of estimating the K-R 20 coefficient and the closely related K-R 21, see Appendix A.

of their errors of measurement. We can compute the variance of the obtained scores (its square root is the standard deviation). Also, we can estimate the variance error of measurement. If only one form of an unspeeded test has been administered, we can split-halve the test and find for each student his score on Half *a* minus his score on Half *b*. We can obtain one such difference for each student. The variance of those differences is the variance error of measurement of scores on the whole test; its square root is the *standard error of measurement* for the whole test. An equivalent formula is $s_{meas} = s_x \sqrt{1 - r_{AB}}$.

If we have given two comparable forms A and B of the same test to a group of students, we find for each student his score on Form A minus his score on Form B. The (variance of these differences)/2 is the variance error of measurement for either Form A or Form B, where variance errors of measurement for the two forms are assumed to be equal. The square root of this variance is the standard error of measurement of either Form A or Form B.

A standard error of measurement is used to infer within what range the student's true score probably lies. Unfortunately, a single obtained score is not itself a good estimator of his true score unless he scored right at the mean of his group. If he scored above the mean, his true score is probably lower than his obtained score by the amount (obtained score − mean)(1 − reliability coefficient). If he scored below the mean, his true score is probably higher than his obtained score by that amount.

This relationship can be simplified and written as follows: Estimated true score = mean + (reliability coefficient)(obtained score − mean). Of course, such estimated true scores are helpful, but how confident can we be about them? If we assume that a student's estimated true scores would be distributed normally around his true score, there are about two chances in three that his true score lies in the range of his (estimated true score) $\pm \sqrt{\text{reliability coefficient}}$ (standard error of measurement).

This is too complex for most test manuals, however, so usually it is stated that, approximately, there are two chances in three that a student's true score lies in the range of his (obtained score) ± (standard error of measurement). Thus if the student has an obtained score of 56, and the standard error of measurement for that test in his group is 5 points, we infer that his true score probably lies somewhere from 51 to 61. There is one chance in six that it is lower than 51, and one chance in six that it is higher than 61. (If the reliability of the test for his group is .81, and its mean is 45, the more exact method mentioned first above gives $[45 + .81(56 − 45)] \pm \sqrt{.81}(5) = 53.91 \pm 4.50 = 49.41$—58.41, an interval of 2(4.5) = 9 instead of 2(5) = 10, with center at 53.91 instead of 56.)

The Standard Error
of Measurement for Differences

Differences between test scores tend to be less reliable than the obtained scores on which they are based. This unreliability makes the interpretation of profiles fraught with hazards. Approximately, there are two chances in three that the difference between a student's true scores on two tests lies in the range of his (obtained score on one test minus obtained score on the other test) $\pm \sqrt{}$ variance error of measurement of one test plus variance error of measurement of other test. If both test scores are z-scores, this reduces to $(z_1 - z_2) \pm \sqrt{2}$ − (reliability coefficient of one test) − (reliability coefficient of other test). If both tests have the same reliability coefficient, then the formula becomes $(z_1 - z_2) \pm \sqrt{2(1 - \text{reliability coefficient})}$.

For example, if Paul has a z-score of 1.32 on a French test and a z-score of -0.55 on a chemistry test, both z-scores being based on the same norm group, and if each test has a reliability coefficient of .92 for that norm group, then there are approximately two chances in three that the difference between his true z-scores on the tests lies within the interval $[1.32 - (-0.55)] \pm \sqrt{2(1 - .92)}$ $= 1.87 \pm 0.40 = 1.47$ to 2.27. The interval 1.47 to 2.27 does not include 0, so we conclude that Paul probably does have a higher true score for the French test than for the chemistry test. In simpler terms, he is better in French, as measured by this test, than he is in chemistry, as measured by that test.[4]

The Standard Error
of Measurement of the Mean

If the standard error of measurement of a certain test is 5 points for your 25 pupils who took it and averaged 44 points, what is the best *estimate* you can make of the mean of the true scores of your class? It is 44. Within what range are the odds 2:1 that the mean of the true scores lies? This range is $44 \pm \dfrac{5}{\sqrt{25}} = 43$ to 45. The mean of 25 obtained scores is only one-fifth as erratic, because of errors of measurement, as a single obtained score is. Therefore, a test that may not be reliable enough for comparing the score obtained by one pupil with the score obtained by another pupil may be adequately reliable for comparing the mean of your class with, say, the mean of a large norm group.

VALIDITY   A definition of validity that appears in many measurement textbooks goes something like this: "A test is valid if it measures what it purports to measure." According to this statement, a test entitled "Clerical Speed" is valid if it actually measures the speed with which persons perform certain clerical tasks. Measurement of

---

[4]We cannot devote more space to the important but complex measurement of change. You may want to see Chester W. Harris, ed., *Problems in measuring change.* Madison: University of Wisconsin Press, 1963. Its chapters were written by Carl E. Bereiter, R. Darrell Bock, Donald T. Campbell, Raymond B. Cattell, John Gaito, Chester W. Harris, Wayne H. Holtzman, Paul Horst, Henry F. Kaiser, Frederic M. Lord, Ledyard R. Tucker, Harold Webster, and David E. Wiley.

speed in the situation itself would seem to be the ideal test, but of course this would be difficult to do and subject to many uncontrolled variations. Therefore, we may decide to try a paper-and-pencil test to see whether or not scores from it correlate well with present speed in the natural setting (here, office), or instead we may use the test with business students to predict later success on the job. In the former instance we want to know whether or not the paper-and-pencil test substitutes adequately for the measure of job performance. In the latter instance we want to predict (estimate ahead of time) future clerical speed. The two may be somewhat different, for the predictor test administered to the student may elicit maximum performance: how fast *can* the student file materials, say, versus how fast *does* the employed file clerk customarily file materials?

The first type of relationship mentioned above might be called *substitutive validity*, indicating how well the test substitutes for a more obviously relevant measuring situation. Most tests are somewhat removed from the actual situation to which we wish to generalize. A coefficient of substitutive validity could be obtained by correlating scores on the test with scores on an ideal criterion, perhaps in many instances an extensive, well-controlled work sample.

The Harvard University educational psychologist Phillip Rulon[5] used 100 addition facts of the following form as his example in discussing a similar type of validity:

$$0 \quad 0 \quad 1 \quad\quad 9$$
$$\underline{+0} \quad \underline{+1} \quad \underline{+0} \ldots \underline{+9} \,.$$

If the teacher's goal is to have the students write the correct answers when the 100 addition problems are presented as above, then her test has perfect curricular relevance—i.e., curricular validity—because its content (a certain 100 addition facts) and operations (add vertically and write the answer) are identical with the content and operations that constitute the teacher's instructional objectives for this portion of her teaching. A test using fewer than the 100 facts or a different way of presenting them, such as $7 + 4 =$ _____, would not be obviously relevant to the teacher's goals, though it might accomplish the same ends. If the changed test correlates as well with the perfectly relevant test as one form of the perfectly relevant test correlates with an equivalent form (rearranged order of items) over the same period of time, then we may substitute the changed test for the original one without losing validity. Otherwise, the substitute test is inferior to the logically relevant one. We might use it, nevertheless, if it is good enough for our purposes, even though not a perfect substitute.

The second type of relationship, already mentioned, is *predictive validity*. A predictor, such as a student's rank in his high-school graduating class, predicts

---

[5] P. J. Rulon, On the validity of educational tests, *Harvard Educational Review,* 1946, 16, 290–296. Reprinted by Harcourt, Brace, and World, New York City, as *Test Service Notebook* No. 3.

a criterion, such as his average college grades during the freshman year. This is an antecedent-consequent relationship, with time intervening between the predictor and the criterion. We try to predict from earlier "aptitude" to later accomplishment. The coefficient of predictive validity is r_{pc}, the coefficient of correlation between *predictor* and *criterion* scores for a number of individuals. It may vary from -1 for perfect inverse relationship (for example, if the most successful high-school students were invariably the least successful college students, and vice versa) to 0 for chance relationship (no matter where the student ranked in high school, we predict that he will make his group's average grades in college), to $+1$ for perfect direct relationship. Actual r_{pc}'s for high-school ranks with college grades usually fall between about .40 and .60, indicating that a person ranking high in his high-school class is more likely to be a good student in college than is one ranking low, and a low-ranking high-school student is more likely to be a low-achieving college student than is one who did well in high school. The relationship indicated by an *r* of .40 or even .60 is far from perfect, however. Anyone who made a large number of predictions of this sort would suffer disappointments about false positives (predicted high, achieved low) but be pleasantly surprised by false negatives (predicted low, achieved high). Most deviations from prediction are not large, however. Seldom does the all-A high-school senior become the all-F college freshman, or the all-C high-school senior become the all-A college freshman.

We can usually predict a criterion better with two or more predictors than with one. Combining rank in high-school graduating class optimally with scores from good tests of verbal and quantitative scholastic aptitude should improve the prediction of college grades over that secured with the high-school ranks-in-graduating-class alone, even though typically the ranks are the best *single* predictor.

A third type of relationship is *content validity,* of which the curricular validity already mentioned is a special case. If you define a population of words as all those in a certain dictionary that are not proper names or technical terms, you may sample this population in some random way to produce, say, 100 words to constitute Form A of your content-valid vocabulary test. From responses of an individual to these 100 words, you could estimate his knowledge of all words in the defined population. To determine the reliability of your test, you would draw another 100 words in the same way and use them as a comparable Form B of the test to secure r_{AB}.

Content validity is usually difficult to ascertain, because rarely do we have a well-defined population from which to draw items randomly. The author[6] has proposed a compromise between Rulon's "curricular" validity and content

---

[6] J. C. Stanley, Teacher-made tests as approaches to the convergence of measurement and instruction, pp. 13–25 in *Proceedings of the Ninth Annual Western Regional Conference on Testing Problems,* Educational Testing Service, 1960.

validity in order to secure tests more relevent to educational objectives and also to sample item content more fully.

A fourth type is *construct validity*. If the test grew out of systematic theory, then scores from it should correlate closely with certain predesignated measures and less highly with certain others. For example, a valid test of numerical reasoning might be expected to correlate well with other numerical tests but less well with a clerical alphabetizing test. Measurement specialists are still fighting the battle of construct validity. Opinions as to the usefulness of this concept are varied. For some psychometricians it is the only scientific type of validity. For others the principal concept is predictive validity. We shall not enter the fray, but some of you will want to trace the argument from Cronbach and Meehl[7] through Bechtoldt[8] and Clark[9] to Campbell[10] and beyond.

Factorial validity is a way of studying the "factors" that a test measures in order to determine construct validity, for unless one has some theoretical framework to guide the selection of the tests that he employs in the factor analysis, the factors that he finds will be less complete and harder to interpret than is desirable. In this connection see Guilford's structure of intellect.[11]

Pseudo-Validity

Years ago Mosier[12] wrote effectively about "the concepts of face validity." His article is a good treatment of uses of the word "validity" beyond the meanings discussed above (substitutive, predictive, content, and construct). Some test manuals make statements which amount essentially to the following: "This test is valid because it was prepared carefully by competent persons," or "This test is valid because we print it on good paper with excellent instructions for its use," or "This test is valid because we are a large, wealthy company and all our tests are excellent." Obviously, these qualitative statements cannot substitute adequately for more relevant information about validity, often expressed in the form of *r*'s.

A frequent objection to a test, voiced by an individual who has scored low on it or thinks he has, is that the test lacks predictive validity for the intended

---

[7]L. J. Cronbach and P. E. Meehl, Construct validity in psychological tests, *Psychological Bulletin,* 1955, 52, 281–302.

[8]H. P. Bechtoldt, Construct validity: A critique, *American Psychologist,* 1959, 14, 619–629.

[9]Cherry Ann Clark, Developments and applications in the area of construct validity, *Review of Educational Research,* 1959, 29, 84–105.

[10]D. T. Campbell, Recommendations for APA test standards regarding construct, trait, or discriminant validity, *American Psychologist,* 1960, 15, 546–553.

[11]J. P. Guilford, B. Fruchter, and H. P. Kelley, Development and applications of test of intellectual and special aptitudes, *Review of Educational Research,* 1959, 29, 26–41. Especially pp. 29–30.

[12]C. I. Mosier, A critical examination of the concepts of face validity, *Educational and Psychological Measurement,* 1947, 7, 191–205.

purpose because its content is not similar to the content of the criterion. More loosely, he may assert that it is not "fair" to him because it is based on irrelevant material. As a hypothetical example, suppose that 100 men want to enter an aircraft mechanics training school. Each is given an aptitude test dealing with sewing machines. A number of those who are denied admittance to the course complain that they know a great deal about airplanes, but that the test did not permit them to show this knowledge. The tester replies that both types of test, sewing machine and airplane, have been tried, and that the sewing-machine questions, being equally strange to nearly all applicants, discriminate better among them and predict grades in the mechanics course better. In other words, the sewing-machine test lacks "face" validity; it does not *seem* likely to predict well, but actually it does predict better than the "obviously" valid airplane test.

The appearance of validity is so important in politically sensitive situations that many Civil Service tests must, according to the rules for constructing them, be plausible. This is one reflection of a larger problem, the rationalizing of low test scores by disappointed, threatened, defensive, angry persons. We all hate to score near the bottom of our class or other group, so our first impulse is to blame the test for the low score. By our implicit definition, if we do not earn a reasonably good score on the test, then it is either a poor test or it tests something of no importance. Only a few unusually mature persons will say, "Yes, I scored low on that test because I am not good in the important function that it measures well."

If we call the test an "intelligence" test, those tested will usually be quite disturbed if they rank low, whereas if we call it a word-meaning or vocabulary test, fewer will be perturbed. Not many individuals are willing to admit that they are unintelligent, stupid, "dumb," because the old word "intelligence" has myriad connotations never intended by Binet, Terman, or Wechsler for their measures of a limited aspect of cognitive functioning.

Validity means that a test must be suitable for our purposes. It must yield the kind of results we need. To determine whether or not it does, we must try it out. A so-called botany aptitude test may be worthless for predicting success in botany courses but valuable as an admissions test for law school. There's no necessary validity in a test's name. Therefore, instead of saying merely that "A test is valid if it *purports* to measure," say "*A test is valid if it yields scores that help us accomplish our purposes.*"

USABILITY   Among the tests that will do what we want done reliably and validly we choose those that offer the most *coverage, convenience, economy,* and *interpretability.* A test may yield more than one reliable score during a single testing period. It may be available in more than one form at more than one grade level. It may be easy to administer properly and to score, or have scored, quickly. Its cost per student tested may be lower than most other similar tests. Results may be expressible conveniently and clearly on forms provided by the publisher. Such considerations of usability are important, but only after questions about reliability and validity have been answered satisfactorily.

With the advent of high-speed electronic test-scoring devices, it is usually undesirable for teachers themselves to score the standardized tests administered in their classes. This is a waste of their energies, expensive when the value of the teacher's time (and morale) per test scored is considered. Most major test publishers now offer to score standardized tests at reasonable rates and to provide a great deal of interpretative information about scores for students, grades, and schools. Some have rental "package" deals, whereby school systems do not even have to buy and store the test booklets.

Rarely does the teacher gain enough diagnostic information about pupil or class by handscoring a standardized test to make the effort worth-while. He would usually be better advised to spend that time studying machine-scored answer sheets, perhaps with a scoring stencil (key) in hand to spot-check answers.

Whether or not the results of a test are easy to interpret and apply depends primarily on the adequacy of the manual accompanying the test. The manual should contain complete norms to facilitate interpretation. Whenever possible, all derived scores should be capable of being read directly from tables of norms without the necessity of computation.

ILLUSTRATION
FROM A TEST MANUAL

In order to make the concepts of reliability and validity more understandable, let's look at an excellent test manual to see what is said there about these characteristics. We consider the 52-page 1962 Manual for the Academic Promise Tests (APT), designed for Grades 6–9 and published by The Psychological Corporation. These tests measure abstract reasoning (AR), numerical ability (N), verbal ability (V), and language usage (LU). In the section entitled "Reliability of the APT" on pages 37–40, we are told that "The coefficients of reliability... are based on scores from alternate forms administered with an intervening time interval. Such reliability coefficients may be described as coefficients of equivalence and stability... the range of reliability coefficients for the single tests, within each of the four grades, is .81 to .90. For the subtotals, AR + N and V + LU, the reliability coefficients range from .88 to .92, with only one of the eight coefficients below .90. The APT Total has extremely high reliability, .93 or .94 for each single grade... a rule-of-thumb estimate of the standard errors of measurement would be: 4 points of raw score for each of the four tests, 6 points for either subtotal, and 8 points for the APT Total, regardless of grade."

For example, in Grade 6 (444 students tested) the reliability coefficient of the abstract-reasoning test scores—the coefficient of correlation between scores on the two comparable forms—was .87. The mean of the sixth-grade group on the form given first was 28.0, with standard deviation 11.6. The standard error of measurement for this grade would be $11.6\sqrt{1 - .87} = 4.2$, so if a student's obtained score is 28, there are two chances in three (i.e., odds of 2:1) that his true score lies within the 8.4-point range 28 ± 4.2, or 23.8–32.2, for which the percentile ranks are approximately 59–71. There is one chance in six that his true score is less than 23.8 and one chance in six that it is more than 32.2.

The authors of the APT battery explicitly reject one-form reliability procedures:

> Procedures which analyze the student's performance on a single administration of one form of a test take advantage of some kinds of irrelevant influences. For example, if odd and even scores on a test are correlated, scores on each half will be similarly affected by whether or not the student is specially alert on the day of the testing. This procedure provides no evidence concerning the stability of the student's performance from day to day. Administering the same form on two different occasions would permit variations in the student's day-to-day performance to be reflected in the reliability coefficient. However this procedure provides evidence only on the specific items which happen to be included in that one form. Whether or not the student would have scored similarly had a different but equally appropriate sample of items been included, can not be ascertained by retesting with the same form. (p. 37)

The Kuder-Richardson 20 formula may yield a good approximation to the comparable-forms reliability that would be obtained with a small time interval between administration of the two forms,[13] though often the comparable-forms coefficient is preferable for the reasons given by the authors of the Academic Promise Tests.

The authors state on page 19 that "The characteristic of a test which is of primary interest to the test user is validity; i.e., to what extent will the test predict future performance?" This is predictive validity, of course. They then say:

> For academic aptitude tests, the criteria to be predicted usually are grades awarded by teachers or scores on an appropriate achievement test, which may in turn be a final school examination or a standardized test. . . . The predictor tests

---

[13] J. C. Stanley, K-R 20 as the stepped-up mean item intercorrelation, *14th Yearbook of the National Council on Measurement in Education,* 1957, pp. 78–92.

are designed solely to appraise intellectual abilities; grades often are assigned not only for what the student has learned, but also for effort, diligence, active participation in discussion, and less relevant (to actual achievement) personal characteristics. Grades are sometimes unreliable; it is not reasonable to expect any test to predict beyond the reliability of the criterion. Despite these deficiencies, however, grades are the basic currency in which school success is evaluated, and tests should therefore be appraised in terms of their effectiveness in forecasting grades.

After this discussion of the limitations and advantage of grades as the criterion, the authors present 15 large pages of tables showing how well the tests, singly and in combinations, predict grades in various courses for Grades 6–9 in a number of communities. These are admirably detailed and complete. For example, on page 21 the predictive validity coefficients for 156 students in an English course in Community 7, Grade 9, North Central region of the U. S., community of 5,000 to 99,000 residents, are as follows: AR, .39; N, .56; V, .52; LU, .66; AR + N, .57; V + LU, .67; and APT Total, .66. For this particular subject and situation, the language-usage test alone predicts about as well (.66) as the best-predicting simple composites of the tests (.67 and .66).

On page 36 the APT authors present expectancy tables for predicting grades in English, social studies, mathematics, and science from scores on the tests of language usage, verbal ability, numerical ability, and abstract reasoning, respectively. They also provide tables of coefficients of correlation of APT scores with "intelligence tests" (p. 43) and achievement tests (pp. 44–45). In addition, they enable you to estimate the Wechsler Intelligence Scale for Children (WISC) full-scale IQ from the APT total raw score, taking into consideration chronological age.

This clear, complete manual contains much other information, such as the "probability that a difference of one inch between APT scores plotted on student report form is due to chance" (p. 18), which of course is based on the standard error of measurement of the difference between APT scores. The probability that a difference of one inch or more is due to chance ranges from .016 for (V + LU) versus (AR + N) in Grade 8 to .096 for V versus N in Grade 6. As we have seen, the APT Manual covers predictive validity extensively for the grade criterion and gives attention to construct and substitutive validity. Content validity is not considered explicitly, probably because it was not the guiding consideration in developing the items.

A diligent user of the APT Manual can learn much from it about the tests' quality and relevance for his classes.[14]

---

[14] For a critique of these tests, see J. C. Stanley, Review of the Academic Promise Tests, Review No. 766 (pp. 998–999) in O. K. Buros (Ed.), *The sixth mental measurements yearbook* (Highland Park, N. J.: Gryphon Press, 1965).

SUMMARY   What, then, are the earmarks of a good measuring instrument? In brief, it possesses three outstanding qualities: validity, reliability, and usability. In other words, *a good test helps the user attain a specific goal, consistently, and with a reasonable expenditure of time, energy, and money.* But the first consideration is always validity. Reliability is a crucial prerequisite for validity, but it only sets the stage for what is to follow.

RECOMMENDED READINGS

Buros, O. K., *Tests in print.* Highland Park, N. J.: The Gryphon Press, 1961. Technical recommendations for psychological tests and diagnostic techniques, pp. 327–366, and Technical recommendations for achievement tests, pp. 367–391.

Cronbach, L. J., Coefficient alpha and the internal structure of tests, *Psychometrika,* 1951, 12, 671–684.

Cureton, E. E., Ch. 16 (pp. 621–694), Validity, in E. F. Lindquist, ed., *Educational measurement.* Washington, D. C.: American Council on Education, 1951.

Ebel, R. L., Content standard test scores, *Educational and Psychological Measurement,* 1962, 22, 15–25.

Ebel, R. L., Must all tests be valid? *American Psychologist,* 1961, 16, 640–647.

Gardner, E. F., Chairman, Educational and psychological testing, *Review of Educational Research,* 1962, 32, whole February issue. 114 pages.

Gulliksen, H. O., *Theory of mental tests.* New York: Wiley, 1950.

Harris, C. W., Ed., *Problems in measuring change.* Madison: University of Wisconsin Press, 1963.

Loevinger, Jane, Objective tests as instruments of psychological theory, *Psychological Reports,* 1957, 3, 635-694 (Monograph Supplement No. 9).

Michael, W. B.; Jones, R. A.; Cox, Anna; Gershon, A.; Hoover, M.; Katz, K.; and Smith, D., High school record and college board scores as predictors of success in a liberal arts program during the freshman year of college, *Educational and Psychological Measurement,* 1962, 22, 399-400.

Nunnally, J. C., Jr., *Tests and measurements,* Ch. 4, The evaluation of psychological measures, and Ch. 6, The reliability of measurements. New York: McGraw-Hill, 1959.

Schutz, R. E., Factor analysis of academic achievement and community characteristics, *Educational and Psychological Measurement,* 1960, 20, 513-518.

Thorndike, R. L., Ch. 15 (pp. 560-620) Reliability, in E. F. Lindquist, ed., *Educational measurement.* Washington, D. C.: American Council on Education, 1951.

Wesman, A. G., Reliability and confidence, *Test Service Bulletin* No. 44, the Psychological Corporation, 1952. Free.

Wesman, A. G., Better than chance, *Ibid.,* No. 45, 1953. Free.

Wood, Dorothy A., *Test construction,* Ch. 3, Principles of psychological measurement. Columbus, Ohio: Merrill, 1960.

GENERAL PRINCIPLES OF TEST CONSTRUCTION

There are at least three important reasons why a teacher must become proficient in constructing informal tests. To begin with, most of the tests he will use will be of just this type.[1] Next, both essay and objective tests will, in the hands of an untrained teacher, usually produce unsatisfactory results. The volume of writing on essay examinations, briefly summarized in Chapter Two, has repeatedly demonstrated this fact. Novices will often do worse with an objective test than with an essay examination; it is possible to make objective tests of even lower reliability than essay examinations.[2] Finally, both logical considerations and statistical analyses have shown that skillfully prepared informal tests can be as reliable and valid as some standardized tests. In fact, where the teaching conditions are unusual, or where the subject matter of a partic-

---

[1] I. H. Hensley and R. A. Davis, What high-school teachers think and do about their examinations, *Educational Administration and Supervision,* 1952, 38, 219–228.

[2] J. M. Stalnaker, The essay type of examination, Ch. 13 in E. F. Lindquist, ed., *Educational measurement* (Washington, D. C.: American Council on Education, 1951).

ular course varies considerably from one locality to another, a "home-made" test will be more appropriate than a nationally published one.

In this chapter, we will consider the general principles of constructing informal tests, the following indicating the four main steps we must take: (1) planning the test; (2) preparing the test; (3) trying out the test; (4) evaluating the test.

PLANNING THE TEST   Constructing a satisfactory test is one of the hardest jobs a teacher has to perform; good ones neither just "happen," nor do they emerge in frenzied moments of creativity. On the contrary, the process is deliberate, time-consuming, and, preferably, calm. Best results will usually be obtained from the sustained efforts of several teachers working together.

If a test is to be successful, careful planning must precede its construction. We must consider the objectives we want to measure, the purpose the scores are to serve, and the conditions under which we will be testing. The following four rules should be followed:

I. Adequate provision should be made for evaluating all the important outcomes of instruction.
II. The test should reflect the approximate proportion of emphasis in the course.
III. The nature of the test must reflect its purpose.
IV. The nature of the test must reflect the conditions under which it will be administered.

I. *Adequate provision should be made for evaluating all the important outcomes of instruction.* From the start, a precise statement of the objectives of the school and of the particular course should be available. Most courses of study do contain some statement of objectives, but, to be helpful in teaching and testing, they should be stated as specifically as possible. The expected *pupil behaviors* that exemplify the sought-after objectives must be stated. Such commonly offered objectives as "good citizenship" and "an integrated personality" are *practically useless.* They must either be stated in more precise and observable form—or discarded.

Armed with a clear and specific list of teaching objectives, a teacher may consider the most appropriate procedures for evaluating progress made towards each objective. He attempts to test what he has tried to teach by using techniques best suited to determine how well each objective is attained.

Classifying Objectives. One writer[3] suggested that instructional objectives might be placed in eight major categories:

1. Functional information
2. Various aspects of thinking
3. Attitudes
4. Interests, aims, purposes, appreciations
5. Study skills and work habits
6. Social adjustment and social sensitivity
7. Creativeness
8. A functioning social philosophy.

Another classification[4] contained ten major types:

1. The development of effective methods of thinking
2. The cultivation of useful work habits and study skills
3. The inculcation of social attitudes
4. The acquisition of a wide range of significant interests
5. The development of increased appreciation of music, art, literature, and other aesthetic experiences
6. The development of social sensitivity
7. The development of better personal-social adjustment
8. The acquisition of important information
9. The development of physical health
10. The development of a consistent philosophy of life.

---

[3]L. E. Raths, Evaluating the program of a school, *Educational Research Bulletin,* 1938, 17, 57–84.

[4]E. R. Smith, R. W. Tyler, and staff, *Appraising and recording student progress* (New York: Harper, 1942).

More recently, Bloom and others[5] classify instructional objectives in what they call three major "domains"—*cognitive, affective,* and *psychomotor.* Thus far, only the cognitive domain has been extensively analysed.

In this scheme, the cognitive domain includes those objectives which deal with the recall or recognition of learned material and the development of intellectual abilities. This domain is at the core of much current test development. In it most of the work in curriculum development has taken place. For it the clearest definitions of objectives are to be found phrased as descriptions of desired student behavior, that is, in terms of knowledge, understanding, and abilities to be acquired.

Bloom states that " ...the affective domain ...includes objectives which describe changes in interest, attitudes, and values, and the development of appreciations and adequate adjustment. ...Objectives in this domain are not stated very precisely; and, in fact, teachers do not appear to be very clear about the learning experiences which are appropriate to these objectives."

Finally, the psychomotor domain deals mainly with physical, motor, or manipulative skills. Many techniques employed in shop, speech, typing, and home economics courses would fall into this classification.

Bloom defines six ascending levels in the cognitive domain: knowledge, comprehension, application, analysis, synthesis, and evaluation. He draws a rather sharp line, however, between "knowledge" and the five higher levels, which involve "intellectual abilities and skills" in addition to simple knowing. We shall discuss and illustrate each of the six levels briefly:

Knowledge involves "the recall of specifics and universals, the recall of methods and procedures, or the recall of a pattern, structure, or setting. For measurement purposes, *the recall situation involves little more than bringing to mind the appropriate material*....The knowledge objectives emphasize most the psychological processes of *remembering*....To use an analogy, if one thinks of the mind as a file, the problem in a knowledge test situation is that of finding in the problem or task the appropriate signals, cues, and clues which will most effectively bring out whatever knowledge is filed or stored." Persons may have various kinds and levels of knowledge, from "knowledge of terminology," e.g., "familiarity with a large number of words in their common range of meanings," to "knowledge of theories and structures," e.g., "knowledge of a relatively complete formulation of the theory of evolution" (pp. 201-204).

Although basic and essential, knowledge is not sufficient for *comprehension,* which "represents the lowest level of understanding....Comprehension is evidenced by the care and accuracy with which the communication is paraphrased or rendered from one language or form of communication to another." Some instructional objectives at the comprehension level are "the ability to understand non-literal statements (metaphors, symbolism, irony, exaggera-

[5]B. S. Bloom, ed., M. D. Engelhart, E. J. Furst, W. H. Hill, and D. R. Krathwohl, *Taxonomy of educational objectives (The classification of educational goals), Handbook I: Cognitive domain* (New York: Longmans, Green, 1956).

tion)," "skill in translating mathematical verbal material into symbolic statements and vice versa," "the ability to grasp the thought of the work as a whole at any desired level of generality," and "skill in predicting continuation of trends" (pp. 204-205).

Application involves the use of abstractions in particular and concrete situations. Illustrative objectives at the application level are: "the ability to relate principles of civil liberties and civil rights to current events," and "the ability to apply the laws of trigonometry to practical situations" (p. 124).

Analysis is defined as "the breakdown of a communication into its constituent elements or parts such that the relative hierarchy of ideas is made clear and/or the relations between the ideas expressed are made explicit." Typical objectives at this level are: "skill in distinguishing facts from hypotheses," "ability to detect logical fallacies in arguments," and "ability to recognize the point of view or bias of a writer in an historical account" (pp. 146-148).

Synthesis involves "the putting together of elements and parts so as to form a whole...not clearly there before." Sample instructional objectives at this level are: "skill in writing, using an excellent organization of ideas and statements," "ability to plan a unit of instruction for a particular teaching situation," and ability to formulate a theory of learning applicable to classroom teaching" (pp. 169-172).

Finally, *evaluation* includes "the making of judgments about the value, for some purpose, of ideas, works, solutions, methods, materials, etc." Examples of this, the highest level of cognitive ability in the taxonomy, are: "the ability to indicate logical fallacies in arguments," "the ability to evaluate health beliefs critically," and "skills in recognizing and weighing values involved in alternative courses of action" (pp. 189-192).

For any course the particular objectives under each classification must be expressed in terms of the specific changes that the teacher is trying to bring about in the mental and physical behavior of pupils. A detailed statement of the particular facts, principles, concepts, and skills of the course is also required, as well as of the levels of cognition the pupils will be expected to employ. In questioning the pupils to see whether *comprehension* has actually occurred, we must try to avoid both the wording of the text and earlier class discussion. Otherwise, we will test only rote memory. Also, we should provide opportunities to apply the material learned to new problems and situations. The center of gravity is the mental activity of the pupils themselves. The teacher must not confuse ends and means. Many years ago a leading psychometrician, E. F. Lindquist, stated this point well: "The real ends of instruction are the *lasting* concepts, attitudes, skills, abilities and habits of thought, and the improved judgment or sense of values acquired; the detailed materials of instruction—the specific factual content—are to a large extent only a means toward these ends."[6]

---

[6]E. F. Lindquist, The use of tests in the accreditation of military experience and in the educational placement of war veterans, *Educational Record,* 1944, 25, 366.

Look back to page 172 at the eight-category system of instructional objectives proposed by Raths. Notice that Nos. 1, 2, and 7 (functional information, various aspects of thinking, and creativeness) belong in Bloom's "cognitive" domain, whereas Nos. 3 and 4 (attitudes; interests, aims, purposes, appreciations) fit into his "affective" domain. No. 5 (study skills and work habits) seems fairly heavily psychomotor. The remaining two (social adjustment and social sensitivity; a functioning social philosophy) appear to have cognitive, affective, and psychomotor components.

Try, in these terms, to analyze the ten categories of the Smith-Tyler list. Which of their objectives lie in the cognitive domain? In the affective or in the psychomotor domain? We shall see later that testing procedures quite properly differ from one domain to another.

Of course, Bloom's six-level classification of the cognitive domain is not the only useful scheme available to us, though it is perhaps the most extensive attempt thus far. Citing Bloom's *Taxonomy,* but not following it specifically, Stecklein offers the following classification above the sheer knowledge level: application, ability to recognize assumptions, comprehension and analysis, ability to judge the validity of inferences, analogous reasoning, problem solving, ability to define problems, and ability to draw valid conclusions.[7]

Ebel's six ascending levels are different again; he attaches to them recommended "ideal" percentages for a good achievement test: content details, 0 per cent; vocabulary, less than 20 per cent; facts, less than 20 per cent; generalizations, more than 10 per cent; understanding, more than 10 per cent; and applications, more than 10 per cent.[8]

The influential Educational Policies Commission (EPC) of the National Education Association stresses "the central role of the rational powers" and devises its own categories:

> The cultivated powers of the free mind have always been basic in achieving freedom. The powers of the free mind are many. In addition to the rational powers, there are those which relate to the aesthetic, the moral, and the religious. There is a unique, central role for the rational powers of an individual, however, for upon them depends his ability to achieve his personal goals and to fulfill his obligations to society.
>
> These powers involve the processes of recalling and imagining, classifying and generalizing, comparing and evaluating, analyzing and synthesizing, and deducing and inferring. These processes enable one to apply logic and the available evidence to his ideas, attitudes, and actions, and to pursue better whatever goals he may have.[9]

---

[7] J. E. Stecklein, How to measure more than facts with multiple choice items, *Bulletin on Classroom Testing, Bureau of Institutional Research, University of Minnesota,* No. 7, 1956.

[8] R. L. Ebel, Obtaining and reporting evidence on content validity, *Educational and Psychological Measurement,* 1956, 16, 269–282.

[9] Educational Policies Commission, *The central purpose of American education* (Washington, D. C.: National Education Association, 1961), pp. 4–5.

What four "powers" does the Educational Policies Commission list? How do these relate to the three domains offered by Bloom's *Taxonomy* (cognitive, affective, and psychomotor), and how does the structuring of the EPC rational-power domain differ from that of Bloom's cognitive domain? Which of the two systems—EPC's or Bloom's—do you prefer for the subject you teach, or plan to teach?

In addition to the various schemes discussed above, there is the structure of intellect proposed by Guilford, which was outlined on page 33.

Why bother to use these classifications in constructing an achievement test? Chiefly, perhaps, to insure the measurement of objectives higher than simple knowledge. In a 1959 booklet, "ETS Builds a Test," the Educational Testing Service of Princeton, New Jersey, offers the grid method shown in Table 6-1 for constructing the National Teacher Examination in biology and general science. The rows consist of 12 subject-matter areas, the top five for general science and the other seven for biology. The nine columns define the different levels of cognitive abilities to be tested in each subject-matter area. Thus there are 108 (12 × 9) "cells" in the grid. The committee of science specialists preparing the test decides in advance how many questions of each type should be included.

Specifications ("dimensions") for the Mathematics section of the College Entrance Examination Board's Scholastic Aptitude Test illustrate this systematic approach to test construction. They consist of seven classifications, with from two to six levels or types within each:

1. Content: (a) arithmetic or algebra, (b) geometry, (c) other;
2. Context of presentation: (a) unusual, (b), familiar;
3. Process for solution: (a) novel, (b) straightforward;
4. Type of thinking: (a) computation, (b) numerical judgment, (c) relational thinking, (d) other;
5. Characteristics of data: (a) adequate, (b) excess, (c) question of sufficiency;
6. Form of presentation: (a) verbal, (b) tabular or graphic;
7. Difficulty: (six classifications from easy to hard).[10]

If just one question of each type were used, there would be $3 \times 2 \times 2 \times 4 \times 3 \times 2 \times 6 = 1728$ items on the test. Actually, the SAT quantitative test usually has less than 4 per cent of that number, so by no means can all the types be represented. The committee might decide to include two questions dealing with geometry, in an unusual context, requiring a straightforward process for solution, evoking a relational type of thinking, involving excess data, presented in graphic form, classified as "easy."

How, according to the above seven-point scheme, would you classify the following item?

---

[10] *ETS builds a test,* p. 6.

TABLE 6-1
Specifications for a Science Test

NTE

Biology and General Science

Item Distribution

SUBJECT MATTER	Understanding of basic scientific concepts and principles	Ability to distinguish basic concepts from those which are irrelevant or inappropriate	Ability to anticipate and diagnose concepts likely to prove easy or difficult for students	Ability to select and devise appropriate demonstrations for effective teaching	Ability to recognize and utilize appropriate sources of information	Ability to give a lucid explanation of scientific concepts and principles	Ability to apply scientific concepts and principles to every-day experience	Ability to evaluate student learning	Ability to stimulate and guide the individual student	TOTAL
ABILITIES										
Chemistry										
Physics										
Astronomy										
Geology										
Meteorology										
Histology										
Botany										
Zoology										
Human anatomy and physiology										
Biology and human welfare										
Ecology										
Heredity and evol.										
TOTAL										

Source: M. R. Katz, ed., *ETS builds a test* (Princeton, N.J.: Educational Testing Service, 1959).

In which one of the following ways could 168 pencils be packaged for shipping?

(A) 11 boxes with 18 pencils in each
(B) 14 boxes with 12 pencils in each
(C) 17 boxes with 14 pencils in each
(D) 24 boxes with 12 pencils in each
(E) 28 boxes with 11 pencils in each[11]

One can readily see that there are many ways to classify educational objectives and test items, each way having its advantages and disadvantages. The simpler plans tend to be too general, the more extensive plans usually too complex to be used by classroom teachers. No plan thus far proposed—not even the 207-page Bloom *Taxonomy* for the cognitive domain—fully covers all situations. Perhaps a reasonable compromise between completeness and usability results when we blend the three-domain view-point (cognitive, affective, psychomotor) with the six-level hierarchy for the cognitive domain: knowledge, comprehension, application, analysis, synthesis, and evaluation. By further adding Guilford's distinction between convergent and divergent thinking,[12] we can guard against the strong tendency to teach and test primarily at the rote-knowledge, undigested-fact level.

Planning a Test for a Teaching Unit. The author[13] has urged that a test covering a teaching unit be cooperatively prepared by two or more teachers in the following way:

1. A team of teachers planning a teaching unit lists a complete set of *specific objectives*—That is, changes in the mental, physical, and affective behavior of the students that constitute the goals of instruction. Two or more teachers independently *classify the objectives* into Bloom's three domains: cognitive, affective, and psychomotor. Still working independently, they further classify the cognitive objectives according to some scheme such as Bloom's, Stecklein's, Ebel's, or ETS's. Then they compare their classifications and try to reconcile differences.

---

[11]*A description of the College Board Scholastic Aptitude Test* (Princeton, N. J.: Educational Testing Service, 1960), Problem No. 60 on p. 47.

[12]Thinking is convergent when "the conclusion or other outcome is a unique one that is essentially determined by the information given ... [Thinking is divergent when] the generated information can be varied or must be varied, alternative outcomes being not only possible but also sometimes demanded. . . . [C]onvergent thinking ... converges upon the unique consequence. . . . [D]ivergent thinking ... goes searching, changes route, and yields multiple answers. It is in the divergent-thinking category that we find the abilities most clearly associated with creative performance—fluency of thinking, flexibility of thinking, and originality." J. P. Guilford, B. Fruchter, and H. P. Kelley, Development and application of tests of intellectual and special aptitudes, *Review of Educational Research,* 1959, 29, 26-41. Quotations are from p. 28.

[13]J. C. Stanley, Teacher-made tests as approaches to convergence of measurement and instruction, pp. 13-25 in H. W. Magnuson, chairman, *Proceedings of the Ninth Annual Western Regional Conference On Testing Problems* of Educational Testing Service, 1960.

Anyone who has tried knows how hard it is to write readily classifiable objectives. Many of these become so complex, grandiose, or just vague that they can barely be classified in one of the three major domains, far less in one of the levels within a domain. Complex, general objectives should be used as major headings under which more specific, classifiable objectives may be grouped. Compound or multiple objectives should be rewritten as two or more objectives. Vague and grandiose objectives should be either brought down to earth or discarded if they prove to be unmeasurable, or, as Edward E. Cureton aptly put it, "intrinsically invalid."[14]

Even when one has specifically defined his educational objectives in terms of student behavior, classification will not necessarily be easy. Systems such as Bloom's *Taxonomy* fall far short of perfection, and, furthermore, the mental activity of classifying is itself rather high in the levels of the cognitive domain, certainly well beyond the rote knowledge level. Close observation of what goes on in classrooms, even at the graduate level, will reveal that teaching and testing often occur to a considerable extent at the lowest level, rote knowledge, so probably we are not encouraged to use our minds enough at the higher levels. This seems least true in mathematics and the physical sciences, where application and analysis must play a large part. This may, in part, explain the great attraction these fields have for the gifted youngster.

A task even more difficult than obtaining classifiable objectives is that of listing all the objectives for a teaching unit. Even though a unit may take only a few weeks' time, it will suggest an almost infinite number of immediate, intermediate, and "ultimate" goals. A teacher, however, will usually most concern himself only with those immediate objectives that will, in his experience, lead to important intermediate and ultimate objectives, attainment of these immediate objectives supposedly showing growth towards the more distant objectives. It is quite important that the teachers try to specify rather completely the changes in behavior—cognitive, affective, and psychomotor—that should come as a result of the unit.

2. After stating and classifying objectives, the teachers—perhaps assisted by their students—*weight each objective according to its relative importance* by determining how much time and effort each one requires. Total unit time, including both class activities and homework, is set at 100 per cent, each objective receiving a percentage equivalent to its determined importance. (It may be helpful to reserve a percentage for such "lost motion" as the routine of washing laboratory equipment; making this stolen time explicit may move both teacher and students towards more efficient ways.)

3. The teachers work toward attainment of the objectives in ways deemed most likely to produce the desired changes in the students' behavior (whether

---

[14]On p. 652 of his Ch. 16, Validity, pp. 621–694 in E. F. Lindquist, ed., *Educational measurement* (Washington, D. C.: American Council on Education, 1951).

mental, physical, or both). We all recognize this as being *the* crucial step, based firmly upon the prior stating, classifying, and weighting of objectives.

4. The teachers *devise evaluative procedures suitable for determining how well each objective has been attained by each pupil.* Ideally, these procedures will evaluate progress towards every stated objective, not confining attention to the cognitive domain only. But, for simplicity and clarity, let us first consider only paper-and-pencil tests calling for cognitive responses. The items that form these tests should cover the cognitive objectives at the same levels as were originally specified for those objectives, if one is to determine how well the objectives were attained.

In the plan of the unit, one must include time for enough evaluation to yield data adequate to make necessary decisions about individual students. Reliable total scores may not be sufficient. Reliable subscores may also be needed to determine whether particular objectives have been attained adequately by each student. This is the diagnostic function of the test.

A teacher will often require complete mastery of certain objectives before permitting a student to attempt later material.[15] Thus, the immediate outcome of evaluation may be remedial assignments—e.g., to study lists of spelling words, basic vocabulary, chemical symbols, fundamental arithmetic operations —which usually fall into the *Taxonomy's* lower *knowledge* levels. However, the balancing of chemical equations, which would be classified as "application," could be treated similarly since students might be required to be proficient in balancing easier equations before being allowed to go on to more difficult ones.

Even when the teacher *does* succeed in writing test questions at what he considers to be the same cognitive level as the particular objective, there still remains the question of whether the items are actually tests of that objective and not some other. Another teacher, working independently, can help by classifying the test items both as to level and objective tested. This second teacher should also write test questions and have them classified by the first teacher. Such cross-classification serves three purposes: (a) to verify the objective of each item; (b) to determine that the items and the objectives are on the same level; and (c) to provide a wider variety of items testing the objective than one teacher would probably prepare, because each item writer tends to write certain types of items more frequently than others. Preparation of tests by teams of two or more teachers appears to be a desirable safeguard.

Let us summarize the suggested steps for constructing achievement tests:

1. List teaching goals, or objectives.
2. Classify them according to domain and level by means of a systematic scheme.
3. Determine the relative importance of each objective.

---

[15]See P. J. Rulon, On the validity of educational tests, *Harvard Educational Review,* 1946, 16, 290–296. Reprinted by World Book Company as *Test Service Notebook* No. 3.

4. Devise and set up learning experiences which will accomplish the objectives.
5. Select evaluative procedures that are appropriate to the domains and levels of the objectives.

Appendix G shows how two mathematics teachers applied this procedure in a two-week introductory algebra unit. Because of the unit's introductory nature, none of their objectives were at the two highest levels, synthesis and evaluation. Of the 10 listed, 8 objectives are in the cognitive domain. Objectives 9 and 10 are affective: to develop a realization of the importance of algebra in the modern world, and to create a friendly attitude toward mathematics. Notice that all ten could have been subdivided and made to specify more fully the behaviors desired. For such a two-week unit, however, their ten objectives would be adequate to guide teaching and testing.

The affective domain. Interests, attitudes, appreciations, and values are difficult to "measure" directly. Usually, we depend on self-reports, inferences made from overt behavior, and comments by others, all of which may be rather unsatisfactory because of varying situational influences, deception, insufficient evidence, and distorted memory. Teachers use many informal methods of evaluating the attainment of affective objectives. Good examples of these are found in the report of the Evaluation Staff of the Eight-Year Study sponsored by the Progressive Education Association. In evaluating an individual's "social sensitivity," for example, the authors recommend the following methods of obtaining evidence: anecdotal records containing descriptions of significant social behavior, writing containing expressions of social attitudes, records of free-choice activities reflecting social concerns, and free-response tests which uncover patterns of social sensitivity.[16]

An affective objective such as "appreciation of literature" may become easier to accomplish if we list ways in which it may manifest itself in pupil behavior. One group of English teachers listed these indications of literary appreciation:[17]

1. *Satisfaction in the Thing Appreciated:* Appreciation manifests itself in a feeling, on the part of the individual, in keen satisfaction in, and enthusiam for, the thing appreciated. The person who really appreciates a given piece of literature finds in it an immediate, persistent, and easily renewable enjoyment of extraordinary intensity.

---

[16]Smith and Tyler, *op. cit.*, pp. 162–168.

[17]L. Raths, Appraising certain aspects of student achievement, *Thirty-Seventh Yearbook of the National Society for the Study of Education, Part I* (1938), pp. 114–115. This reference contains some ingenious tests designed to measure appreciation of literature, attitudes toward important social issues, and important aspects of thinking. Also see W. A. Brownell, chairman, The measurement of understanding, *Forty-Fifth Yearbook of the National Society for the Study of Education, Part I* (Chicago: University of Chicago Press, 1946).

2. *Desire for More of the Thing Appreciated:* Appreciation manifests itself in an active desire . . . for more of the thing appreciated. The person who really appreciates a given piece of literature is desirous of prolonging, extending, supplementing, renewing his first favorable response toward it.

3. *Desire to Know More about the Thing Appreciated:* Appreciation manifests itself in an active desire . . . to know more about the thing appreciated. The person who really appreciates a given piece of literature is desirous of understanding as fully as possible the significant meanings which it aims to express and of knowing something about the genesis, its history, its locale, its sociological background, its author, etc.

4. *Desire to Express One's Self Creatively:* Appreciation manifests itself in an active desire . . . to go beyond the thing appreciated, to give creative expression to ideas and feelings of his own which the thing appreciated has chiefly engendered. The person who really appreciates a given piece of literature is desirous of doing for himself, either in the same or in a different medium, something of what the author has done . . .

5. *Identification of One's Self with the Thing Appreciated:* Appreciation manifests itself in the individual's active identification of himself with the thing appreciated. The person who really appreciates a given piece of literature responds to it very much *as if* he were actually participating in the life situations which it represents.

6. *Desire to Clarify One's Own Thinking with Regard to the Life Problems Raised by the Thing Appreciated:* Appreciation manifests itself in a desire . . . to clarify [one's] own thinking with regard to specific life problems raised by the thing appreciated. The person who really appreciates a given piece of literature is stimulated by it to rethink his own point of view toward certain of the life problems with which it deals and perhaps, subsequently, to modify his own practical behavior in meeting these problems.

7. *Desire to Evaluate the Thing Appreciated:* Appreciation manifests itself in a conscious effort . . . to evaluate the thing appreciated in terms of such standards of merit as [oneself] at the moment, tends to subscribe to. The person who really appreciates a given piece of literature is desirous of discovering and describing for himself the particular values which it seems to hold for him.

One of the least tangible but most valued objectives of instruction is creativity.[18] Grimes and Bordin[19] proposed that creative expression in art should result in the development of certain personality traits. These traits would be evaluated by the art teacher through observation of, and conversation with his pupils. This process is guided by a check list on which the teacher's record is entered. Grimes and Bordin suggest that this technique would be more valuable if a group of teachers cooperated in the construction of a check list of their own, rather than adopting their list wholesale.

It must be remembered that the objectives of a course represent *directions* of progress rather than *destinations* to be arrived at by individual pupils at any

---

[18]For developments on this topic see V. Lowenfeld, Current research on creativity, *Journal of the National Education Association,* 1958, 47, 538–540, and Creativity, *Carnegie Corporation of New York Quarterly,* 1961, 9(3).

[19]J. W. Grimes and E. S. Bordin, A proposed technique for certain evaluations in art, *Educational Research Bulletin,* 1939, 18, 1-5 and 29.

particular time. As far as possible, the progress of each pupil should be measured in terms of his own abilities, interests, and needs. How well this aim of the modern school is accomplished depends not only on the material resources available, but also on the educational philosophy and skill of the teaching staff.

II. *The test should reflect the approximate proportion of emphasis in the course.* Proper balance of question emphasis requires the outlining of a sort of "job analysis" or "table of specifications"[20] that will guide the test maker just as blueprints and specifications guide the building contractor. It is well to indicate not only the various objectives in mind, but also, at least roughly, the relative amount of emphasis each objective has received in the actual teaching of the course. For example, the same test might not be equally valid for two teachers of a course in general science using the same textbook. This would be the case if one teacher emphasized the memorization of isolated facts, while the other was concerned with the understanding of facts in relation to each other, and in their application to practical problems. The test should be a faithful mirror of teaching emphasis. The amount of time devoted to the different phases of the course is a fair indication of their relative importance. The content of the test should show similar proportion. The time devoted to a topic can indicate only the *number* of test items to be included and not the *type* of items (e.g., essay, multiple-choice, matching, ranking, performance). This will depend on the nature of the objective to be measured. The table of specifications should also indicate the approximate teaching emphasis from the standpoint of the cognitive, affective, and psychomotor skills that have been sought.

III. *The nature of the test must reflect its purpose.* If the purpose of the test is to provide a basis for school marks or classification, it will rank the pupils in order of their total achievement. But if its purpose is diagnostic, its value will lie in its ability to reveal specific weaknesses in individual pupil achievement. Diagnostic tests cover a limited field but in much greater detail than general achievement tests, and are designed to yield scores on the separate parts. The range of item difficulty and the individual discriminating power[21] of the items are relatively less important in diagnostic tests. This is also true of mastery tests administered at the end of a teaching unit to determine whether the minimum essentials have been achieved.

IV. *The nature of the test must reflect the conditions under which it will be administered.* In planning the test, attention must be given not only to the age and experience of the pupils being tested, but also to such factors as the time

[20]For a systematic approach to specifying the content of individual items see J. C. Flanagan, The use of comprehensive rationales in test development, *Educational and Psychological Measurement*, 1951, 11, 151–155.
    [21]If an item is more often marked correctly by pupils with high total scores on a test than by the pupils with low total scores, we say that the item discriminates between high scorers and low scorers, or simply that it has discriminating value or power. See page 200 and Appendix A.

available for testing, facilities for duplicating the test, and the cost of the materials.

PREPARING THE TEST   The second step is the actual preparation of the test. Experience has shown the following rules or suggestions to be helpful:

1. *Begin the preliminary draft of the test as soon as possible.* Many teachers find it helpful to jot down possible test questions as the teaching progresses, day by day. In this way, they make sure that no important points are omitted. If this is not done, supplementary material which is not found in the textbook (but which may be of unusual value) will probably be overlooked. This practice also permits the material to "cool off" and so to be appraised more correctly before it is included in the final draft of the test.

2. *The test may include more than one type of item.* A test with a variety of item-types is less likely to be monotonous than one using a single form. This is especially true of long tests. Also, the requirement that the question types be suited to the material covered may automatically require that a number of objective item-forms be used. These varied objective items are frequently teamed with one or more discussion questions to make up the test.

3. *Most of the items in the final test should be of approximately 50 per cent difficulty* after being "corrected for chance" by the procedure described in footnote 37 on page 200. That is, only half of the group should "know" the answer to each item. This requirement is hard to meet in the typical school situation, however, because item difficulties in the preliminary form of the test will vary considerably. There will usually be too few items to permit discarding those not close to the 50 per cent mark. A rule-of-thumb method for constructing the final (post-tryout) form is this: For motivational purposes, let Items 1 and 2 be so easy that almost nobody will miss them. Discard all other items whose correct answer was "known" by less than 10 per cent or more than 90 per cent of the tryout group. Then let Item 3 be the easiest of the remaining items, one "known" by about 90 per cent of those tested. Arrange the remaining items in an ascending order of difficulty, with the hardest ones at the end of the test.

This implies that for maximum discrimination among the students tested, the difficulty of the entire test should be such that, when allowance is made for chance, the average pupil in the group makes about 50 per cent of the possible score. Thus, a test which is of ideal difficulty for one class may be too easy or too difficult for other classes of abler or less able students.

One of the worst and most common defects of teacher-constructed tests is their lack of difficult items, this probably due to the influence of the "70 per cent is passing" tradition. In order to pass all but a few students, the teacher who grades on a 100-base, percentage-right system must build tests for which the average score is 80 per cent or more. The result is a test that is too easy for efficient measurement.

A few exceptions to this principle should be noted. Where the objective is *rate* rather than extent of knowledge, as in speed tests in simple arithmetic and routine clerical work, all items should be quite easy. Also, in both mastery and diagnostic tests, the content should be determined primarily by the *importance* of the subject matter rather than its *difficulty.* An adequate diagnostic test in fundamental arithmetic might yield many nearly perfect scores in a strong class, and scores well below 50 per cent in a weak class.

4. *It is usually desirable to include more items in the first draft of the test than will be needed in the final form.* This will permit a later culling of the items that appear weak or not needed to provide proper balance. For each section of the test, from 25 to 50 per cent more items should be prepared than are likely to be required.

5. *After some time has elapsed, the test should be subjected to a critical revision.* The items should be checked with the original outline to see that the test shows the desired emphasis on the various topics. A careful reading of the test at this time will usually reveal some objectionable items. It is also wise to have the test criticized by other teachers of the same subject. In this way some items may be found which test points of doubtful importance, and others which are either unclearly stated or about which there is disagreement as to the answers. The wording of the items should be checked critically for ambiguity. A very serious error is wording items so that one answer is correct with one interpretation but, with another interpretation, a different answer is also reasonably correct.

6. *The items should be phrased so that the content, rather than the form of the statement, will determine the answer.* A common flaw is the telltale word or phrase that provides an unwarranted clue to the answer. These so-called *specific determiners* are especially common in true-false items. It has been found that statements containing emphatic words such as "always," "never," "entirely," "absolutely," and "exclusively" are much more likely to be false than true. On the other hand, words or expressions that weaken a statement, such as "may," "sometimes," "as a rule," and "in general," are much more likely to make it true than false. These expressions should be avoided entirely. But, if this is difficult, the "offending items" should be balanced to provide a nearly equal number of false and true. Avoiding the exact wording of the text will prevent pupils with good rote memories from answering items they do not understand. Sometimes, even spelling or grammatical form can provide clues. It is very likely that one reason why many bright pupils seem to prefer objective tests is that these often contain items so worded as to require a minimum knowledge of the subject matter involved. Such defects, however, are not inherent in objective testing and may be avoided by the alert test maker. Administering the test to persons unfamiliar with the specific content of the course will often reveal items which can be answered from general intelligence or from a general knowledge of language forms and usage.

The opposite mistake is also made. Figurative language, needlessly heavy vocabulary, or involved sentence structure may so obscure the meaning of an item that it is answered incorrectly by pupils who really understand the point.

Unless a test is definitely supposed to measure reading ability or general intelligence, the form and wording of its items should neither block the pupil's way nor provide unwarranted clues. Both defeat the intended purpose of the test.

7. *An item should be so worded that its whole content functions in determining the answer, rather than only a part of it.* There is often a wide discrepancy between what actually determines the pupil's response to an item and what the teacher intended. One of the main reasons for this is often that only a part of a question's content functions; the rest is wholly inert as far as the pupil is concerned. Lindquist[22] gives some excellent examples of this difficulty, two of which should make the problem clear. In the first:

> The leader in the making of the compromise tariff of 1833 was (1) Clay, (2) Webster, (3) Jackson, (4) Taylor, (5) Harrison.

That the majority of the pupils who responded to this item correctly did so on the superficial basis of the strong verbal association between the words "compromise" and "Clay" is shown by the fact that fewer than half of them answered correctly when the item appeared in the following form:

> The leader in the tariff revision of 1833 was (1) Clay, (2) Webster, (3) Jackson, (4) Taylor, (5) Harrison.

That the matching type of test is also subject to this error is shown by the next illustration:

> DIRECTIONS: Below are two columns of items. Match the items in the two columns by placing on the line before each group of words in the "Items" column the right *letter* from the "Options" column.

Items	Options
____1. a Phoenician contribution to civilization	A. Mason-Dixon Line
____2. most famous building of the ancient Greek world	B. Spanish Armada
____3. the fleet whose defeat in 1588 gave England the control of the Atlantic Ocean	C. Saratoga
____4. a boundary between two colonies that later became famous as the division between free and slave territory	D. Dred Scott Decision
	E. Parthenon
	F. Missouri Compromise
	G. alphabet
	H. printing press
	I. Ordinance of 1787

---

[22] H. E. Hawkes, E. F. Lindquist, and C. R. Mann, *The construction and use of achievement examinations* (Boston: Houghton Mifflin, 1936), pp. 73–81.

    ____5. the victory which caused
         France to come to our aid
         during the Revolutionary War
    ____6. the law that forbade slavery
         north of the Ohio River
    ____7. a ruling by the Supreme
         Court which opened all
         territory to slavery

In most of these items, a single word gives the clue. "Boundary" in item 4 suggests "Line" in option A. Likewise, either "ruling" or "court" in item 7 suggests "Decision" in option D. If a pupil knows that "armada" means "fleet," he will be able to match item 3 with option B without knowing the date, the country, or the event involved. (It should be noted, however, that even after we correct the wording, this matching question will still be poor because the items included are so diverse in character.)

The test maker should try to anticipate how the pupils will arrive at their answers to each item. The teacher should ask himself whether a pupil can ignore *any* part of the item and still answer correctly. What is the least amount of knowledge he will need to answer correctly?

8. *All the items of a particular type should be placed together in the test.* Completion, true-false, and multiple-choice items (of varying numbers of choices) are sometimes thrown together in random order. This arrangement is undesirable. Similar item types should be placed together. Such an arrangement not only speeds up scoring and evaluation, but enables the pupil to take full advantage of the "mind-set" imposed by a particular item form.

9. *The items of any particular type in the test should be arranged in ascending order of difficulty.* It is especially important to have the easiest items at the beginning of the test and the hardest ones at the end. The psychological justification for this is the wholesome effect it has on the morale of the pupils. Also, placing very difficult items at the beginning produces needless discouragement in the pupils, particularly those of average ability and below. If the most difficult items appear at the end of the test, only the more capable pupils will probably get to them. This is certainly valid since the only function of these items is to discriminate among the high-ranking pupils.

Before an actual tryout of the test, it is impossible to do more than estimate the difficulty order of the items, unless one has the time to obtain the judgment of several persons.[23] The opinion of even one experienced teacher is likely to have some validity. In any case, it is usually possible to pick out those items that will be at the extremes of the scale and, fortunately, this is what is needed most. After the test has been administered, its items can be placed in a more exact order of difficulty for later use.

[23]I. Lorge and Lorraine Kruglov, A suggested technique for the improvement of difficulty prediction of test items, *Educational and Psychological Measurement,* 1952, 12, 554–561.

10. *A regular sequence in the pattern of correct responses should be avoided.* The order of correct responses should be random, rather than of a regular pattern.[24] If, for example, items are arranged alternately true and false, or two true and two false, the pupil is apt to discover the arrangement. In a desire to ease scoring, some suggest that the correct responses to multiple-choice items be arranged in an easily remembered "date-like" pattern such as 1342. But there is still the risk that the pupil will "catch on" to the pattern and be able to answer without even having to consider the content of the item.

11. *Provision should be made for a convenient written record of the pupil's responses.* Such a record may be a check list, or some form of rating scale which will serve as a systematic and permanent record of a pupil's behavior under specified conditions. It is particularly difficult, though not impossible, to keep a satisfactory written record of responses on oral quizzes.[25] In the written test, however, the pupil makes his own record either on a test paper or a printed answer sheet. The problem then is merely that of arranging the test so as to minimize the labor of scoring. Numbering or lettering multiple-choice responses and completion-item blanks so that the responses will be recorded in a column rather than scattered irregularly over the page will save time and reduce the possibility of scoring error. Special answer sheets and punched-out scoring stencils may be helpful. Simply grouping the items by fives, instead of spacing them uniformly, reduces eyestrain in scoring the test.

12. *The directions to the pupil should be as clear, complete, and concise as possible.* The aim should be to make the instructions so clear that the least able pupil in the group knows what he is expected to do, although he may not be able to do it. The pupil should know how and where to mark the items, how much time he has to do so, and the extent to which he should "guess." The amount of detail necessary will depend on the age of the pupils and their experience with that type of test. It is better, for example, to tell very young children to "draw a line under" rather than "underline," and to "draw a ring around the right answer" rather than "encircle the correct response." In the lower grades, the teacher should read the directions aloud while the pupils silently follow the written directions on their test papers. Wherever the form of the test is unfamiliar or complicated, the generous use of correctly marked samples and practice exercises (or even practice tests) is recommended. Sometimes, a blackboard demonstration is the only way to make sure a procedure is clear. When the pupils become familiar with the various types of items, the directions may be abridged greatly.

A single illustration should make these points clear. The following direc-

---

[24]Scarvia B. Anderson, Sequence in multiple choice item options, *Journal of Educational Psychology,* 1952, 43, 364–368.
[25]M. M. Kostick and Belle M. Nixon, How to improve oral questioning, *Peabody Journal of Education,* 1953, 30, 209–217.

tions may be considered reasonably satisfactory for a class unfamiliar with objective tests:

> DIRECTIONS TO THE PUPIL: Here are thirty statements about measurement in education. Examine each one and decide whether it is true or false. In the ( ) before each statement you think is true, put +; in the ( ) before each one you think is false, put 0. You will have ten minutes for the test. Your score will equal the number right minus the number wrong. You should mark an answer even when you have only a slight hunch, but *do not waste time guessing.* Study the following samples. They are answered correctly.
>
> SAMPLES:
> (0) A. High reliability insures high validity in a test.
> (+) B. Group tests of intelligence originated in the United States.

After the pupils have become familiar with true-false tests and the method employed in scoring them, the directions may be shortened to a form somewhat as follows:

> DIRECTIONS: In the ( ) before each item put + if it is true, and 0 if false. You will have ten minutes for the test.

One other point warrants consideration. Should pupils be encouraged to guess when they are unsure of an answer? Some test specialists would require the pupils to attempt all items on objective tests, by giving some such direction as, "If you do not know, *guess!*" Others would go to the other extreme and say, "Do *not* guess!" And some would simply tell the pupil what correction formula[26] is to be employed and let him use his judgment about guessing. Unfortunately, the experimental evidence on this point is neither extensive nor convincing. Most of the studies have merely attempted to compare the relative effect of do-guess and don't-guess instructions on the validity and reliability of the scores, without considering the intermediate approach (stating that a certain correction formula will be used for scoring).

The results have usually favored do-not-guess-*wildly* instructions by a slight margin. Davis is particularly opposed to forced guessing:[27]

> To force students to mark answers to items based on reading passages available for reference is undesirable, but to force them to mark answers to items testing specific subject matter that they do not know and cannot figure out is far worse. It is not only frustrating to the students but it goes contrary to good teaching practices and compels the students to break habits of carefulness that the schools try hard to inculcate. Once in a while it is possible that students might be told that as part of an experiment they are required to mark every item in a test even when

---

[26] One such formula is discussed on pages 195-198.

[27] F. B. Davis, Item selection techniques, in E. F. Lindquist, ed., *Educational measurement* (Washington, D. C.; American Council on Education, 1951), pp. 274-275.

they have no idea what to mark, but in systematic testing programs this would be inadvisable as well as impractical. It might eliminate variations in the number of omissions and thus wipe out some of the effects of differences in personality, but it would do this at a cost of antagonizing teachers and frustrating students. It would also introduce additional chance variance into the scores.

Cronbach[28] and others have found some evidence of "acquiescence" (marking a T-F item true if one doesn't know the correct answer) and other response sets (such as a student's tendency to mark Option A most of the time when he doesn't know the correct answer) sometimes operating in taking certain types of tests. Do-not-guess instructions may place bold students at an advantage over submissive students. Such instructions may reduce the validity of achievement tests, which then become, in some degree, measures of personality traits. Some investigators have also found that good students tend to improve their scores when they guess, whereas poor students do not.

All things considered, we offer the following seven recommendations:

1. Whenever possible, provide at least four responses (options) for each multiple-choice item. This will decrease the probability of answering correctly by sheer guessing.

2. Except in unusual circumstances, avoid true-false items. Recast them into the form of a multiple-choice item, with two or more explicit options. For example, the "Group tests of intelligence originated in the United States" true-false question above might be reworded as follows:

> In what country did group tests of intelligence originate?
> A. France
> B. Germany
> C. Great Britain
> D. The United States
> E. The Netherlands

Note, however, that we were more or less forced to use a specific determiner, long option length, for the correct response, No. D, and therefore to camouflage this option by having as other options "Great Britain" and "The Netherlands." This could have been avoided by substituting "America" for "The United States," but, strictly speaking, America is not a country. Also, the initials "U. S. A." would be too conspicuous. One way to avoid the lengthier options is as follows:

> In what country did group tests of intelligence originate?
> A. England
> B. France
> C. Russia
> D. Germany
> E. None of the above. They originated in_____.

---

[28]L. J. Cronbach, Studies of acquiescence as a factor in the true-false test, *Journal of Educational Psychology,* 1942, 33, 401–415; Further evidence on response sets and test design, *Educational and Psychological Measurement,* 1950, 10, 3–31.

Which one of the two forms do you prefer, and why? Can you devise better wording?

3. Arrange the items in increasing order of difficulty.

4. Allow enough time for practically all students to work as far into the test as their knowledge permits.

5. Encourage students to attempt every item for which they have *even the slightest hunch.* A hunch will probably work to increase a student's score over pure chance and need not be discouraged. On the other hand, students should be encouraged *not* to guess blindly. Pure chance guessing of this sort is not only pedagogically unsound, but it also decreases the reliability of total scores on the test.

6. Students should be allowed to omit items which they can answer only by blind guessing. It is very important that they do not waste time puzzling over items which are completely obscure to them. Their time should be devoted to items about which they are better informed.

7. The correction of a student's total score for "guessing," (no. of items correct) minus [(no. of items incorrect) divided by (no. of options minus 1)], is actually a correction for different number of omissions from student to student.[29] If every student omitted exactly the same number of items, there would be no need for correction, because the z-scores of the students would be the same with or without the correction. If there are few items omitted by anyone, no correction is needed from the measurement standpoint, though it may still be desirable to use one to remind the students that their "true" level of knowledge is lower than that indicated by the uncorrected scores (see page 196).

If, however, some students omit appreciably more items than others,[30] it becomes desirable to employ a correction formula. Suppose that a test contains 100 five-option items. Students Dave and Paul each know 50 items and are ignorant of the other 50 (an overly simplified situation, to be sure, but necessary for clarity here). Cautious Dave *omits* the 50 that he does not know, and receives a score of $50 + 0 = 50$. Gambler Paul *guesses* at all 50 that he does not know and, because he has a one-in-five chance of answering any given item correctly gets, on the average, $50 + (1/5 \times 50) = 60$, 10 points ahead of Dave. These 10 points may make Dave rank considerably lower in the class than Paul. If, however, both scores were "corrected for chance," Dave and Paul would receive the same score of 50 points because $60 - \dfrac{40}{5-1} = 50$, cancelling the advantage the latter gained through pure chance. (The correction procedure is detailed in the following section.)

It is, however, often difficult to justify the use of the correction formula logically even to graduate students (particularly when negative scores result, as

[29]See J. C. Stanley, "Psychological" correction for chance, *Journal of Experimental Education,* 1954, 22, 297–298.

[30]Some students prefer to gamble, while others do not. Robert C. Ziller has derived "A measure of the gambling response-set in objective tests" that is a personality variable, essentially independent of the examinee's score on the test. See *Psychometrika,* 1957, 22, 289–292.

a few usually will). Probably, no such attempt should be made at the time of the test; the procedures of Steps 1—6, above, should be sufficient. Only when corrected tests are returned is it desirable to discuss the rationale behind the use of the correction procedure.

Rarely are the directions on standardized tests adequate with respect to guessing. It is extremely difficult to make students see the fine separation between an informed hunch and a wild guess. However, if every student does not enter the test situation with the same "set" or approach towards the items, scores between individuals or groups will not be strictly comparable. This is due to the fact that the gambling student may be able to increase his total score through his willingness to take calculated risks on items about which he is unsure, whereas the overly-cautious student is penalized for omitting an unduly large number of items simply because he is not perfectly sure. In this case, the test becomes, to some extent, a measure of personality type, confounding its function as a measure of achievement.

As an illustration, let us look at the somewhat ambiguous directions in the test booklet for a certain test of verbal ability. Part I states, "...Omit those items that you could answer only by pure guess, but answer all you *think* you know, even if you are not quite certain. Do not study long over any pair." For Part II, the caution is, "...Omit those that you would have to answer by pure guess." Undoubtedly, one student's "pure guess" may be another's shrewd hunch, and the interpretations of "not quite certain" will probably differ appreciably. Usually, the examiner will be expected to interpret these directions. If he urges students to try items for which they have even the slightest hope of beating chance, he may considerably increase some scores over what they would be if he cautioned strongly against "gambling."

The Sequential Test of Educational Progress (E.T.S., 1957) does not employ a correction for guessing and can therefore be a bit more explicit in its directions. "You will make your best score by answering *every* question because your score is the number of correct answers you mark.... If a question seems to be too difficult, make the most careful guess you can, rather than waste time puzzling over it."

In effect, the problem of devising adequate test instructions is essentially a problem of equalizing the test-taking attitudes of all students. On one hand, the examiner wants them to exhibit the *full range* of their achievement by encouraging them to consider all items; but he also wants to control the pedagogically unsound practice of blind guessing and the possibility that some scores will be inflated by the element of chance much more than others will be. The element of chance can be reduced by using items with at least 4 options. Influence of the gambling versus the overly-cautious attitudes, leading to more omissions by some students than by others, can be controlled to a degree by the correction-for-chance. The *best* assurance of obtaining scores which reflect the students' optimum achievement, without being confounded seriously by personality and chance factors, however, lies in the examiner's ability to provide clear, precise, and explicit directions which will allow the student to do his best—in fair competition with his fellow students and the test norms.

TRYING OUT THE TEST After the test has been prepared according to plan, it is ready to be given a trial. Since it is impossible to know in advance just how good the test is, or to eliminate all the poor items, a tryout is essential. The following four principles should govern the tryout. With the possible exception of the second, these principles also apply to the later use of the test in its final form.

1. *Every reasonable precaution should be taken to insure excellent testing conditions.* This is important because the responses to any test are determined not only by the test itself, but by surrounding conditions as well. It is usually best to administer the test to the pupils in the familiar environment of their own classroom. Any tendency to cheat should be forestalled by careful supervision. Where cheating is likely to be a special problem, pupils may be placed so that every other seat is vacant, or the test items may be arranged in different orders for pupils seated close together. Instead of these precautions, you may wish to try a plastic device called Answer Guard, shown as Figure 6-1, which makes seeing another's answers quite difficult.[31]

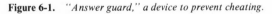

[31]Available from ANSWER GUARD, 5751 Baja Drive, San Diego 15, California.

Figure 6-1. *"Answer guard," a device to prevent cheating.*

2. *The time allowance for the test should be generous.* This is more important in the tryout than in later uses of the test. One reason for this is that the tryout items are, at best, arranged in only a rough order of difficulty, and, if not enough time is allowed, the pupils may not be able to try items at the end of the test, which they may be able to answer correctly. Short time allowances should be avoided, therefore, in order to secure the data needed to determine the difficulty of each item and its discriminating value (that is, whether more of the students who score high on the test as a whole answer the item correctly than do students who score low on the test). What may be considered a generous time allowance depends on both the purpose of the test, and the ability and experience of the pupils. For example, it is obvious that the time limits of tests designed to measure speed of work should be so short that even the best pupil will not have time to finish the test. On the other hand, more time should be allowed for diagnostic tests than for tests of general achievement; and purely factual tests can be answered even more quickly than those involving the higher mental processes.

Some arbitrary rules of thumb may be useful. For the final version of general achievement tests, the time allowance should be such that at least 90 per cent of the students have time to consider all items in a timed section of the test—that is, can attempt virtually all items within their power. For fairly short factual items, three recall or four recognition items per minute may be reasonable above the third grade. For items above the knowledge level, the time allotments should be increased appropriately on the basis of time needed by the tryout group. Younger pupils and longer or harder items may demand still more time.

These standards apply to the use of a test in its final form, rather than to the tryout, for which more time should be allowed. Since so many factors influence the time demands of a particular test, we suggest that sufficient time be allowed in the tryout so that nearly all the pupils have time to finish. If, at certain times during the progress of the test, the examiner records the number of pupils still at work, the information he gathers will be useful in setting time allowances for later revisions of the test.

3. *The scoring procedure should be fairly simple.* As a rule, the best procedure in scoring objective tests is to give the same credit for each correct response. In multiple-choice tests, this means the same credit for one properly marked item as for another, and in recall tests, the same credit for each correctly filled blank. It is usually unnecessary to weight the items according to estimated difficulty or importance, for even in essay examinations weighting is far less important than is ordinarily assumed. Almost all pupils will be in nearly the same rank order regardless of whether the individual items are weighted alike or differently.[32]

---

[32]See J. P. Guilford, *Psychometric methods,* 2nd ed. (New York: McGraw-Hill, 1954), pp. 445–447.

The correction-for-chance formula actually corrects for omissions rather than for guessing, as such. If the students omit no items, or if they all omit the same number of items, their relative scores will be the same, whether or not the formula is applied. The most commonly used formula[33] is as follows:

$$S = R - \frac{W}{o - 1}$$

In this formula
   S is the score corrected for guessing;
   R is the number of *right* responses;
   W is the number of *wrong* responses, *not* counting omitted items; and
   o is the number of *options* presented for each item.
For two-option items, including true-false, this becomes

$$S = R - \frac{W}{2 - 1} = R - W.$$

For three-option items the formula is

$$S = R - \frac{W}{3 - 1} = R - \frac{W}{2}.$$

For four-option items the formula is

$$S = R - \frac{W}{4 - 1} = R - \frac{W}{3}.$$

For five-option items it is

$$S = R - \frac{W}{5 - 1} = R - \frac{W}{4}.$$

If the items have six or more options, it is probably not worth while to correct the "rights" scores for chance.

These formulas will, on the average, reduce to zero the scores of students who, totally ignorant of the subject material presented in the test, guess with a chance degree of success that depends only on the number of options each item has. If a test contains 100 true-false items and a student guesses at each of these, he should, by chance, answer about 50 items "correctly." Thus, we expect the typical wholly uninformed person to score 50 right and 50 wrong.

---

[33] J. E. Doppelt, The correction for guessing, *Test Service Bulletin* No. 46, The Psychological Corporation, 1954. Free.

However, since he richly deserves a final score of zero, which, by our definition, represents his true knowledge of the material, 50 wrongs are subtracted from 50 rights: $R - W = 50 - 50 = 0$.

If, however, he answers 50 items correctly and *omits* the other 50, his score will be $50 - 0 = 50$. Had he tried the 50 omitted items he would, on the average, by chance have answered half of them (25) correctly and missed the other 25, making his "rights score" 50 known + 25 guessed = 75, and his "wrongs score" 25. He would therefore receive $75 - 25 = 50$, the same score he would have secured without any guessing. There is a possible fallacy in this argument, though, for a student is unlikely to know the answers to half the questions and be absolutely ignorant concerning the other half. More likely, he has various degrees of partial information and misinformation about many of the items and, in some test situations, these contributing and detracting influences seem to balance each other, thereby making the $R - \dfrac{W}{o - 1}$ formula suitable.[34]

It should be re-emphasized that the correction formula is needed *only* when some students omit a fairly large number of items, and others omit few. If this is not the case, the student ranking will be virtually unchanged, whether or not their scores are corrected for "chance." But, for psychological reasons, the teacher may return corrected scores to the students, even though few items have been omitted. This is especially advisable with two-option tests, where the poorest students may not realize the extent of their ignorance and hence may protest if given low grades on the basis of uncorrected test scores that to them seem to indicate considerable knowledge.[35] For example, 60 correct out of 100 two-option items marked may represent only 20 per cent knowledge of content, but the student may think that he knew 60 per cent.

If every student tested answers every item, the standard deviation of scores corrected for chance is $\dfrac{o}{o - 1}$ times the standard deviation of the rights scores. From this relationship, it is apparent that correcting scores from a "do-guess" test composed of two-option items will double their standard deviation: $\dfrac{o}{o - 1} = \dfrac{2}{2 - 1} = 2$. Likewise, if there are no omissions, the standard deviation of corrected-for-chance five-option-item test scores is $5/4 = 1\ 1/4$ times the standard deviation of the uncorrected scores. We therefore recommend using the correction formula with true-false and two and three-option multiple-choice test scores, even when omissions are negligible, so as to emphasize the range of knowledge within the group tested.

The Educational Testing Service uses the $R - W/4$ formula to obtain raw scores on its Preliminary Scholastic Aptitude Test (PSAT) and Scholastic Apti-

---

[34] Davis, *op. cit.*, p. 271.
[35] Stanley, *op. cit.* 1954, p. 298.

tude Test (SAT), which are composed of five-option multiple-choice items. Negative SAT scores will result occasionally, because if an examinee's "true" ability on the SAT is 0, the score he will obtain may (if he marks any items) depart by chance from 0 in either direction.

Suppose a student has absolutely no knowledge of the material on a 90-item test, each item containing five options. He chooses one option for each item entirely by chance. Curve 2 of Figure 6-2 shows the probabilities of his receiving various scores. Notice that he will, on the average, receive a score of 18 out of 90 correct by chance alone, because one-fifth of 90 is 18. Other less likely but probable scores group themselves in a rather narrow range on both sides of this most likely score of 18. We would expect a chance score of 10 (18 − 8) correct about as often (1 per cent vs. 1.2 per cent) as we would expect a chance score of 26 (18 + 8) correct—about once each in 100 trials. Ninety-eight times in 100 the student's purely chance score will fall in the range of 9.63-27.32 correct answers as shown. The most probable individual score is 18, which would be obtained by 10.5 per cent of a large group of guessers.

Also notice what happens to the range of chance scores when the correction-for-guessing formula (in this case R − 1/4W) is applied (Curve 1). The

Figure 6-2. *Frequency distributions of corrected-for-chance scores (curve 1) and of number-right scores (curve 2) caused by guessing answers to 90 five-option multiple-choice items.*

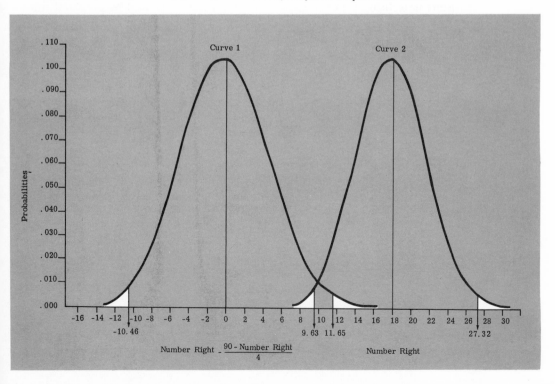

most probable no-information score becomes, appropriately, 0. Also possible, though less probable, are scores as low as −10 or as high as +10, each of these having a probability of approximately .01 (one in a hundred). Ninety-eight times in 100 the student's score will fall within the range −10.46 to +11.65 with a most probable individual score of 0. The figure shows graphically two important results of applying the correction for guessing to chance scores: 1) the average chance score is reduced to 0, and 2) the range of possible scores is increased—in this instance from 0-90 to −22½-90, or 25 per cent. The standard deviation of the "number-right" distribution is 3.80, whereas the standard deviation of the corrected-for-chance distribution is $\frac{5}{5-1}$ × 3.80, or 4.75.

Although guessing may produce variations among the scores, one should not pay serious attention to the beaming student who insists that he "guessed his way" to a high score on a long test (even on one composed of two-option items). The probability is great that he approached the items in some non-chance fashion, although he may not have been aware of it.

Compare the "guessing directions" of several tests whose scores are corrected for chance with tests whose scores are not. Do they differ? How can they be improved?

4. *Before the actual scoring begins, prepare answer keys and scoring rules.* Satisfactory scoring keys for teacher-made objective tests can be prepared simply by filling in the correct responses on an unused copy of the test. Scoring then consists of comparing the pupil's responses with those on the key placed beside his paper. Scoring rules for objective tests usually say merely that one point will be allowed for each correct response and that no fractional credits will be allowed, also indicating whether a correction formula will be used. In essay examinations, the key would be a paper containing a set of model answers, together with the maximum point value to be allowed for each. The scoring rules for essay examinations, besides giving the weight for each question, tell whether deductions are to be made for errors in spelling, grammar, and usage. In mathematics tests, the rules should cover such points as whether the answers to problems must be reduced to lowest terms, and whether credit will be allowed for solutions that are correct in principle but have the wrong answer.

If the students' answers have been recorded on a special answer sheet, such as the IBM general-purpose answer sheet, a punched-out cardboard key will speed up scoring considerably. One of the most useful of the various answer sheets is shown in Figure 6-3.[36]

---

[36]Answer sheets and the key-punch may be purchased from International Business Machines Corporation, Endicott, New York.

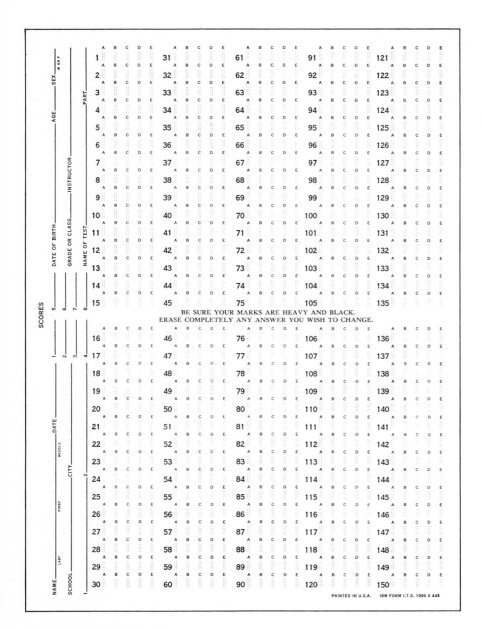

Figure 6-3. *IBM general-purpose answer sheet.*

EVALUATING THE TEST   After the papers have been scored, the results should be interpreted and evaluated in terms of both the quality of the pupils' responses and the quality of the test itself. Although a teacher must ultimately be interested in the achievement of his pupils, as shown by the test results, he should first be concerned with the quality of his test. Only good tests afford suitable information. To what extent, then, did his test possess the essential characteristics of a satisfactory measuring instrument? The five principles that follow are suggested for test evaluation.

1. *The difficulty of the test is a rough indication of its adequacy.* The over-all difficulty of the test is determined by calculating what percentage the average obtained score (corrected for chance, if appropriate) is of the maximum possible score. In general achievement tests, the nearer this average is to 50 per cent, the better. The difficulty of an individual test item is obtained by finding its percentage of successful response, usually corrected for "chance" in the same manner as the total score.[37] Items answered correctly by few or nearly all of the pupils are of little value in a test of general achievement for distinguishing the ablest students from the least able. However, item difficulty becomes a relatively unimportant consideration in mastery and diagnostic tests.

2. *Individual items in the test should discriminate between pupils who rank high and those who rank low on the test as a whole.* There are several methods of determining this, but only the simplest of these are practical for use with informal tests. A satisfactory procedure for the classroom teacher is to determine the number of correct responses (or of incorrect responses) to each test item by the pupils who rank in the highest 27 per cent of the class on the test as a whole, and to compare this with the corresponding number in the lowest 27 per cent of the class.[38] The items for which the number of correct responses of the high group *most* exceeds that of the low group are most discriminating; those in

---

[37]Proportion of students who "know" the answer to an item $=$ $\left(\text{number who marked it correctly} - \dfrac{\text{number who marked it incorrectly}}{(\text{number of options item has}) - 1}\right)$ divided by the total number of students. In symbols:

$$p = \frac{R - \dfrac{W}{o - 1}}{N}$$

This formula is appropriate only when nearly all students have had time enough to try the item. Otherwise, see Davis, *op. cit.,* pp. 278-280.

[38]The reasons for selecting contrasting groups from the 27 per cent at the extremes of the distribution are given by Truman L. Kelley in The selection of upper and lower groups for the validation of test items, *Journal of Educational Psychology,* 1939, 30, 17–24. Also see his *Fundamentals of statistics* (Cambridge: Harvard University Press, 1947), pp. 300–301; and E. E. Cureton, The upper and lower twenty-seven per cent rule, *Psychometrika,* 1957, 22, 293–296.

which the number of correct responses of the high group falls behind that of the low group, and those in which the numbers are the same, are not discriminating. Items showing negative discrimination (more correct in low group than in high) or zero discrimination (same number correct in both groups) should be rewritten or discarded.[39]

3. *It is a good practice to have the items interpreted and criticized by persons who have taken the test.* It is impossible to anticipate all the approaches pupils will employ in marking a test item, but these can be determined to some extent by questioning pupils who have taken the test.[40] Very often, wholly unsuspected irrelevancies and ambiguities will be revealed. A slight change in wording may remedy the difficulty. Sometimes, the item must be discarded. If a test contains too many unsuitable items, the scores on the test should not be counted in determining a student's class record. Inviting members of the class to assist in this critical evaluation will tend to create a favorable attitude toward the testing process used by the teacher, and is, for the students, a valuable educational experience in itself.

4. *Whenever possible, the results on the test should be checked against an outside criterion.* For short tests covering small units, this is likely to be difficult and of little value. But, even here it is sometimes helpful to compare the ranks of the pupils on the test with their class standing before the test was given. The validity of a longer and more important test can be determined better by comparing a class's scores with their standings on a good standard test covering the same material, given at about the same time.

5. *It is sometimes desirable to estimate the reliability of the test.* We recognize that it is rather easy to overemphasize "reliability" coefficients,[41] a mistake formerly made in the construction of standardized tests. Low reliability coefficients will indicate tests of doubtful merit, *but a high reliability coefficient will not necessarily establish the worth of a test.* To be of real value these coefficients must be supported by information about validity and usability.[42]

The construction of a teacher-made test, then, involves these four steps: planning, preparing, trying out, and evaluating. It is perhaps more correct to say that such activities constitute a *cycle* in the construction of a test, for it is often necessary to repeat these steps, particularly the last three, several times before a test is brought to its finished form.

---

[39] A complete item analysis of a classroom test is set forth in Appendix A.

[40] See B. S. Bloom and Lois J. Broder, *Problem-solving processes of college students* (Chicago: University of Chicago Press, 1950).

[41] Discussed in Chapter Five.

[42] In Appendix A simplified methods for securing one-form reliability coefficients are applied to a typical classroom examination.

RECOMMENDED READINGS

Anderson, Scarvia B., Katz, M. R., and Shimberg, B., *Meeting the test.* Scholastic Magazines, Inc., Englewood Cliffs, N. J., 1959. Especially "Checking your achievement," pp. 8-13.

Diederich, P. B., Short-cut statistics for teacher-made tests, *Evaluation and Advisory Service Series* No. 5, Educational Testing Service, 1960. Free.

Downey, M. T., *Carl Campbell Brigham.* Princeton, N. J.: Educational Testing Service, 1961. Professor Brigham was an outstanding pioneer in the construction and analysis of multiple-choice items.

Downie, N. M., *Fundamentals of measurement: techniques and practices,* Part II, Achievement tests. New York: Oxford University Press, 1958.

Dyer, H. S., A psychometrician views human ability, *Teachers College Record,* 1960, 61, 394–403.

Ebel, R. L., The problem of evaluation in the social studies, *Social Education,* 1960, 24, 6–10.

Ebel, R. L. and Hill, R. E., Jr., Development and applications of tests of educational achievement, *Review of Educational Research,* 1959, 29, 42-56.

Educational Testing Service, Differences in problem-solving styles affect the essential nature of a test, *ETS Developments,* Nov. 1963, 11, p. 2.

Furst, E. J., *Constructing evaluation instruments,* Part II, Constructing achievement tests. New York: Longmans, Green, 1958.

Hill, W. H. and Dressel, P. L., The objectives of instruction, Ch. 2 (pp. 27-53) in Dressel, ed., *Evaluation in higher education.* Boston: Houghton Mifflin, 1961.

Katz, M. Improving tests by means of item analysis, *The Clearing House,* 1961, 35, 265-269.

Krathwohl, D. R., Bloom, B. S., and Masia, B. B., *A taxonomy of educational objectives, Handbook II: the affective domain* (New York: David McKay, 1964).

Lindquist, E. F., Preliminary considerations in objective test construction, Chapter 5 in E. F. Lindquist, ed., *Educational measurement.* Washington, D. C.: American Council on Education, 1951.

McLaughlin, K. F., How is a test built? *Test Service Notebook* No. 25 Harcourt, Brace & World, 1961. Free.

Merwin, J. C. and Gardner, E. F., Development and application of tests of educational achievement, *Review of Educational Research,* 1962, 32, 40–50.

Messick, S., Separate set and content scores for personality and attitude scales, *Educational and Psychological Measurement,* 1961, 21, 915–923.

Nunnally, J. C., Jr., *Tests and measurements; assessment and prediction,* Ch. 8, Test construction. New York: McGraw-Hill, 1959.

Odell, C. W., *How to improve classroom testing,* Ch. 4, Test construction: general. Dubuque, Iowa: William C. Brown, 1953.

Stanley, J. C., Simplified test-analysis statistics, *Journal of Higher Education,* 1956, 27, 498–500.

Travers, R. M. W., Rational hypotheses in the construction of tests, *Educational and Psychological Measurement,* 1951, 11, 128–137.

Traxler, A. E., Jacobs, R., Selover, Margaret, and Townsend, Agatha, *Introduction to testing and the use of test results in public schools,* Ch. 2, What do tests contribute to understanding the individual pupil? New York: Harper, 1953.

Wood, Dorothy Adkins, *Test construction; development and interpretation of achievement tests.* Columbus, Ohio: Merrill, 1960.

CONSTRUCTING
SPECIFIC TYPES
OF OBJECTIVE TESTS

In the previous chapter we considered basic principles for constructing objective test items. Now we develop specific rules and procedures for writing good items of several types. In certain respects this chapter is the most important one in the book, because unless the unit of an objective test—the item itself—is prepared insightfully and skillfully, the test cannot be excellent. No amount of statistical computation will make badly written items acceptable, though of course such techniques as item analysis enable us to locate the items that demand close scrutiny.

The main types of objective test items used by classroom teachers are (1) free-response types: complete question; incomplete statement or question; and (2) limited-response types: alternative response, including two-option multiple-choice and true-false; multiple-choice, with three or more options; matching; and rearrangement.

Limited-response items provide all the options that the student must decide among. The most common is the four- or five-option multiple-choice item, used in most published tests. Here is an example from a social studies test:[1]

The House of Representatives has the authority, within limits, to determine who shall become President in case:
A. No candidate receives a majority of the popular votes.
B. No candidate receives a majority of the electoral votes.
C. No candidate receives a majority of both the popular and electoral votes.
D. The elected candidate dies before he can be inaugurated.

Only one of the four options correctly completes the stem to form a "true" statement. Which one is it? The other three options are designed to detect the uninformed, and are variously known as *foils, decoys,* or *distracters.* Such options must be plausible, more tempting to the less able students than to the able ones, and less correct in relationship to the stem than is the keyed option. There are two kinds of keyed options: correct answer and best answer. Above, *B* is the correct answer. Sometimes, a student will produce what he considers to be a more "correct" option than the item provides him. If this happens, something is wrong either with him or with the item, and one of the two should be set aright.

Formerly, multiple-choice items were simply referred to as "recognition" items, as if they were capable of testing only rote knowledge. Obviously, they can be as high-level as the effort and ingenuity of an able item writer can make them. Even a simple arithmetical reasoning item like "How many apples can I buy for 42¢ when each apple costs 7¢?" involves application. A teacher can

---

[1]H. D. Berg, Suggestions for increasing the thought content of objective test items (Mimeographed, 1958), 9 pp.

leave a blank at the end of such a question, or he can provide several options and let the student choose the correct option. In neither case is "recall" alone involved, as it might be if we asked what year England entered World War I.

FREE-RESPONSE ITEMS   The *free-response* test is one in which each item appears as a direct question, a stimulus word or phrase, a specific direction, or an incomplete statement or question. The response must be *supplied* by the pupil rather than merely *identified* from a list of suggested answers supplied by the teacher. This kind of test differs from the essay examination primarily in the length of response required; the typical response to the free-response item is short, preferably a single word or phrase. Thus it is sometimes called a short-answer objective test. Example: Who devised the 1916 Stanford-Binet Intelligence Scale? _____

Advantages and Limitations

This type of test has the obvious advantage of familiarity and "naturalness." It may almost completely eliminate guessing, because the student chooses among the (usually large) number of options he himself can think of. The free-response test is particularly valuable in mathematics and the physical sciences, where the stimulus appears in the form of a problem requiring computation. It also has wide application to test situations presented in the form of maps, charts, and diagrams in which the pupil is required to supply, in spaces provided, the names of parts keyed by numbers or letters.

One limitation of the free-response test is that in actual practice it tends to measure highly factual knowledge, consisting of isolated bits of information, because questions with unrelated short answers are used. Confinement to the isolated knowledge level is not inevitable, however, if the item writer is ingenious. Also, the scoring is somewhat laborious and not always entirely objective. For example, which of the following answers to the above completion item ("Who devised the 1916 Stanford-Binet Intelligence Scale?) is correct? Lewis M. Terman, Professor of Psychology at Stanford University in Stanford, California; Lewis M. Terman; Lewis Terman; L. M. Terman; Terman; Louis Terman; Termen; or Tarmen. Probably most teachers will consider any of the first five responses (through "Terman") fully correct, because they indicate that the student has differentiated between Terman and, say, Wechsler. Some would want to penalize the last three because of inaccurate spelling, even though the student's intent is clear. Far more difficult decisions about grading completion and other short-answer items must be made when several different answers to an item seem plausible.

These limitations need not be very serious when tests are carefully prepared.

Illustrations of Free-response

Below are a few sample free-response test items that have been taken from standard tests.[2] Excellent examples of this and other test forms used in a variety of school subjects on all educational levels are to be found in Rinsland's book.[3]

STONE REASONING TESTS IN ARITHMETIC[4]

1. James has 5 cents. He earned 13 cents more and then bought a top for 10 cents. How much money did he have left?   *Answer:* _____
2. How many oranges can I buy for 35 cents when oranges cost 7 cents each?   *Answer:* _____

SONES-HARRY HIGH SCHOOL ACHIEVEMENT TEST, PART II[5]

1. What instrument was designed to draw a circle?   _____ 1
2. Write "25% of" as "a decimal times."   _____ 2
3. Write in figures: one thousand seven and four hundredths.   _____ 3

COOPERATIVE GENERAL MATHEMATICS TESTS FOR COLLEGE STUDENTS, FORM 1934[6]

28. How many axes of symmetry does an equilateral triangle have? ... (   )
29. Eight is what per cent of 64?... (   )
30. Write an expression that exceeds M by X .... (   )
31. Solve the formula $V = \dfrac{Bh}{3}$ for h .... (   )

IOWA PLACEMENT EXAMINATIONS, CHEMISTRY-TRAINING[7]

1. The atomic weight of K is 39; of Cl, 35.5; of O, 16. What is the molecular weight of $KClO_3$?   _____
2. If 7 gm. of iron unite with 4 gm. of sulphur, how many gm. of iron sulphide will be produced?   _____

---

[2] In the examples of the various types of objective tests that follow, an effort has been made to illustrate a wide variety of mechanical arrangements of items as well as of subject matter. It is recognized that they are not all of equal merit. Some of the tests referred to are out of print but are needed as illustrations, because recent published tests are largely of the multiple-choice variety.

[3] H. D. Rinsland, *Constructing tests and grading in elementary and high school subjects* (Englewood Cliffs, N. J.: Prentice-Hall, 1938), pp. 23–222.

[4] Devised by C. W. Stone, and published by Bureau of Publications, Teachers College, Columbia University.

[5] Devised by W. W. D. Sones and D. P. Harry, Jr., and published by Harcourt, Brace & World. (Out of print.)

[6] Devised by H. T. Ludholm and L. P. Siceloff, and published by Cooperative Test Division of ETS.

[7] Devised by G. D. Stoddard and J. Cornog, and published by Extension Division, State University of Iowa.

TESTS ON EVERYDAY PROBLEMS IN SCIENCE, UNIT XII[8]

What device is used in a vacuum cleaner to pump air into the dust bag? ....(15) ——————

What is the pressure in pounds of ordinary air per square inch?........(16) ——————

AN EXERCISE FROM A BIOLOGY WORKBOOK[9]

DIRECTIONS: As you locate each part using a hand lens on an actual specimen, find the corresponding part in the accompanying illustration and label it. Consider how each part functions in the life of the grasshopper.

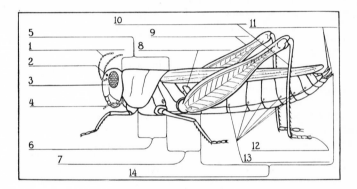

Parts of the Grasshopper.

The following items from an informal class test illustrate the possibilities of free-response tests with more than one response to each item:

Event	*Country*	*Year*	*Person*
First psychological laboratory	——————	——————	——————
First general intelligence test	——————	——————	——————
First standardized achievement test	——————	——————	——————

Rules for Constructing

Free-Response Items

The free-response is one of the most familiar test forms and one of the easiest to prepare. The main problem is how to phrase the items so that they will call forth responses of a higher intellectual level than mere rote memory, and so that they can be scored with a minimum expenditure of time and effort.

1. *The direct-question form is often preferable to the statement form.* It is more natural for the pupil and is likely to be easier to phrase.

---

[8] Devised by C. J. Pieper and W. L. Beauchamp, and published by Scott, Foresman.

[9] Prepared by A. O. Baker and L. H. Mills to accompany their *Dynamic biology today* (Chicago: Rand McNally, 1943).

EXAMPLE: The first president of the United States was_____

BETTER: Who was the first president of the United States? _____

2. *The questions should be so worded that the response required is as brief as possible, preferably a single word, number, symbol, or at most a short phrase.* This will both ease scoring and increase objectivity.

3. *The blanks provided for the responses should be in a column, preferably at the right of the questions.* This arrangement eases scoring and is more convenient for the pupil. The illustrations above show various ways of arranging the answer column.

4. *Avoid using textbook wording in phrasing items.* Unfamiliar phrasing will reduce the possibility of correct responses that represent mere meaningless verbal associations, and also will eliminate the temptation of pupils to memorize the exact wording of the book.

5. *The questions should be so worded that there is only one correct response.* This standard is difficult to reach, since pupils are ingenious in reading into questions interpretations which the teacher never intended. When challenged on a history test to "name two ancient sports," one resourceful student answered "Anthony and Cleopatra." This possibility would not have arisen if the question had taken the form, "What were two popular athletic contests in ancient Greece?" But when it becomes clear that more than one legitimate interpretation of a question *will* be possible, all acceptable replies must be listed on the scoring key. Extra care in wording the questions at first will prevent much of this sort of trouble.

COMPLETION TESTS   The *completion* item, a special free-response item form, may be defined as a sentence in which certain important words or phrases have been omitted, with blanks left for the pupil to fill in. The sentence may contain one or more blanks. The sentences in the test may be disconnected, or they may be organized into a paragraph. Each blank usually counts one point.

As far as subject matter is concerned, completion tests have wide applicability. But, unless they are prepared with extreme care, they are likely to measure rote memory rather than real understanding; or they may turn out better measures of general intelligence or linguistic aptitude than of school achievement, requiring more brightness and reading ability than knowledge of the subject matter itself.

Scoring is likely to be even more laborious than it is with simple-recall tests, especially if the missing words are written in blanks scattered all over the page, rather than in a column. While these limitations cannot be eliminated entirely, they can be greatly reduced, as is evident from the illustrations below.

Illustrations of Completion Tests

STANFORD ACHIEVEMENT TEST, PARAGRAPH MEANING, 1940 EDITION[10]

DIRECTIONS: [Abridged] Write JUST ONE WORD on each line. *Be sure to write each answer on the line that has the same number as the missing word in the paragraph.*

---

[10] Devised by T. L. Kelley, G. M. Ruch, and L. M. Terman, and published by Harcourt, Brace & World. (Superseded by the 1953 and 1964 editions.)

1–2–3   Answer

    In olden days men made their own pens from the quills of
feathers. It required considerable skill to cut a pen properly so as to 1 _____
suit one's individual taste in writing. Students were always on the
lookout for good goose, swan, turkey, or other bird feathers. Goose 2 _____
quills made the most satisfactory —1— for general —2—, but school-
masters liked pens made from the —3— of swan feathers because they
fitted best behind the ear.   3 _____

PUBLIC SCHOOL ATTAINMENT TESTS FOR HIGH SCHOOL ENTRANCE[11]

3. *Question:* Did this team have a coach?
    Answer: No, they taught __(3)__ how to play without any
    coach.   (3) _____

TESTS OF EVERYDAY PROBLEMS IN SCIENCE, UNIT XI[12]

A pry-pole is an example of a machine called the .... (11) _____
A capstan is an example of a machine called the .... (12) _____
A screw is an example of a machine called the .... (13) _____
Your teeth are examples of machines called.......................... (14) _____

GREGORY TESTS IN AMERICAN HISTORY[13]

	Write your words and dates here.
2. The man who headed the first expedition to circumnavigate the globe was......................................	2 _____
7. The Articles of Confederation were in force from 1781 to .	7 _____
9. The "Old Liberty Bell" rang out the decision of Congress to be free from England in the year	9 _____

COOPERATIVE ENGLISH TEST, SERIES 1[14]

20. Write on the lines to the right the contractions—shortened forms to represent how
    the words are naturally spoken—for the seven groups of words underlined in the
    following sentences. For instance, for *do not,* you would write *don't.* You need not
    copy the sentence, but only the seven contractions.

I have read his story, but I *cannot* believe   _____
that *he will* get a passing grade on it,
for *it is* not well written and *has not*   _____
a clear-cut plot. The characters *are*
not at all interesting; *they are* not even human.   _____

Rules for Constructing

Completion Items

    Most of the suggestions on pages 208-209 for
constructing free-response items apply equally well to completion items. The

---

[11] Prepared by H. D. Rinsland and R. L. Beck, and published by Public School Publishing
Company. (The form of completion with all responses in a column, instead of staggered within
sentences, was devised by Rinsland.)

    [12] Devised by C. J. Pieper and W. L. Beauchamp, and published by Scott, Foresman &
Company.

    [13] Devised by C. A. Gregory, and published by C. A. Gregory Company.

    [14] Devised by S. A. Leonard and others, and published by Cooperative Test Division of Edu-
cational Testing Service, Princeton, N. J.

dangers to be avoided are largely the same for both forms. A few suggestions may be offered, however, that have special reference to completion items. The three main problems in constructing completion tests are (1) how to phrase the statements so as to indicate the *type* of response desired, (2) how to avoid giving the pupil unwarranted clues to the correct, or keyed responses, and (3) how to arrange the items so as to ease scoring. The first two suggestions below apply to the first problem, the next five apply to the second problem, and the last six suggestions are for the third problem.

1. *Avoid indefinite statements.* A pupil has a right to know the *type* of response desired, and when this is done the scoring is far more rapid. First phrase a simple direct question; then write a complete statement in answer to the question, employing all the applicable wording of the question, but omitting the crucial word or words of the answer.

> EXAMPLE: When was Abraham Lincoln born? (Vague question, probably leading to the poor completion item "Abraham Lincoln was born in _____ .")
> BETTER: In what year was Abraham Lincoln born? (This leads to the completion item, "Abraham Lincoln was born in the year _____ .")

The first example leads to a completion item which fails to indicate specifically whether the desired response is the date, the place, or the circumstances of his birth. In that form, legitimate answers might be "February" or "1809," "Kentucky," or possibly "The South," and even "poverty," or "a log cabin." By a slight change in wording the statement is made quite definite.

2. *Avoid overmutilated statements.* If too many key words are left out, it is impossible to know what meaning was intended.

> EXAMPLE: The (1) is obtained by dividing the (2) by
> the (3) .   1. _____
>   2. _____
>   3. _____

In its present form, it is impossible to tell to what the statement refers.

> BETTER:
> 1. The IQ is obtained by dividing the (1) by the (2)   1. _____
>   2. _____
> 2. The (1) is obtained by dividing the (2) by the CA.   1. _____
>   2. _____

3. *Omit key words and phrases, rather than trivial details.* If this is not done the response may be as obvious as the first example below, or as unnecessarily difficult as the second example.

> EXAMPLES:
> 1. Abraham Lincoln was born February . . . , 1809.   _____
> 2. Abraham Lincoln was born in . . . County, Kentucky. _____

4. *Avoid lifting statements directly from the text.* This puts too great a premium on rote memory.

5. *Whenever the indefinite article is required before a blank, write it in the form a(n), so that the pupil must decide for himself whether the correct answer begins with a consonant sound or with a vowel sound.*

> EXAMPLE: (following a paragraph to be read by the student):
> Mary picked an . . . off the tree and ate it.   _____
>
> BETTER: Mary picked a(n) . . . off the tree and ate it.   _____

Clearly, such words as "pear," "peach," "plum," "cherry," "lemon," and "pineapple" could not be used in the first statement. In fact, the choice tends to narrow down to two familiar fruits, "apple" or "orange." The second statement contains no specific determiner.

6. *Make the blanks of uniform length.* If the blanks vary in length the pupil has a clue to the length of the correct answer. Even more of a clue is afforded by using a dot or a dash for each letter in the correct word. Perhaps it is best to use an ellipsis (. . .) for each omitted word in a completion item and put standard-length answer blanks at the right of the item, each blank being long enough for the longest correct response.

> EXAMPLE:
> 1. The second president of the United States was _ _ _ _   _ _ _ _ _ _ from the state of _ _ _ _ _ _ _ _ _ _ _ _ _.
> 2. The president in office during the Mexican War was _ _ _ _ _ _   _ _ _ _ _ from the state of _ _ _ _ _ _ _ _ _.
>
> BETTER:
> 1. The second president of the United States was   1._____
>   . . . (1) . . . from the state of . . . (2) . . .   2._____
> 2. The president in office during the Mexican War was   1._____
>   . . . (1) . . . from the state of . . . (2) . . .   2._____

7. *Avoid grammatical clues to the correct answer.*

> EXAMPLE: The authors of the first performance test of intelligence were . . . . _____
>
> BETTER: The first performance test of intelligence was prepared by . . . . _____

8. *Try to choose statements in which there is only one correct response for the blanks.* The scoring is far more objective if only one specific word or phrase can be used to complete the statement.

9. *The required response should be a single word or a brief phrase.* The more the scorer has to read the longer scoring will take, because the more words

there are in the intended answer the more different patterns the scorer will have to evaluate subjectively.

10. *Arrange the test so that the answers are in a column at the right of the sentences.* The illustrations above show how this may be done. If the sentences contain more than one blank, scoring will be faster if the blanks are numbered and the pupil is directed to write his response in the correspondingly numbered blank in the answer column at the right. The wording of the following directions should be clear to pupils above the fourth grade:

DIRECTIONS: In each of the sentences below, one or more words, numbers, or dates are needed in the numbered dotted spaces to make the sentence complete and true. Place the word or words in the same-numbered blank to the right.

11. *Avoid unordered series within an item.* They are difficult to grade. Request that they be listed in unique order, perhaps alphabetical or numerical.

EXAMPLE: The three colors of the United States flag are 1._____
..(1)., ..(2)., and .(3).   2._____
                                                                              3._____

The typical student is likely to respond 1. red, 2. white, and 3. blue, because he learned the colors in that order, but five other orders are also correct. If the item had been

"The five lightest gases are ..(1)., ..(2)., ..(3).., ..(4).., and ..(5).," students could list the five correctly in 120 ways. What a headache the teacher may get trying to score this item! Sometimes teachers try to justify their insisting on just one "correct" series, saying that they taught the things in that particular order. Does this argument have any merit? It would seem better to specify that the gases be listed alphabetically, but to give full credit for correct responses even though not in alphabetical order.

12. *Prepare a scoring key that contains all acceptable answers.* Although it is desirable to have only one "correct" response for each blank, it is not always possible. As a rule, a satisfactory scoring key can be made by writing in red all the correct answers in each blank on an extra copy of the test.

13. *Allow one point for each correctly filled blank.* Avoid fractional credits or unequal weighting of items based on difficulty or importance, because complicating scoring usually fails to improve reliability or validity.

Even at best, however, the completion item usually proves less than fully satisfactory. Disillusioned writers of completion items may wish to try casting them into multiple-choice form. Here are two examples from the practice booklet entitled "A Description of the College Board Scholastic Aptitude Test":[15]

---

[15] Published annually by the College Entrance Examination Board, c/o Educational Testing Service, Princeton, N. J., and obtainable without cost. These two examples are from p. 30 of the 1963 edition.

Each of the sentences below has one or more blank spaces, each blank indicating that a word has been omitted. Beneath the sentence are five lettered words or sets of words. You are to choose the one word or set of words which, when inserted in the sentence, *best* fits in with the meaning of the sentence as a whole.

14. Science is always _____, expecting that modifications of its present theories will sooner or later be found necessary.
   (A) final
   (B) original
   (C) tentative
   (D) practical
   (E) improving

15. Since growth is not a _____ process for all people, the importance of studying the _____ growth pattern has been emphasized.
   (A) uniform . . individual
   (B) healthy . . normal
   (C) unique . . varying
   (D) simple . . fundamental
   (E) normal . . typical

Apparently, no more than two omissions appear in any of these SAT multiple-choice completion items, nor is more than one word required for any blank. Which option did you choose as being correct for Item 14? The keyed option is (C). For Item 15 the keyed option is (A). Any conscientious clerk can score this kind of completion item, whereas scoring free-response completion items usually requires much expert judgment, since decisions concerning the correctness of various answers must be made by the scorer.

ALTERNATIVE-RESPONSE

TESTS
An *alternative-response* test is made up of items which each permit only two possible responses. The usual form is the familiar true-false test. Other similar forms are right-wrong, correct-incorrect, yes-no, same-opposite, and two-option multiple choice.

Advantages and Limitations
Obvious advantages of the alternative-response test are its apparent ease of construction, applicability to a wide range of subject-matter, objectivity of scoring, and wide sampling of knowledge tested per unit of working time. The true-false test, a form very popular with class-

room teachers, has been the object of more research and criticism than any other form of objective test. For example, the negative-suggestion effect (i.e., the presumably undesirable effect of incorrect statements on students) and the factor of guessing are often pointed out as its greatest limitations. While the use of the correction formula may provide a fairly satisfactory adjustment for guessing in the total score, the true-false form is not well adapted to educational diagnosis because the alternatives other than the statement itself are not specified. For instance, if a student answers "False" to the statement, "Columbus discovered America in 1492," what other date—if any—does he have in mind?

The danger of negative suggestion when pupils see statements which are false has apparently been overestimated, but perhaps it is wise not to use true-false tests as pretests, when untaught points might be learned incorrectly, or with young children, who may be susceptible to misinformation. In such cases it is better to avoid the true-false format by using, instead of a declarative statement, a question that can be answered *YES* or *NO*.

Several modifications of the true-false test have been proposed. One writer,[16] for example, suggested having students cross out the part of the statement that is in error, while other studies[17] have shown that having students córrect the wrong statements increases the reliability of the test. Still others[18] have proposed that items be weighted according to the judgment of the pupil, or be marked *true, false,* or *doubtful.* All of these suggestions add to the labor of scoring and have not been widely accepted. And strictly speaking, when these modifications are followed, the test is no longer of the alternative-response type. As a rule, the most obvious way to "improve" the true-false test is also the best; *make the test longer and prepare it more carefully.* At least 75 items are desirable, and unless the test covers a very narrow range, or is used for instructional purposes only, 50 may be set as an absolute minimum. One advantage of the true-false test is that it can cover more items in the same time than most other types can. The same-opposite vocabulary item ("Does *hot* mean the same as *cold,* or the opposite?") may be answered even faster.

Should pupils be advised to look over true-false tests when they have completed them and change the answers on doubtful items? Several studies have attempted to answer this question. One writer[19] made an extensive investiga-

---

[16]W. A. Barton, Jr., Improving the true-false examination, *School and Society,* 1931, 34, 544–546.

[17]E. E. Bayless and R. C. Bedell, A study of comparative validity as shown by a group of objective tests, *Journal of Educational Research,* 1931, 23, 8–16; F. D. Curtis, W. C. Darling, and N. H. Sherman, A study of the relative values of two modifications of the true-false test, *Journal of Educational Research,* 1943, 36, 517–527; W. H. E. Wright, The modified true-false item applied to testing in chemistry, *School Science and Mathematics,* 1944, 44, 637–639.

[18]Kate Hevner, A method for correcting for guessing in true-false tests and empirical evidence in support of it, *Journal of Social Psychology,* 1932, 3, 359–362.

[19]G. E. Hill, The effect of changed responses in true-false tests, *Journal of Educational Psychology,* 1937, 28, 308–310.

tion of the problem and came to the conclusion that there is "not much advantage to be gained by changing one's answers on a true-false test," although the advantage was somewhat greater in changing from true to false than in the reverse. There is some evidence that the better pupils profit most from rechecking and revising their work. And even if the scores are not always improved, it is probably a good work habit to encourage.

The low regard test experts have for the alternative-response type of test, especially the true-false form, is indicated by the absence of the form in most recent standardized achievement tests. Although this type of test has been sorely overworked by classroom teachers, it does have a legitimate, although restricted, use in informal tests. For example, the true-false test seems well adapted to testing the persistence of popular misconceptions and superstitions. In some situations, it is difficult or impossible to construct more than two plausible responses for a multiple-choice test. There are many situations of this sort in language usage. Common examples include the case forms of pronouns (e.g., *who* vs. *whom*), correct use of singular and plural verbs, confusions of past tense and past participles, the use of *sit* and *set, lay* and *lie,* and many others. A safe rule would be to *restrict the use of the alternative-response test to situations in which other test forms are inapplicable, and then give particular care to the wording of the items.*

Illustrations
of Alternative-Response Tests

CALIFORNIA ACHIEVEMENT TESTS—ADVANCED BATTERY, FORM AA[20]

DIRECTIONS: In the following sentences, mark as you have been told the number of each correct word.

Test 5—Section C

36. ([1]Isn't [2]Aren't) the baskets filled with flowers? _____36
47. I approve of ([1]his [2]him) going. _____47

For each statement given below that is a complete sentence, mark YES; for each that is not, mark NO.

51. When we approached the deserted farmhouse at night.   YES   NO   51
56. The mountains resounded with peals of thunder
which indicated the storm's fury.   YES   NO   56

IOWA SILENT READING TESTS, NEW EDITION, SENTENCE MEANING,
ELEMENTARY, FORM AM[21]

DIRECTIONS: Read each question. If the answer is "Yes," fill in the space under YES in the margin. If the answer is "No," fill in the space under NO. Study the sample. Do not guess.

---

[20]Devised by E. W. Tiegs and W. W. Clark, and published by California Test Bureau.
[21]Devised by H. A. Greene and V. H. Kelley, and published by Harcourt, Brace & World.

1. Is a dime less in value than a nickel? 1   YES   NO

2. Can we see things clearly in a thick fog? 2   YES   NO

3. Is geography studied in public schools?.................3   YES   NO

ALLPORT-VERNON-LINDZEY "STUDY OF VALUES"[22]

DIRECTIONS: A number of controversial statements or questions with two alternative answers are given below. Indicate your personal preferences by writing appropriate figures in the boxes to the right of each question . . . . For each question you have three points that you may distribute in any of the following combinations.

1. If you agree with alternative (a) and disagree with (b), write 3 in the first box and 0 in the second box. . . .
2. If you agree the (b); disagree with (a), write [0 in the first box and 3 in the second box].
3. If you have a slight preference for (a) over (b), write [2 in the first box and 1 in the second box].
4. If you have a slight preference for (b) over (a), write [1 in the first box and 2 in the second box]. . .

1. The main object of scientific research should be the discovery of truth rather than its practical applications.

(a) Yes   (b) No

10. If you were a university professor and had the necessary ability, would you prefer to teach: (a) poetry; (b) chemistry and physics?

TESTS IN ENGLISH FUNDAMENTALS: GRAMMAR[23]

DIRECTIONS: Classify the italicized words in the sentence below as adjectives or adverbs by placing check marks in the proper columns:

		Adjective	Adverb
3. That was a *silly* remark.	3		
6. Those flowers smell *sweet*.	6		
11. You can *hardly* expect him to wait.	11		

---

[22] Devised by G. W. Allport, P. E. Vernon, and G. Lindzey, and published by Houghton Mifflin Company, 1960.

[23] Devised by R. Davis, and published by Ginn and Company.

THE IOWA EVERY-PUPIL TESTS IN BASIC SKILLS[24]

DIRECTIONS: In each of the following sentences there are two or more numbered words or phrases enclosed in brackets. If you think the *first* word or phrase is correct, place an X in the *first* box of the corresponding row on the answer sheet. If you think the *second* answer is correct, place an X in the *second* box of the proper row, etc.

7. Ted is $\left\{\begin{array}{l} 1.\ a \\ 2.\ an \end{array}\right\}$ industrious man.

54. My father $\left\{\begin{array}{l} 1.\ has \\ 2.\ hasn't \end{array}\right\}$ no money.

62. I want everyone to help $\left\{\begin{array}{l} 1.\ himself \\ 2.\ themselves \end{array}\right\}$.

COOPERATIVE PLANE GEOMETRY TEST, REVISED SERIES Q[25]

DIRECTIONS: Read these statements and mark each one in the parentheses at the right with a plus sign (+) if you think it is always true, or with a zero (0) if you think it is always or sometimes false.

1. The opposite angles of a parallelogram are equal .....1 ( )

2. A diameter of a circle divides the circle into two equal parts ....2 ( )

17. If two triangles are similar, their areas are in the same ratio as the medians drawn to corresponding sides ....17 ( )

18. All similar polygons are equilateral ....18 ( )

TESTS ON EVERYDAY PROBLEMS IN SCIENCE: UNIT III[26]

DIRECTIONS: There are 25 incomplete statements in this test, each followed by parts (a), (b), (c), and (d). One or more of these parts, or perhaps none of them, correctly complete the incomplete statement. You are to place a plus sign (+) in the parentheses (near the right margin) opposite each part which correctly completes the statement, and a minus sign (−) opposite each part which does not correctly complete the statement.

13. Minerals in our food supply
    (a) furnish heat and energy to the body..( )
    (b) are the only materials of which cells can be built ....( )
    (c) are good regulators of certain of the body activities ....( )
    (d) help particularly to build bone and blood ....( )

---

[24] Devised by H. A. Greene, and published by Extension Division, State University of Iowa, 1939.

[25] Devised by Emma Spanney and L. P. Siceloff, and published by the Cooperative Test Division, Educational Testing Service, Princeton, N. J.

[26] Devised by C. J. Pieper and W. L. Beauchamp, and published by Scott, Foresman.

COOPERATIVE SOLID GEOMETRY TESTS[27]

DIRECTIONS: Read these statements and mark each one in the parentheses at the right with a plus sign (+) if you think it is true, or with a zero (0) if you think it is false, wholly or in part.

 4. Any number of planes may be passed through a given straight line.   ( )
27. Two planes parallel to the same straight line are parallel to each other. ( )
41. The square of a diagonal of a cube is three times the square of its edge. ( )

GEORGE WASHINGTON UNIVERSITY ENGLISH LITERATURE TEST[28]

T   F   1. "Il Penseroso" describes the charms of a merry social life.

T   F   2. "Pilgrim's Progress" is one of the greatest prose allegories in literature.

Rules for Constructing
Alternative-Response Items

Experienced test-makers are convinced that preparing excellent alternative-response items requires great skill. The true-false test is generally thought to be one of the easiest types to prepare. This superiority is more apparent than real, however. Unusual care must be exercised in wording true-false statements so that the *content* rather than the *form* of the statement will determine the response. The aim should be to phrase the statement so as to provide no unwarranted clues, but also in such a way as not to make its meaning needlessly obscure. With practice and care, you can attain this balance. The following suggestions may be found helpful in constructing true-false tests. Many of the suggestions for constructing multiple-choice tests (found in the next section) are also applicable here.

1. *Avoid specific determiners.* It has been found that teachers' strongly worded statements are much more likely to be false than true, while moderately worded statements are much more likely to be true than false. (As a wit once said, "Every generalization, including this one, is false.") Examples of the first are those containing "all," "always," "never," "no," "none," and "nothing"; examples of the second are those containing "may," "some," "sometimes," "often," "frequently," "generally," and "as a rule." For example, "The gas xenon never combines chemically with any other element" is a false statement, whereas "The gas xenon is generally inert" would probably be considered true, because only with certain rather active elements does it form compounds. If you are careful to balance the number of true and false statements containing any one expression, that expression ceases to be a specific determiner that affords a clue to the answer.

---

[27]Devised by H. T. Lundholm and others, and published by Cooperative Test Division, Educational Testing Service, Princeton, N. J.

[28]Devised by K. T. Omwake and others, and published by Center for Psychological Service.

"All" and "always" creep in because the teacher is aware of a relatively minor exception; but once the pupil has been tricked in this fashion, it is necessary only that he recognize "always" as meaning there is an exception in this teacher's items, and he need not know what that exception is. If an exception is significant, the true-false statement should be made about the exception itself, and not in terms of the generalization. For example, instead of the statement "All but the smallest sea creatures lay eggs," say "Whales are mammals" or "A mammal living in the sea is the _____."

2. *Avoid a disproportionate number of either true or false statements.* Several studies have shown that false statements are more valid than true statements, because pupils who do not know the correct answer tend to mark "true." For this reason, it is sometimes suggested that a test have more false statements than true. But if this were generally done, the validity of the false statements would probably be reduced, since the pupil would then tend to mark all doubtful statements false. Make *approximately* half of the statements true, the other half false, and *tell* the students this before they take the test.

3. *Avoid the exact wording of the textbook.* Lifting true statements directly from the textbook or making true statements false by changing a single word or expression puts too great a premium on rote memory.

4. *Avoid trick statements.* These are usually statements which appear to be true but which are really false because of the petty insertion of some inconspicuous word, phrase, or letter.

> EXAMPLES: 1. "The Raven" was written by Edgar Allen Poe. [Notice spelling of Allan.]
> 2. The Battle of Hastings was fought in 1066 B.C. [Notice B. C.]

> BETTER: 1. "The Raven" was written by Edgar Allan Poe. [True]
> 2. The Battle of Hastings was fought in 55 B.C. [Correct answer: 1066 A.D.]

5. *Limit each statement to the exact point to be tested.* Do not use two or more stimuli to elicit one response, as in the following partly true, partly false statement: Poe wrote "The Gold Bug" and "The Scarlet Letter."

6. *Avoid double negatives.* Such statements are especially bad, since pupils well versed in English grammar might conclude that two negatives equal an affirmative, whereas other pupils would interpret such statements as emphatic negatives. Logically, "I do not have no money" means that I do have some money. Subtler versions are such as "He was not unmindful of my poverty."

7. *Avoid ambiguous statements.* With one interpretation the statement may be true and, with another equally plausible interpretation, it may be false. It is impossible to tell what is being measured when a statement has more than one legitimate interpretation. "The Aztecs were a backward people" is true if we compare them with Europeans of the same period, but false if they are compared with U. S. Indians of that time.

8. *Avoid unfamiliar, figurative, or literary language.* The experience of the learner must be considered. A statement is badly worded if a pupil who understands the point involved misses it because of the language employed. "A gorilla is hirsute" tests knowledge of the meaning of that unfamiliar adjective much more than it tests knowledge of the hairiness of the gorilla.

9. *Avoid long statements, especially those involving complex sentence structure,* for the same reason as for the preceding suggestion.

10. *Avoid qualitative language wherever possible.* Quantitative language conveys more exactly the meaning intended. Expressions such as "few," "many," "large," "small," "old," "young," "important," and "unimportant" are vague and indefinite. Notice that "more than" and "most" are specific enough to make the truth or falsity of a statement containing them determinable (by measurement or counting), whereas "many" cannot be agreed upon in any way. "Many people voted for Jones in the recent election" can be replaced by "Jones received a majority of the votes cast in the recent election."

11. *Commands cannot be "true" or "false."* They do not state or assert anything; they simply *direct*. Teachers of young children are especially likely to produce such gems as, "Eat the seven basic foods," "Brush your teeth three times a day," and "Start each sentence with a capital letter."

12. *If a statement is to test for the truth or falsity of a reason, the main clause should be true and the reason either true or false.* Say either "As it ages, pure copper turns green [true] because it oxidizes [true]" or "As it ages, pure copper turns green [true] because it attracts green algae [false]," and *not* "As it ages, pure copper turns brown [false] because it oxidizes [true]."

13. *Require the simplest possible method of indicating the response.* Instead of requiring the pupil to write *True* and *False* or *Yes* and *No,* let him write *T* and *F, Y* and *N,* or underline the correct response. The symbols "+" for true and "0" for false are so distinct as to make scoring still easier. When the pupil must choose between two words or expressions, the responses should be numbered so that they can be indicated simply by writing the correct number.

14. *Indicate by a short line or by ( ) where the response is to be recorded.* The responses may be arranged in a column at either the left or right of the statements. Most scorers prefer the answers to the right.

15. *Arrange the statements in groups.* There is less eyestrain in scoring if the items are arranged in groups of five, with double spacing between each group.

MULTIPLE-CHOICE
TESTS

Definition: A multiple-choice test is made up of items each of which presents two or more responses, only one of which is *correct* or *definitely better* than the others. (It is also possible, especially in English-usage and spelling tests, to have several correct options and only one incorrect or least desirable option, which is to be chosen in each item.) Each item may be in the form of a direct question, an incomplete statement, or a word or phrase. This form of test is to be distinguished from the multiple-response type, which requires that two or more responses be made to a single item.   Here is a simple multiple-choice item:

The first president of the United States was
A Lincoln
B Kennedy
C Grant
D Washington
E Jefferson

In multiple-response form, a similar question would be:

Which one(s) of the following men served as president of the United States?
A Davis
B Grant
C Hamilton
D Polk
E Jefferson

For the first item, the keyed response is, of course, D, Washington. For the second item the keyed answer is B D E, because Grant, Polk, and Jefferson were presidents of the United States.

The typical true-false item should not be considered a two-option multiple-choice item because the alternatives to the statement are not specified. For example, whereas "Columbus discovered America in the year 1492" has as its implied alternative all dates other than 1492, "Columbus discovered America in the year (A) 1492 (B) 1776" offers the specific distracter "1776" only. Choosing between two stated alternatives can probably be done more objectively than can differentiating a stated alternative from an unspecified multitude of possible ones.

Possibilities and Limitations
The multiple-choice type of item is usually regarded as the most valuable and most generally applicable of all test forms. The prominent measurement specialist Lindquist asserted that it is "definitely superior to all other types" for measuring such educational objectives as "inferential reasoning, reasoned understanding, or sound judgment and discrimination on the part of the pupil."[29] Another leading psychometrician[30] regards

---

[29] H. E. Hawkes, E. F. Lindquist, and C. R. Mann, *The construction and use of achievement examinations* (Boston: Houghton Mifflin, 1936), p. 138.

[30] L. J. Cronbach, Further evidence on response sets and test design, *Educational and Psychological Measurement,* 1950, 10, 3–31.

it as being practically free from "response sets," the tendency for students to select a given option position, such as the second option, **B**, more often than would be predicted on the basis of chance alone. (Position preferences of this kind would tend to lower the validity of the test.)

One study[31] suggests 14 question types which may be used in multiple-choice test items. The list is not all-inclusive and is not supposed to prescribe exact wording, but it should serve as a guide in formulating the questions.

1. Definition
   a. What means the same as . . . ?
   b. What conclusion can be drawn from . . . ?
   c. Which of the following statements expresses this concept in different form?
2. Purpose
   a. What purpose is served by . . . ?
   b. What principle is exemplified by . . . ?
   c. Why is this done?
   d. What is the most important reason for . . . ?
3. Cause
   a. What is the cause of . . . ?
   b. Under which of the following conditions is this true?
4. Effect
   a. What is the effect of . . . ?
   b. If this is done, what will happen?
   c. Which of the following should be done (to achieve a given purpose)?
5. Association
   What tends to occur in connection (temporal [same time], causal [one causes the other], or concomitant association [varying together]) with . . . ?
6. Recognition of Error
   Which of the following constitutes an error (with respect to a given situation)?
7. Identification of Error
   a. What kind of error is this?
   b. What is the name of this error?
   c. What recognized principle is violated?
8. Evaluation
   What is the best evaluation of . . . (for a given purpose) and for what reason?
9. Difference
   What is the important difference between . . . ?
10. Similarity
    What is the important similarity between . . . ?
11. Arrangement
    In the proper order (to achieve a given purpose or to follow a given rule), which of the following comes first (or last, or follows a given item)?
12. Incomplete Arrangement
    In the proper order, which of the following should be inserted here to complete the series?

---

[31]C. I. Mosier, Claire Myers, and Helen G. Price, Suggestions for the construction of multiple-choice test items, *Educational and Psychological Measurement*, 1945, 5, 261–271.

13. Common Principle
   All of the following items except one are related by a common principle:
   a. What is the principle?
   b. Which item does not belong?
   c. Which of the following items should be substituted?
14. Controversial Subjects
   Although not everyone agrees on the desirability of _____, those
   who support its desirability do so primarily for the reason that _____.

In constructing multiple-choice items, you must be especially careful to
avoid the inclusion of irrelevant or superficial clues, and to insure that the tests
measure something more than the memory of factual knowledge. The value of
multiple-choice tests in diagnosis depends on the skillful selection of the incorrect choices presented in the items.[32]

Illustrations

of Multiple-Choice Tests

The items below, taken from standard tests,
illustrate several different arrangements of multiple-choice tests in a variety
of subjects.[33] This type of test is widely used in all school subjects and on all
educational levels for measuring a variety of teaching objectives.

KUHLMANN-FINCH INTELLIGENCE TESTS, TEST IV[34]

13. **Early** is to **begin** as **late** is to

1	2	3	4	5	
start	end	awake	enter	prompt	13_ _ _ _ _ _ _

22. **Flour** is to **bread** as **sugar** is to

1	2	3	4	5	
sweet	candy	fruit	cook	eat	22_ _ _ _ _ _ _

THE MODERN SCHOOL ACHIEVEMENT TESTS, LANGUAGE USAGE[35]

DIRECTIONS: In each sentence, choose the word or group of words that makes the best
sentence. Then on the dotted line at the right, copy the number that is before the
correct form.

	1. **off**		
4. I borrowed a pen	2. **off of**	my brother.	_ _ _ _ _ _ _ _
	3. **from**		

---

[32] E. Weitzman and W. J. McNamara, Apt use of the inept choice in multiple-choice testing,
Journal of Educational Research, 1946, 39, 517–522.

[33] These tests are not all equally good, however. The reader will note that some of them are
not wholly consistent with the principles set forth in this chapter.

[34] Devised by F. H. Finch, F. Kuhlmann, and G. L. Betts, and published by American
Guidance Service, Inc.

[35] Devised by A. I. Gates and others, and published by Bureau of Publications, Teachers
College, Columbia University.

```
                         1. your
 7. Every student must do 2. his    best.                    _ _ _ _ _ _ _ _
                         3. their
            1. has got
17. He 2. has         his violin with him.                   _ _ _ _ _ _ _ _
            3. has gotten
```

THE BARRETT-RYAN LITERATURE TEST: SILAS MARNER[36]

A. ( ) An episode that advances the plot is the--1. murdering of a man. 2. kidnapping of a child. 3. stealing of money. 4. fighting of a duel.

B. ( ) Dolly Winthrop is--1. an ambitious society woman. 2. a frivolous girl. 3. a haughty lady. 4. a kind, helpful neighbor.

C. ( ) A chief characteristic of the novel is--1. humorous passages. 2. portrayal of character. 3. historical facts. 4. fairy element.

WESLEY TEST IN POLITICAL TERMS[37]

1. An embargo is
   1. a law or regulation 2. a kind of boat 3. an explorer 4. a foolish adventure
   5. an embankment   ( )

2. An injunction is a
   1. part of speech 2. wreck 3. union of two things 4. court order 5. form of advice   ( )

UNIT SCALES OF ATTAINMENT IN FOODS AND HOUSEHOLD MANAGEMENT[38]

2. The spoon should be placed
   1. at the top of the plate
   2. at the left of the fork
   3. in the spoon holder on the table
   4. at the right of the knife ....( )

40. We get the most calories per pound from
   1. proteins 2. carbohydrates
   3. fats 4. mineral matter
   5. vitamins...( )

TRAXLER SILENT READING TEST, WORD MEANING[39]

8. The *commendation* is deserved.
   (1) success (2) blow (3) popularity (4) good fortune
   (5) praise   ( )

---

[36] Devised by E. R. Barrett, T. M. Ryan, and H. E. Schrammel, and published by Kansas State Teachers College, Emporia.

[37] Devised by E. B. Wesley, and published by Charles Scribner's Sons.

[38] Devised by Ethel B. Reeve and Clara M. Brown, and published by Educational Test Bureau.

[39] Devised by A. E. Traxler, and published by Public School Publishing Company.

9. His actions received *condemnation.*
  (1) approval (2) applause (3) censure (4) sympathy
  (5) contempt   ( )

COLLEGE ENTRANCE EXAMINATION BOARD FOREIGN-LANGUAGE ITEMS[40]

1. C'est la fin de l'entracte, et la pièce est très amusante.
  Vous dites à votre camarade:
  (A) La pièce va commencer tout de suite.
  (B) Qu'allons-nous faire maintenant?
  (C) Allons reprendre nos places.
  (D) Voulez-vous aller fumer une cigarette?

4. I am glad to see you.
  Es freut mich, . . . zu sehen.
  (A) Ihnen
  (B) Sie
  (C) ihn
  (D) sie

COLLEGE ENTRANCE EXAMINATION BOARD ENGLISH ITEMS[41]

DIRECTIONS: The following sentences contain problems in grammar, usage, word choice, and idiom.
  Some sentences are correct.
  No sentence contains more than one error.
  You will find that the error, if any, will be underlined and lettered, and that all other elements of the sentence are correct and cannot be changed.
  If there is an error, select the *one underlined part* that must be changed in order to make the sentence correct, and blacken the corresponding space on your answer sheet.
  If there is no error, mark answer space E.

EXAMPLE: He spoke bluntly and angrily to we spectators. No error
A   B   C   D   E
SAMPLE ANSWER: A B ■C D E

1. Had we known of your desire to go with us, we most certainly would of
    A   B   C
  invited you to join our party. No error
        D   E

----

[40] From *A description of the College Board achievement tests* (Princeton, N. J.: College Entrance Examination Board, 1963). The two items are from pp. 33 and 38. The student marks a separate answer sheet readily scored by counting right and wrong responses through perforated scoring stencils. For mass testing of the CEEB, scoring is done very quickly by electronic devices.
[41] *Ibid,* pp. 17 and 22-23.

2. Neither Harriet nor Claire was completely convinced by Joan's insisting
   <u> </u>   <u> </u>

       A   B   C

   that it was <u>them</u> who were to blame. <u>No error</u>

            D   E

3. Big Konrad's new helper, though somewhat <u>slighter</u> of build than <u>him,</u>

                                     A   B

   set out <u>to prove that</u> skill <u>may</u> compensate for lack of brute strength.

              C   D

   <u>No error</u>

     E

DIRECTIONS: Each group of sentences in this section is actually a paragraph presented in scrambled order. Each sentence in the group has a place in that paragraph; no sentence is to be left out. You are to read each group of sentences and decide the best order in which to put the sentences so as to form a well-organized paragraph.

Before trying to answer the questions which follow each group of sentences, jot down the correct order of the sentences in the margin of the test book. Then answer each of the questions by blackening the appropriate space on the answer sheet. Remember that you will receive credit only for answers marked on the answer sheet.

The first group of sentences on page 23 is a sample, and the questions following it are answered on the sample answer sheet.

SAMPLE PARAGRAPH

P . The Empire State Express, loaded with passengers, left New York.

Q. Unlike the businessmen, however, a few reporters on board had been told that this run would be newsworthy and were eagerly waiting for something unusual to occur.

R. At last the big day, May 10, arrived.

S . If some of the important businessmen on board had known what was going to happen, they might have found an excuse to leave the train at Albany.

T . Her secret had been carefully kept.

U. Only a few officials knew that a record was to be tried for.

CORRECT
ORDER
OF
SENTENCES

R
P
T
U
S
Q

SAMPLE QUESTIONS   SAMPLE ANSWER SHEET

i. Which sentence did
   you put first?
   (A) Sentence P
   (B) Sentence R   A   B   C   D   E
   (C) Sentence S   i ☐   ■   ☐   ☐   ☐
   (D) Sentence T
   (E) Sentence U   A   B   C   D   E
                                   ii ☐   ☐   ☐   ■   ☐

ii. Which sentence did   A   B   C   D   E
    you put after Sen-   iii ☐   ☐   ☐   ☐   ■
    tence P?
    (A) Sentence Q
    (B) Sentence R
    (C) Sentence S
    (D) Sentence T
    (E) Sentence U

iii. Which sentence did
     you put after Sen-
     tence Q?
     (A) Sentence P
     (B) Sentence R
     (C) Sentence T
     (D) Sentence U
     (E) None of the
         above. Sentence
         Q is last.

COOPERATIVE TEST OF SOCIAL STUDIES ABILITIES, EXPERIMENTAL FORM Q[42]

Interpreting Facts

DIRECTIONS: The exercises in this part consist of a series of paragraphs each followed by several statements about the paragraph. In the parentheses after each statement, put the number

 1. if the statement is a reasonable interpretation, fully supported by the facts given in the paragraph.
 2. if the statement goes beyond and cannot be proved by the facts given in the paragraph.
 3. if the statement contradicts the facts given in the paragraph.

[The sample exercise and its explanation are omitted.]

   I. The nineteenth century witnessed a rapid growth in Germany's industrial power. Like England, Germany came to have a fairly satisfactory balance between the amount

---

[42] Devised by J. W. Wrightstone, and published originally by Cooperative Test Service (now Cooperative Test Division of ETS).

of its export and import trade. Heavy exports of coke supplied full cargoes for ships to foreign ports and helped to balance heavy importations of raw materials. The imports especially provided a means for distributing freight rates to the advantage of the German trader competing overseas. By these means Germany was constantly obtaining larger portions of world trade. German wares were carried into every trading realm, and trade meant political as well as commercial power in foreign lands.

1. Through growth in foreign trade, Germany's industrial power increased in the nineteenth century .... 1 ( )
2. Germany had an export trade equal in volume to that of England .... 2 ( )
3. Germany exported very little coke to foreign countries .... 3 ( )
4. England was unable to balance the tonnage of her import and export shipments .... 4 ( )
5. By reducing freight rates Germany was constantly gaining a greater percentage of world trade.. 5 ( )
6. The sale of German wares in every part of the world resulted in added political influence and commercial growth .... 6 ( )

Sequential Tests of Educational Progress (STEP), Science[43]

Level 4 (Grades 4-6)

Situation: Tom wanted to learn which of three types of soil—clay, sand, or loam—would be best for growing lima beans. He found three flowerpots, put a different type of soil in each pot, and planted lima beans in each. He placed them side by side on the window sill and gave each pot the same amount of water.

LOAM   CLAY   SAND

The lima beans grew best in the loam. Why did Mr. Jackson say Tom's experiment was NOT a good experiment and did NOT prove that loam was the best soil for plant growth?

  A The plants in one pot got more sunlight than the plants in the other pots.
  B The amount of soil in each pot was not the same.
  C One pot should have been placed in the dark.
  D Tom should have used three kinds of seeds.

Level 3 (Grades 7-9)

Situation: Tom planned to become a farmer and his father encouraged this interest by giving Tom a part of the garden to use for studying plant life.

[43] *A prospectus for the Cooperative Sequential Tests of Educational Progress.* Princeton, N. J.: Cooperative Test Division, Educational Testing Service, 1957. We illustrate only one test item for each situation, but STEP Science itself has several.

Tom wanted to find out what effect fertilizer has on garden plants. He put some good soil in two different boxes. To box A he added fertilizer containing a large amount of nitrogen. To box B he added fertilizer containing a large amount of phosphorus. In each box he planted 12 bean seeds. He watered each box with the same amount of water. One thing missing from Tom's experiment was a box of soil with

A both fertilizers added
B neither nitrogen nor phosphorus fertilizers added
C several kinds of seeds planted
D no seeds planted

Several test publishers provide excellent practice materials. The College Entrance Examination Board's extensive booklets are splendid.[44] While far shorter, the California Test Bureau's "Practice exercises for marking answers to tests on machine-scoring answer sheets, scoreze, or Cal-cards"[45] can be very helpful for introducing pupils, particularly in the lower grades, to new types of items and new ways of marking them. Here is an item from the practice exercises and one from the sample test:

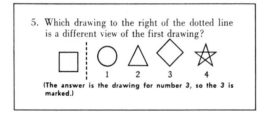

Thirty-four sample items from social science, natural science, and the humanities are contained in an announcement of the Area Tests of the Grad-

[44] See the current *A description of the College Board Scholastic Aptitude Test* and *A description of the College Board achievement tests,* both obtainable without cost from the College Entrance Examination Board, Princeton, N. J. or Berkeley, Calif.

[45] California Test Bureau, Del Monte Research Park, Monterey, Calif. Four pages, including seven practice items and a 15-item sample test to be marked on two different answer sheets.

uate Record Examinations of the Educational Testing Service.[46] One sample:

3. "I am tired of being lectured to about these schedules . . . Let us recognize the fact that with a tariff bill it is just as it is with the river and harbor bills. There is no use denying it. You tickle me and I tickle you."
    In this statement, Senator Knute Nelson was
    (A) holding that the tariff is a form of pork-barrel legislation
    (B) defending protection because it unifies the country
    (C) favoring internal improvements
    (D) arguing for less government intervention in business
    (E) questioning the usefulness of tariffs

Several kinds of multiple-choice items, including analogies, are illustrated in Appendices A and B of the book you are now reading.

Rules for Constructing
Multiple-Choice Items

Testing specialist Harry D. Berg gives suggestions for increasing the thought content of objective test items in the social studies, which he illustrates with four- or five-option multiple-choice items.[47] Jason Millman offers 22 "Multiple-choice test item construction rules"[48] under the headings "Communicate well" and "Don't give away the answer." Fourteen of Berg's rules are similar to Millman's, but the other 14 represent an ingenious attempt to pitch the level of items above rote knowledge or general intelligence. See Berg's chapter, cited in footnote 47. Here are 21 of Millman's rules, in expanded and somewhat altered form:

Communicate Well

1. *The stem should contain the central problem and all qualifications,* including words that would otherwise be repeated in each alternative. For example, if the incomplete statement form is used, it must clearly imply a specific question. The pupil should not be required to make up his own question by consulting the options. In two of his examples, Berg illustrates faults of these sorts.

I. "The study of the price system narrows down to an analysis of these two sets of prices and the interrelationships between them" (Knight, *Social Economic Organization*). The two sets of prices referred to are
    (A) those for consumption goods and those for capital goods.
    (B) those for consumption goods and those for productive services.
    (C) those for labor and those for the other productive factors.
    (D) those for economic and those for non-economic goods.

---

[46] *Assessing the broad outcomes of education in the liberal arts* (Princeton, N. J.: Educational Testing Service, n.d)., 15 pp.

[47] Berg's suggestions that we consider here come from his mimeographed "Suggestions for increasing the thought content of objective test items in the social sciences" (1958, 9 pages), but for a more complete treatment see H. D. Berg, Evaluation in social science, Ch. 4 (pp. 79–112) in P. L. Dressel, ed., *Evaluation in higher education* (Boston: Houghton Mifflin, 1961).

[48] Ithaca, New York: Cornell University, 1961. Mimeographed, 7 pp.

Obviously, the second sentence of the stem should have read "The two of prices referred to are those for," because "those for" occurs as the first t, words of every option. If the incomplete form of stem is used, it must include all the language that is exactly applicable in every option, in order to avoid wasting the pupil's time by repetition in each option.

II. Consumer cooperatives
  (A) are to consumers what labor unions are to laborers.
  (B) have recently been declared illegal.
  (C) originated in the United States and later spread to Europe.
  (D) have been criticized as not paying their equitable share of taxes.

Here we have four true-false questions, each concerning some aspect of consumer cooperatives and only one of which is keyed as being true. The stem, "Consumer cooperatives," does not constitute a statement of a central problem, so this is not a suitable multiple-choice item.

2. *Each item should be as short as possible,* consistent with clarity. Otherwise, it may be more a test of reading ability than is desirable.

3. *Try to avoid negatively stated stems,* but if the negative form is used, emphasize the fact by underlining or using italics. As Berg says, "Negative items increase testing opportunities, but it is well to group them together and to underscore such words as 'not,' 'never,' and 'least.' Another technique to use with such items is to end the stem with the words 'with one exception. Select the exception.'"[49] For example, "Each of the following men *except one* was president of the United States. Which one was *not?*"

4. *The stem should, without aid from other items, state the problem of the question fully.* Items should be largely independent of each other, though several of them may refer to a common passage, as for instance when four or five questions are based on the same paragraph to be read.

5. *Ask for the best answer or use terms such as "most" and "primary" if more than one answer is at least partially correct.* One alternative should clearly be best. For example, "The one factor generally considered most important in causing the United States to enter World War II at the time that it did was . . ."

6. *The omissions in incomplete statements should usually not occur early in the stem.* This might lead to confusion and necessitate excessive rereading of the stem, but note the following item (No. 20 from page 31 of the 1963 SAT sample booklet), to which the "rule" does not seem applicable:

_____ no physical basis for the disorder can be found with the tests now available, doctors refuse to say that the cause must be _____ .
  (A) Although . . . mental
  (B) Insofar as . . . hereditary
  (C) Since . . . unknown
  (D) When . . . mysterious
  (E) Because . . . serious

---

[49] Berg, *op. cit.,* p. 8.

7. *The linguistic difficulty of items should be low.* Berg states the rule more explicitly and gives an example: "The incidental vocabulary and phrasings used in items should not be above the general level, nor should technical terms which have not been studied be used.

"Of the following, the chief difference between man and the lower animals is that the lower animals

(A) are incapable of any communication.
(B) cannot develop true conditioned responses.
(C) lack adaptive instincts.
(D) do not become objects to themselves.
(E) are independent of the homeostatic principle" (p. 8).

"Homeostatic" and perhaps "conditioned responses" seem too technical for the context.

8. *Each item should test only one idea,* though of course the idea may be a complex one such as evolution.

9. *When there is logical sequence in which alternatives can occur (as in order of magnitude, temporal sequence, etc.), use it,* but be sure that in the test as a whole each option occurs as the keyed response approximately as frequently as any other option. Avoid regularly recurring patterns of correct responses, for pupils are likely to detect them.

Don't Give Away the Answer

10. *Foils should be plausible and attractive.* Distracters (foils, decoys) are the incorrect options. They must be prepared at least as carefully as is the keyed option, or else they will not decoy the unknowledgeable. As we noted earlier, for ideal discrimination among pupils a five-option item should be of 50 per cent difficulty when corrected for chance. Therefore, it should be answered correctly by about 60 per cent of the students who mark it (because 60 per cent − 40 per cent/4 = 50 per cent), and 10 per cent of the students should mark each incorrect option. The item writer will usually try to aim the various incorrect options at several levels of knowledge, from nearly enough to answer the item correctly to very little. After the item has been administered, he will tally responses to options (including "omit" and "not reached" as options) to determine how well the distracters actually distracted and then replace unattractive distracters with seemingly better options, unless the item already discriminates so well between high and low scorers on the test as a whole that he considers it unwise to disturb the options.

For example, a teacher of junior-high general mathematics might devise the following test item, hoping that its various options would attract students from five levels of ability in his class:

The positive fourth root of 16 is: A 2   C 12   E 16^4
                                       B 4   D 64

The correct answer is A (because $2 \times 2 \times 2 \times 2 = 16$), which can be expressed as $16^{1/4}$. A student who confused "root" with "power" might choose E. Perhaps such students would be abler, on the average, than students who chose Option B, 4, which is the second root of 16. Students who chose D, 64, which is 4×16, might be abler than students who marked C, 12, which is $16 - 4$.

Of course, the options may not function as the teacher planned, but even then the item would discriminate the able students from the less able ones if the better students on the test marked A and the poorer ones distributed their choices among Options B—E.

Devising excellent multiple-choice items is a highly creative process, particularly with respect to preparation of distracters.

11. *Make all optional responses grammatically consistent with the stem.* Inconsistent articles, changes in tense, and the like may nullify otherwise excellent distracters. We mentioned earlier how an item such as the following gives a strong grammatical clue to the keyed option:

Which of the following men were famous explorers?
    A Lewis and Clark
    B Van Gogh
    C Rogers and Hart
    D Aaron Burr
    E Benjamin Franklin

The plural wording, men and explorer*s*, points to Options A and C only. One might get around this problem by substituting the following options for B, D, and E:

    B Gauguin and Van Gogh
    D Burr and Hamilton
    E Franklin and Jefferson

12. *The length, explicitness, or degree of technicality of alternatives should not vary with correctness.* This rule is related to No. 7, above, but differs in that here the above characteristics give clues to the keyed answer, whereas there the technicality tended more to confuse students. A highly qualified, cautiously worded option is likely to be both long and correct. A strange technical word in an option often signifies a distracter, for if a reasonably competent student cannot recall having ever seen it before, the chances are good that it is not the keyed answer. Inexperienced item writers are prone to use such options, as are item writers who are not completely familiar with the topic being tested.

A general-science item may help clarify this rule:

An atom is
    A an amalgam.
    B a compound.
    C a mixture.

D a molecule.
E the basic "building block" of matter, consisting of a nucleus surrounded by electrons in orbits.

Probably the class has not yet studied amalgams, so the test-wise student will probably ignore Option A. He will notice immediately that Option E is much longer than the other answers. Even without having a clear idea of the relationship of atoms to compounds, mixtures, and molecules (much less to amalgams), he will have little doubt that the keyed answer is E, because it "stands out" from the others. Some experienced item writers will occasionally choose to lure this test-wise type of student astray by making one or more of the incorrect options long and elaborate but leaving the correct option short and simple.

13. *Alternatives should be rather homogeneous in subject content, form, and grammatical structure.* The following illustration[50] shows how the degree of required discrimination increases with homogeneity of the options presented:

    I. Engel's law deals with
       (A) the coinage of money.
       (B) the inevitableness of socialism.
       (C) diminishing returns.
       (D) marginal utility.
       (E) family expenditures.
   II. Engel's law deals with family expenditures for
       (A) luxuries.
       (B) food.
       (C) clothing.
       (D) rest.
       (E) necessaries.
  III. According to Engel's law, family expenditures for food
       (A) increase in accordance with the size of the family.
       (B) decrease as income increases.
       (C) require a smaller percentage of an increasing income.
       (D) rise in proportion to income.
       (E) vary with the tastes of families.

To respond correctly to Item No. I, the student must know only that Engel's law deals with family expenditures. For II, he must know that the specific item of expenditure is food. The maximum degree of discrimination, however, is required for answering III, where still more information is given in the stem.

These three items also illustrate the last portion of Rule 13: *Make all optional responses for a given item parallel in grammatical structure.* Note that grammatical consistency is least true in I, but that even there the basis of each option is a modified noun. All five responses in II are single-word nouns. All responses in III begin with a verb in the present tense, third person plural.

---

[50] Hawkes, Lindquist, and Mann, *op. cit.,* pp. 146-147.

14. *Avoid unintentionally allowing the correct response to occur appreciably more often in one option position than in another.* This is the reverse of the logical-sequence suggestion in Rule 9, above, and was covered there. Four options for a given item may occur in any one of $4 \times 3 \times 2 \times 1 = 24$ orders, five options may occur in 120 different orders, and six options can be arranged in 720 ways! (Try this with books on a library shelf. Three books can be arranged in $3 \times 2 \times 1 = 6$ ways.) Cooperative Test Division editor Scarvia Anderson[51] has published a table that may be used to randomize the order of options. At least, be sure that you use the various option positions (A, B, C, ...) approximately equally frequently for the keyed response, even when logical considerations suggest certain orders for some items. You will want to vary a bit from *exactly k/o* occurrences in each option position, where k is the number of items and o is the number of alternatives (that is, *o*ptions) for each item, because having precisely the right number of options correct in each position might help the best students, who know most of the answers, to infer answers to items about which they are uncertain.

15. *Have at least four alternatives per item* unless doing so would require using implausible options. Five alternatives per item are optimal for many situations, but sometimes six or more excellent options may be available. For certain materials, as few as two options per item may be best. You may even choose to vary the number of options from item to item.

16. *Avoid poetic repetition of sounds or repetition of words or phrases between the stem and the correct answer.* Berg qualifies the rule as follows: "It is legitimate, even desirable, to incorporate in the incorrect responses phrasing, etc., which would be weaknesses in the correct response. Such things as lengthiness, repetition of words appearing in the stem, and 'pat' phrases are examples." Like all rules, this can be overdone. If all distracters are loaded with irrelevant lengthiness, false technicality, and words from the stem, while the correct response stands out because of clarity and simplicity, test-wise students will be able to "spot" it without much knowledge about the point being tested. The test constructer must be clever and versatile, reading the students' minds in advance (and in retrospect, too, from the item analysis) without permitting his own intentions to be discernible.

For example, in the following question the word "battle" appears in the stem and in the keyed option only, thereby giving a clue to the observant pupil:

A decisive battle between United States soldiers and American Indians was the
    A   battle called "Custer's last stand."
    B   fighting at Yorktown.
    C   War of 1812.
    D   storming of the Alamo.

---

[51] Scarvia B. Anderson, Sequence in multiple-choice item options, *Journal of Educational Psychology*, 1952, 43, 364–368.

Notice, also, that Option C, "War of 1812," is poor because the stem specifies a single battle, whereas a war usually involves more than one battle. The test-wise student will ignore Option C.

The question might be reworded as follows:

An important battle between United States soldiers and American Indians was the
    A   last stand of Custer.
    B   fighting at Yorktown.
    C   Battle of Gettysburg.
    D   Battle of the Alamo.

Now the word "Battle" appears in two incorrect options but not in the keyed option, so it may distract test-wise students who do not know the correct keyed answer.

17. *Avoid textbook wording or stereotyped phraseology,* except perhaps in distracters as discussed above.

18. *One item should not help the student answer another item* that is meant to be independent of it. Therefore, the assembled items that form the test must be reviewed carefully in relation to each other. It may help, where time permits, to have a competent person check the entire test for overlap. Long or highly important tests may require even more elaborate precautions, such as indexes of words and concepts. Casual scrutiny is never sufficient.

19. *Alternatives should not overlap, include, or be synonymous with one another,* especially within a given item but also between items because of the previous rule. Each of the k items in the test should have a independent alternatives, so the ak options that compose the entire test should be independent of each other. For instance, a 50-item test composed of 4-option items should have 200 different options. Otherwise, sampling of knowledge and understandings is reduced and test-wiseness brought too prominently into play.

Inexperienced, unimaginative, or lazy item writers sometimes reuse the same or similar alternatives in different items to such a great extent that they in effect prepare wordy matching tests (discussed in the next section) and not proper multiple-choice tests. The matching-test format is appropriately used when merely the matching of stimuli with responses is the mental operation to be tested.

20. *Avoid specific determiners* such as "always" and "never," except occasionally to foil wise-guys who know about specific determiners, because students know that few things are always true or never true. This requires that the usually determining word be employed in the non-determined way part of the time, as for example "The product of 4 and 3 is (a) always 12; (B) not always the same as 3×4; (C) 7." For instance, options containing "always" would have to be true statements as often as they are false, so that the student could not reject them automatically. Even then, some test-wise pupils may outsmart the teacher. The skillful use of words that are usually specific determiners is a task only for expert writers of options and stems.

21. *In testing for the understanding of a term or concept, you should usually present the term first, followed by a series of definitions or descriptions from which the choice is to be made.* If the order is reversed, so that from a series of terms the one that best fits the definition or descriptive statement is chosen, the selection frequently can be made on the basis of superficial verbal associations without genuine understanding. This is not inevitably so, however. Consider the two following items, in the first of which the term (reliability coefficient) is in the stem, with definitions as options, whereas in the second item the definition is in the stem, with terms as options. Which item seems easier to you?

The reliability coefficient of a test was originally defined as the
A   standard error of measurement.
B   stepped-up split-half *r*.
C   correlation between scores on two comparable forms of the test.
D   Kuder-Richardson Formula 20 coefficient.
E   average intercorrelation of the test's items, stepped up by the Spearman-Brown formula.

The correlation between scores on two comparable forms of a test is called the coefficient of
A   equivalence.
B   stability.
C   equivalence and stability.
D   predictive validity.
E   error of measurement.

For both items the keyed option is C.

To these 21 rules we add six more:

22. *Try to test a different point with each item.* A long test may actually cover only a few points if it repeatedly tests the same point with slightly different items. Usually, many more aspects can be tested if some care is taken, with consequently better sampling of instructional objectives.

23. *"None of these" may be a useful last option* for correct-answer items, especially in mathematics. Avoid it when the keyed response is merely the best answer among the responses given, rather than the wholly correct or best possible answer, because if the very best possible answer is not offered, the student will have to mark "None of these" instead of the keyed best option. Which answer would you mark to the following item?

49 divided by 6 equals
A   294   .
B   55   .
C   43   .
D   8.17 .
E   None of the above answers.

The exactly correct answer is 8 1/6, or 8.1666.... Probably the teacher who prepared this item keyed it D, because 8.17 is the correct answer to two decimal places. How can the student who knows how to divide 49 by 6 decide whether to mark D or E? E here serves only to confuse.

If we leave off E, Option D is still objectionable because it is a specific determiner, the only one of the four numbers that is a decimal fraction. We can remedy this somewhat by making the options

    A   294.00 .
    B   55.00 .
    C   43.00 .
    D   8.17 .
    E   0.12 .

The four distracters involve the use of an incorrect operation (multiplication, addition, or subtraction instead of division) or inverted division: 49×6, $49 + 6$, $49 - 6$, and $6/49$, respectively.

Also, be careful that "None of these" is the correct response approximately $1/o$th of the time that it occurs, where o is the number of options the item has—2, 3, 4, 5 or more. If it is used as the fifth option in each of 10 five-option items, then, on the average, it should be the keyed response two times. "None of these" should not be a desperation response, resorted to when inspiration fails. Apparently, it is used rather infrequently by professional item writers. The 1963 practice booklets for the College Entrance Examination Board Scholastic Aptitude Test and the Achievement Tests do not contain it, although the final option (E) for some geometry problems is an equivalent "It cannot be determined from the information given."

24. *"All of the above" or "More than one of the above" may sometimes be suitable options,* but usually the alternatives are made more specific, as in the two following examples from p. 86 of the 1963 CEEB "A description of the College Board achievement tests":

    18. Given $\triangle PQR$ with median RS. Which of the following *must* be true?

        I.   RS is perpendicular to PQ.
        II. RS bisects $\angle QRP$.
        III. $\triangle PQR$ is a right triangle.

        (A) None   (B) I only   (C) II only
        (D) III only   (E) I, II and III

The keyed answer to the above question is (A) None. Does the *must* in the stem function as a specific determiner?

20. If h, k, m, and n are positive numbers, k is greater than m, and n is greater than h, which of the following is (are) true?

I. n + h may equal k + m.
II. k + h may equal n + m.
III. k + n may equal m + h.

(A) None (B) I only (C) I and II only (D) I and III only
(E) I, II, and III

Notice that the I, II, and III above may be combined in eight ways, producing eight possible options: *none* (1), *any one* (3), *any two* (3), *and all* (1). In the first question *none,* the three *ones,* and *all* are used. In the second question *none, one* (once), *two* (twice), and *all* occur. Would it be desirable to offer all eight alternatives for each such item, instead of just five? If feasible from the scoring standpoint, the eight options would be useful because they cover all possible alternatives and also reduce the number of chance successes.

Form

25. *Paragraph each option,* unless all options are so brief that they can be put on a single line without crowding. This reduces the time and effort needed to locate the correct answer.

26. *Number items and letter options,* as illustrated above.

27. *Punctuation for options:* If the stem of the item is an incomplete statement, each option (*not the series of options*) is by itself a possible completion of the statement. Therefore, each should begin with a lower case letter and be followed by a terminal mark of punctuation (period, question mark, exclamation point) and not by a semicolon, as is often found. If the stem is a direct question, and each option a sentence that might possibly answer it, begin each option with a capital letter and follow it by a terminal mark of punctuation. If the stem is a question, but the options are words or phrases and not complete sentences, begin each option with a capital letter but do not put any mark of punctuation at its end. Other possibilities occur, as shown in the illustrations below from various unrevised teacher-made tests:

The defeat of the Danes by King Alfred prevented them from
(A) destroying Christianity in England.
(B) driving the older tribes from England.
(C) conquering all the Anglo-Saxons.

A rose is a
(A) box.
(B) flower.
(C) home.
(D) month.

Ingor is a new child in school. He has been in this country only a year. He can speak English but still has difficulty with some words. He also has an accent. What would be best for you to say to the boys and girls who are teasing him?

(A) He is better than you, anyway. He knows two languages.
(B) Why don't you go tease somebody else?
(C) He is trying. Why not give him a chance?
(D) You are too ignorant to listen and understand him.

The woods listed below are used in furniture construction. Which one is classified as a hardwood?
(A) White pine
(B) Walnut
(C) Red cedar

In the following group of words, one word does not belong in the group because of its part of speech. Mark the letter of that word on the answer sheet. (A) toward (B) beyond (C) before (D) running (E) on

Tommy reached greedily for his dessert, but, noticing his mother's disapproving look, he . . . pulled toward himself a half-finished dish of vegetables.

(A) slowly
(B) cautiously
(C) eagerly
(D) reluctantly

HUGE, TINY

(S) same
(O) opposite

Other types of multiple-choice items occur, of course. Test specialist Raymond Gerberich[52] classifies and illustrates a variety of types. You will want to try many sorts; do not succumb to the human tendency to specialize prematurely.

Though even the best rules have exceptions and must be tempered with good judgment, careful consideration of the 27 suggestions above should help you write better multiple-choice items.

MATCHING EXERCISES   *Definition:* A matching exercise typically consists of two columns, each item in the first column to be paired with an alternative in the second column. In the simplest form of matching exercise, the number of responses is exactly the same as the number of items. But frequently, matching exercises are made which provide more responses than items, in order to reduce success by guessing. Sometimes the items in the first column are incomplete sentences, each requiring a word or phrase from the second column for its completion. Occasionally, two or more columns of responses are given, and a choice must be made from each of

---

[52] J. R. Gerberich, *Specimen objective test items, a guide to achievement test construction* (New York: Longmans, Green, 1956).

these response columns for each item in the first column. The matching exercise is also useful for identifying numbered places or parts on maps, charts, and diagrams.

Advantages and Limitations

Many types of learning involve the association of two things in the mind of the learner. Common examples are events and dates, events and persons, events and places, terms and definitions, foreign words and English equivalents, laws and illustrations, rules and examples, and tools and their use. The matching exercise is a very convenient form for measuring such learning. "The matching exercise is particularly well adapted to testing in *who, what, when,* and *where* types of situations, or for naming and identifying abilities."[53]

Its principal limitations are as follows: (1) It is not well adapted to the measurement of understanding as distinguished from mere memory; (2) With the exception of the true-false test, the matching exercise is the form most likely to include irrelevant clues to the correct response; (3) Unless skillfully made, it is time-consuming for the pupil. The suggestions that follow are designed to overcome the last two limitations. The matching exercise can hardly be designed to measure genuine understanding of a high level or the ability to interpret complex relationships.

Illustrations of Matching Tests

Because matching exercises usually have too many options (more than 5 or 6) for typical multiple-choice answer sheets, they appear far less frequently in recent published tests than they did before 1940. Some teachers still use them, however. Here is a "square," 10-by-10, unrevised matching exercise from a social-studies quiz:

_____ 1. The country that aided Columbus with money and ships	A. Philadelphia
_____ 2. The oldest town in the United States	B. St. Augustine
_____ 3. A famous Quaker	C. William Penn
_____ 4. The first English settlement in America	D. Pilgrims
_____ 5. A city in Massachusetts	E. Cartier
_____ 6. "City of Brotherly Love"	F. Spain
_____ 7. First French explorer in America	G. Jamestown
_____ 8. He founded Connecticut.	H. Magellan
_____ 9. They landed at Plymouth Rock.	I. Thomas Hooker
_____10. His ship sailed around the world.	J. Boston

Is the above material too heterogeneous to be put into a single matching exercise? Four of the options are names of cities, four are names of persons, one is the name of a country, and one is a plural noun. How much does a stu-

---

[53] Hawkes, Lindquist, and Mann, *op. cit.,* p. 150.

dent really have to know about early United States history to be able to puzzle out the correct answers? For No. 1, he has only to recognize that Spain is the only country in the list of alternatives. His choice for No. 2 lies among A, B, G, and J. For No. 3, he is likely to reject Cartier and Magellan as not sounding "Quakerish," leaving just C, William Penn, and I, Thomas Hooker. No. 4 uses the same four options as No. 2, and perhaps St. Augustine does not sound like an English name. No. 5 has an oddly contemporary, non-historical ring, out of context with the other nine items. No. 6 is the fourth, and last, of the "city" items, automatically answerable if he surmised the correct answers to Nos. 2, 4, and 5. In effect, then, the city questions constitute a 4 × 4 matching exercise that might better have been presented as such, instead of being buried in the 10 × 10 format and thereby favoring test-wiseness and clerical ability.

"Persons" also constitutes an imbedded 4 × 4 matching exercise. No. 7 contains the give-away "French," which points to Cartier, the only French-sounding name among the four. Ignorant but shrewd pupils will probably choose the answer to No. 8 from just C and I, since it seems unlikely that Connecticut was founded by a person with a name such as Cartier or Magellan. (True, that is hazardous procedure and requires a little knowledge, but with this sort of teacher-made exercise it usually pays off.) No. 9 is ridiculous, for the "They" who landed at Plymouth Rock *must* be the only plural word among the ten alternatives. By the time the average pupil comes to No. 10, the fourth person in the list of 10 items (he may not save it for last), he probably must feel that cunning is more important than knowledge in getting through this maze. It need not have been so, for the teacher could have prepared far better exercises to cover the material.

This 10-item matching exercise appeared in a 40-item social-studies test, along with 10 three-option multiple-choice items, 10 true-false items, and 10 completion items. It was administered to 33 students who had just completed a unit of instruction on U. S. colonial history. The four teachers who constructed the test claimed that the objectives for the social studies course were: (1) to help pupils understand how America developed into a great nation; (2) to teach the children the pertinent facts about the discovery and colonization of our country; and (3) to intensify pupil interest in the workings of democracy. Obviously, the matching exercise emphasized the second objective.

Results of the item analysis based on the 33 pupils tested are interesting. First the papers were graded for all 40 items.[54] They were then arranged ac-

---

[54]Each item in a matching exercise is usually scored either right (1 point) or wrong (0 points), as was done with these 10 items. Correction for chance success is possible, however. If you wish to delve into that aspect, start with these three references: D. W. Chapman, The scoring of matching tests with unequal series of items, *Journal of Educational Psychology,* 1936, 27, 368–370; E. Shen, Note on the scoring of matching tests, *Ibid.,* 1940, 31, 625–626; and L. Chen, The correction formula for matching tests, *Ibid.,* 1944, 35, 565–566. An excellent guide to early research in test construction, scoring, and norming is *Selected references on test construction, mental test theory, and statistics, 1929–1949,* by H. W. Goheen and S. Kavruck, U. S. Government Printing Office, Washington 25, D. C., 1950. For 1950 and subsequent years, see the *Psychological Abstracts,* the *Education Index, Educational and Psychological Measurement,* and *Psychometrika.*

cording to total score, from the highest to the lowest (33rd). Then the highest 27 per cent (9 papers) and the lowest 27 per cent (also 9 papers) were compared for responses to each item. The most discriminating item was No. 9, "They landed at Plymouth Rock," which we have already decided could be answered wholly on the basis of the correspondence of the "They" to the plural "Pilgrims," these being the only plurals among either the items or the alternatives. The 9 top-scoring pupils on the test as a whole all marked this item correctly, while the 9 lowest-scoring pupils all marked it incorrectly! It *may* be that this is the central theme of the unit and that the ablest students would have got it right even without the specific determiner, but it is uncomfortable to suspect that the primary determinant of score on the test *might* be verbal ability, reading ability, and test sophistication (in various proportions, perhaps), and not specific knowledge of the topic studied.

The least discriminating of the 10 matching items, and fourth from the bottom of the 40 items in discrimination, was No. 2, "The oldest town in the United States." Eight persons of the 9 in the low group and 6 of the nine in the high group missed it. The most difficult item on the entire test was No. 6, "City of Brotherly Love," missed by 9 in the low group and 6 in the high group. By looking at the actual options marked, a teacher can to some extent "read the pupils' minds" and determine what remedial teaching is needed. For example, are a number of pupils misinformed, so that they think St. Augustine is the City of Brotherly Love, or are they just ignorantly marking No. 6 at random among the four cities offered?

Despite all its limitations, suggested by our analysis of the 10 matching items, this test was of middle difficulty for the group tested (mean rights score, not corrected for guessing, 19.5), had a large standard deviation (9.1), and yielded a high estimated internal-consistency (reliability) coefficient of .92. Whatever it measured, scores on this test ranked the students reliably, and the various items measured the same type of knowledge or ability rather accurately. With practice, the four teachers could devise items much freer of the kinds of faults we noticed. Even at worst, though, the test is probably superior to a teacher's casual judgments about a pupil's knowledge.

Here is another type of matching exercise, devised as part of a test for a Grade 9 English class:

She and Margaret have probably gone to the little grocery store around the corner.
14   15   16   17   16   18   19   20

_____14. She   A. noun
_____15. Margaret   B. pronoun
_____16. have gone   C. verb
_____17. probably   D. adjective
_____18. little   E. adverb
_____19. grocery   F. preposition
_____20. around

This is a 7 × 6 matching item. Any number of items could be used with just the 6 alternatives (i.e., responses). On the test itself, 40 items were used, with 15 sentences and a six-column arrangement for checking the part of speech. Nos. 16 and 19 were the most discriminating items of the 7 above, and No. 15 was the least discriminating. All 7 discriminated well between high and low scorers on the test, though. The most difficult of the 7 items was No. 19, which was missed by 11 of the 12 lowest scorers but by only one of the 12 highest scorers. Incidentally, the only perfectly discriminating (12:0) one of the 93 items was the adjective "hearty" in the sentence "The hearty breakfast was soon finished." Most of the lowest scorers thought it an adverb because of the "y" ending.

A little knowledge can be a dangerous thing, and sometimes student misapplication of knowledge is detectable from the item analysis. As an aside from our discussion of matching exercises, consider the following item: "No one but (A. he) (B. him) came to the meeting." Five of the 12 lowest-scoring students chose "he," but nine of the highest scorers did also. Apparently, the more able students knew that "but" is usually a conjunction and concluded that this is a compound sentence, "he" being the subject of the verb "came." The lowest-scoring students, not knowing much about parts of speech, may have proceeded by the sound of the sentence. They were probably used to saying, "This is him," and "him" sounded right in the test sentence. We are merely speculating, of course. To check this hypothesis, high and low scorers could be questioned about their reasons for marking A and B.

Another negatively discriminating item was the part of speech of the pronominal adjective "their" in "The strong yellow soap stung their chapped hands." It was keyed as an adjective. Whereas 7 of the 12 lowest scorers mistakenly thought otherwise, 11 of the 12 highest scorers were also in error. Most of the highest scorers noted that it precedes the adjective "chapped" and concluded incorrectly that therefore it modified "chapped" and must be an adverb! The remedy for such imperfect knowledge is not a new item, but remedial teaching.

We now present three other examples of matching exercises.[55] The first goes readily with six-option printed answer sheets where options are lettered.

DIRECTIONS: Famous inventions are listed in the left-hand column below. In the right-hand column are names of famous inventors. Place the letter corresponding to the inventor in the space before the invention for which he is famous.

Inventions	*Inventors*
_____1. steam boat	A. Alexander Bell
_____2. cotton gin	B. George Washington Carver
_____3. sewing machine	C. Robert Fulton
_____4. reaper	D. Elias Howe
	E. Cyrus McCormick
	F. Eli Whitney

[55]J. E. Stecklein, How to write matching test items. *Bulletin on Classroom Testing* No. 6, Bureau of Institutional Research, University of Minnesota, 1955.

DIRECTIONS: Quotations from poetry written during the Romantic Period are listed in the column at the left below. In the column at the right, names of famous poets are listed. You are to indicate the author of each of the quotations by writing in the space before the number of the quotation the letter corresponding to the name of the author in the right-hand column.

Quotation (Romantic Period)	*Poet*
_____1. Hail to thee, blithe Spirit! Bird thou never wert, That from Heaven, or near it, Pourest thy full heart in profuse Strains of unpremeditated art.	A. Robert Burns B. Lord Byron C. Samuel Taylor Coleridge D. John Keats
_____2. She walks in beauty, like the night of cloudless climes and starry skies; And all that's best of dark and bright meet in her aspect and her eyes.	E. Percy B. Shelley F. Alfred Lord Tennyson G. William Wordsworth
_____3. My heart leaps up when I behold a rainbow in the sky; So was it when my life began; So is it now I am a man; So be it when I shall grow old, or let me die!	
_____4. A thing of beauty is a joy forever: Its loveliness increases; it will never Pass into nothingness; but still will keep A bower quiet for us, and a sleep Full of sweet dreams, and health, and quiet breathing.	

DIRECTIONS: Three lists are presented below. Famous English authors of plays are listed in the column farthest to the right, names of well-known plays are listed in the center column, and in the column farthest to the left are names of characters in some of these plays. You are to look at the name of the character listed, decide in which play this character appears, and identify the author of this play. Indicate your answers as follows: Place the small alphabet letter corresponding to the play in which the character appears in the first space before the name of the character; place the capital alphabet letter corresponding to the author of this play in the second space before the name of the character. Note that there are more names of plays and authors than there are names of characters, so not all answers will be used.

____ ____1. Mildred Tresham	a. The Silver Box	A. John Millington Synge
____ ____2. Ralph Rackstraw	b. Riders to the Sea	B. Clemence Dane
____ ____3. Algernon Moncrieff	c. Easy Virtue	C. Robert Browning
____ ____4. Elizabeth Saunders	d. H. M. S. Pinafore	D. W. Somerset Maugham
____ ____5. Marion Whittaker	e. A Bill of Divorcement	E. Henry Authur Jones
____ ____6. Bartley	f. A Blot on the Scutcheon	F. Noel Coward
____ ____7. Montague Lushington	g. Our Betters	G. Oscar Wilde
	h. The Masqueraders	H. W. S. Gilbert
	i. The Importance of Being Earnest	I. John Galsworthy

Suggestions for Constructing
Matching Exercises

1. *Be careful about what material is put into the question column and what is put into the option column.* It is wrong, for example, to use authors in the question column and novels in the option column; for this, in effect, asks the question, "What did Sinclair Lewis write? Guess which one of his many novels I have put over there in the option column for you to seek." Some teachers try to justify this frustrating arrangement by saying, "But I just taught them one!" Unfortunately, the absurdity of this reply is not at all apparent to some of them.

In the case of a one-to-one correspondence, as chemical element—chemical symbol, it makes no difference; in the many-to-one correspondence, it is an item of the many that belongs in the question column, with the unique correspondent in the option column. For example, *Main Street* is the item, with Sinclair Lewis the option to be chosen.

2. *Include only homogeneous material in each matching exercise.* Do not mix such dissimilar items as persons and places in a single exercise. We saw above in the Colonial-America exercise why this kind of heterogeneity is undesirable.

3. *Check each exercise carefully for unwarranted clues that may indicate matching pairs.* For each item ask yourself this question: What is the least amount of information that must be known in order to select the right response?

4. *Be sure that the students fully understand the bases on which matching is to be done.* May an option be used for more than one item? May the desired response to a given item consist of more than one option? Communicate your exact intent to the pupil.

5. *Put items on the left and number them; put options on the right and designate them by letters.* Item numbers run consecutively throughout the test, but option letters begin anew with each matching exercise.

6. *Arrange items and options in systematic order.* If the list consists of dates, put them in chronological order. Option words may be alphabetized to make it easier for the student to locate the desired response.

7. *Place all the items and options for a matching exercise on a single page,* if possible. Turning the page back and forth in search of desired responses is both confusing and time-consuming.

8. *Limit a matching exercise to not more than 10–15 items.* Longer lists tend to be too heterogeneous and therefore afford clues for the test-wise; they waste time; and if testing time is brief, they put too much premium on the students' clerical speed and accuracy.

Chapter Three and Appendix E have material on the preparation and scoring of rearrangement (ranking, sequence, chronology, continuity) exercises and should be consulted at this point. Appendix E makes scoring them rather simple, thus eliminating one of the chief objections to this item type.

Probably the chief difficulty in preparing rearrangement exercises is keeping the material homogeneous. Each thing to be ranked in a given set should, for the group tested, be just about as difficult as every other thing. For historical chronologies, this requires that unfamiliar events not be included with far more familiar events, and perhaps that the events be spaced approximately equally. If one event is wholly unknown to most of the students, as compared to the rest of the events, then the location of that event in the ranked series will have to be made by sheer chance, thereby decreasing the reliability of the ranking exercise. If two events are much closer together in time than are the other events, they may be confused with each other, even though the chronological location of either with reference to the other events is known. This seems to be a lesser difficulty than the unknown event, for half the time by chance the two close-together events would be ranked correctly, and the other half of the time they would be interchanged.[56]

The rearrangement exercise is a promising type for quite a few fields. Home economics teachers might use it for such chronologies as steps in baking a cake. Chemistry teachers may wish to have equations for a certain process put in order. English teachers may ask (as the College Entrance Examination Board's English Composition Test sometimes does) that a set of randomly ordered sentences be regrouped to make the best possible paragraph, or that the sequence of events in a story be ordered. Mathematics teachers may be able to test for sequence of operations in solving a problem. Science teachers may present colors to be ranked according to wave length.

There are $N(N - 1)(N - 2) \ldots 1$ possible orders for N things. For example, there are $4(4 - 1)(4 - 2)(4 - 3) = 24$ different orders of the letters ABCD. Ideally, each rearrangement exercise should have its items presented in a purely random order. Up through six, you can randomize by rolling a die (singular of dice) and arranging each item according to the number on the die. Suppose, for example, that your rearrangement exercise consists of five events in a story to be put into the correct order. You start with the five events listed in any order. Now, how shall the first one be relisted? You roll the die and get a

---

[56]Unfortunately, although we know how to score rearrangement exercises to take into account amount of discrepancy and degree of misinformation, little is known about how to construct them well. For that reason, our suggestions in this paragraph are few and tentative. Systematic research in the construction of rearrangement items is greatly needed.

two, so the first event in your list will be placed second in the exercise. You next roll a five, so your second event will be fifth in the exercise. Continue until all five events are put in some order. If you throw a six, disregard it and roll the die again. (Should you prefer not to use a die, write the numbers 1, 2, 3, 4, and 5 on each of five slips of paper respectively, shuffle them thoroughly, and draw randomly.) Numbers from 7 through 12 can be handled by using 7-12 slips of paper.

A novel use of 15 four-item rearrangement exercises occurs in Part II of the "Study of Values."[57] The authors pit each one of six "evaluative attitudes" against all possible combinations of three of the other five attitudes. There are 15 possible combinations of six things taken four at a time, and they use each possible combination once. Here are two of their exercises. Each of the four items in an exercise typifies one of the six values. The student is told, "Each of the following situations or questions is followed by four possible attitudes or answers. Arrange these answers in the order of your personal preference by writing, in the appropriate box at the right, a score of 4, 3, 2, or 1.[58] To the statement you prefer most give 4, to the statement that is second most attractive 3, and so on."

Here are two of the 15 ranking items from the Study of Values:

2. In your opinion, can a man who works in business all the week best spend Sunday in—

    a. trying to educate himself by reading serious books

    b. trying to win at golf, or racing

    c. going to an orchestral concert

    d. hearing a really good sermon

13. To what extent do the following famous persons interest you—

    a. Florence Nightingale

    b. Napoleon

    c. Henry Ford

    d. Galileo

---

[57] Devised by G. W. Allport, P. E. Vernon, and G. Lindzey, and published by Houghton Mifflin, 1960.

[58] It would be just as appropriate to employ a 3, 2, 1, 0 scoring system for the "Study of Values" as the 4, 3, 2, 1 scores actually used, if this did not confuse the test taker.

The four options in item 2 represent Evaluative Attitudes A, B, C, and D, while the options of Item 13 represent E, B, F, and A. What do "trying to educate himself by reading serious books" and "Galileo" have in common, being representatives of Evaluative Attitude A? What do "trying to win at golf, or racing" and "Napoleon" have in common, both being items for Attitude B? If you rank "trying to educate himself by reading serious books" 4—the highest possible—you award 4 points to Attitude A. Because there is no "correct" (i.e., keyed) order against which to score the Study of Values ranking exercises, by an r_{ranks} formula (see Chapter Three) or otherwise, you award to the attitude (one of the six attitudes ABCDEF) represented by each item the number of points (4, 3, 2, or 1) you allotted that item.

There are 4 items per ranking exercise and 15 exercises, making a total of $4 \times 15 = 60$ items covering the 6 attitudes equally, so there are $60/6 = 10$ items per attitude. Because the maximum number of points for any item is 4, the largest possible score on the 15 ranking exercises is $10 \times 4 = 40$ for any *one* of the 6 attitudes. The smallest possible score is $10 \times 1 = 10$. There are 15 $(4 + 3 + 2 + 1) = 150$ points for all 6 attitudes, so the average attitude score for any person on the ranking exercises must be $150/6 = 25$. In other words, each student has the same average (or total) attitude score as any other student. The Study of Values is an *ipsative* scale because of the forced-choice (i.e., ranking) nature of its items, so strictly speaking we cannot compare one student's *scores* on the various attitudes with another's scores but only the profiles of their respective scores. What is the student's highest attitude? His lowest attitude? Does he have the same rank-order of attitudes as some other student? Are his scores on the 6 attitude scales considerably more variable than another student's? If so, he has more sharply differentiated evaluative attitudes.

The Study of Values is an interesting rearrangement and alternative-response test. There are no "right" or "wrong" answers for it, and each person who completes the SV has the same "total" score as any other person. In order to understand it better, you may wish to obtain a copy of the SV booklet and the Manual of Directions, perhaps via your instructor, fill out the booklet, score it, and study the results. In Chapter Nine, "Self Reports and Reports by Others," we shall consider why inventories such as the Study of Values are not "tests" in the same sense that a vocabulary or an arithmetic test is.

CONCLUDING REMARKS   Item writing is an art, assisted but not superseded by the statistical procedures of item
analysis. As automation takes over the scoring of tests, obtaining of frequency distributions and norms, and efficient distribution of results, we hope that the heart of the test—its items and exercises—will not be neglected by test publishers. Great emphasis on mechanical procedures can lead to undesirable consequences. Too great a preoccupation with indices of item discrimination, for example, may result in neglect of the item's logical, motivational, and literary properties. A paragraph in a reading test, for instance, should be acceptable to

an expert in the subject it pertains to, well written in an aesthetic sense, and interesting to the student. An item may discriminate well between high and low scorers on a test as a whole and still be inaccurate, uninteresting, and confusingly written. This situation usually comes about when items are not constructed with loving care and consummate artistry by well trained, experienced item specialists who genuinely know the subject being tested. Brightness and mastery of the principles of measurement are necessary but not all-sufficient; knowledge of subject matter, sufficient time, and hard work are essential, too. Also, the items should be thoroughly reviewed by other well-qualified persons *who are not aware how the items are keyed by the writer,* and the items must be edited on the basis of their comments. This must be done to compensate for the inevitable limitations of any one person. Further editing of all but the most discriminating items on the basis of a detailed item analysis (carried out on the answer sheets of a substantial number of students) is an important step that is too frequently omitted. This may be because items are often in short supply, and because of the usually unwelcome prospect of having to try out the re-edited items again.

Perhaps elements of automation can help systemize and facilitate item writing, for computers have excellent "memories" that might be harnessed to speed up the man-pace somewhat. Also, you can look forward to the time when test booklets, answer sheets, and scoring keys will give way to fully computerized testing, probably tailored optimally to each individual pupil. Teachers may even be able to ask a machine, "In which section of algebra should Eric be placed?" and get an answer of stated precision on the basis of information already known about Eric as supplemented by further personalized testing via the machine.

But, probably for a long while, test items and exercises themselves will be devised mainly by human beings in the current painstaking manner, so the prospective or present teacher might as well learn the art. We have introduced you to it. With practice and further study you will be able to prepare better tests for *your* classes than anyone else can, and certainly much better than anyone else will.

RECOMMENDED READINGS

Anderson, Scarvia B., Katz, R., and Shimberg, B., *Meeting the test.* New York: Scholastic Magazines, 1959. Especially articles No. 4 and 5.

Barnette, W. L., ed., *Readings in psychological tests and measurements.* Homewood, Ill.: Dorsey Press, 1964.

Buros, O. K., ed., *The sixth mental measurements yearbook.* Highland Park, N. J.: Gryphon Press, 1965.

Buros, O. K., ed., *Tests in print.* Highland Park, N. J.: Gryphon Press, 1961.

Chauncey, H. and Dobbin, J. E., *Testing: its place in education today.* New York: Harper & Row, 1963. Especially pages 185-217, Multiple-choice questions: a close look.

Downie, N. M., *Fundamentals of measurement: techniques and practices.* Ch. 7, Multiple-choice items, Ch. 8, Other types of objective-test items, and Ch. 10, Item analysis. New York: Oxford University Press, 1959.

Dressel, P. L., and associates, *Evaluation in higher education.* Boston: Houghton Mifflin, 1961.

Findley, W. G., ed., The impact and improvement of school testing programs, *62nd Yearbook of the National Society for the Study of Education,* Part II, 1963, especially Chapter VIII, The improvement of tests, by M. D. Engelhart and J. M. Beck.

Flanagan, J. C.; Dailey, J. T.; Shaycoft, Marion F.; Gorham, W. A.; Orr, D. B.; and Goldberg, I., *Design for a study of American youth.* Boston: Houghton Mifflin, 1962. Especially Chapters Five and Six, The tests: their history and content.

Furst, E. J., *Constructing evaluation instruments.* New York: Longmans, Green, 1958. Part II, "Constructing achievement tests."

Gardner, E. F., chairman, *Proceedings of the 1962 Invitational Conference on Testing Problems of Educational Testing Service.* Princeton, N. J.: Educational Testing Service, 1963. Especially Session I, Creativity, pages 11-54.

Goslin, D. A., *The search for ability.* New York: Russell Sage Foundation, 1963.

Katz, M., Improving classroom tests by means of item analysis, *Clearing House,* 1961, 35, 265–269.

Lindquist, E. F., ed., *Educational measurement.* Washington, D. C.: American Council on Education, 1951. Especially Chapter Seven, Writing the test item, by R. L. Ebel.

Lyman, H. B., *Test scores and what they mean.* Englewood Cliffs, N. J.: Prentice-Hall, 1963.

Merwin, J. C. and Gardner, E. F., Development and application of tests of educational achievement, *Review of Educational Research*, 1962, 32, 40–50.

Myers, S. S., The kinds of thinking required in current mathematics tests, *New Jersey Mathematics Teacher,* 1961, 18, 11-15.

Nunnally, J. C., Jr., *Tests and measurements: assessment and prediction,* Ch. 12, Achievement tests. New York: McGraw-Hill, 1959.

Palmer, O., Sense or nonsense? The objective testing of English composition, *English Journal,* 1961, 50, 314-320.

Remmers, H. H., Gage, N. L., and Rummel, J. F., *A practical introduction to measurement and evaluation,* Ch. 8, Constructing teacher-made tests. New York: Harper, 1960.

Stanley, J. C., The ABCs of test construction, *NEA Journal,* 1958, 47, 224–226. Reprinted as Selection No. 45 (pp. 490–496) in V. H. Noll and Rachel P. Noll, *Readings in educational psychology.* New York: Macmillan, 1962.

Stecklein, J. E., *Bulletins on classroom testing* of the Bureau of Institutional Research, University of Minnesota, Minneapolis, Minnesota, Nos. 4, 5, and 6 (1955), and 7 (1956): How to write multiple-choice test items, How to write true-false test items, How to write matching test items, and How to measure more than facts with multiple-choice items.

Stodola, Q., and others, Making a classroom test: a guide for teachers, 2nd ed. *Evaluation and Advisory Service Series* No. 4 of Educational Testing Service, 1961.

Test Development Division, Educational Testing Service, *Multiple-choice questions: a close look.* Princeton, N. J.: Educational Testing Service, 1963.

Tyler, Leona E., *Tests and measurements.* Englewood Cliffs, N. J.: Prentice-Hall, 1963.

Wood, Dorothy Adkins, *Test construction: development and interpretation of achievement tests.* Columbus, Ohio: Merrill, 1960. Especially Ch. 7, Constructing objective test items.

CONSTRUCTING AND USING ESSAY TESTS

Thus far we have, for the most part, considered only tests that can be scored objectively, with little need for teacher judgment during scoring. As all of you know, the typical teacher asks many test questions whose answers require subjective scoring, since each pupil's answer to a particular question will differ somewhat from the answers of his classmates. "What were the principal political considerations that led to the War Between the States?" "Write an essay about 1000 words long concerning the cinema as an art form." "Distinguish between 'connotation' and 'denotation.'" "Is logic a branch of mathematics, or mathematics a branch of logic? Why?" "Discuss the relative influence of heredity and environment on the development of verbal 'intelligence.' Support your points by citing relevant studies."

Teachers usually refer to such questions or statements as "essay questions." One or more essay questions will constitute an "essay test," if the answers are graded (note that teachers do not "score" essay tests, whereas they score objective tests because a key can be prepared in advance of the scoring). An essay test differs from a short-answer-item test in that for the latter the teacher knows at the time the test is prepared what responses he expects. "Name the inert gases" permits just one set of names, with no display of individuality by the student except in the order that they are written down. Essay questions limit "universal discourse" less than do other item forms. The teacher does not say merely, "Write something," but on the other hand he does not specify the form of the answer completely.

Because the grading of essay questions calls for expert judgment, they cannot be graded by clerks or machines, as objective items can; nor can they be graded quickly and without thought. Even with the best of efforts by skilled teachers, the reliability of many essay tests is low. For many years, major efforts have been made to find feasible ways to obtain adequate reliability of grading of essay tests, particularly of English compositions written by high-school juniors and seniors applying for entrance to selective colleges. Ever since its beginning early in the century, the College Entrance Examination Board (CEEB) has had the grading of essay questions as a major item on its agenda. Two "camps" have developed in recent years, one decrying objective testing and the other insisting that most important mental processes, including the composing of essays, can be measured well by objective items. Let us consider the argument favoring essay tests, as expressed well by John M. Stalnaker, who was an official of the CEEB during a number of years when some of the most important work in this area was done. He compares the merits of essay and objective tests in a thorough and impartial manner, concluding that *both* have considerable value when used properly. The summary to his chapter is especially interesting:

The essay test has been the subject of repeated and often unfair attacks by psychologists and educationalists interested in the measurement of achievement as a science. As a result, the essay test remains largely undeveloped, although it continues to be used widely by the classroom teacher. The values claimed for it have not been generally established, yet it may well be a basic test form which, properly controlled, can measure important outcomes of learning not yet otherwise measured. It also has other potential values which have been described. It has several important and unique advantages as an educative influence. The fact that it continues to be a test form widely used by the teacher preparing his own test would alone seem to justify further development and research.[1]

CEEB publications, *The College Board Review* and the *Annual Report of the Director,* contain valuable reports of work with essay tests. For College Board achievement tests in English, see the current "A description of the College Board achievement tests." In 1963, only the objectively scored English Composition Test and the essay Writing Sample were offered. The 1963 booklet's description of the Writing Sample on pages 12–13 shows the type of essay test of compositional ability that colleges may require their applicants to take:

> The Writing Sample, as its name suggests, is an essay-writing exercise which provides colleges with direct evidence of your competence in written expression. You are given one hour to write an essay on a single assigned topic, and copies of your essay, exactly as written, are sent to your school and to the colleges you specify at the time you write the essay.
>
> The essay will not be graded by the College Board. It will be used by the college to supplement the information provided by your school grades in English, your score on the English Composition Test (if you are asked to take it), and any other evidence that may be submitted relating to your writing ability (such as teachers' recommendations or ratings).
>
> Here is an example of the kind of topic you will be asked to write on if you are requested by a college to take the Writing Sample:
>
> "Loyalty is a quality which, in the abstract, we delight to honor. In practice, however, it is something that may vary with circumstances and conditions. There is 'loyalty among thieves,' 'loyalty to self-interest,' 'loyalty to a pal at the expense of truth,' as well as 'loyalty to an ideal, to country, or to cause.'"
>
> Define your concept of loyalty and arrive at a principle regarding its use or abuse.
>
> DIRECTIONS: Express your ideas in a well-planned essay of 300 to 500 words, using several paragraphs to organize your discussion. Your point of view should be supported by and illustrated from your own experience, or by appropriate references to your reading, study, or observation. Be specific. You are expected to express your best thought in your best natural manner. After you have written your essay, *underline the sentence* which you think comes closest to *summarizing your central idea.*

The fact that the CEEB does not mark or grade the Writing Sample in any way, but leaves to each college that requires the Writing Sample the decision

---

[1] J. M. Stalnaker, The essay type of examination, Ch. 13 in E. F. Lindquist, ed., *Educational measurement* (Washington, D. C.: American Council on Education, 1951), p. 530.

as to how it shall be handled, points up the difficulties of grading such an essay test reliably and validly. Many colleges (by no means all of them) want a Writing Sample from each applicant, but they differ in how these are used. Some colleges turn the papers over to the English department to be graded, while others make them available for scrutiny by members of the admissions committee when the applicant cannot be accepted or rejected on the basis of other information.

English composition is just one subject in which subjectively graded tests are used, of course. Some teachers in most areas, especially the social studies, use them regularly or even exclusively. To limit the use of informal teacher-made tests to those classified as objective would be an unwarranted restriction. The so-called traditional or essay test still has a legitimate place in the modern school. In this chapter we will consider some of the limitations and advantages of this type of test, and offer suggestions for its improvement and use. Throughout, let us keep in mind this wise admonition:[2]

> The intelligent point of view is that which recognizes that whatever advantages either type may have are *specific* advantages in *specific* situations; that while certain purposes may be best served by one type, other purposes are best served by another; and, above all, that the adequacy of either type in any specific situation is much more dependent upon the ingenuity and intelligence with which the test is *used* than upon any *inherent* characteristic or limitation of the *type* employed.

LIMITATIONS OF THE ESSAY TEST

As ordinarily employed, the essay test has certain serious limitations. It suffers in comparison with most forms of objective tests on the three important criteria of a satisfactory measuring instrument—validity, reliability, and usability.

Low Validity

As it is commonly used in classrooms, the essay examination has low content validity (see page 162). Several factors contribute to this condition. The limited subject-matter sampling of the essay test is often pointed out. For example, an early measurement specialist, Giles Ruch,[3] produced evidence to show that the essay called forth less than half the knowledge the average pupil actually possessed on the subject as determined by objective tests, and required twice the time to do it. The essay scorer is also faced with many irrelevant factors such as the quality of the spelling, handwriting, and English used, as well as bluffing, for which no correction formulas

---

[2]H. E. Hawkes, E. F. Lindquist, and C. R. Mann, *The construction and use of achievement examinations* (Boston: Houghton Mifflin, 1936), p. 20.
[3]G. M. Ruch, *The objective or new-type examination* (Chicago: Scott, Foresman, 1929), p. 54.

exist. It has been suggested that the essay overrates the importance of knowing how to say a thing and underrates the importance of having something to say.

Low Reliability

The essay test is also usually low in reliability. Since short tests are usually less reliable than long tests (see page 156), the limited sampling, that is the small number of points covered by essay tests, would tend to restrict its reliability. Still more serious is the subjectivity of scoring. Numerous studies have shown that teachers cannot agree with each other in scoring essay tests. Studies have also shown that the same teachers cannot agree with themselves on a second series of values assigned independently to the same papers. Part of this is due to different standards of marking and different weighting of the questions. Certain other factors, such as the physical and mental condition of the person marking the papers, also tend to influence the mark that is assigned to a paper.

In a study[4] made at the University of West Virginia, it was found that "the passing or failing of about 40 per cent depends, not on what they know or do not know, but on *who* reads the papers" and that "the passing or failing of about 10 per cent depends . . . on *when* the papers are read." It has been observed that the grades assigned tend to be greatly influenced by those grades allowed the papers immediately preceding. For example, one writer asserts that, "A *C* paper may be graded *B* if it is read after an illiterate theme, but if it follows an *A* paper, if such can be found, it seems to be of *D* caliber."[5]

This situation is not peculiar to American education. In fact, one writer[6] asserts that evidence showed that the unreliability of essay tests in Europe was "even more serious" than had been revealed many times in America. In support of this conclusion, he says: "In the English studies, examiners were found to reverse their judgments almost completely when asked to mark the same papers they had scored a year before."

Bowles'[7] comments concerning England's examination system for college entrance are illuminating. He concludes that it is quite deficient when judged by American standards of reliability and statistical validity, but that because of various safeguards for the individual, such as regrading of marginal papers, "the system works" well.

In fairness to the essay test, however, it should be pointed out that many of the studies reported have been with unimproved forms given under unfavor-

---

[4]R. R. Ashburn, An experiment in the essay-type question, *Journal of Experimental Education,* 1938, 7, 1–3.

[5]J. M. Stalnaker, The problem of the English examination, *Educational Record,* 1936, 17, Supplement No. 10, 41.

[6]W. C. Ryan, Jr., The seventh world conference of the New Education Fellowship, II, *School and Society,* 1936, 44, 364.

[7]F. H. Bowles, *The College Entrance Examination Board. 51st Annual Report of the Director, 1951* (New York: College Entrance Examination Board, 1952), pp. 23–30.

able conditions. Often, the essay test at its worst has been compared with an improved objective test. Under such conditions, the essay type is bound to show up badly. If objective tests had been scored under similar conditions, without scoring rules or keys, the agreement of the scores would be less impressive. As a matter of fact, even with scoring rules and keys, the agreement among the scores on objective tests marked by amateur scorers is less than perfect. Under highly favorable conditions the agreement among scorers of essay tests may approximate that reported for essentially objective tests. One study[8] reports that the average correlation coefficient between first and second scorings of an essay test in history by three experienced scorers was .98. Another study[9] reports that the median coefficient obtained between two independent readings of certain College Entrance Examination Board tests was .97. The twenty coefficients were above .90, except for English, which was .84. It must be kept in mind, however, that these tests were so worded as to make the scoring more objective than is usually possible with ordinary essay tests. The items were much more specific than the "Discuss the history of Western civilization" type, which is almost impossible to score reliably.

It is significant that most studies having to do with the "reliability" of essay tests deal with between- or within-grader agreement in *marking the examination* and not with the reliability of the *examination* itself. A few studies have been reported of the correlation between two forms of an essay test designed for a particular purpose which were given to the same pupils and carefully marked by experienced examiners. McGregor and Ruch[10] used this procedure in studying eighth-grade tests in 16 subjects from 952 pupils in 11 states. Each paper in the two sets of examinations was marked independently by two experienced teachers. This study made it possible to compare the reliability of the *test* with the agreement in *marking the test*. The agreement of the two independent markings of the same papers is represented by an average correlation of .62, while the agreement of the two sets of examinations marked by the same teacher is represented by an average correlation of only .43. One of Ruch's students, W. E. Gordon,[11] made a similar study of the New York Regents' Examinations with comparable results. He found the average agreement of the two independent markings of the same papers was .72, while the average agreement of the two sets of tests marked by the same teacher was only .42. Another study[12] conducted at the University of Chicago High School showed that two independent sets of marks assigned by two "experienced readers of essay ex-

[8]R. E. Cochran and C. C. Weidemann, Improvement of consistency of scoring the "explain" and "discuss" essay examination, a paper read before Section C of the American Educational Research Association at Cleveland, Ohio, 1 March 1939.

[9]J. M. Stalnaker, Essay examinations reliably read, *School and Society,* 1937, 46, 671–672.

[10]Ruch, *op. cit.,* pp. 91–96.

[11]*Ibid.,* pp. 97–98.

[12]A. E. Traxler and H. A. Anderson, The reliability of an essay examination in English, *School Review,* 1935, 43, 534–539.

aminations" agreed to the extent of .94 on Form A and .84 on Form B, but that the correlation between Form A and Form B was only .60. These three studies illustrate an important point: *Agreement in marking the essay test is higher than the reliability is of the test itself.*

The reliability coefficient of an essay test is the correlation across both graders and comparable forms of the essay test. In simplest form, it is the correlation between Teacher 1's grades for Form A papers with Teacher 2's grades for the Form B papers of those same students. To improve reliability, we would have more than one teacher grade the Form A papers and more than one other teacher grade the Form B papers. We would then find for each pupil his total score on Form A for the, say, *a* teachers who graded the Form A papers, and his total score on Form B for the *b* teachers (different from the Form A graders) who graded Form B. We would then correlate the total scores of the pupils on Form A with their total scores on Form B.

Notice, however, that a student's total score on the two forms, A and B combined, would be more reliable than his total score on Form A or Form B alone. If r_{AB} is the reliability coefficient for either form, A or B, then the reliability coefficient of (A + B) is estimated in the following way: $2r_{AB}/(1 + r_{AB})$. For example, if $r_{AB} = .50$, then $2r_{AB}/(1 + r_{AB}) = 2(.50)/(1 + .50) = .67$. If there were three comparable forms, A, B, and C, each with reliability coefficient .50, the reliability of total scores on all three forms combined, A + B + C, is even higher: $3(.50)/[1 + (3 - 1)(.50)] = .75$. Therefore, *to increase the reliability of essay-test scores, increase the number of graders and/or the number of forms of the test* administered to all pupils. First, however, prepare the forms of the essay test carefully so that the r_{AB} for Teacher 1 grading Form A with Teacher 2 grading Form B will be as high as possible.

There is some as yet unpublished evidence from studies conducted at the Educational Testing Service that when ratings of overall merit of essays are made, a four-point rating scale is most efficient.

Low Usability

The essay test also ranks low in usability (see p. 164). There seems no escape from the fact that this type of test is time consuming, both for the pupil and for the teacher. In fact, the additional expenditure of time and energy over that needed for objective tests is so serious a limitation that the use of essay tests can be justified only if it can be shown that the values realized are commensurate with this investment.

ADVANTAGES
OF THE ESSAY TEST

Even the most enthusiastic advocate of essay tests would scarcely claim their superiority over objective tests on the grounds of reliability or usability. The best that can be hoped for essay tests is that by the use of improved techniques their reliability may approach that of objective tests. Regarding usability, the fact that the questions can be written on the blackboard is an advantage only in those schools which lack duplicating facilities. The reduction in time required to prepare essay tests is more apparent than real, if the work is well done, and any such advantages are more than offset by the extra time required for administering and scoring.

It is apparent that if the use of essay tests is to be justified, it must be in terms of their superior value for certain purposes. What, then, are the unique functions of these tests?

Unfortunately, there is only a little experimental evidence in this area. One study[13] indicated that true-false items did not measure 30–40 per cent of the mental functions measured by improved essay tests. Two similar studies by Cochran and Weidemann[14] compared one-word fact tests with essay tests of the improved "explain" and "discuss" types covering the same material, and concluded that about 40 per cent of the mental functions measured by the latter were not measured by the former. The important question of just what unique mental functions each type of test measures remains to be answered, though the results of these three studies do suggest that essay tests may require somewhat different thinking than is required by certain types of objective-test items. Guilford's distinction between divergent and convergent thinking (see page 178) may be relevant to the issue of essay versus objective tests. If you want novel responses to a question such as "List in two minutes time all the possible uses you can devise for a book," it seems necessary to seek free responses rather than to provide a large number of uses to be checked in some manner. On the other hand, if you want to determine whether or not pupils can reason ingeniously to a single "correct" solution, the multiple-choice format is usually excellent.

Essay tests, as distinguished from short-answer items, are probably not used as much as we generally think they are. Sims,[15] for example, analyzed 458 questions ordinarily classified as being of the essay type and found that fewer than half in the high school and fewer than one in five in the elementary school involved discussion, the others being almost equally divided between simple-recall and short-answer questions requiring not more than one sentence for a response. Such items are probably graded more reliably than essay items, but of course they do not permit the free expression that is generally considered the principal advantage of the essay item.

Several experimental studies have shown that the type of test used by a teacher influences the type of study procedures pupils use. When pupils expect

[13]C. C. Weidemann and L. F. Newens, Does the "compare and contrast" essay test measure the same mental functions as the true-false test? *Journal of General Psychology,* 1933, 9, 430–449.

[14]R. E. Cochran and C. C. Weidemann, "Explain" essay vs. word answer fact test, *Phi Delta Kappan,* 1934, 17, 59–61 & 75, and A study of special types of tests, *Phi Delta Kappan,* 1937, 19, 113-115 & 131.

[15]V. M. Sims, Essay examination questions classified on the basis of objectivity, *School and Society,* 1932, 35, 100–102.

an essay test, they seem more likely to employ such desirable study techniques as making outlines and summaries, and seeking to perceive relationships and trends, than is done when objective tests are used exclusively.

It follows then that neither essay nor objective tests should be used exclusively. From the Hensley-Davis study[16] it appears that teachers believe this, for they prefer to use a combination of the two types.

SUGGESTIONS
FOR IMPROVING
ESSAY TESTS   Although the essay test has been in existence for hundreds of years, the amount of research that has been devoted to it has been far less than that devoted to the objective test, which is comparatively new. Furthermore, much of the research relating to essay tests has been of a negative kind. Its purpose has been only to show how poor unimproved essay examinations are, rather than to find ways to improve them. However, a study of the meager experimental literature available does yield several positive suggestions. In the following sections, we shall consider some of the most promising of these.

*Improving the Construction
and Use of Essay Tests*

     It is just as important to know *when* to use the essay test as it is to know *how* to use it. It is wise to restrict the use of the essay test to the measurement of those organizing and expressive abilities for which it is best adapted. There would usually appear to be no good reason for employing subjective measurement where objective tests measure the same abilities as validly. What, then, does the essay test attempt to do? Several writers have tried to answer that question.

Weidemann[17] distinguished eleven definable types of improved essay tests. Arranged in a series from simple to complex, these types are as follows: (1) *what, who, when, which,* and *where;* (2) *list;* (3) *outline;* (4) *describe;* (5) *contrast;* (6) *compare;* (7) *explain;* (8) *discuss;* (9) *develop;* (10) *summarize;* and (11) *evaluate.* The first two types seem almost the same as items of the objective type. The others appear to permit freer responses.

Years ago, Monroe and Carter classified[18] essay questions into 20 types.

---

[16]I. H. Hensley and R. A. Davis, What high-school teachers think and do about their examinations, *Educational Administration and Supervision*, 1952, 38, 219–228.

[17]C. C. Weidemann, Written examination procedures, *Phi Delta Kappan*, 1933, 16, 78–83; also, C. C. Weidemann, Review of essay test studies, *Journal of Higher Education*, 1941, 12, 41–44.

[18]W. S. Monroe and R. E. Carter, The use of different types of thought questions in secondary schools and their relative difficulty for students. Urbana, Illinois: Bureau of Educational Research Bulletin, Number 14, University of Illinois, 1923.

These types, together with sample questions from the field of measurement and some discussion, appear below:

1. *Selective recall—basis given*
   Name three important developments in measurement that occurred during the first decade of the twentieth century.
2. *Evaluation recall—basis given*
   Name the three persons who have had the greatest influence on the development of intelligence testing.
3. *Comparison of two things—on a single designated basis*
   Compare essay tests and objective tests from the standpoint of their effect on the study procedures used by the learner.
4. *Comparison of two things—in general*
   Compare standardized and non-standardized tests.
5. *Decision—for or against*
   In which, in your opinion, can you do better, oral or written examinations? Why?

Score for its truth and logical relevance the evidence offered in support of the decision. There is no justification for scoring the *opinion,* since it was asked for and given.

Sometimes this kind of question appears as "What is your favorite X and why?" In this case nothing is scorable but the mechanics of composition. Notice that "why" is ambiguous because it may call either for an account of the student's psychological development or for a list of qualities of X that have special appeal for him.

6. *Cause or effects*
   How do you account for the popularity of objective tests during the last 50 years?
7. *Explanation of the use or exact meaning of some word, phrase, or statement in a passage*
   What is the meaning of "objective" in the above question?
8. *Summary of some unit of the text or of some article read*
   Summarize in not more than one page the advantages and limitations of essay tests.

A comment on the meaning of "summary" may be helpful. If a pupil responds with a mass of detail, yet omits the main ideas that the details support, he has not responded adequately; the ability to summarize is a manifestation of a high order of thinking, and a properly scored summary item should have considerable discriminating power with respect to degree of understanding of the matters involved.

Our example above is faulty in that it specifies a quantity of verbiage ("one page"). When this is the case, there is a tendency on the part of the scorer to evaluate in terms of the quantitative requirement, and on the part of the pupil to respond in terms of it. The same comment is applicable to attempts to "limit" the *discuss*-type question (No. 14, below). A glib student, acquainted with the possibilities of the English language, can use five words where two would do, thereby meeting the requirement of "in not less than 300 words."

EXAMPLE: Discuss X in not less than 300 and not more than 500 words.

"In my opinion, for whatever it may be worth, which probably is not very much in view of the fact that I was not present at the time and have no direct knowledge of the central issue involved in the controversy between the contending parties. . ."

This means no more than "I have no justification for thinking that . . . ," but it achieves 45 of the desired 300 words instead of just seven.

9. *Analysis (The word itself seldom appears in the question.)*
   Why are many so-called "progressive educators" suspicious of standardized tests?
10. *Statement of relationships*
    Why is it that nearly all essay tests, regardless of the school subject, tend to a considerable extent to be measures of the learner's mastery of English?
11. *Illustrations or examples (the pupils's own) of principles in science, construction in language, etc.*
12. *Classification*
    What type of error appears in the following test item? "With what country did the United States fight during World War II?"
13. *Application of rules, laws, or principles to new situations*
    In the light of experience in the United States with examinations for selecting college students, what public-relations problems would you expect to arise in England because of the Age 11+ examinations there?
14. *Discussion*
    Discuss the role of Sir Francis Galton in the development of the Pearson product-moment coefficient of correlation, *r.*
15. *Statement of aim—author's purpose in his selection or organization of material*
    Why are individual mental tests not treated in greater detail in this book?
16. *Criticism—as to the adequacy, correctness, or relevancy of a printed statement, or a classmate's answer to a question on the lesson*
    Criticize or defend the statement, "The essay test overrates the importance of knowing *how* to say a thing and underrates the importance of having something to say." "To criticize" assumes a set of standards given or known. Many persons are under the impression that it means "Tell something good about and tell something bad about, but mostly good, so that it will be constructive." Teachers should not foster this misconception. For further clarification, see Bloom and others.[19]
17. *Outline*
    Outline the principal steps in the construction of an informal teacher-made test.
18. *Reorganization of facts (a good type of review question to give training in organization)*
    Name ten practical suggestions from this book that are particularly applicable to the subject you teach or plan to teach.
19. *Formulation of new questions—problems and questions raised*
    What are some problems relating to the use of essay tests that require further study?

---

[19] B. S. Bloom and others, *Taxonomy of educational objectives* (New York: Longmans, Green, 1956), pp. 185–200.

20. *New methods of procedure*
    Suggest a plan for proving the truth or falsity of the contention that exemption from semester examinations for the ablest students is a good policy in high school.
21. *Inferential thinking*
    Is the author of this book likely to use essay tests frequently in *his* measurement classes?

Notice that the classifications by Weidemann and by Monroe and Carter distinguish a considerable number of rather distinct abilities that can be measured by essay tests. Teachers should study each type of essay question carefully until they are familiar with its distinguishing characteristics.

There is some evidence that a more valid sampling of the pupil's knowledge can be obtained by increasing the number of questions and reducing the length of discussion expected on each. In many cases, a well-constructed paragraph is a sufficient answer. Very few discussions need exceed one or two pages in length. In any case, the question should be so worded as to restrict the responses toward the objective which is to be measured. For example, the question, "Explain the reasons for the strike at Consolidated Electronics in 1964," is too general and would be improved if it were restricted by the addition of the phrases "to show (a) the labor grievances of the employees; (b) the practices of the employer; (c) related national, social, and economic factors; (d) the rival labor unions; and (e) the method of striking." It must be recognized, however, that such suggestions take away some of the uniqueness of the traditional essay examination in that they improve its reliability by the obvious device of making it more like the objective test.

Many teachers, especially beginning teachers, believe that the essay test is the easiest kind to construct. As a matter of fact, *it is probably more difficult to construct essay tests of high quality than it is to construct objective tests of high quality.* Much care and thought must be given to their construction, if they are to measure anything but mere memory for factual knowledge. Many of the general principles of testing outlined in earlier chapters are as applicable to essay tests as to objective tests, and the special suggestions of this chapter should help you devise questions above the rote-knowledge level. Finally, there is always the risk that, in attempting to phrase essay questions so that they can be answered more specifically and scored more objectively, the results may not even be as good as an out-and-out objective test. In any case, it is especially important that the test be critically reviewed, with the help of a colleague's judgment, if possible.

Preparing Students
to Take Essay Tests

A number of writers have emphasized the importance of training students to take examinations of all kinds. This training can be done well in classrooms by teachers. Wider experience and training in preparing for and in taking tests of all types is likely to increase the accuracy of measurement and therefore the fairness of scores for the students tested. In the essay, pupils should be taught the meanings of the words used in the various types of thought questions. They should be taught that "Compare" requires a statement of similarities *and* differences and that their answer to such an item is not complete if it omits either. "Contrast" requires only a statement of differences. "Compare and contrast" is therefore incorrect. This sort of thing is of much more educational value than the emphasis upon certain mechanics in the appearance of the paper.

By way of summary, three important suggestions for the construction and use of essay examinations are as follows:

1. Restrict the use of the essay *test*, a measuring instrument whose results are *graded*, to those functions to which it is best adapted. When it is not clear that the essay-type test is required for measuring the desired objectives, use an objective test. This does not rule out the use of ungraded essay *exercises*, however, for instructional purposes.

2. Increase the number of questions asked and reduce the amount of discussion required on each. Always indicate clearly the type of response desired.

3. Make definite provisions for teaching pupils how to take examinations. Specific training in preparing for and in taking tests and examinations of the various types commonly encountered is a legitimate objective of instruction. Perhaps the best way is to find or devise good practice tests, administer them, and discuss the results with the students.

IMPROVING THE GRADING OR RATING OF ESSAY TESTS

There is a distinction between the terms *scoring* and *grading*. Scoring is an objective process of counting right or wrong responses, whereas grading always means interpreting quality subjectively in terms of some criterion. Strictly speaking, then, it is more correct to speak of grading or rating essay examinations than it is to speak of scoring them.

All claims made for the value of the essay test as a measuring instrument are, of course, based on the assumption that the papers can be read accurately. For example, not only must the essay test *call forth* from superior pupils responses which are consistently superior, but the teachers marking the papers must be able to *recognize* consistently that they are superior responses. The same is true of responses with other degrees of merit. The grading of the essay examination, therefore, occupies a strategic position.

To begin with, certain preventive measures are important. A careful wording of the questions and directions to the pupil that indicate clearly just what type of response is expected will simplify the problem of marking the papers.

The use of optional questions should be discouraged,[20] because each student should take the *same* test as any other student if their scores are to be compared. The simple precaution of having the pupil record his name inconspicuously either on the back or at the end of the paper, rather than at the top of each page, is likely to decrease the bias with which the paper is graded.

Cochran and Weidemann[21] outline a procedure for evaluating essay examinations, the essentials of which can be taught in ten minutes. This is shown by the fact that the majority of the consistency coefficients of two series of scorings made five weeks apart were between .80 and .90 for teachers with ten minutes of training. Independent scores by experienced readers showed an average agreement of .98 when the procedure given below in a slightly modified and abridged form was used. (Much depends on the particular questions used and on situational factors, such as heterogeneity of the group of students, however; *r*'s *far* lower than these sometimes result, despite the teacher's best efforts.)

SUGGESTIONS FOR MARKING ESSAY EXAMINATIONS

(After Cochran and Weidemann)

1. I read over a sampling of the papers to obtain a general idea of the grade of answer I may expect.
2. I score one question through all of the papers before I consider another question. I have found two outstanding advantages in scoring one question through an entire set of papers. The first is that the comparison of answers appears to make the grades more exact and just. The second is that having to keep only one list of points in mind saves time and promotes accuracy.
3. Before scoring any papers I read the material in the text which covers the questions, and also the lecture notes on the subject.
4. I make a list of the main points which should be discussed in every answer. Each of these points must be weighed and assigned a certain value if the scoring is to approach accuracy. This value assigned to the main points needed for a reasonably adequate answer is designated as the minimum score. If a pupil elaborates and discusses points not required yet pertinent to the question, his answer is given an additional value, called the extra score. This extra score may vary for different pupils, but may not exceed a certain set maximum.
5. After the points have been weighed, the actual scoring begins. I read the answer through once and then check back over it for fact details. I attempt to mark every historical mistake on the paper and write in briefly the correction. As I read the answer I make a mental note of the points omitted and the value of each point, so that when the end of the question is reached, I have the minimum grade figured. If there is any additional or extra percentage to be given, it is added to the minimum score, and then the value of the question is written in terms of the per cent deducted rather than the positive per cent. Then when every question on a paper is scored, it is a simple matter to add the negative quantities and obtain the final grade.

---

[20] J. M. Stalnaker, The essay type of examination, *op. cit.,* pp. 505–506.
[21] R. E. Cochran and C. C. Weidemann, *op. cit.*

It is difficult to overemphasize the importance of three things: (1) the preparing in advance of a list of answers which are considered adequate for the objectives of the test; (2) the assigning of a specific value to each essential part of the answers; and (3) the grading of one question through all the papers before going on to another question. Most students of the problem recommend attempting to distinguish a relatively small number of degrees of merit in an answer. Perhaps as good a plan as any is to allow credit for each part of the answer considered essential to a question as follows: 4 for excellent, 3 for good, 2 for fair, 1 for inferior, and 0 for an omission or wrong reply. Stalnaker[22] found that the weighting of essay questions (i.e., giving more points for some than for others) was of negligible value, the correlation between weighted and unweighted scores on the College Entrance Board Examinations varying from .97 to .997.

Grading by Sorting

In addition to the points made by Cochran and Weidemann, several specialists have found another suggestion helpful. The suggestion is to make a sorting of the papers into three to five piles, according to the merit of the discussion of each question on the basis of a brief preliminary examination of the answers. Sims describes one such procedure as follows:[23]

1. Quickly read through the papers and on the basis of your opinion of their worth, sort them into five groups as follows: (a) very superior papers, (b) superior papers, (c) average papers, (d) inferior papers, (e) very inferior papers.
2. Reread the papers in each group and shift any that you feel have been misplaced.

Flanagan[24] has shown that when the ability being measured is normally distributed, the optimum percentages for five groups are 9, 20, 42, 20, and 9. Therefore, about 10 per cent of the papers might be called "very superior" and 10 per cent "very inferior." Twenty per cent would be "superior" and a like percentage would be "inferior." The remaining 40 per cent are "average." These are rough approximations, of course, dependent upon the ability level of the particular student group being graded.

The preliminary sorting of the papers into piles of approximately equal merit before assigning numerical values to them will help to avoid the difficulty pointed out by Stalnaker: namely, that the values allowed a paper are often greatly influenced by the merit of the paper which happens immediately to precede it in the order of scoring. It is also easier to locate papers distinctly out

---

[22] J. M. Stalnaker, Weighting questions in the essay-type examination, *Journal of Educational Psychology,* 1938, 29, 481–490.

[23] V. M. Sims, The objectivity, reliability, and validity of an essay examination graded by rating, *Journal of Educational Research,* 1931, 24, 216–223.

[24] J. C. Flanagan, The effectiveness of short methods for calculating correlation coefficients, *Psychological Bulletin,* 1952, 49, 342–348.

of line with those in a particular group supposedly of similar quality. It is a good idea to throw the papers into a single group after each question has been evaluated and before they are re-sorted into piles according to the merits of the discussions of the next question. This procedure will make it easier to conceal the identity of the particular pupil whose paper is being judged and so to avoid one of the most disturbing factors in marking essay examinations.

The Role of English Composition

Each teacher should adopt a policy regarding what factors shall be considered, and what factors shall not be considered, in evaluating a written examination. *Only those factors should be taken into account which afford evidence of the degree to which the pupil has attained the objectives set up for that particular course.* Except in English classes, this may rule out making arbitrary reductions for such things as faulty sentence structure, paragraphing, handwriting, and the spelling of nontechnical words. These factors will be considered only when they affect the clarity of the pupil's discussion. It is always legitimate to hold the pupil responsible for the spelling, as well as the meaning, of the vocabulary that is peculiar to the course.

This does not mean that the quality of the written English used in examinations is unimportant and should therefore be disregarded. On the contrary, it is always very important. But it should be considered only in relation to that for which it may be accepted as valid evidence: namely, in determination of the pupil's mark in English. Where the teacher has complete charge of an entire grade, this adjustment is easy to make. But where the school is departmentalized the problem is more difficult. Even here it should be possible to work out a system whereby at intervals the papers in other subjects, after having been graded as to content, may be turned over to the English teacher to be judged from the viewpoint of their merits as English compositions. In this way it may be possible to sample the pupil's characteristic performance in written English better than when he writes a paper specifically for the English teacher. And, what is equally important, it makes the pupil's mark in other subjects more nearly a measure of achievement in those subjects, rather than to a considerable extent a measure of skill in English composition.

NOT AN EITHER-OR SITUATION

Despite its critics, who have found a number of valid objections to essay tests as often employed, it seems likely that such tests are here to stay. As teachers, you can use them wisely as an essential *part* of your measuring and evaluating equipment. You will not be misled into abandoning objective tests because of the attacks by well-intended persons, among them several college professors, in professional and popular magazines and in books.[25] During 1961 these assaults

---

[25] Among these, see B. Hoffman, *The tyranny of testing* (New York: Crowell-Collier, 1962).

against objective testing became so virulent that Henry Chauncey, President of the nonprofit Educational Testing Service in Princeton, New Jersey, made clarification of the role of objective tests the central theme of his 1960–61 Annual Report. There he showed the relationship of standardized tests to the objectives of education: supplementing the teacher's instructional tools rather than supplanting them or changing the goals of the school. His comments are applicable also to objective tests that the teacher prepares locally. Properly constructed objective tests can measure the attainment of a considerable number of educational objectives well.

Some persons who wish to abolish objective testing may be confusing testing with teaching. The two are related, of course, but not completely. Compositions, essays, and discussion questions that prove to be poor *tests* may nevertheless be worthwhile *exercises*. If the teacher goes through the material carefully and makes constructive remarks, perhaps followed by oral discussion of the paper, the student may be benefited greatly even though no grade is assigned—perhaps partly *because* none is. If, on the other hand, the teacher merely marks the paper "A," "B," or the like without commenting, his grading may be highly unreliable and, to boot, the student probably will not have learned how to improve his next paper. It is possible to do both, grading and commenting, in which event the comments may be helpful[26] even if the grading is unreliable.

RECOMMENDED READINGS

Advocate of Writing Sample puts judgment to the test, *ETS Developments,* Jan. 1963, 11, 2.

College Board Review, Reading conference, 1953, No. 19, 324–326.

Composition test shows high validity on reliable criterion of writing ability, *ETS Developments,* Jan. 1963, 11, pp. 1, 4.

Dressel, P. L. and Nelson, C. H., Testing and grading policies, pp. 227–252 in P. L. Dressel, ed., *Evaluation in higher education.* Boston: Houghton Mifflin, 1961.

Flanagan, J. C. The use of comprehensive rationales in test development, *Educational and Psychological Measurement,* 1951, 11, 151–155.

Kostick, M. M. and Nixon, Belle M., How to improve oral questioning, *Peabody Journal of Education,* 1953, 30, 209–217.

Odell, C. W., *How to improve classroom testing.* Dubuque, Iowa: Wm. C. Brown Company, 1958. Chs. V and VI, "Discussion of essay examinations" and "Short-answer tests: general."

Palmer, O., Sense or nonsense? The objective testing of English composition, *English Journal,* 1961, 50, 314–320.

---

[26] E. B. Page, Teacher comments and student performance: a seventy-four classroom experiment in school motivation, *Journal of Educational Psychology,* 1958, 49, 173–181.

Remmers, H. H., Gage, N. L., and Rummel, H. F., *A practical introduction to measurement and evaluation.* New York: Harper, 1960. Chapter 8, "Constructing teacher-made tests."

Stalnaker, J. M., The essay type of examination, Ch. 13 in E. F. Lindquist, ed., *Educational measurement.* Washington, D. C.: American Council on Education, 1951.

Stecklein, J. E., Essay tests: why and how? *Bulletin on Classroom Testing* No. 2, Bureau of Institutional Research, University of Minnesota, Minneapolis, 1955.

Torgerson, W. S. and Green, B. F., Jr., The factor analysis of subject matter experts, *Journal of Educational Psychology,* 1952, 43, 354–363.

SELF-REPORTS AND REPORTS BY OTHERS

"Who was the third President of the United States?" Historians agree that Thomas Jefferson was, so if you respond "Thomas Jefferson" you are correct. "Do you like spinach?" There is no "right" answer to that question, although it *might* be found that high-school science teachers who answer it "Yes" tend to be rated by their principals as being more intelligent than those who say "No." This illustrates the difference between *a priori* keying of responses and empirical keying. We know in advance that the keyed answers for the first question will be "right" for Thomas Jefferson and "wrong" for anything else. We cannot in advance designate an always-right answer for the spinach-preference question, because there are no generally correct or incorrect responses in this matter of personal preference. An in-between type of question, keyed in advance, would be "How well do you like spinach? Loathe it. Dislike it. Indifferent. Like it. Love it." Scores for the five responses would be 0, 1, 2, 3 or 4.

A third type of question partakes of both

C H A P T E R   N I N E

the knowledge aspect of the president question and the self-report nature of the spinach query. If you ask an acquaintance, "Have you ever lived in Chicago, Illinois?", his "Yes" response may be correct or incorrect. Either he did live in Chicago or he didn't, but you may find it difficult to verify his statement. This sets you to speculating about his memory and motives, and that may lead you to seek reports about him from others who know him better. If several persons who have known him all his life assure you that he has always lived near them, far from Chicago, probably you will mark his "Yes" response "wrong" unless you suspect their motives. The correct answer to a self-report question depends on the person queried, whereas the correct answer to an ability question is the same for all respondents and depends on the agreement of the authorities who developed the key.

Many evaluative devices involve self-reports or reports by others. Among the former are interest inventories, personality inventories, attitude scales, questionnaires, aptitude indices, projective techniques, and interviews. Chief among the latter are procedures, including sociometry, for rating, ranking, or comparing others. Although the names sound dissimilar, a common difficulty runs through all such methods: they are situationally unstable. Much more usually depends on who reported, when, where and for what purposes, than is the case for "ability" measures. (This instability arises in part from the instability of what is measured, i.e., the attitudes, interests, etc.)

For instance, your reported liking for classical music during an interview for a summer position in a music store may differ greatly from what you would tell a close friend, whereas very likely your score on an "ability" test of music vocabulary would not be affected much by your desire for employment, unless you were forewarned and could "cram" for the test. It is necessary only that you have enough motivation to take the vocabulary test conscientiously in order to reveal your knowledge. Even large inducements simply won't compensate for lack of information about fugues and Bach.

It is helpful to define ability tests as those *a priori* keyed tests on which one cannot fake a high (i.e., favorable) score, although of course one can fake a low score (i.e., deliberately score poorly on the test). On self-report devices one can usually fake in either direction: we tell the music-store owner that we prefer classical music, while we tell our friends that we prefer jazz, when in fact we dislike both forms, actually preferring folk music. Some test specialists would point out that sometimes a perceptive student deliberately answers an item on an ability test incorrectly in order to have his response scored as being correct, as when a misinformed teacher insists that the third president was James Madison; but this is merely faulty keying. (Few students nowadays would let their teachers get away with so obvious an error as this for long.) Also, some self-report and other-report devices are fairly resistant to extreme faking; the individual being tested cannot ascertain readily what the teacher is trying to assess. Properly constructed and administered ability tests yield measures of well-motivated performance, whereas self-report devices more nearly reflect desire to conform to the special situation, as perceived by the examinee, because self-report devices do not lend themselves to intrinsic right-wrong scoring. Liking spinach may be "right" for one purpose and "wrong" for another, whereas the correct spelling of "separate" is independent of the context in which the word appears. This distinction has important implications, as we shall see below while discussing various self-report and other-report devices. You are encouraged to reread Chapter Two, where a discussion of historical background appears, before going further in this chapter.

VOCATIONAL INTEREST INVENTORIES

Two vocational interest inventories have dominated the field for many years: the Strong Vocational Interest Blank (VIB) for Men[1] and the Kuder Preference Record— Vocational.[2]

Strong Vocational Interest Blank for Men

The Strong inventory, which dates from 1925,[3] was designed to discriminate successful men in a given occupational group from men in general. Most of its 400 items require the individual to indicate

---

[1] E. K. Strong, *Vocational Interest Blank for Men: Manual* (Palo Alto, Calif.: Consulting Psychologists Press).

[2] G. F. Kuder, *Kuder Preference Record—Vocational* (Chicago: Science Research Associates).

[3] See Footnote 90 on page 45.

his preference by marking a phrase D for "dislike," I for "indifferent," or L for "like," as in the following three artificial examples (not from the VIB itself):

Moving a piano	D	I	L
Multiplying one number by another	D	I	L
Purchasing a new automobile	D	I	L

How *should* successful mechanical engineers, say, respond to "Moving a piano"? We might *infer* (that is, make a shrewd guess) from their known characteristics that more of them than of men in general would mark it *L,* but only actual data will tell us whether or not they in fact do. Suppose that we took a random sample of 500 male mechanical engineers from all successful male mechanical engineers in the United States and asked them this question. Suppose also that we took a random sample of 500 male college-graduate non-engineers of about the same ages as the engineers and asked them the question. If all 1000 responded, we would have a 2 × 3 table such as Table 9-1.

TABLE 9-1

Responses of 500 Successful Male Mechanical Engineers
and 500 Male College Graduates to "Moving a Piano" (Hypothetical Data)

Group	D(islike)	I(ndifferent)	L(ike)	Totals
Mechanical Engineers	100	150	250	500
Men-in-General	300	150	50	500
Totals	400	300	300	1000

Scoring weights for mechanical-engineer scale
D: $(100 - 300)/400 = -1/2$
I : $(150 - 150)/300 = 0$
L : $(250 - 50)/300 = 2/3$

We notice that one-half of the engineers (250 out of 500) said they like moving a piano, while only one-tenth of the college-graduate men-in-general (50 out of 500) did. Therefore, if *you* respond with *L* to "Moving a piano," you have marked the item more like mechanical engineers than like college-graduate men-in-general.

What if you mark *I*? Thirty per cent of the engineers (150 out of 500) and 30 per cent of the men-in-general did, so this item gives no evidence of your being more like one than like the other. What if you mark *D*? One-fifth of the engineers and three-fifths of the men-in-general did, so you are more like men-in-general than like successful male mechanical engineers.

A simple scoring scheme would be to give *D* a weight of $(100 - 300)/400 = -\frac{1}{2}$ points for engineers. *I* would get a weight of $(150 - 150)/300 = 0$ points for engineers, and *L* would get $(250 - 50)/300 = 2/3$ points. [With this scheme, the largest possible score weights would be -1 and 1, because $(0 - 400)/400 = -1$ and $(400 - 0)/400 = 1$.]

Therefore, if you marked *D*, you would be credited with $-\frac{1}{2}$ points for the mechanical engineer scale. If you marked *I*, you would receive 0 points for the mechanical engineer scale. If you marked *L*, you would receive 2/3 points for the mechanical engineer scale. This is not Strong's scoring procedure, but it is a simple illustration of empirical keying.

Each item is scored again and again, once for each occupational scale to which it contributes. Scoring weights are determined by the discrepancies between the markings of the professional group and of men-in-general. Strong and others have found scoring weights for more than 45 occupations for men and 25 on the women's form. The VIB for men is generally considered to be superior in quality to the form for women, probably because it was prepared more carefully. For occupations where women compete directly with men, it may be desirable to administer the men's form to women, rather than using the women's form.

Whenever empirical or criterion keying, such as discussed above, is employed, one must plan in advance to cross-validate his keying of the scales in order to determine whether or not he is doing more than merely capitalizing on the peculiar characteristics of the occupational samples he has drawn. This might be done by having 1000 engineers and 1000 men-in-general initially. A random 500 of each group would be used to establish one set of weights for the items. These weights would then be tried on the other two 500's to see how well they "work." Similarly, weights might be obtained for the second two 500's and tried out on the first two 500's. The schematic illustration of such double cross-validation is shown in Figure 9-1. Further details are too complex to be included in this book.[4]

Kuder Preference Record—Occupational

The KPR[5] differs from the SVIB in its method of construction. The KPR-O consists of 100 sets of three phrases each, of the "You like most to . . ." variety, such as this actual item (No. 6):

R. Play a game that requires mental arithmetic
S. Play checkers
T. Work mechanical puzzles

---

[4]See Symposium: The need and means of cross-validation, in *Educational and Psychological Measurement*, 1951, 11, 5–28, particularly the papers by C. I. Mosier, Problems and designs of cross-validation (pp. 5–11) and R. A. Katzell, Cross-validation of item analysis (pp. 16–22). Before you study this symposium, however, be sure to read the classic satire by E. E. Cureton, Validity, reliability, and baloney, *Educational and Psychological Measurement*, 1950, 10, 94–96.

[5]This KPR for males only, more recent than the KPR-Vocational or the KPR-Personal, includes items representing all 15 of the vocational and personal areas covered by those forms. See the *Manual for the Kuder Preference Record—Occupational*, Form D (Chicago: Science Research Associates).

The examinee is to indicate which one of the three activities he likes most, and which one he likes least. This is equivalent to ranking the three activities in order of preference, because obviously the one he does not mark ranks in the middle. Each of the 100 KPR-O items has this forced-choice triad (three-part) form.

There are 120 different combinations of 3 things each taken from 10 things $[(10 \cdot 9 \cdot 8)/(3 \cdot 2 \cdot 1) = 120]$, so with 10 different phrases one can create 120 sets of three phrases each. On the other hand, if each phrase differs from every other phrase, you need $3 \times 100 = 300$ phrases to yield 100 triadic items. Most of the KPR-O phrases are different.

How are responses scored? Let us examine the scoring of the above item for five keys. First, this item does not contribute to the Verification (sincerity vs. faking) scale. Not surprisingly, by empirical scoring you get 1 point on the bank cashier scale if you most like to "Play a game that requires mental arithmetic." You get 1 point on the Librarian scale if you most like to "Play checkers." You get 1 point on the "X-ray Technician" scale if you most like to "Work mechanical puzzles." You get 1 point on the Pharmaceutical Salesman scale

Figure 9-1. *Schematic illustration of double cross-validation: scoring weights from each half applied to the other. Engineers and men-in-general randomly chosen.*

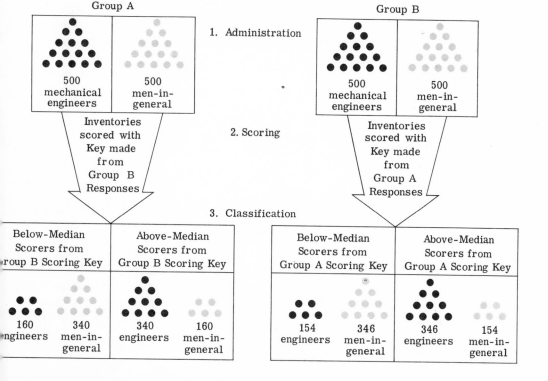

if you *least* like to "Work mechanical puzzles." Thus these four occupational scales use four of the six possible like-most and like-least responses to the item. Other scales probably use the like-least responses for mental arithmetic and checkers, too.

There are 100 items to be marked. Your total score on a scale is merely the total number of points you receive. There are 119 holes in the Bank Cashier scoring stencil, but no one can earn a score as high as that because in a number of items two "Mosts" or two "Least" markings are keyed, but the examinee is instructed to mark just one "Most" and one "Least" in each triad. Scores of 61 or higher are extremely characteristic of bank cashiers, as contrasted with the men-in-general group. The Librarian scoring stencil has 146 holes, with 63 points or more indicating close resemblance to male librarians in the way that they react to KPR-O items.

In the cross-validation group, only 20 per cent of the men-in-general score above the cutting point of the Librarian scale when the cutting point between men-in-general and male librarians who like their work is halfway between the means of these groups. This shows that high scores on the Librarian scale are much more characteristic of such male librarians than of men-in-general. The chief methodological difference between Strong's approach and Kuder's forced-choice scheme is that the former uses a considerable number of rating-scale type items that one may mark as he pleases—all *L*, for instance, or all *I*—whereas the latter uses a ranking-type triadic item that may be more resistant to response sets caused by the tendency to prefer one category on a rating scale. Kuder says in effect, "Mark exactly 100 'Mosts,' one per item, and exactly 100 'Leasts,' one per item." Strong does not say, "Mark one-third of the 400 items *D*, one-third *I*, and one-third *L*," although he does use some forced-choice items elsewhere in the VIB.

The Strong VIB has the advantage of long development and much research. Standardization of the Kuder PR-O utilizes much more recent occupational groups. Probably there will be comparative studies to determine which, if either, discriminates substantially better.

PERSONALITY
INVENTORIES   Another frequently-used self-report device is the personality inventory. For an example of this, let us look at the widely used Mental Health Analysis, Elementary (Grades 4–8),[6] which is one of the paper-and-pencil personality inventories constructed and keyed along "common-sense" lines. It consists of 200 questions to be answered *Yes* or *No* and yields 10 scores, five for "Mental Health Assets" and five for freedom from "Mental Health Liabilities." The Assets are Close Personal Relationships, Inter-Personal Skills, Social Participation, Satisfying

---

[6] Published by the California Test Bureau. Illustrative items are from the 1959 revision.

Work and Recreation, and Adequate Outlook and Goals. The Liabilities are Behavioral Immaturity, Emotional Instability, Feelings of Inadequacy, Physical Defects, and Nervous Manifestations. Each score is based on the responses to 20 questions, so the five-Assets score is based on 100 questions, as is the five-Liabilities score. The first, 100th, and 200th questions are as follows: Do your folks usually let you have some of the friends you want? (Close Personal Relationships); Are you bothered with eye strain? (Nervous Manifestations); Do you believe that most people spend too little time playing? (Adequate Goals and Outlooks). The desired (i.e., positively keyed) responses to these questions are *Yes, No,* and *Yes,* respectively.

Individual items of paper-and-pencil personality inventories may be of more value to the teacher or counselor in suggesting "leads" for further study —tentative hypotheses about the pupil—than are the subscores and total score as measures of mental health. A number of things plague us when we try to treat self-report items in the same way that we consider ability items.

1. One, already mentioned, is situational instability. We cannot tell from the manual of the Mental Health Analysis how stable its scores are from one time to another, for the only "reliability" coefficients reported "were computed by using the Kuder-Richardson formula 21" (p. 5 of the *MHA Manual*), which deals with the *internal* consistency of the inventory scores.

2. Even when responses are stable, however, they may be invalid each time, because of untruthfulness, lack of self-insight, or atypical interpretation of words such as "often," "usually," "some," and "most."

3. We may be a little uneasy about how legitimate it is to add together points from items as different as these which appear in the Physical Defects scale; for example: "Do you think your hair is too straight or too curly to look nice?" "Are you troubled because something is the matter with your arms or hands?" "Are you troubled about the size of your mouth?" In other words, do these items measure the same thing?

4. Closely related to this is the question of whether items are in the right subtests. For instance, "Do you seem to catch cold very easily?" contributes to the Nervous Manifestations score, rather than to Physical Defects.

5. Also, there is the matter of keying each response right or wrong, either by "common-sense" agreement of several persons, or in terms of an outside criterion. The Mental Health Analysis items were keyed in the former way, judgmentally.

6. All Assets items are keyed *Yes,* while all Liabilities items are keyed *No* in order that high scores on assets will have the same meaning as high scores on Liabilities (that is, freedom from Liabilities). If a person has a tendency to mark most questions *Yes,* perhaps without even reading them, he will score high on Assets and low on freedom from Liabilities, meaning that he has a large number of both assets and liabilities. Similarly, if he marks mostly *No,* he will appear to have few assets (low score) and few liabilities (high score).

Such response sets would result in a negative correlation of the assets and liabilities scores.

There are, however, technical methods for meeting these problems:

1. A personality inventory can be administered twice to the same individuals after a *short* interval of time, perhaps with the order of the items rearranged the second time. Then the correlation between scores the first and second times tells us how stable they are. If scores fluctuate wildly from one time to another, they cannot be useful. (Many self-report devices can be expected to show considerable fluctuation in scores over a short period of time because of actual fluctuations in the individual, even when errors of measurement and situationally distorting aspects are small.)

2. Various "lie" scales have been devised for personality inventories. The usual procedure is to insert items to which a particular response very likely indicates intent to deceive, such as "Have you ever been somewhat unhappy at any time?" Since every mortal has his unhappy moments, however fleeting they may be, a "No" response to this question would be suspect. It follows, then, that answers to other items may also be suspect.

3 and 4. Each item in a homogeneous subtest should have a higher "true" correlation with each item in that subtest than with any item in any other subtest. Various ways exist for resolving a group of items into maximally homogeneous subtests.[7] That the problem is not simple will be apparent when you note that an astronomically large number of different sets of 10 subtests, each containing 20 items, can be formed from 200 items, that number being 181 followed by 182 zeroes. Even then, the 10 most homogeneous subtests that can be formed from a particular set of 200 items may not be very homogeneous when cross-validated, and some of the subtests may differ little from others in what they measure. Another approach is to ask how many subtests of at least a specified degree of homogeneity can be formed from the 200 items. The number might be appreciably different from 10.

5. The simplest way to check the judgmental (i.e., a priori) keying of personality items is to ask several competent persons to key them independently and then determine how well they agree. This may represent a pooling of ignorance or bias, but at least it can reveal disagreements. Empirical keying against an outside criterion (something other than the inventory items themselves) may be useful in certain situations, such as developing a test to predict insurance-selling ability or success in college, but it is less helpful in the personality area, where the available criteria usually aren't excellent themselves.

6. A number of attempts to negate the effects of response sets have been made.[8]

---

[7]Loevinger, Jane; Gleser, Goldine C.; and DuBois, P. H., Maximizing the discriminating power of a multiple-score test, *Psychometrika,* 1953, 18, 309–317.

[8]For example, see S. Messick, Separate set and content scores for personality and attitude scales, *Educational and Psychological Measurement,* 1961, 21, 915–923.

The most thoroughly developed paper-and-pencil adjustment inventory is the Minnesota Multiphasic Personality Inventory (MMPI), which first appeared in 1940.[9] Its items are declarative sentences with which the individual either agrees or disagrees. Scores are secured for a number of psychiatric categories (depression, hypochondriasis, schizophrenia, etc.) and for masculine vs. feminine interests. A tremendous amount of research and re-analysis of the MMPI has taken place since its appearance. Because the MMPI is a complex instrument that requires highly trained admnistrators and interpreters, we shall not discuss it further here. It has been widely used at the college level, but only rarely in the elementary and secondary schools. A good, brief description of its rationale and items is given by Nunnally.[10]

ATTITUDE SCALES   In the 1920's at the University of Chicago, Louis Thurstone and his students and colleagues[11] developed techniques for constructing scales to ascertain various "attitudes" (e.g., toward God, war, Negroes). Such scales, with modifications, persist to the present day. (We presented Thurstone's attitude-toward-movies scale on pages 42-44.) The Thurstone-Chave experimental "attitude toward the church" scale is illustrated in the following extract from their work. Mark those statements in the manner prescribed, *now*.

EXPERIMENTAL STUDY OF ATTITUDE TOWARD THE CHURCH[12]

This is an experimental study of the distribution of attitude toward the church. You will be asked to read a list of statements about the church and to indorse those that express your own sentiment. Let your own experience with churches determine your indorsements.
1.   Name _____
     (You need not sign your name, if you prefer to give your opinions anonymously.)
2.   Group _____
3.   Underline your classification:
     Freshman, Sophomore, Junior, Senior, Graduate, Faculty, Unclassified
4.   Department of major work: _____
5.   Do you attend church frequently?   Yes   No   (underline one)
6.   Are you an active member of a church?   Yes   No   (underline one)
7.   Before turning this page write a brief statement indicating your general attitude toward the church as you know it.

_____

_____

[9]S. R. Hathaway and J. C. McKinley, A multiphasic personality schedule (Minnesota): I. Construction of the schedule, *Journal of Psychology,* 1940, 10, 249–254.

[10]J. C. Nunnally, *Tests and measurements—assessment and prediction* (New York: McGraw-Hill, 1959), pp. 324–327.

[11]L. L. Thurstone and E. J. Chave, *The measurement of attitude* (Chicago: University of Chicago Press, 1929).

[12]*Ibid.,* pp. 60–63.

8. Write an *x* somewhere on the line below to indicate where you think you belong.

Strongly favorable to the church	Neutral	Strongly against the church

Check (√) every statement below that expresses your sentiment toward the church. Interpret the statements in accordance with your own experience with churches.

1.   I think the teaching of the church is altogether too superficial to have much social significance.
2.   I feel the church services give me inspiration and help me to live up to my best during the following week.
3.   I think the church keeps business and politics up to a higher standard than they would otherwise tend to maintain.
4.   I find the services of the church both restful and inspiring.
5.   When I go to church I enjoy a fine ritual service with good music.
6.   I believe in what the church teaches but with mental reservations.
7.   I do not receive any benefit from attending church services but I think it helps some people.
8.   I believe in religion but I seldom go to church.
9.   I am careless about religion and church relationships but I would not like to see my attitude become general.
10.   I regard the church as a static, crystallized institution and as such it is unwholesome and detrimental to society and the individual.
11.   I believe church membership is almost essential to living life at its best.
12.   I do not understand the dogmas or creeds of the church but I find that the church helps me to be more honest and creditable.
13.   The paternal and benevolent attitude of the church is quite distasteful to me.
14.   I feel that church attendance is a fair index of the nation's morality.
15.   Sometimes I feel that the church and religion are necessary and sometimes I doubt it.
16.   I believe the church is fundamentally sound but some of its adherents have given it a bad name.
17.   I think the church is a parasite on society.
18.   I feel the need for religion but do not find what I want in any one church.
19.   I think too much money is being spent on the church for the benefit that is being derived.
20.   I believe in the church and its teachings because I have been accustomed to them since I was a child.
21.   I think the church is hundreds of years behind the times and cannot make a dent on modern life.
22.   I believe the church has grown up with the primary purpose of perpetuating the spirit and teachings of Jesus and deserves loyal support.
23.   I feel the church perpetuates the values which man puts highest in his philosophy of life.
24.   I feel I can worship God better out of doors than in the church and I get more inspiration there.
25.   My experience is that the church is hopelessly out of date.
26.   I feel the church is petty, always quarreling over matters that have no interest or importance.
27.   I do not believe in any brand of religion or in any particular church but I have never given the subject serious thought.

28. I respect any church-member's beliefs but I think it is all "bunk."
29. I enjoy my church because there is a spirit of friendliness there.
30. I think the country would be better off if the churches were closed and the ministers set to some useful work.
31. I believe the church is the greatest institution in America today.
32. I believe in sincerity and goodness without any church ceremonies.
33. I believe the church is the greatest influence for good government and right living.
34. I think the organized church is an enemy of science and truth.
35. I believe the church is losing ground as education advances.
36. The churches may be doing good and useful work but they do not interest me.
37. I think the church is a hindrance to religion for it still depends upon magic, superstition, and myth.
38. The church is needed to develop religion, which has always been concerned with man's deepest feelings and greatest values.
39. I believe the churches are too much divided by factions and denominations to be a strong force for righteousness.
40. The church represents shallowness, hypocrisy, and prejudice.
41. I think the church seeks to impose a lot of worn-out dogmas and medieval superstitions.
42. I think the church allows denominational differences to appear larger than true religion.
43. I like the ceremonies of my church but do not miss them much when I stay away.
44. I believe the church is a powerful agency for promoting both individual and social righteousness.
45. I like to go to church for I get something worth while to think about and it keeps my mind filled with right thoughts.

Then look on page 284 for the item "intensities." Your score on the attitude scale is the mean of the intensities of the item(s) you marked. If you marked just one item, its intensity is your score. If you marked two or more items, average their intensities.

What does your score mean, and how were the item intensities secured? It will be interesting to tabulate the scores of your class, perhaps separately by sex, keeping the identity of individuals anonymous, in order to make a normative comparison with the absolute meaning of the mean-intensity scores. The lower your score, the more favorable your attitude toward the church; the higher the score, the less favorable. The scale of intensities is considered to run from 0 through 11. Do the scores in your class average approximately $(0 + 11)/2 = 5.5$? (Remember that this scale was constructed many years ago, and attitudes may have changed somewhat meanwhile. Also, your class may be atypical.) How far above or below the median of your class are you? In your opinion, is your attitude actually more favorable or less favorable toward the church than the average intensity for the items you checked indicates, as compared with your classmates? If so, how do you explain your score?

Thurstone-type attitude scales are developed by giving several hundred persons ("judges") a large number of statements such as those which appear above, and asking each judge to assign each statement to one of 11 categories that range from "extremely favorable" through "neutral" to "extremely un-favorable." Each statement is on a separate slip of paper. The judges are asked to rate the intensity of each statement, not the extent to which they agree with it. Those statements for which the judges agree reasonably well as to intensity are candidates for the final scale. It consists of about 20 statements that spread evenly over the 11-point intensity scale, as determined by the median category to which the judges assigned a given statement, in order to discriminate well at all levels of "favorableness." On the final printed form the order of these state-ments is random. As you did above, the examinee is asked to mark those statements with which he agrees, and his score is the mean intensity of those statements. Intensities for the "attitude toward the church" items are listed in Table 9-2.

TABLE 9-2

*Scale-Values for the "Attitude toward the Church" Scale
(from Thurstone and Chave, pp. 78–79)*

Statement No.	Scale-Value	Statement No.	Scale-Value
1	8.3	24	6.9
2	1.7	25	9.1
3	2.6	26	8.6
4	2.3	27	5.9
5	4.0	28	8.8
6	4.5	29	3.3
7	5.7	30	10.5
8	5.4	31	0.2
9	4.7	32	6.7
10	10.5	33	0.4
11	1.5	34	10.7
12	3.1	35	7.4
13	8.2	36	5.9
14	2.6	37	9.6
15	5.6	38	1.4
16	3.9	39	7.2
17	11.0	40	10.4
18	6.1	41	9.2
19	7.5	42	7.2
20	4.0	43	5.1
21	9.5	44	1.2
22	1.0	45	2.2
23	0.8		

The statement most favorable to the church is No. 31, "I believe the church is the greatest institution in America today."

The other commonly used procedure for constructing attitude scales was devised by Likert in 1932.[13] It also begins with a large number of negative and

------

[13]R. Likert, A technique for the measurement of attitudes, *Archives of Psychology*, 1932, 22, No. 140, 55 pages.

positive statements concerning an institution, object, or class of persons, but no judges are employed. Instead, a large number of items are tried out on a considerable number of persons who mark each item on a five-point scale: strongly disagree, disagree, undecided, agree, strongly agree. For positive statements, each "strongly disagree" response is scored 1, each "disagree" 2, each "undecided" 3, each "agree" 4, and each "strongly agree" 5. For negative items the scoring system is reversed: "strongly disagree" receives 5 points, with 4 points for "disagree," and so on. (Weights of 0, 1, 2, 3, and 4 are as useful, and computationally easier.)

Scoring weights for the responses by the various examinees to a given item (they will be 1's, 2's, 3's, 4's, and 5's) are correlated by the Pearson r method with total scores on the inventory, which may range from the number of statements (if someone obtains all 1's) to five times that number. Those items having high correlations with total scores are retained for the final inventory. The other items are discarded, for either they are unreliable or they concern some attitude factor not typical of the bulk of the items. This is a method of item analysis somewhat similar to the one we considered in Appendix A.

In Figure 9-2 there are five modified Likert-type items, a page taken from Sister M. Jacinta Mann's questionnaire. The options are arranged in scrambled order to diminish "response sets," that is, the tendency to mark the same position, such as 3, for each item. The weights for the first item are 0 for Option 1, 4 for Option 2, 1 for Option 3, 3 for Option 4, and 2 (the indifference point, midway between 0 and 4) for Option 5.

The Likert procedure uses five categories per item, while the Thurstone method employs just two (checked or not checked), so the former furnishes more information than the latter. Likert-scale scores have no absolute (direct) meaning, however, whereas Thurstone-scale scores do *if* judgments of intensity are independent of the attitudes of the judges, though under a number of conditions they may not be.

The Thurstone scale is an example of a check list, which is the simplest form of a rating scale. The Likert scale is a five-category rating scale. Under some conditions it may be useful to have as many as 7, or perhaps even more, categories to be rated. Usually the number of categories employed is odd (3, 5, 7, . . .), so that there will be a middle, neutral category available.

Another method of attitude-scale construction is the Bogardus Social-Distance Scale for assessing attitudes toward different national groups.[14] It usually involves these seven categories:

With respect to _____ (a certain national group), I would
1. admit them to close kinship by marriage.
2. admit them to my club as personal chums.
3. admit them to my street as neighbors.

---

[14]E. Bogardus, Measuring social distance, *Journal of Applied Sociology,* 1925, 9, 299–308, and A social distance scale, *Sociology and Sociological Research,* 1933, 17, 265–271.

4. admit them to employment in my occupation.
5. admit them to citizenship in my country.
6. admit them only as visitors in my country.
7. exclude them from my country.

The respondent checks the categories with which he agrees. Probably the order of the categories should be random. Also, it may be necessary to have an eighth or even ninth category, more negative than the seventh, such as "exterminate them from the earth," in order to detect extremely hostile feelings.

Figure 9-2. *Sample Job-Satisfaction Rating Scale Item. From Sister M. Jacinta Mann, Relationships among certain variables associated with college and post-college success. Unpublished Ph.D. dissertation, University of Wisconsin, 1958.*

HERE ARE SOME QUESTIONS ABOUT HOW WELL YOU ARE SATISFIED WITH *YOUR JOB.* IF NOT PRESENTLY EMPLOYED, CONSIDER HERE YOUR LAST FULL TIME JOB.

Please circle the number of the alternative which comes closest to your answer.

Which statement *best* tells how well you *like* your job?

   1 I hate it.
   2 I am enthusiastic about it.
   3 I don't like it.
   4 I like it.
   5 I am indifferent to it.

Which statement *best* shows how much of the time you feel *satisfied* with your job?

   1 About half of the time
   2 Occasionally
   3 A good deal of the time
   4 Seldom
   5 Most of the time

Which statement *best* tells how you feel about *changing* your job?

   1 I would quit this job at once if I could get anything else to do.
   2 I would like to change both my job and my occupation.
   3 I would like to change my present job for another job in the same line of work.
   4 I am not eager to change my job but would do so if I could get a better one.
   5 I would not exchange my job for any other.

Which statement *best* shows how you think you *compare* with other people in feelings about your job?

   1 No one likes his job better than I like mine.
   2 I like my job better than most people like theirs.
   3 I like my job about as well as most people like theirs.
   4 I dislike my job more than most people dislike theirs.
   5 No one dislikes his job more than I dislike mine.

Which statement *best* expresses your present feeling about your place in the working world?

   1 I haven't gotten started at all. I'm no farther along than when I left school.
   2 I've made so little progress that I'd dislike to think it were going to be like this all the time.
   3 It could be better, but I suppose I really don't have much to complain about.
   4 I might have done better in places, but on the whole, I think I have done pretty well.
   5 I think I have made an excellent start in my life's work.

A rather different scaling procedure, devised by Guttman,[15] is of considerable theoretical but limited practical importance because it requires items more reliable than we can almost ever find. If you are especially interested in scaling, however, read his basic article for its nice analogy of attitude assessment to the measurement of physical characteristics such as height and weight.

Attitude assessment is complex, especially because the relationship of stated attitudes to actions is uncertain—even under the most deception-free circumstances. A man who would greatly prefer that members of a certain national group not marry his daughter, belong to his club, live on his street, or even visit his country, might sit next to such a person on the bus and talk with him cordially because there was no other unobtrusively reached seat, or because he is aware of his prejudice and ashamed of it, or because he is running for political office and needs the vote, or for any one or more of a number of other reasons. Thurstone himself was once heard to say that one should not expect much correspondence between scores on a paper-and-pencil attitude scale and behavior that might appear to reflect that attitude. This would seem especially likely with the largely unvalidated social-distance scale, where one's score may reflect at least as much geographical difference and unfamiliarity as dislike. For example, how socially distant do you feel from the inhabitants of the Republic of San Marino? (On the other hand, *some* kind of attitude is being measured when a person says in effect that he can't abide *X*, of which he has no knowledge or experience.)

QUESTIONNAIRES   Much used in educational research, and probably considerably overused in comparison with manipulative experimentation and personal observation, are sets of self-report questions, usually mimeographed or printed and sent through the mail or administered to captive audiences such as groups of teachers. The questions making up questionnaires may be of virtually any kind that we have discussed in this book. The questions may begin with background data, such as sex (Male or Female—check one), date of birth (month, day, and year), and number of years of school completed. After this, the questions may remain factual (How many students are enrolled in your classes? Which subject do you teach?) or the instrument may become an opinionnaire, typically of the rating-scale or ranking kinds. One might, for instance, send the Thurstone-Chave "Attitude toward the Church" scale to be filled out and returned, but more likely he would use materials of his own devising instead. See Figure 9-3 below for the first page of a well-prepared eight-page questionnaire.

Questionnaires have all the usual limitations of self-report devices, plus some special problems of their own. If they are mailed to individuals to be filled

---

[15]L. Guttman, The Cornell technique for scale and intensity analysis, *Educational and Psychological Measurement,* 1947, 7, 247–279.

1) What is the DATE OF YOUR BIRTH? _____
                                   (month)   (day)   (year)

2) What is your MARITAL STATUS? (circle one)

            Female   1. single   Male   3. single
                            2. married   4. married

3) In what CITY AND STATE
             do you live? _____

4) If married, please give number of children. _____

5) Please give the *number of months,* if any, that you have spent in the MILITARY SERVICE.

    World War II _____ ; Korean War _____ ; Peacetime tour of duty _____

    Other _____ (please specify) _____

6) Have you taken ADDITIONAL COLLEGE OR UNIVERSITY WORK since receiving your bachelor's degree? (circle one)

    1. Yes   If yes, give: Semester credits earned _____

    2. No   Degrees received _____

                                      College or university _____

7) Circle the LAST SCHOOL YEARS YOUR FATHER AND MOTHER (or guardians) *completed* at these levels.

Father	Mother	Levels
1 2 3 4 5 6 7 8	1 2 3 4 5 6 7 8	Elementary School
1 2 3 4	1 2 3 4	High School
1 2 3 4	1 2 3 4	College
1 2 3 4	1 2 3 4	Graduate or Professional School
1 2 3 4	1 2 3 4	Other (specify) _____

8) If your parents or guardians were granted college degrees, please list these.

Father _____ Mother _____

Figure 9-3. *First page of a mailed questionnaire (from Sister M. Jacinta Mann, Relationships among certain variables associated with college and post-college success, unpublished Ph.D. dissertation, University of Wisconsin, 1958; see same author and title,* Educational and Psychological Measurement, *1959, 19, 351–362).*

out at whatever time(s) and under whatever circumstances happen to prevail in the home or office of the recipient, the results may vary greatly from individual to individual, depending on the time and care he chooses or is able to give. Some questionnaires will probably be returned with responses made carelessly and perhaps quite incompletely, unless respondents are in some way wooed into allotting the time and care required. Other questionnaires will not be returned at all, unless their receivers are reminded several times. And despite the best efforts of the investigator, there will probably be some persons who do not return questionnaires in usable form. These non-returners and unsatisfactory answerers are the non-respondents who bias the generalization he can make legitimately from his survey.

Suppose, for example, that you sent out a double postal card to every female fourth-grade teacher in your state and asked her how many years she has taught in that grade. If in two weeks half of the cards have been returned, you would not be in a good position to tabulate your results and announce them because you would not know which half of the teachers had responded, the ones who have taught the shortest time in the fourth grade or those who have taught the longest. Of course, you could *assume* that you have secured a *random* 50 per cent of the teachers, so far as years of teaching are concerned, but readers of your report might not be willing to permit you that assumption without further justification. That is why it is essential to build initially into your study careful plans for several *follow-ups* in order to reduce non-respondents to as small a percentage as possible.

Even with 100 per cent returns, however, you would still need to qualify your conclusions from the self-report returns. Your figures represent how long the teachers *say* they have taught in the fourth grade, not necessarily how long they have actually taught. Careless errors, fallible memories, and willful deception color your findings in ways largely unknown to you.

Even a simple mail survey demands great care in the construction of the questionnaire, and so does use of such devices with large "captive" audiences. We leave further intricacies to books on questionnaire methodology, such as Festinger and Katz's.[16]

SELECTING PREDICTORS
EMPIRICALLY

One may use an empirical approach to *predicting* a certain criterion, such as amount of life insurance that will be sold in three years by an insurance salesman when this amount is adjusted for the potential of his territory. You may try various possible predictors, such as age, marital status, score on an intelligence test, and responses to certain other self-report items. Some of these will predict the criterion better than chance in a group of beginning insurance salesmen. Others

---

[16]L. Festinger and D. Katz, *Research methods in the behavioral sciences* (New York: Dryden Press, 1953).

won't. By retaining just those antecedent measures that do contribute to predicting the later criterion, and by "weighting" them optimally to predict that criterion, you may be able to devise a set of questions that improves appreciably the productivity of your sales force by enabling you to avoid hiring persons likely to be poor producers. For further information about this method, see the historical survey by industrial psychologist Leonard Ferguson.[17]

PROJECTIVE
TECHNIQUES   Clinical psychologists use two self-report instruments, the Rorschach Ink-Blot Test and the Thematic Apperception Test (TAT), or variants thereof, in making many of their personality assessments. We discussed the development of these on pages 39-51. They are called "projective tests" because a person is expected to project into the ink blots or the ambiguous pictures his needs, wants, desires, aversions, fears, anxieties, and the like. Procedures for administering, scoring, and interpreting the two tests are quite different, but they have in common their ambiguous stimuli, the "nonsensical" ink blots or the provocative pictures.

We shall not discuss how the Rorschach is scored for whole versus detail responses, figure versus ground, rare versus usual responses, form, and color, or how the TAT is scored for press and need. Much background in the psychology of personality and in clinical psychology is required before one is well equipped to use projective techniques. For a number of references and some discussion, see the chapter on projective techniques in the February issue of the *Review of Educational Research.*[18]

A word of caution: Many measurement specialists have far less regard for projective techniques than do most clinical psychologists. To some of the former, the Rorschach and TAT rate little higher than the reading of tea leaves. Validity is not well established psychometrically even for the Rorschach and the TAT, much less for newer projective techniques. Perhaps a great part of their popularity with clinical psychologists rests on what might be called "faith validity" assumed by the users.

A number of persons have attempted to devise multiple-choice versions of the Rorschach to replace or at least precede the much more arduous interview-type procedure by which the Rorschach is usually administered. A good example, with attractive format, is the experimental version being tried by the California Test Bureau.[19] It is as yet too early to know whether or not ob-

[17]L. W. Ferguson, A look across the years 1920 to 1950, pp. 1–17 in L. L. Thurstone, ed., *Applications of psychology* (New York: Harper, 1952).

[18]The "Educational and psychological testing" issue appears every three years—February 1953, 1956, 1959, 1962, etc. See H. Ricciuti, Development and application of projective tests of personality, *Review of Educational Research,* 1962, 32, 64–77.

[19]J. B. Stone, *Structured-objective Rorschach test, preliminary edition* (Monterey, Calif.: California Test Bureau, 1958).

jectively scorable projective tests will be more useful than the standard paper-and-pencil personality inventories such as the Mental Health Analysis or the Minnesota Multiphasic Personality Inventory that we have already considered.

INTERVIEWS   Perhaps the most widely used assessment procedure is the interview. Throughout our lives we converse with persons in many situations, and usually we evaluate the remarks we hear. The "formal" interview differs from casual conversation in that it has structure and explicit purpose. It differs from tests, however, in that the interviewer may adjust his questions to the answers he is getting and thereby probe and explore. In this respect the interview is analogous to an individual intelligence test used by a clinical psychologist to "test the limits"—that is, to ask many questions not in the test manual that the examinee's responses suggest. Since such questions are unique to the examinee, his answers cannot be compared with the answers of other examinees, who are asked different questions. A main strength of the usual test is that it compares all examinees on the same questions. When one departs from this model, whether with a test or a "flexible" interview, he loses direct comparability of responses. This may permit the interviewer's prejudices and biases to operate rather freely.

Thus the price of flexibility is subjectivity of interpretation. Let us take an example. Suppose that you are chairman of the admissions committee of Midstate College. Five hundred high-school graduates have applied for admission to the freshman class at M.C., but you can take only two hundred. Which 40 per cent will you accept? You know for each applicant his rank in high-school graduating class, his verbal and quantitative academic aptitude test scores, and his scores on three achievement tests. You decide that there should be an interview with each applicant. Who will do the interviewing, and how? You do not see how you could get a really high-level faculty member to devote the necessary time to interviewing, and you would not know which one to use, anyway. Professor Jones prefers one sort of student, Professor Smith another, and Professor Doe yet another. You hesitate to ask five professors to interview 100 students each, for they do not have comparable frames of reference; this would be like giving five different tests, one test to each 100 students, and trying to compare the 500 students with each other.

You do not want to assign a routine administrative assistant to do the interviewing, however, for he might recommend rejection of the very students whom the faculty desires. For instance, if he was a mediocre high-school student himself, he may be subconsciously prejudiced against students who ranked high in their graduating classes. Usually, he would not state his objections this way, but would instead say that the applicant lacked poise, or sincerity, or "creativity."

When properly planned and conducted, interviews can be of some value for certain purposes, such as telling you whether or not you like the person on first acquaintance. Even at best, however, they probably add little to the prediction of most objective criteria when the best objective predictors are at hand. They may even hurt predictability by interfering with the efficacy of the objective predictors, as for example when an academically inferior principal refuses to employ "A" students as teachers. In particular, interviews for academic selection are greatly overrated. Academic predictors such as previous grades, verbal and quantitative aptitude, and scores on achievement tests are usually vastly more important than poise and acting ability at an interview, rationalizations of previous inadequacies, and eloquent promises to study hard. The single best predictor of future success is past success.

As an illustration of this (and you know that an illustration is not a proof), note that a number of years ago the University of Wisconsin admitted as "early entrants" at the end of the tenth or eleventh grade a number of men and women from far-off New York State. These students could not get into local universities for the Ford Foundation experiment because there were so many applicants from that state. They were accepted at Wisconsin on the basis of test scores and letters of recommendation alone, without interviews because of the great distance. Their academic, social, and emotional success was at least as great as that of students elsewhere whose admission had been heavily contingent upon the results of interviews.[20]

The contribution of interviews to academic prediction can be studied in a given situation, but since the interviewers themselves and their procedures may change from year to year, it is difficult to generalize across time even within one setting, much less to determine the validity of *the* interview in general.

Actually, the prime value of the interview is probably for imparting information and aiding the interviewee to make good choices on the basis of all the information he has. Interviews can be friendly, helpful sessions, with the evaluating of interviewee by interviewer minimized in favor of their both concentrating on helping the former make wise choices. This is the guidance function of interviews. It is widely applicable in schools and colleges. To learn more about it, see R. H. Byrne, *The school counselor.*[21]

REPORTS BY OTHERS   You may rate yourself on such qualities as sociability, altruism, and beauty, or others may rate you. Various techniques can be used, from straight rating scales (e.g.: extremely unsociable, unsociable, not particularly unsociable or sociable, sociable, and extremely sociable) to sociometric techniques ("Name the three most sociable pupils in the room." "Which one of these two persons is the more sociable?").

---

[20]Fund for the Advancement of Education, *They went to college early* (New York: Fund for the Advancement of Education, 1957).

[21]Boston: Houghton Mifflin, 1963.

During World War II, the Office of Strategic Services (OSS) tried out a number of structured situations in which tasks were assigned to a person, usually serving as leader of a group, and his performance was observed and rated by psychologists. Many of the situations were designed to be frustrating. "Co-workers" might be psychologists in disguise whose primary function was to confuse the person being observed and to thwart him in accomplishing a difficult task, such as building a bridge across a stream with inadequate materials. See page 36 for further discussion.

SOCIOMETRIC
TECHNIQUES   Teachers may study the social structure of a classroom by asking students to make certain *meaningful* choices: With which student would you rather study tomorrow's arithmetic lesson? With which three pupils would you rather play at recess? Which two pupils would be the most fun at a party at your home?

A more complex variation is to present the personality sketch of a hypothetical pupil and ask each youngster to name, say, the three persons in the class who seem to him most like the individual described.

We shall illustrate the sociometric process with actual data from a fourth-grade class that contained 14 girls and 17 boys.[22] The teacher gave each child a dittoed sheet that read as follows:

My three best friends in this class are:
1. My very best friend _____
2. My second best friend _____
3. My third best friend _____

The results are shown in Table 9-3, where the capital letters from A through N designate girls, and the small letters from a through q represent boys.

How does one read Table 9-3? Let us start with Girl A. In Row A we see that she chose Girl D as her very best friend, because there is the number 1 at the intersection of Row A and Column D. Girl A listed Girl C as her second best friend. Girl A listed Boy c as her third best friend.

Who chose Girl A? Look at Column A, where you see from top to bottom the following numbers: 1 (first choice of Girls D and N and Boy k), 2 (second choice of Girls C, F, and G and Boy d), and 3 (third choice of Boys c and f). Thus Girl A was named by nine pupils—three times as first choice, four times as second choice, and twice as third choice. You will find the summary 3, 4, and 2 in column A of the first three rows below the choices.

In the lower left quadrant of Table 9-3 you can tell that Girl A was chosen by four boys, while no other girl was chosen by more than one boy. Also, you

---

[22]We thank Elaine M. Williams for lending us a paper that she prepared at the University of Wisconsin. We have rearranged a portion of her data somewhat.

TABLE 9-3

Choices of Three Best Friends by 14 Girls and 17 Boys

		Girls Were Chosen By													Boys Were Chosen By																
		A	B	C	D	E	F	G	H	I	J	K	L	M	N	a	b	c	d	e	f	g	h	i	j	k	l	m	n	o	p	q
	A			2	1														3													
	B					2			3														1									
	C	2						3											1													
	D	1		3			2																									
	E		1					2												3												
	F	2			1																				3							
Girls	G	2		3																		1										
Chose	H	1								3		2												2								
	I	1			3																				2							
	J						2		1																					3		
	K		2	1																3												
	L							2												1	3											
	M						2									1									3							
	N	1				2	3																									
	a																						2	1			3					
	b																	1	2							3						
	c	3																1		2												
	d	2																1						3								
	e					2																1										
	f	3		1											2								2			3					
Boys	g													1									2			3				
Chose	h							2											1									3
	i	2												2		1		3									
	j													1	2				3								
	k	1		3	2																						
	l						2							1													
	m														2		3				1		3				
	n														2	1											
	o														3			2		1							
	p	1													3		2			1							
	q																			1							
1st choice		3		4	1	2			1							5	3	3	1	2	2	1	1		1	1						
2nd choice		4	1	1	1	2	3	2	1	1	1	1				2	3		2	1	2		1	1								
3rd choice		2		3		2		1			2							3	3	2		2		2	1		2	1	1	1		
Times chosen		9	5	4	3	4	3	3	2	3	1	1				7	6	6	6	5	4	3	2	3	2	1	2	1	1	1		
"Score"		19	14	8	8	6	6	5	5	4	2	2	0	0	0	19	15	12	10	10	10	5	5	4	4	3	2	1	1	1	0	0
		A	B	C	D	E	F	G	H	I	J	K	L	M	N	a	b	c	d	e	f	g	h	i	j	k	l	m	n	o	p	q

can determine that no girl chose only boys, whereas Boy *k* chose only girls. (Did any girl choose Boy *k*?)

If we give 3 points for being chosen as "very best friend," 2 points for "second best friend," and 1 point for "third best friend," the highest scorers are Girl *A* and Boy *a*, each with 19 points, even though Girl *A* was chosen by two more pupils than Boy *a*. This happens because Boy *a* was chosen as very best friend by five pupils, worth 15 points, while Girl *A* was chosen as very best friend by only three pupils, worth just 9 points. For Girl *A* the computation is $(3 \times 3) + (4 \times 2) + (2 \times 1) = 19$. For Boy *a* it is $(5 \times 3) + (2 \times 2) = 19$.

The lowest scorers, whom nobody chose, are Girls *L*, *M*, and *N* and Boys *p* and *q*. They may be the fourth best or fifth best friends of some of the pupils, for all we know, but they weren't listed as first, second, or third. In Table 9-3 the girls are arranged in order of total number of points from *A* with most to *L*, *M*, and *N* with least. The boys are arranged in the same way.

Every girl listed three names, but Boys *e*, *l*, and *q* did not. Inspect Rows *e*, *l*, and *q* to see which choices they omitted. (Do you suppose that fourth-grade boys typically are less careful about such tasks than fourth-grade girls?).

The 31 very-best-friend choices went to just 15 pupils. How many of these were mutual—for example, where Mary listed Susan as her very best friend and Susan listed Mary as hers? By searching in Table 9-3 we see that *A* chose *D* and was chosen by *D*, that *B* chose *f* and was chosen by *f*, that *C* chose *c* but was not chosen by *c*, and so on. The five mutual-first-choice pairs are *AD*, *Bf*, *ag*, *bc*, and *eh*. Fifteen mutual first choices were possible. Probably it would have been better to have asked each pupil to name his very best friend and second best friend of each sex, rather than just his three best friends. Girl *E*, for instance, listed Girl *B* as her very best friend, but Girl *B* listed Boy *f* as her very best friend and Girl *E* as her second best friend, probably meaning that Girl *E* is her best *girl* friend. Failure to consider the sexes separately can make it difficult to interpret results or make them appear to be less consistent than they are.

Girl *A*, the most-chosen pupil, has perfect mutuality with all three of her choices. She listed Girl *D* as her very best friend, and Girl *D* listed her likewise. She chose Girl *C* as her second best friend, and Girl *C* reciprocated. She named Boy *c* as her third best friend, and he named her as his third best friend.

Girl *B*'s three choices all named her as very best friend. Girl *C* listed Boy *c* as her very best friend, but he did not choose her at all, instead choosing boys for 1 and 2 and designating her second best friend, *A*, as his third best friend.

One could go on analyzing these 89 "chose" and "was chosen by" listings for a long time, uncovering various interesting relationships. It is somewhat tedious to do this from a two-way table such as Table 9-3 however, so usually a sociogram like the one in Figure 9-4 is constructed in order to depict mutualities more obviously.[23] Note that all girls except *L* are at the left. *L* chose two boys and was not chosen by anyone, as was also true of *M*. *N*, however, chose only girls (and was chosen by nobody), so she appears at the left. The two "stars," *A* and *a*, are in the center near each other, though neither chose the other.

Arrangement of the sociogram follows definite rules, but because of the

[23] Horace Mann—Lincoln Institute of School Experimentation, Columbia University, *How to construct a sociogram* (New York: Bureau of Publications, Teachers College, Columbia University, 1947).

enormous number of ways that the "chosens" and "were chosen bys" can be depicted in two dimensions, some variations from teacher to teacher for identical data can be expected. In general, "isolates" (unchosen pupils) are near the periphery, while "stars" (much-chosen pupils) are near the center. Because we used *A* and *a* to represent the most-chosen pupils, *B* and *b* the next-most-chosen ones, etc., letters at the start of the alphabet tend to be in the middle of Figure 9-4, while letters nearer the end (*M, N, p, q*) are further out.

For clarity, girls are doubly denoted by a capital letter in a circle, and boys are identified by a small letter in a square.

Solid black lines represent first choices, white lines second choices, dashed lines third choices. Arrows with points on each end represent mutual choices. For example, *A* and *D* chose each other as "very best friend"; *A* and *C* were mutual "second best friends"; and *A* reciprocated with *c* for "third best friend." Inspection of the table will convince you that strict mutualities, indicated by the double-headed arrows, are rare except for mutual "very best friends" (i.e., mutual first choices).

Sociometric techniques should be meaningful to the students and provide useful data for the teacher. Nothing beneficial can be expected to happen merely because the pupils have been asked to list their three best friends. Responses to this kind of question constitute the starting point from which the

Figure 9-4. *Sociogram, based on data in Table 9-3.*

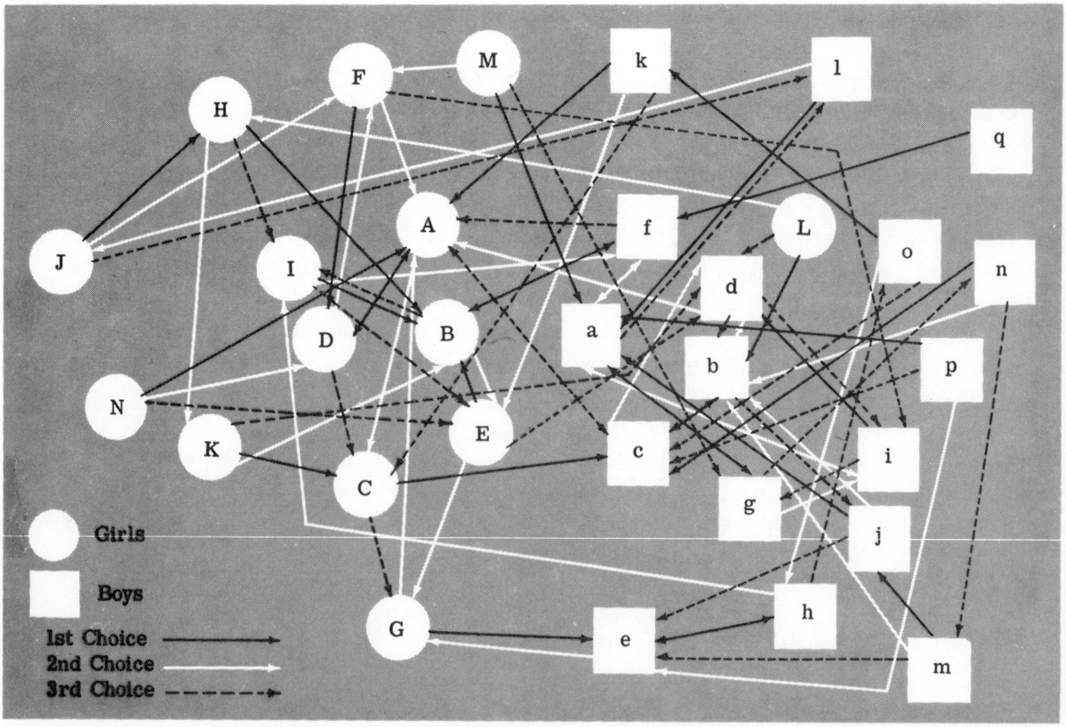

ingenious teacher studies the social structure of his classroom and devises ways to help it facilitate his teaching. He may try to alter the structure somewhat in carefully thought out ways, such as by forming study groups of low mutuality in the hope that this will permit the "friendless" to make friends. The teacher needs to understand the social psychology of his group rather well in order to do this extensively or radically, however. He is well advised to proceed with caution, but to proceed. In particular, the "isolates" such as L, M, N, p, and q may need help.

Self-report and other-report devices rank with objective and essay tests as aids for the teacher in attaining the objectives of education. They can be used with profit more extensively and systematically than is usually done at present.

RECOMMENDED READINGS

Cattell, R. B., Scheier, I. H., and Lorr, M., Recent advances in the measurement of anxiety, neuroticism, and the psychotic syndromes, *Annals of the New York Academy of Sciences,* 1962, 93, 813–856.

Boy, A. V. and Pine, G. J., *Client-centered counseling in the secondary school.* Boston: Houghton Mifflin, 1963.

Fiske, D. W., Homogeneity and variation in measuring personality, *American Psychologist,* 1963, 18, 643–652.

Gardner, E. F. and Thompson, G. G., Measuring and interpreting social relations. *Test Service Notebook* No. 22, Harcourt, Brace and World, New York City, 1959. Free.

Getzels, J. W. and Thelen, H. A., The sociopsychological structure of the instructional group. *Fifty-Ninth Yearbook of the National Society for the Study of Education, Part II* (The dynamics of social groups). Chicago: University of Chicago Press, 1960, pp. 53–82.

Kuder, G. F., A rationale for evaluating interests, *Educational and Psychological Measurement,* 1963, 23, 3–10.

Lambert, P., Administration of the F-scale to a sample of elementary school principals and teachers, *Journal of Educational Research,* 1960, 53, 336–340.

McCleary, L. E., Restructuring the interpersonal relations of a junior high school class, *School Review,* 1956, 64, 346–352.

Medley, D. M. and Mitzel, H. E., Measuring classroom behavior by systematic observation, Ch. 6 (pp. 247–328) in N. L. Gage, ed., *Handbook of research on teaching.* Chicago: Rand McNally, 1963.

Remmers, H. H., Rating methods in research on teaching, Ch. 7 (pp. 329–378) in N. L. Gage, ed., *Handbook of research on teaching.* Chicago: Rand McNally, 1963.

Stern, G. G., Measuring noncognitive variables in research on teaching, Ch. 9 (pp. 398–447) in N. L. Gage, ed., *Handbook of research on teaching.* Chicago: Rand McNally, 1963.

Swartz, J. D. and Holtzman, W. H., Group method of administration for the Holtzman Inkblot Technique, *Journal of Clinical Psychology,* 1963, 19, 433–441.

Torgerson, W. S., *Theory and methods of scaling.* New York: Wiley, 1958.

THE TESTING

PROGRAM

One of the chief weaknesses of many attempts to use standard tests is that there has been no program worthy of the name. The word "program" has certain important implications, such as *order, system, planning*. It implies a sequence of events that has been determined after careful thought.

Testing programs call for the planned use of a variety of tests to supplement the teacher's own testing and other evaluative activities. Results should be viewed cumulatively, so that over the years a number of different abilities and aptitudes can be assessed. It should not be necessary to repeat a given kind of test very often, not more than every three years or so, if information obtained from other tests supplements it. For example, a test of verbal "intelligence" is often remarkably similar to the word-meaning, reading, and vocabulary sections of achievement tests. Similarly, the arithmetic reasoning subtest of an achievement test may measure much the same thing as a test of quantitative intelligence.

One must not assume that the testing pro-

CHAPTER TEN

gram should be restricted to the use of standardized tests. As noted above, *teacher-made tests will have a large place in any complete testing program.* Schools should have a carefully thought out general policy on such matters as the frequency of testing, the importance of final examinations, the factors to be considered in determining final marks, and, most important, the uses to be made of the results.

Regardless of its scope, the complete testing program at any particular time will ordinarily consist of the following eight steps, or stages, in chronological order:

1. Determining the purpose of the program
2. Selecting the appropriate test or tests
3. Administering the tests
4. Scoring the tests
5. Analyzing and interpreting the scores
6. Applying the results
7. Retesting to determine the success of the program
8. Making suitable records and reports

DETERMINING
THE PURPOSE
OF THE PROGRAM It must be recognized at all times that tests are only tools and that measurement is always a means to an end, never an end itself. Thus, the value of any testing program depends on the use made of results. Merely "giving tests" without rhyme, rule,

299

or reason is money, time, and effort wasted. The author once heard an experienced educator say that he had wondered for years what many people did with standard tests after they had been "given." At last he found out. They filed them! A testing program should have a more serious purpose than that. The first step, therefore, in planning a program is to determine its purpose. In so doing, three things should be kept in mind: the program should be *cooperative, practical,* and *definite.*

A Cooperative Program

As a rule, the program should not represent the judgment of any one person alone, but that of a group. It should be a truly cooperative enterprise. The teachers and administrators alike should be made to feel that it is "our" program, as indeed it should be. This is not likely to be the case, however, if the principal, superintendent, or research department determines the program and then "hands it down" to the classroom teachers. The entire staff should have a voice in determining the purpose of the program and in formulating the plans, and all should have the opportunity of participating in it in every way possible from beginning to end. If this is not done, the teachers are not likely to understand the program fully or to appreciate what it is attempting to do. Without the hearty cooperation of the entire staff, the program is almost sure to fall short of its highest possibilities. It is suggested, therefore, that in a small school or school system the purpose of the program be decided upon after discussion in a general teachers' meeting or series of meetings in which everyone has a chance to participate. In the larger school systems, it is better to entrust the responsibility of planning the program to a committee representing all interested groups. Even then it should be brought before the entire staff before final action is taken. It cannot be emphasized too strongly that the success of the program largely depends on cooperative action. An important part of the program, then, is the educating of the staff so that they can participate intelligently in it. The teacher's attitude is probably the most important single factor to be considered.

A Practical Program

The general purpose of the testing program is to provide data which will help in the solution of practical school problems. As a rule, this means that the problems whose solutions are sought will have to do with administration, instruction, or research, or with some combination of these three. Even when tests are used primarily for administrative purposes, such as classification, they can also be used by the classroom teachers for diagnostic purposes. Unless the school has had considerable experience with testing, it will be better not to undertake a program primarily for research, although under favorable conditions research is a legitimate interest both of classroom teachers and of administrators. Even when a program is undertaken for research purposes, it should ordinarily be one which bears directly on some practical issue in the school, such as determining the relative efficiency of different teaching methods or of administrative organizations.

A Definite Program

It is not enough that the program be cooperative and practical. It must also be definite. The scope of the program may vary all the way from a single subject in one grade to measurement involving the entire school system. A common mistake of a staff inexperienced in the use of tests is to undertake too much. The danger then is that the program will drag along until everybody is more or less "fed up" with it. Much of the value of the information sought from the tests will be lost unless the information is made available without delay. It is usually best, particularly with inexperienced teachers, to run the risk of undertaking too small a program rather than one too large.

Another mistake is in stating the purpose of the program in too general terms. "To improve instruction" is too vague and inclusive. "To motivate study" or "to diagnose weaknesses and provide a basis for remedial instruction" would be better. Best of all would be a still more definite formulation, such as "to motivate study in fifth-grade arithmetic" or "to make a diagnosis of characteristic weaknesses in first-year algebra and to formulate a program of remedial teaching to eliminate them." The purpose should state specifically both the nature and the scope of the program to be undertaken. In a long-range program, the purpose for each year will have a definite relationship to the whole. No matter how stated, however, there is really one fundamental purpose in all measurement: namely, the better understanding of the individual pupil. To accomplish this purpose the information must be as definite and as complete as possible.

SELECTING THE APPROPRIATE TEST OR TESTS

When the purpose of the testing program has been determined, and not until then, the selection of the test, or tests, is in order. In Chapter Five, attention was called to the fact that a test may be superior for one purpose and worthless for another. Great care must be exercised to obtain the tests most appropriate for the purpose. Three questions require consideration:

1. Who should select the test or tests?
2. What type of tests should be used?
3. What is the best procedure in making the selection?

Who Should Select the Tests?

In larger school systems, the director of research or of pupil personnel services is most often the person best qualified to make the selection. But, even then, in the selection of achievement tests for specific subjects, the teachers of these subjects should be consulted, since their knowledge is essential in judging the curricular validity of the tests. In smaller schools, the major responsibility is usually assumed by the principal or superintendent, or assigned to a guidance counselor. However, in the selection of achievement tests, a committee of teachers will be helpful in judging the content of the tests. In evaluation that involves a subjective element, it is a sound principle to rely, whenever possible, on the combined judgment of a group of competent persons, rather than on the judgment of just one individual.

What Types of Tests Should Be Used?

Ordinarily, an adequate testing program will involve the use of more than one type of test. It will be desirable, except in a few cases such as in the beginning of the kindergarten or first grade, to use both intelligence and achievement tests. If considerations of time and money make it advisable to limit the testing program to one standard test for determining the present status of the class or school, the best choice will usually be a test battery.[1]

For a general survey of the intellectual status of the class or school, one good group test of intelligence will usually be adequately reliable. However, for comparing pupils with each other, the mean of two test scores is better than just one. In any measurement of intelligence involving group tests, especially if only one test is used, it is desirable to retest with an individual intelligence test, such as the Revised Stanford-Binet Intelligence Scales[2] or one of the Wechsler Scales,[3] pupils who test very low, say below an IQ of 80, and those whose scores are considerably out of line with the judgment of the teacher. The Revised Stanford-Binet is particularly trustworthy at the low IQ levels. The distinctive advantage of the individual intelligence test is the opportunity afforded the examiner to observe the behavior of the child under standardized conditions. As a diagnostic instrument, such a test is likely to be much superior to the group test. Pupils who have serious language difficulty should be tested individually, perhaps with a performance test.

---

[1] Nearly every major test publisher has such a battery. The interested administrator or other person responsible for helping with the planning of testing programs will want to have test catalogues of some of the companies listed in Appendix J.

[2] L. M. Terman and Maud A. Merrill, *Stanford-Binet Intelligence Scale; manual for the Third Revision, Form L-M* (Boston: Houghton Mifflin, 1960).

[3] *The Wechsler Intelligence Scale for Children (WISC)* and the *Wechsler Adult Intelligence Scale (WAIS),* both sold to trained individual mental testers by The Psychological Corporation, 304 E. 45th Street, New York 17, N. Y.

Because of the relative stability of the commonly measured mental factors, it is unnecessary to administer intelligence tests each year. The mental level of most pupils can be predicted closely enough from intelligence tests scheduled several years apart. (On page 311 we outline intelligence testing programs adapted to various types of school organization.) At times, aptitude tests in specific fields, rating scales, check lists, personal interviews, and the like will also be required. The particular combination of measuring techniques needed in any given situation will depend on the specific purposes to be served. As a rule, classroom teachers will find a larger place for nonstandardized, teacher-made tests in the solution of instructional problems than will school administrators in the solution of administrative problems. The reverse condition will tend to be true for standardized tests. Table 10-1 is a sort of "balance sheet" which briefly summarizes some of the chief advantages and limitations of various types of achievement tests. It is evident that there is a legitimate place for all kinds of tests, but no one test is equally good for all purposes.

What is the best procedure? Regardless of the purpose of the testing program or who makes the selection of tests, it is important that a systematic procedure be followed. Users of standard tests will find the information contained in *The Mental Measurements Yearbooks* of great value. The comprehensive character of the tests reviewed in this publication is indicated by the "Classification of Tests" in *The Fifth Mental Measurements Yearbook,* which is shown in Table 10-2.[4]

As an illustration of the type of evaluations in this volume, we offer the following evaluative excerpts from reviews of the seven Sequential Tests of Educational Progress (STEP),[5] which were reviewed for the first time in the 1959 volume.

The battery was discussed by Robert W. B. Jackson, Professor of Educational Research and Director of the Department, University of Toronto, Toronto, Canada, and by Wilbur L. Layton, Chairman of the Department of Psychology at Iowa State University, Ames, Iowa. In addition to this, each of the seven tests was reviewed by two or three persons. In all, 21 different persons reviewed some portion or portions of the STEP battery. Here indeed is a great deal of help for the prospective user of these tests, particularly if he reads a number of reviews carefully in order to average out the preferences of the reviewers.

Jackson described the tests, praising various aspects. Then on page 64 he expressed concern about what "seems to be an unjustified tendency to offer understanding and application of knowledge as alternatives to the acquisition of factual information. . . . The tests in mathematics, science, and social studies might well be improved by increasing the proportion of items requiring fac-

---

[4]O. K. Buros, ed., *The fifth mental measurements yearbook* (Highland Park, N. J.: Gryphon Press, 1959), p. vii.

[5]Essay, listening, mathematics, reading, science, social studies, and writing, published by the Educational Testing Service of Princeton, N. J.

TABLE 10-1

Advantages and Limitations of Standardized

STANDARDIZED

Criterion	Advantages	Limitations
1. Validity a. Curricular	Careful selection by competent persons. Fit typical situations.	Inflexible. Too general in scope to meet local requirements fully, especially in unusual situations.
b. Statistical	With best tests, high.	Criteria often inappropriate or unreliable. Size of coefficients dependent upon range of ability in group tested.
2. Reliability	For best tests, fairly high—often .85 or more for comparable forms.	High reliability is no guarantee of validity. Also, reliability depends upon range of ability in group tested.
3. Usability a. Ease of Administration	Definite procedure, time limits, etc. Economy of time.	Manuals require careful study and are sometimes inadequate.
b. Ease of Scoring	Definite rules, keys, etc. Largely routine.	Scoring by hand may take considerable time and be monotonous. Machine scoring preferable.
c. Ease of Interpretation	Better tests have adequate norms. Useful basis of comparison. Equivalent forms.	Norms often confused with standards. Some norms defective. Norms for various types of schools and levels of ability are often lacking.
Summary	Convenience, comparability, objectivity. Equivalent forms may be available.	Inflexibility. May be only slightly applicable to a particular situation.

And Nonstandardized Tests of Achievement

NONSTANDARDIZED

Essay		*Objective*	
Advantages	Limitations	Advantages	Limitations
Useful for English, advanced classes; afford language training. May encourage sound study habits.	Limited sampling. Bluffing is possible. Mix language factor in all scores. Usually not known.	Extensive sampling of subject matter. Flexible in use. Discourages bluffing. Compares favorably with standard tests.	Narrow sampling of functions tested. Negative learning possible. May encourage piecemeal study. Adequate criteria usually lacking.
	Reliability usually quite low.	Sometimes approaches that of standard tests.	No guarantee of validity.
Easy to prepare. Easy to give.	Lack of uniformity.	Directions rather uniform. Economy of time.	Time, effort, and skill are required to prepare well.
	Slow, uncertain, and subjective.	Definite rules, keys, etc. Largely routine. Can be done by clerks or machine.	Monotonous.
	No norms. Meaning doubtful.	Local norms can be derived.	No norms available at beginning.
Useful for part of many tests and in a few special fields.	Limited sampling. Subjective scoring. Time consuming.	Extensive sampling. Objective scoring. Flexibility.	Preparation requires skill and time.

TABLE 10-2

Classification of Tests in the Fifth Mental Measurements Yearbook (1959)

	Page		Page
ACHIEVEMENT BATTERIES	1	MISCELLANEOUS	
CHARACTER AND PERSONALITY	86	Miscellaneous	655
Nonprojective	86	Philosophy	655
Projective	212	Psychology	655
ENGLISH	324	Record and Report Forms	658
Composition	356	Religious Education	659
Literature	363	Safety Education	661
Speech	367	Socioeconomic Status	661
Spelling	368	Testing Programs	663
Vocabulary	373	MULTI-APTITUDE BATTERIES	667
FINE ARTS	376	READING	721
Art	376	Miscellaneous	756
Music	377	Oral	767
FOREIGN LANGUAGES	388	Readiness	772
English	388	Special Fields	780
French	398	Speed	780
German	408	Study Skills	781
Greek	411	SCIENCE	799
Hebrew	412	Biology	806
Italian	412	Chemistry	811
Latin	412	Geology	823
Spanish	413	Physics	824
INTELLIGENCE	415	SENSORY-MOTOR	831
Group	415	Hearing	831
Individual	535	Motor	832
MATHEMATICS	561	Vision	834
Algebra	575	SOCIAL STUDIES	841
Arithmetic	582	Economics	850
Geometry	611	Geography	850
Trigonometry	614	History	850
MISCELLANEOUS	615	Political Science	858
Business Education	615	Sociology	870
Computational and Scoring Devices	628	VOCATIONS	871
Education	628	Clerical	871
Etiquette	641	Interests	879
Handwriting	641	Manual Dexterity	901
Health	641	Mechanical Ability	904
Home Economics	648	Miscellaneous	920
Industrial Arts	650	Specific Vocations	932
Listening Comprehension	650		

tual knowledge not obtainable by reading a supplied passage; reading with understanding is not, after all, the primary objective in these areas."

He continued with "a more serious question to be raised with respect to the STEP series. . . . In their desire to keep clear of specific subject matter, the authors have apparently tended to arrive at something not too far from a *set* of measures of general intelligence. Further evidence in this connection, particularly in regard to intercorrelations among the tests of the different STEP series, will be awaited with interest. The basic similarity among certain reading, science, and social studies items . . . leads to the expectation that these may be uncomfortably high" (p. 64).

Layton prefaces his critique with the following cautions: "The STEP authors have attempted a tremendous task in designing and developing the STEP materials. Actually, the development project has only just begun. Consequently, in the early stages of the project this review may be too critical. A reviewer several years hence may find many of the present criticisms not applicable" (p. 67). Layton then argues that too high a price has been paid for the "sequential" feature, which attempts to span Grades 4 through 14.

John S. Diekhoff, Dean of Cleveland College, Western Reserve University, says of the STEP Essay Test: "Accepting as he does the assumption that the best test of writing is writing, this reviewer does not see how it could be done much better. The essay topics are appropriate to the several school levels. The sample essays present clear differences in quality—one wishes student themes were always so clearly 'high,' 'low,' or 'middle.'. . ." (p. 357).

Julian C. Stanley (author of this textbook) and Sister M. Jacinta Mann, Director of Admissions at Seton Hill College, concluded in their review that: "Overall, the STEP Science tests meet excellently the need for a well planned, coordinated survey series stressing application of common curricular material to familiar situations. . . ." To them, however, "The great amount of reading these tests require is somewhat disturbing . . . , even though the test authors do have an explicit rationale for their long contexts" (p. 804).

Reviewers do not always agree concerning the characteristics a test should have. For example, in contrast to Jackson's concern about inattention to facts, Stanley and Mann fear that the STEP Science test is oriented too heavily toward rote knowledge instead of toward comprehension, application, analysis, synthesis, and evaluation. Such discrepancies motivate Buros to have at least two, and preferably three, independent reviewers for each new test, when possible. Only the Listening Test is reviewed by just two persons; each other STEP test is reviewed by three independent reviewers or sets of reviewers.

If the test is not new, it has probably been reviewed in earlier *Mental Measurements Yearbooks,* which should be consulted. Buros has made this easy by providing a 479-page index of *Tests in Print*[6] that cites such reviews. The *Yearbooks* and *Tests in print* make it easier for a teacher, guidance counselor, or administrator to decide which tests he would like to inspect. He can then send to the publishers for sample ("specimen") sets to compare and contrast, assisted further by the *Yearbooks.*

---

[6]O. K. Buros, *Tests in print* (Highland Park, N. J.: Gryphon Press, 1961).

Many aspects determine the suitability of a given test for given purposes. For many years, test specialists have been offering various rating procedures designed to give a "score" to each of the tests being considered for use, so that various characteristics will be weighted properly.

In Table 10-3 we provide a simple scheme that involves assigning half of the 100 points to validity, one-fifth to reliability, and the remaining three-tenths

TABLE 10-3

A Simple Scale for Rating Published Tests

Category		Number of Points
Validity		50
Content and Curricular	30	
Statistical	20	
Reliability		20
Internal consistency	8	
Comparable forms	8	
Test-retest	4	
Usability		30
Ease of administration	10	
Provisions for scoring	10	
Other aspects	10	
Total		100

to usability. Within each of these three categories there are subdivisions, such as 30 points for content and curricular validity, and 20 points for statistical (predictive, concurrent, and construct) validity.

Two points have probably occurred to you: the weights one uses are arbitrary, and some test characteristics are essential, while others are desirable but not crucial. In the early 1950's, a committee appointed by the American Psychological Association (APA), working in collaboration with other professional groups, carefully devised "Technical recommendations for psychological tests and diagnostic techniques." These were supplemented a year later, in 1955, by "Technical recommendations for achievement tests," issued by the American Educational Research Association (AERA) and the National Council on Measurement in Education (NCME). Both sets of recommendations appear in the back of Buros' *Tests in print*,[7] which is another good reason why every school system should have at least one copy of that book. These test recommendations are likely to be revised every ten years or so.

The APA recommendations are made under six major headings: dissemination of information, interpretation, validity, reliability, administration and scoring, and scales and norms. The AERA-NCME report has the same head-

[7] Buros, *ibid.*, pp. 327–366 and 367–391, respectively.

ings. Probably the most important single feature of the recommendations is the treatment of validity.[8] Several excerpts from those discussions will help reveal the tenor of the recommendations, though of course the serious student will want to read the two sets of recommendations himself.

Here is the introduction to the section on validity in the APA report. We considered a number of these concepts in Chapter Five.

> Validity information indicates to the test user the degree to which the test is capable of achieving certain aims. Tests are used for several types of judgment, and for each type of judgment a somewhat different type of validation is involved. We may distinguish four aims of testing:
>
> a) The test user wishes to determine how an individual would perform at present in a given universe of situations of which the test situation constitutes a sample.
>
> b) The test user wishes to predict an individual's future performance (on the test or on some external variable).
>
> c) The test user wishes to estimate an individual's present status on some variable external to the test.
>
> d) The test user wishes to infer the degree to which the individual possesses some trait or quality (construct) presumed to be reflected in the test performance.
>
> Thus, a vocabulary test might be used simply as a measure of present vocabulary, as a predictor of college success, as a means of discriminating schizophrenics from organics, or as a means of making inferences about "intellectual capacity."
>
> To determine how suitable a test is for each of these uses, it is necessary to gather the appropriate sort of validity information. These four aspects of validity may be named content validity, predictive validity, concurrent validity, and construct validity. Content validity is evaluated by showing how well the content of the test samples the class of situations or subject matter about which the conclusions are to be drawn. Content validity is especially important in the case of achievement and proficiency measures. . . . Predictive validity is evaluated by showing how well predictions made from the test are confirmed by evidence gathered at some subsequent time. The most common means of checking predictive validity is correlating test scores with a subsequent criterion measure. . . . Concurrent validity is evaluated by showing how well test scores correspond to measures of concurrent criterion performance or status. Studies which determine whether a test discriminates between presently identifiable groups are concerned with concurrent validity. Concurrent validity and predictive validity are quite similar save for the time at which the criterion is obtained. . . . Construct validity is evaluated by investigating what psychological qualities a test measures, i.e., by demonstrating that certain explanatory constructs account to some degree for performance on the test. To examine construct validity requires both logical and empirical attack. Essentially, in studies of construct validity we are evaluating the theory underlying the test. The validation procedure involves two steps. First, the investigator inquires: From this theory, what predictions would we make regarding the variation of scores from person to person or occasion to occasion? Second, he gathers data to confirm these predictions.

---

[8]Technical recommendations for psychological tests and diagnostic techniques, *Supplement to the Psychological Bulletin,* 1954, 51, No. 2, Part 2, 38 pp. (201–238).

This rather extensive introduction continues for several pages. Then, 67 recommendations are made and discussed. Of these, 46 are labeled ESSENTIAL, 18 VERY DESIRABLE, and 3 DESIRABLE. Here are examples of each category:

> C.1. When validity is reported, the manual should indicate clearly what type of validity is referred to. The unqualified term "validity" should be avoided unless its meaning is clear from the context. ESSENTIAL
>
> *Comment*: The manual should make clear what type of inference the validation study reports. No manual should report that "this test is valid." In the past, evidence that is not appropriately termed evidence of validity has been presented in the manual under that heading. For example, the "validity" report of the Thurstone Interest Schedule deals solely with item-test correlations. The discussion of item-test correlations in the manual of the Heston Personal Adjustment Inventory illustrates how such data may be used in reporting test validity without risk of misleading readers. . . .
>
> C.6.12. When validity of a clinical test is indicated by agreement with psychiatric judgment, the training, experience, and professional status (e.g., diplomate) of the psychiatrist should be stated. VERY DESIRABLE
>
> C.15.2. Validity of predictions from interest tests should be estimated separately at different levels of mental ability. DESIRABLE

You can check off the characteristics of prospective tests against the APA-AERA-NCME recommendations, supplemented by reviews in the *Mental Measurements Yearbooks,* before using them. This may seem to be a long, somewhat tedious process, but it is your best guarantee of using wisely the large number of pupil-hours and teacher-hours allotted to testing. We shall not offer you any scale for rating tests, other than the brief one in Table 10-3, because the technical recommendations themselves can serve this evaluating function best.

Long ago, Brownell pointed out "some neglected criteria for evaluating classroom tests"[9] that go beyond the recommendations discussed above. Does the test:

1. elicit from the pupils the desired types of mental processes?
2. enable the teacher to observe and analyze the thought processes which lie back of the pupil's answers?
3. encourage the development of desirable study habits?
4. lead to improved instructional practice?
5. foster wholesome relationships between teacher and pupils?

Brownell's criteria are especially important for achievement tests. Such tests can be evaluated by means of Bloom's *Taxonomy of educational objectives,*[10] which emphasizes the higher thought processes of comprehending, ap-

---

[9]W. A. Brownell, Some neglected criteria for evaluating classroom tests, *National Elementary Principal,* 1937, 16, 485-492.

[10]B. S. Bloom, M. D. Engelhart, E. J. Furst, W. H. Hill, and D. R. Krathwohl, *Taxonomy of educational objectives; the classification of educational goals. Handbook I: Cognitive domain* (New York: Longmans, Green, 1956).

plying, analyzing, synthesizing, and evaluating as being important steps beyond the purely factual, but of course basic and essential, knowledge level.

In selecting a test for a particular purpose, consider the grade level at which it is to be administered. Test publishers often suggest a considerable grade range in which the test may be used, but both test authors and publishers tend to be too optimistic concerning the range of usefulness of their tests. For example, a scholastic aptitude test that is supposed to be suitable for grades three through eight may be found too difficult for half the students in the typical third grade and too easy for the abler students in the eighth grade. Usually, a test discriminates best among a group of students if the average score obtained is half-way between the chance level and the perfect score, and if very few students make chance or perfect scores. Remember, however, that for diagnostic and mastery tests the discriminating function may be relatively unimportant.

ADMINISTERING
THE TESTS   In order to insure that tests are properly administered, three questions must be answered:

1. When should the tests be administered?
2. Who should administer the tests?
3. What is the correct procedure to follow?

Each of these questions is considered carefully below.

When Should the Tests Be Administered?

As problems concerning the use of "intelligence" tests differ somewhat from those concerning the use of achievement tests alone, it is better to consider the two separately. When should intelligence tests be administered? There is general agreement that it is not necessary to give the same pupils intelligence tests every year, but there is also agreement that possible fluctuations on group tests are great enough to warrant giving such tests more than once. The fluctuations are likely to be larger in the primary grades. A reasonable plan employed by many school systems is to give intelligence tests at transitional points in the pupil's school career. Procedure would therefore vary according to the school organization. A suggested minimum program is as follows:

Type of Organization	Grades in Which to Give Intelligence Tests
Six-six plan	First and sixth or seventh
Seven-five plan	First and seventh or eighth
Eight-four plan	First and eighth or ninth
Six-three-three plan	First, sixth or seventh, and ninth or tenth

If possible, it would be well to add to this minimum program a test at about the fourth grade and one near the end of the high-school course.

In recent years, testing in the eleventh and twelve grades by outside agencies such as the College Entrance Examination Board (verbal and quantitative scholastic aptitude, plus as many as three or more achievement tests), the American College Testing Program, and the National Merit Scholarship Corporation have provided high schools and colleges with a wealth of comparative information about students. This can be used wisely for both guidance and selection, in helping the student make thoughtful and satisfying educational and vocational choices. Such information may make extensive ability testing by the senior high school staff unnecessary.

There is some disagreement regarding the best time of year to give intelligence tests. Of course, if the tests are to have maximum value, their results must be made available at the very beginning of transitional periods, such as entrance to the first grade or junior high school. This means they should be given early in the first grade if the pupils have not attended kindergarten. The reliability and validity of the test may be increased by postponing testing until at least two weeks after entrance to kindergarten or the first grade. The later tests can be given either at the beginning of the transitional year or at the close of the year preceding. There is a growing tendency to have scholastic aptitude tests for college entrance administered in the junior year of high school and achievement tests during the senior year. This is obviously necessary if such tests are to be used in counseling seniors regarding the advisability of continuing their education. Also, for interim testing, there will usually be a few pupils who will transfer into the school system and who have not had intelligence tests, and other pupils about whom teachers may feel serious doubt regarding the validity of the existing record.

The frequency with which achievement tests should be used will depend mainly on the purpose they are to serve. Most purposes, however, will require at least two series of tests administered alternately every year or two. Most achievement tests have norms for the middle and the end of the year, but often for no other time. When tests are given at these periods, comparisons with norms are easiest. There is also the fact that many studies have shown a considerable decline in knowledge of certain subjects by the end of the summer vacation. This would seem to favor giving the tests at the end of the school year, when the pupil's status is more normal. A comparison between the records made by pupils at the end of each of two successive years is usually more trustworthy than that between the beginning and end of one year.

There are some advantages in having the tests administered in the fall. Almost always, some pupils will enter the school for the first time and their status in the group can best be determined by administering tests to all the pupils. The teachers will then have the entire school year in which to remedy any deficiencies revealed. Fall testing also avoids the undesirable practice of cramming. If too much emphasis is placed on "improvement" shown during the year, however, pupils may be tempted not to do their best on the first series of tests. This would not be the case if progress is measured between two series of tests administered at the end of the preceding year and at the end of the current school year.

Administering the tests at the end of the school year will make it possible to have the information serve several purposes. It can be used partially as a basis for determining promotion from the grade, for educational guidance, and possibly for sectioning the next grade. Also, there seems to be no good reason why an analysis of the errors revealed cannot serve equally well as a basis for remedial teaching in the succeeding grade, as if the new teacher had given the test at the beginning of the year. Of course, sometimes there might be considerable value in repeating the test at the beginning of the year in order to determine the effects of the summer vacation, apart from the better-established weaknesses which were present when the vacation started. Moreover, the estimation of achievement level is more trustworthy when based on two samplings of performance than on one.

Who Should Administer the Tests?

It is not always an easy matter to tell who is really competent to administer standardized tests. In the case of individual tests of the Stanford-Binet or Wechsler type, only persons who have had sufficient specific instruction should attempt to administer them. There should be at least one person in every school who is qualified to give such individual tests. When group tests are used for purposes of research, or when they are used to compare one grade, class, or school with others, they should usually be given by one person, or a small group of specially trained examiners. But in the ordinary testing program, the regular classroom teachers should usually administer the group tests. Most teachers will welcome an opportunity to do so. At the present time there seems no good reason for selecting a group test whose administration is so difficult as to be beyond the mastery of most teachers in the public schools. The point of view of the pioneer measurement specialist William McCall seems as sound today as it was when first stated:[11]

> Many years ago certain specialists sought to secure a monopoly of the privilege of using standard tests by trying to persuade educators to regard the tests as possessing certain mystic properties. A few of us with Promethean tendencies set about taking these sacred cows away from the gods and giving them to mortals. Can teachers be entrusted with tests? If not, then teachers ought not to be trusted with 90 per cent of their present functions. We now entrust them with the far more difficult task of teaching reading, creating concepts, and building ideals. Let us not strain at a gnat when we have swallowed fifty elephants.

---

[11] W. A. McCall, in *The Test Newsletter,* published by Bureau of Publications, Teachers College, Columbia University, December 1936.

But it is well not to take the competency of the examiners for granted. One of the best plans is to get the group of examiners together and demonstrate the administration of the tests to be used. A good way to do this is to give a demonstration with a regular class and to follow this by a discussion with the examiners of the procedure they have seen. Another way is to administer the test to the examiners themselves. This should be followed by a full discussion of the procedure involved. It is usually well to suggest that after each examiner has studied the manual he try the procedure on some other person, perhaps on a member of his family; or two teachers may try it out on each other. If questions then arise, they can be settled by a conference with the person in general charge of the program before the examiner goes before his own students to administer the test. It has been found that, if such measures are taken, the regular classroom teachers can obtain practically the same results with group tests as can be obtained by special examiners.

What Procedure Should Be Followed?

Although the procedure of administering group intelligence tests and achievement tests is not beyond the mastery of classroom teachers and school administrators, some difficulties may arise. In fact, good group testing may be more difficult than individual testing. First, the conditions for the test must be favorable. It is usually best to have the tests given in the familiar environment of the pupils' own classrooms. This is especially true with younger children. It is well always to have the tests given at regular class time without permitting them to run over into lunch hour or play time. For the same reason it is desirable not to have tests just before or just after an important event, such as a holiday, a school party, or an athletic contest. Precautions should be taken to avoid distractions and interruptions during the test. It is a good plan to attach to the outside of the classroom door a card which reads: *Tests Going On. Please Do Not Disturb.* Pupils should be instructed to remove everything from the tops of their desks except two well-sharpened pencils with good erasers. The examiner should also have ready several extra pencils in case any of the children forget theirs. All these things must be looked after in order to insure favorable testing conditions.

As a rule, a group test can be successfully administered by anyone who meets the following three requirements. First is being able to read well. Good silent reading is required for the mastery of the directions printed in the manual which accompanies the test. Good oral reading ability is required, for the directions to the pupils should be *read*, not recited from memory. To undertake to give the test from memory is to run a serious risk of leaving out some important word or phrase or of paraphrasing the directions in such a way as to change their meaning. But the examiner should be so familiar with the manual that he can read the directions with his eyes off the page a good part of the time. The directions should be read with proper emphasis in a clear voice just loud enough to be heard throughout the room. The aim should be to make the meaning understood without arousing excitement, anxiety, or hostility.

The second requirement for administering a test is accurate timing. If the test has a single time limit of, say, 20 minutes or more, it is probably preferable to time it with an ordinary pocket watch rather than a stop watch, since the latter may on occasion be erratic. When a pocket watch is used, set its hands to some convenient time such as the beginning of an hour and give the starting signal just as the second hand reaches 12 (which is also 0). It will usually help students and examiner alike to have a clock in the room, preferably at the front, which shows everyone the correct time.

The aim should be to keep time to the very second. On most tests the signal to start is, "Ready, go!" or "Ready, begin!" When this signal is given, the examiner should note—that is, write down—the *exact* time—hour, minute, and second. This should be *recorded immediately,* preferably on a small card or specially prepared blank. The record for Test 1 would look like this:

Test 1	Hr.	Min.	Sec.
Time test began	9	0	0
Time allowed		5	
Time to stop	9	5	0

Experienced examiners know that *it is never safe to trust one's memory to keep the time.* A written record must be made.

The third requirement for administering a test is the ability to follow directions accurately. The manual should be followed verbatim; no deviation whatsoever is permissible. To add anything to the directions, or to modify them in any way, means that the test can no longer be called standardized. The norms are made on the assumption that a specified procedure is to be used. As a part of the preliminary instructions, pupils are almost always told not to ask any questions after the test starts. Occasionally a pupil forgets this instruction and holds up his hand for a question. The examiner should walk over to him and, if it is a reading test or an intelligence test whose purpose is following directions, should say in a quiet voice, "Read it carefully and do just what it says." If it is an achievement test and the pupil is concerned about where to put his answer or some other point of mechanics that does not involve the answer to a question in the test or modify the directions already given, it is permissible to set the pupil at ease without causing disturbance. The teacher should be free to say or do anything that does not disturb or delay pupils at work, that does not help the individual child do the things for which he is being tested, and that does set him to work again after some foolish or trivial issue has distracted him. Examples of permissible statements are: "Yes, you may change your answer if you decide it is wrong," "Just work on the side of the sheet; you do not need scratch paper," "When you have finished the first column go right on to the next one," and "No, you must not go back to a test you have passed." *In case of doubt, the examiner should err on the side of saying nothing.* While the test is in progress the examiner must be alert constantly to see that the pupils neither help nor hinder each other nor are distracted by external factors. A test is more than a measuring device; it presents a standardized situation in which to observe pupil behavior. Anything observed during the progress of the test that may throw light upon the interpretation of the results should be carefully recorded.

SCORING THE TESTS It is desirable to have the tests scored as quickly as possible, and with the highest possible degree of accuracy. As a rule, then, the best system is the one that accomplishes these objectives with the minimum expenditure of money, time, and energy. There are two questions involved: Who should score the tests? What technique should be used?

Who Should Score the Tests?

There are a number of extremely fast electronic test-scoring machines. It is desirable for any school system to consider having the tests it uses scored by them, rather than burdening the administrative staff and teachers with this essentially clerical operation at which people are far less efficient than the machines. By negotiating with major test companies, the superintendent or his representative may be able to contract for "package deals" that include, at reasonable rates, rental of test booklets and answer sheets, accurate, fast scoring, and reporting of desired scores and other statistics. He may also want to request supervisory assistance for administering the tests. In these ways he disrupts teaching as little as possible while securing just the information he needs, which may even include counts of the various responses to individual test items, if that data is wanted for diagnostic purposes. By renting tests and answer sheets, he eliminates storing and inventory problems. Also, he will always be using the current forms of the tests, whereas if he purchased copies it might be necessary to continue using an obsolescent form because of the expense of buying the later version.

Therefore, *we recommend that electronic-machine scoring be utilized as much as possible,* freeing teachers and administrators from costly, inefficient clerical labor. In actual practice, however, standardized tests are often scored locally by a variety of persons, so we shall give certain suggestions for improving manual procedures. Where objective tests with special answer sheets such as the one shown in Figure 6-3 on page 199 are used, scoring by means of cut-out cardboard stencils can be made quite efficient. Each answer sheet should be scored independently by two scorers. If they do not agree, the answer sheet may be rescored by them or, preferably, by a third scorer in order to reconcile the differences. If answers are marked in test booklets, scoring may have to be slower and more elaborate.

Sometimes, especially in larger systems, the work is done by a clerical staff at a central bureau, or by the use of old-type (i.e., electric rather than electronic) scoring machines; sometimes it is done by advanced students under supervision; but the most common method seems to be to have the work done by the teachers. Except in the larger systems where there is a bureau of research equipped with special facilities, the scoring is probably best done by the classroom teachers. In that way not only can the work be done promptly, but the teachers can perhaps learn something of value about the types of errors made on the achievement tests. But it is important to get the scoring done without producing an unfavorable attitude toward it on the part of the teachers. Some schools have found it advisable to dismiss classes at noon when the testing is in progress, so that the teachers can devote the afternoon to the work of scoring. This would seem an effective way of emphasizing the important fact that *teaching and testing are intimately related processes.*

What Techniques Should Be Used?

Every reasonable precaution should be taken to assure a high degree of accuracy in scoring. It must not be assumed that merely because the directions are clear, the key complete, the separate answer sheets well-designed, and the process entirely objective, perfect protection against errors is thereby afforded. Numerous studies give abundant evidence to contradict this assumption. They reveal two distinct types of errors in scoring: *constant errors* and *variable errors.* A common example of the former type is misunderstanding the scoring directions—for instance, by counting omissions the same as errors, when using a correction-for-chance scoring formula. Such errors are especially serious, because there is no possibility of their offsetting each other according to any so-called "law of averages." Variable errors, on the other hand, sometimes tend to make the score too high and at other times too low. Although such errors may do serious harm to individual pupils, they tend to cancel each other in group measures such as averages. Examples of variable errors are errors resulting from carelessness, errors in counting the scores, errors in entering the scores on the front of the test booklet or on the record sheet, and errors in adding up the total score. Some of the most serious errors found are not in marking the paper at all, but in counting and in addition.

Clearly, then, accuracy in scoring cannot be taken for granted. What is to be done about it? The first thing is to prevent the occurrence of errors. The scorers must be *taught* how to score the papers and not merely *told* how to do it. They should be given an opportunity to study the manual and the scoring keys, and whenever possible, an actual demonstration of scoring should follow. It is a good idea, also, .o check carefully the first few papers marked by beginners to detect errors at the outset. This procedure should reveal any constant errors and the principal types of variable errors. It is usually desirable to have each page or part of the test, or each answer sheet, scored through all the papers in a set before going on to the second page, part of the test, or answer sheet. If the scorers work in groups, as is usually desirable, each one can specialize in marking one part of the test, and pass the test when scored to the next scorer, who is specializing in marking the next part of the test. This procedure will reduce the risk of error and at the same time will increase the speed of scoring. It is usually an especially poor technique to have one person read the answers while the scorers mark the papers. This is slow, because the slowest scorer sets the pace. It also increases the risk of error, owing to the possibilities of losing the place or of failure to hear correctly.

Colored pencils are desirable. Inexperienced scorers should mark each item in the test being scored in some uniform manner, such as + for correct, − for incorrect, and 0 for omitted items. Experienced scorers will save time by marking only the incorrect and omitted items. It is, of course, unnecessary to mark the items below the last one the pupil attempts. But it is well to draw a horizontal line across the test under the last item attempted. Figure 10-1 illustrates the scoring of an alternative-response test of word meaning, using the formula Score = R − W.

The simple device of keeping a written record of who marks, checks, transcribes, or totals each part of the test reduces the likelihood of error. If the scoring is organized systematically, it is a simple matter to keep such a record on a mimeographed sheet attached to each package of tests when scored, as shown in Figure 10-2.

But in spite of these preventive measures, certain errors are likely to occur. The safest plan, therefore, is to have each set of papers marked a second time by different scorers, using pencils of a different color. If a complete rescoring does not seem practical, a sampling method may be followed. Each fifth or tenth paper, for example, may be selected and carefully rescored, and if only an occasional minor error is found, the whole set may be safely accepted. On the other hand, if frequent or serious errors are found in these sample papers, the entire set should be rescored. In any event it is important to have some person other than the original scorer check the totals for each part of the test and for the whole test, all substitutions in the scoring formulas, all transcribing of scores, and all transmuting of point scores into derived scores.[12] It is possible to locate many serious errors by examining closely the profile of each individual pupil on all tests with this form of record. Any score much higher or much lower than the general level should be suspect. Also, when two or more tests are used which purport to measure the same function, any serious discrepancies should be scrutinized, on the supposition that a high positive correlation is to be expected. The standard of absolute accuracy should be accepted by all scorers. *The possibilities of serious injustice to individual pupils by errors in scoring should be recognized fully.*

---

[12] Derived scores are obtained from tables of norms. Each point score is expressed in some equivalent unit, such as an age or percentile rank. The interpretation of these units is considered in Chapter Four.

When two words mean the SAME, draw a line under "SAME."
When they mean the OPPOSITE, draw a line under "OPPOSITE."

SAMPLES	fall—drop	<u>same</u>—opposite		
	north—south	same—<u>opposite</u>		

1	expel—retain..	same—<u>opposite</u>	1	+
2	comfort—console	<u>same</u>—opposite	2	+
3	waste—conserve	same—<u>opposite</u>	3	+
4	monotony—variety	same—<u>opposite</u>	4	+
5	quell—subdue	<u>same</u>—opposite	5	+
6	major—minor..	<u>same</u>—opposite	6	−
7	boldness—audacity...	<u>same</u>—opposite	7	+
8	exult—rejoice	<u>same</u>—opposite	8	−
9	prohibit—allow	<u>same</u>—opposite	9	O
10	debase—degrade	<u>same</u>—opposite	10	+
11	recline—stand	same—<u>opposite</u>	11	+
12	approve—veto...	same—<u>opposite</u>	12	+
13	amateur—expert...	<u>same</u>—opposite	13	−
14	evade—shun	same—<u>opposite</u>	14	+
15	tart—acid	same—<u>opposite</u>	15	−
16	concede—deny	same—<u>opposite</u>	16	O
17	tonic—stimulant...	<u>same</u>—opposite	17	+
18	incite—quell	<u>same</u>—opposite	18	−
19	economy—frugality	<u>same</u>—opposite	19	+
20	rash—prudent	same—<u>opposite</u>	20	+
21	obtuse—acute	same—<u>opposite</u>	21	O
22	transient—permanent.......................................	same—<u>opposite</u>	22	O
23	expel—eject	<u>same</u>—opposite	23	+
24	hoax—deception...	same—<u>opposite</u>	24	O
25	docile—submissive...	<u>same</u>—opposite	25	+
26	wax—wane	same—opposite	26	
27	incite—instigate...	same—opposite	27	
28	reverence—veneration	same—opposite	28	
29	asset—liability	same—opposite	29	
30	appease—placate..	same—opposite	30	

Right ....**15**....Wrong .....**5**...Score ....**10**......

Figure 10-1. *An illustration of the procedure followed in scoring Test 3 of the Terman Group Test of Mental Ability, Form A (Copyright by World Book Company).*

ANALYZING AND INTERPRETING THE SCORES

After the tests have been scored and checked, the next step is the analysis and interpretation of the results. Both processes go on together, for analysis is worthless without interpretation, and interpretation is impossible without analysis. Analysis is of two main types, statistical and graphical. Before either can be undertaken, how-

STANDARD TEST SCORING RECORD

Name of Test Modern School Achievement Test Form 1

School Williamsdale Grade 4

No.	Scored by	Errors	Checked by	Comment
1.	Mary Anderson	5	John Long	In adding
2.	Julia Jones	0	Mabel Adams	not reduced to lowest terms
3.	James Johnson	3	Lee Cross	
4.	Jeanette Long	4	Ed Howard	Decimals
5.	Jessie Lee	20	William Jameson	Misunderstood Directions
6.	Alma Wright	0	Jed Smith	
7.	Walter Justice	2	Ruth Alton	Carelessness
8.	Oscar Wilson	2	Ray Kelley	"
9.	Mildred White	1	June Hunt	
10.	Anna Camp	3	Henry Luther	"

Transcribed by	Errors	Checked by	Comment
Betty Brown	0	Walter Coleman	
Edith Raymond	1	Elizabeth Kent	

Scores added by	Errors	Checked by	Comment
Judson Allen	1	Alice James	Too low by 100

Norms, etc., by	Errors	Checked by	Comment
Edsel Harvey	0	Susan Clay	

Class record by	Table made by	Median by	Graph by
Martha Rule	Bill Tate	Norma Gill	Sarah Garr

Figure 10-2. *A sample standard test scoring record.*

ever, there is the important preliminary step of classification and tabulation. An analysis of errors appearing in the test papers is usually of major importance to the classroom teacher. Chapters Three and Four are concerned with a discussion of the whole problem of analysis and interpretation; only an outline will be given here to indicate the steps involved:

1. Classification and tabulation of scores
2. Statistical analysis of scores
3. Graphical analysis and representation
4. Use of norms and standards
5. Analysis of errors

In a complete testing program all five of these steps will receive attention, although not always to the same degree. If the primary purpose of the testing program is diagnosis, for example, the fourth step would be relatively unimportant and the fifth step relatively important. The reverse would be true of a program whose main objective is a study of the comparative efficiency of various grades, classes, and schools.

APPLYING THE RESULTS   The application of the results is the crux of the whole testing program. Everything that has gone before is preliminary. Whatever value the tests are to have depends in the last analysis on the use made of the results.

Just what is to be done, of course, depends on the purpose of the program. In several chapters we have considered in some detail procedures to be followed for several administrative and instructional problems. It will be sufficient at this point to give some idea of how the procedure will vary with the purpose.

Suppose, for example, that the purpose of the tests is to determine the present status of a particular school in order to improve it, and that the test data are before the principal. The question now is, what is to be done? On the basis of the test scores and other pertinent data, such as the teachers' estimates, health reports, age-grade status, and the like, several pupils are given trial promotions to the next higher grades. A small group of pupils, whose achievement and intelligence scores are well below the central tendency of their respective grades, is organized into an ungraded class which is assigned to a specially prepared teacher. Ability groups are also organized in several grades and classes, with appropriate differentiation in curricula and methods.

Similarly, suppose the primary purpose of the testing program is to determine whether or not the teaching emphasis is correct in the various subjects in the grades, and, when the test results are in, it is apparent that most of the grades are strong in arithmetic and spelling, about average in reading, and weak in language and the social studies. Now what is to be done here? The principal calls the teachers together and presents the situation in tables and graphs, with interpretive comment. Then they discuss the findings. One or more committees are appointed to study the situation and to make recommendations at a later meeting. After discussion and deliberation, a course of action is decided upon, looking to the improvement of the situation in the weaker subjects.

The procedure will again be somewhat different in essential respects if the primary purpose is diagnosis and remedial work in reading. Here the test results should be analyzed in some detail in each grade. An analysis of the test papers, item by item, is often very revealing. Special effort should be made to locate the specific nature of the reading difficulties. There may be found some general weaknesses, such as the inability to use the index and table of contents in a book, or possibly to locate the central idea in a paragraph. In addition, there are usually other weaknesses, which appear in some pupils and not in others. Some of these will not be revealed at all by the usual paper-and-pencil reading tests, but will require special tools and techniques. After considering these facts, the staff will try to plan a remedial program to be followed during the year.

The essential point in all these cases is that *something is done about the situation revealed by the test scores.* To fail to apply the results in some practical way is to fail in the testing program.

RETESTING TO DETERMINE
THE SUCCESS
OF THE PROGRAM   Most testing programs stop with applying the results, if, indeed, they go that far. But an essential step yet remains. After a reasonable time has been allowed for a trial of the remedial measures which were agreed upon in the light of the test data, a checkup should be made to determine the success of this program. Most tests are not sufficiently accurate to reveal progress over a shorter period than one-half year. As a rule, a second comparable form of the test or tests used in the beginning should be employed in retesting. If this is not done, it will usually be very difficult to express the results in terms sufficiently comparable to make an accurate measure of progress possible. Of course, not all the change from one form to another can be correctly attributed solely to the remedial program. Some of it is doubtless due to practice effect, or familiarity with the test itself, part of it to instruction outside the school, part of it to natural growth, and part to difference between forms.[13] Often, however, the improvement will be so marked as to indicate beyond a reasonable doubt the effectiveness of the program attempted. At other times the improvement will be disappointingly small. It is then usually wise to modify the remedial program in the view of the results obtained.

The essential point is that the success of the remedial program must not be taken for granted. On the contrary, a definite effort must be made to assess its effectiveness. To fail to do this is to leave the testing program incomplete. There

---

[13] If two forms of the test are available, it is probably wise to administer Form A to half the students at the beginning of the year and Form B to the other half of the students then. At the end of the year, those students who took Form A first can take Form B, and vice versa. This procedure permits us to determine whether Forms A and B are equally difficult. For a way to ascertain this, see J. C. Stanley, Statistical analysis of scores from counterbalanced tests, *Journal of Experimental Education,* 1955, 23, 187-207.

is no better reason for taking the efficiency of the remedial program on faith than there was for taking the earlier results of teaching on faith.

MAKING SUITABLE
RECORDS AND REPORTS   Certain records and reports are essential to the success of the testing program. But by no means do all these records and reports come chronologically at the end of the program. Some of them are essential to the last three stages already discussed.

In general, it may be said that five groups have an interest in knowing what the tests show: pupils, teachers, administrators, parents, and the general public. Naturally, the nature of the report will vary somewhat with the group to whom it is made, and the nature of the record with the specific function it is to serve. In Chapter Eleven we consider ways test results may be used and reported.

SUMMARY   We have considered eight steps in the testing program, from determining the purpose of the program to making suitable records and reports. Buros' *Mental Measurements Yearbooks* and his *Tests in Print,* plus such classifications of educational objectives and test items as Bloom's *Taxonomy of Educational Objectives,* constitute basic resources that should be available to help educational personnel set up test programs, carry them out competently, and use the results well. Good testing requires thought, time, and money, but probably in no other way can teachers learn as much about pupils in such a short period of time. The better the planning, the more that can be learned per dollar spent.

RECOMMENDED READINGS

Anderson, Scarvia B. and Maier, M. H., 34,000 pupils and how they grew, *Journal of Teacher Education,* 1963, 14, 212–216.

Bauernfeind, R. H., *Building a school testing program.* Boston: Houghton Mifflin, 1963.

Buros, O. K., *Tests in print.* Highland Park, N. J.: Gryphon Press, 1961.

Buros, O. K., *The sixth mental measurements yearbook.* Highland Park, N. J.: Gryphon Press, 1965.

Chauncey, H. and Dobbin, J. E., *Testing: Its place in education today.* New York: Harper & Row, 1963.

Cottle, W. C. and Downie, N. M., *Procedures and preparations for counseling.* Englewood Cliffs, N. J.: Prentice-Hall, 1960.

Findley, W. G., ed., The impact and improvement of school testing programs, *Sixty-Second Yearbook of the National Society for the Study of Education, Part II.* Chicago: University of Chicago Press, 1963.

Katz, M., Selecting an achievement test: principles and procedures, 2nd ed., *Evaluation and Advisory Service Series* No. 3, Educational Testing Service, 1961. Free.

Traxler, A. E., Ten essential steps in a testing program, *Education,* 1959, 79, 1–6.

GRADING, REPORTING, AND PROMOTING

At some point most teachers must convert scores into grades. They must then convey the import of these grades to parents and pupils, perhaps even in the form of a recommendation for non-promotion. Changing scores into grades is at best a rather arbitrary process, and this arbitrariness is further complicated by public-relations aspects of reporting to parents. Frequently these difficulties produce double-talking teachers and confused, defensive parents.

Nowadays, however, the teacher or counselor often is not only reporting to parents about grades, but is also helping them interpret scores from teacher-made tests and from standardized tests in terms of local and/or national norms. This sort of reporting is less threatening to teachers and parents alike, but calls for special skills of the kind that we hope you have acquired by now, especially familiarity with percentile ranks, standard scores, errors of measurement, and predictive validity.

C H A P T E R E L E V E N

MARKING TESTS   First let's look at the process of assigning grades to tests. Sometimes the grade is given directly, as when an English teacher says that this is an "A" theme and that is a "C" theme. In his mind, some sort of evaluative process has gone on, moderated by his usual standards of grading. Implicitly, he is accustomed to giving approximately a certain percentage of A's, of B's, and so on. Typically, he is a "hard," an average, or an "easy" marker, as compared with other teachers of the same course in the same school. His percentages fluctuate from time to time, of course, particularly if he uses grades as a motivating or disciplining device, but year after year his grades tend to average higher or lower than the grades of certain other teachers of the same course.

Quite a few teachers give a paper a total point score that is the percentage grade directly, as when each of 25 questions counts four points. Either percentages are used directly or the letter equivalent of a percentage is set by school regulations (e.g., 70—79 = C, 80—89 = B, 90—100 = A). This can result in much cut-and-trying of successive tests in order not to fail most of the pupils or give most of them A's. Since the difficulty of a test depends on the particular items that happen to be used, and since teachers are not expert judges of such difficulty (nobody is, for that matter), direct percentage marking usually forces the teacher to grade some tests leniently and others severely in order to make the grades come out "right." If percentages are running low, he can give points for partially-correct answers, unless the questions are wholly objective. If percentages are running too high for his tastes, he can choose to credit only the most unimpeachable answers and count all the others wrong. If all this adjusting of scoring methods still results in a distribution of grades different from that desired by the teacher, he can make the next test easier or harder in order to bring the average grade up or down.

Changing standards from test to test in the above ways must be confusing to students. Actually, it is unnecessary. If the teacher simply scores the test for number of points earned, expressed neither as a grade nor as a percentage, (e.g., with 25 items the maximum number of points might be 25, each item counting 1 point), then he can make the arbitrary conversion of points into grades according to his best judgment. The basic question he must answer is: "How many A's, B's, C's, D's, and F's shall I give this class on this test?" Thus he is face to face with the arbitrariness of his decision, rather than having it hidden by sleight-of-hand grading procedures.

No one has ever been able to devise a sure-fire way to make the savage grader more lenient and the easy one more stringent, but there may be help in faculty discussion of grading practices, together with consideration of anonymous distributions of grades actually assigned by various teachers. If a certain teacher insists year after year that he gets the worst students in his classes, it may be desirable to set up an explicit partitioning of available students at the beginning of the year so that his contention may be shown invalid. However, it is difficult, if not impossible, to raise the grading level of the teacher who argues that his severe grading is indicative of good teaching. (Grading differences among instructors are at least as great at the college level as they are in high schools and elementary schools.)

In desperation, some schools have set up percentages of the various grades, especially of failing grades, that all teachers are urged or even required to follow: not more than 10 per cent of F's in general mathematics at the end of the year, for example. Such prescription is of limited value, though, for the ability of students in various sections even of the same course can vary considerably, because of scheduling difficulties and year-to-year variation, as when none of the pupils taking advanced mathematics can enroll for one section of physics but must all be in the other. Probably it would not be fair to require the same distribution of grades in these two sections.

Some of you may have heard of "grading on the normal curve," which became popular during the 1920's and 1930's. Stripped of its unnecessary complexities, this amounted simply to determining in advance just what percentage of the class would get A's, what percentage B's, etc. Some amusing and revealing tales are told about how this prejudgment might backfire. On the first day of class a graduate professor of Latin informed the seven students taking his advanced course that he had learned of grading on the curve the previous summer and would use it in this class, resulting in certainty that one of the seven students would fail the course. As the students left at the close of class, one of them muttered to the other six, "I'm sure to be the one who fails, so I'm dropping the course right now."

"But you can't do that," the others exclaimed, "because we don't know which one of us would fail then."

So the six pitched in and paid the predestined failure to stay in the course and absorb the failing grade.

Another story is similar. At a certain large university during the first few years after World War II, the wives of veterans who were studying there enrolled for the more difficult courses in sufficient numbers to absorb all the failing grades themselves. They simply did little or no work and received F's and D's, while their husbands got grades of C or better with only moderate effort.

We deplore this much rigidity, of course, but the fact remains that the number of A's or F's given is rather arbitrarily dependent upon the philosophy or even the whim of the instructor or of some policy-making group such as a committee. Setting the percentage of each grade in advance may be justifiable for, say, the 2,000 persons enrolled for a required college course in physical science that has a common final examination for all sections. Even then, however, some discretion is usually left to the instructor of each section to count daily assignments and his own quizzes in determining the final grades. A compromise of uniformity with individuality of grading seems desirable.

ACHIEVEMENT
VERSUS EFFORT   Thus far we have been talking chiefly about marking tests. In assigning quarter, semester, and yearly grades for a course, many teachers consider not only achievement as measured by tests but also more subjectively evaluated characteristics such as "effort," punctuality, behavior, and neatness of written work. Usually these non-test aspects get much more weight in elementary school than in high school, even to the point that in some schools children who are "working up to capacity" get the highest obtainable grade, even though they are not learning much, while those who seem not to be expending "enough" effort are graded lower, despite better achievement. This extreme system is confusing to pupils and parents, especially when a child moves from elementary to junior high school and his grades change sharply because the bases for them change.

Just as one does not average oranges and bicycles, so it is wise to *keep marks for achievement separate from ratings of essentially non-cognitive aspects.* Achievement can be judged in terms of teacher-made tests, homework assignments, work in class, and standardized tests. Sometimes these various sources do not agree, in which event both the written and oral reporting procedures should reveal the discrepancies. It is informative to know that Johnny does rather poorly on his fifth-grade teacher's general science tests, but leads the same class on the Sequential Tests of Educational Progress (STEP) science test.[1] In one sense he may be termed an "underachiever," but in another he is not.

---
[1] See pages 143-148.

Far too little use is typically made of information from standardized tests when reporting to pupils and parents. Caution may stem from unhappy effects of divulging IQ's in the early days of their use (1920-35), but achievement-test results seem far less threatening to parents and pupils than are scores or IQ's from intelligence tests. If David can't read well, that is something to be remedied. But if he isn't very "bright" the picture looks hopeless and uncomplimentary to the whole family. In reporting to parents and pupils, one is usually well advised to avoid words with undesirable connotations such as IQ, intelligence, and brightness. Instead, talk or write about reading ability, vocabulary knowledge, and knowledge of word meanings. Be even more specific and diagnostic, if possible, for Mary may be considerably better with synonyms and antonyms than she is with verbal analogies, or better with spatial-relations items than with arithmetical reasoning.

In the elementary school it is helpful to present local-norm profiles to parents at a teacher-parent conference where they can be considered and explained. These profiles, which can show achievement graphically without using any numbers at all, indicate the pupil's strengths and weaknesses relative to his peers in the grade or school system. A sample is shown in Figure 3-2 on page 70, if the numbers are deleted from the profile. Points are plotted with a plastic, wooden, metal, or cardboard template that itself contains the percentile ranks or standard scores. Parents see that their child is, for example, in the "High" section on certain tests, "Average" on others, and perhaps "Low" on some. Titles of the tests are simplified so that they will be readily understandable and non-threatening.

This same profile scheme can be continued in junior and senior high school or even college for measures common to all students. It would not be correct, however, to compare local norms for most elective subjects directly with local norms for required subjects, because the ability level of students in the former might not be comparable to that in the latter. For instance, students who take Latin or physics are usually abler than typical students in their grade. On local norms their average would have to be set above the 50th percentile for required subjects in order to make the point on the profile representing Latin (or physics) comparable to points representing required subjects. Standard scores for achievement tests of the College Entrance Examination Board are "pegged" in this way. A standard score of 500 on the Scholastic Aptitude Test, Verbal, is approximately the 59th percentile of senior applicants tested for college, while a score of 500 is only the 14th percentile of the advanced mathematics achievement test, because persons taking the latter are an exceptionally capable group as judged by their scores on the *SAT*.[2]

We saw on page 159 that only the highest and lowest points on a profile are likely to differ significantly from each other in the statistical sense—that is, to

---

[2]*College Board score reports: a guide for counselors* (Princeton, N. J.: College Entrance Examination Board, 1962), pp. 11, 14.

represent "real" differences that would continue to appear upon retesting the pupil with comparable forms of the same tests. Even if a pupil's "true" profile were a straight line right across the middle of the "Average" region of the graph, his "obtained" profile would have peaks and valleys because of errors of measurement. The difference between the true and the obtained profile will be greatest when points on the profile are based on short, poorly-prepared tests, and least when points are based on long, well-prepared tests. For stability of scores, length of test is usually even more important than the care with which it is devised. Quite a few manuals for multi-score tests now illustrate the effect of errors of measurement on the difference between obtained scores at two points on a profile. In any event, don't pay much attention to small differences between standard scores on two tests.

REPORT CARDS   Most modern report cards contain both grades and check-list items; some also contain achievement-test scores. The trend is toward informing parents more by interpreting and supplementing the grades themselves. It seems important to keep achievement separate from judged effort, neatness, citizenship, and the like. Parents usually want to know both aspects: how does my child compare with his classmates in knowledge of each subject being studied, and how does he seem to the teacher in other respects? Also, is he doing as well as he can be expected to do on the basis of measures of general ability? How does he rank on national norms in the subject, as shown by an achievement test?

No one report card can be offered as a model. Each school or school system must work out its own reporting system in terms of the local situation. You would like to see a few reasonably typical cards, however, so we present three, as Figures 11-1, 11-2 and 11-3. Each carries the year's report for a single subject—fine arts, social studies, and typing, respectively. These cards were used at the Wisconsin High School (Grades 7-12) in Madison during the academic year 1963-64. They have the first part in common. Grades of A, B, C, D, F, Inc., or NM are given for "Scholastic Achievement" each of the four quarters. Citizenship ratings of S, N, and U are also given each quarter. Check lists on the lower part of each card differ from subject to subject, the categories for fine arts being the most numerous and detailed.

Like most secondary schools, Wisconsin High School maintains a cumulative record of test scores for each student, which can be used in parent-teacher or student-counselor conferences. It does not have an official parent-teacher conference report form, however, so the form in Figure 11-4 comes from another school system. It is a check list to be used twice, in triplicate each time (the original is white, the first carbon copy is yellow, and the second carbon copy is pink).

The four report forms were devised by teachers for local use, so they should

Report of _____

Ratings are for first quarter, first semester, second quarter, second semester	Semester I		Semester II	
Scholastic Achievement				
Citizenship				

Scholastic Achievement Ratings: A-Excellent; B-Good; C-Fair; D-Poor (D-not recommended for college entrance); F-Failure; Inc.-Incomplete; NM-Non-Mastery. Marks of Inc. and NM can be converted into passing marks through supplementary work.

Citizenship Ratings - S-Superior; N-Normal; U-Unsatisfactory.

Items checked here offer partial explanation of ratings given above	Superior	Average	Unsatisfactory
INITIATIVE Ability to initiate ideas with minimum stimulation from instructor Comment _____			
WORK HABITS Expresses ideas in an original, inventive and imaginative way Comment _____			
Demonstrates an understanding of some basic art principles Comment _____			
Uses time in an effective way Comment _____			
Cares for tools and equipment _____			
Demonstrates craftsmanship and an understanding of materials Comment _____			
EVALUATION OF WORK Ability to judge and improve own work Comment _____			
Ability to work congenially with others and accept criticism Comment _____			
Shows growth in expression Comment _____			
General quality of completed work Comment _____			

Red-1st 9 weeks; Black-1st Semester; Green-3rd 9 weeks; Purple-2nd Semester

Signature of Teacher _____

Figure 11-1. *A sample report card for fine arts.*

Report of _____

Ratings are for first quarter, first semester, second quarter, second semester	Semester I		Semester II	
Scholastic Achievement				
Citizenship				

Scholastic Achievement Ratings: A-Excellent; B-Good; C-Fair; D-Poor (D-not recommended for college entrance); F-Failure; Inc.-Incomplete; NM-Non-Mastery. Marks of Inc. and NM can be converted into passing marks through supplementary work.

Citizenship Ratings - S-Superior; N-Normal; U-Unsatisfactory.

Items checked here offer partial explanation of ratings given above	Semester I		Semester II	
1. Organizes material well				
2. Thinks independently and critically				
3. Has growing understanding of current problems				
4. Takes active part in class discussion				
5. Works up to capacity				

_____

_____

_____

_____

_____

_____

_____

_____

_____

Signature of Teacher _____

Figure 11-2. *A sample report card for social studies.*

Report of _____

Ratings are for first quarter, first semester, second quarter, second semester	Semester I		Semester II	
Scholastic Achievement				
Citizenship				

Scholastic Achievement Ratings: A-Excellent; B-Good; C-Fair; D-Poor (D-not recommended for college entrance); F-Failure; Inc.-Incomplete; NM-Non Mastery. Marks of Inc. and NM can be converted into passing marks through supplementary work.

Citizenship Ratings - S-Superior; N-Normal; U-Unsatisfactory.

Items checked offer partial explanation of the ratings given above.

	Semester I				Semester II			
	LOW	HIGH	LOW	HIGH	LOW	HIGH	LOW	HIGH
1. Technique								
2. Stroking rate								
3. Accuracy in stroking								
4. Proofreading								
5. Ability to apply skill								
6. Promptness in completing assignments								

Signature of Teacher _____

Figure 11-3. *A sample report card for typewriting.*

BIRNAMWOOD PUBLIC SCHOOLS
Birnamwood, Wisconsin

Parent-Teacher Conference Report   Teacher's Name ....

Name of Student..Name of Parent..

Date........................	Date........................
First Conference	**Second Conference**

PHYSICAL

General Health — — — — —

Specific difficulties — —

Attendance record............days pres.

Regular sleeping hours — —

Personal appearance — — —

EMOTIONAL

Getting along at home — —

Is he having trouble in school?

Courtesy — — —

Special friends — —

WORK HABITS

Follows directions —

Neatness — —

Does he give up easily ?

Work independently?

Others — — —

ACADEMIC GROWTH

Language	ave. above below
Arithmetic	ave. above below
Reading	ave. above below
Writing	ave. above below
Music	ave. above below
Others	ave. above below

TEACHER'S COMMENTS

Suggestions:

PHYSICAL

General Health — — — — —

Specific difficulties — —

Attendance record............days pres.

Regular sleeping hours — —

Personal appearance — — —

EMOTIONAL

Getting along at home — —

Is he having trouble in school?

Courtesy — — —

Special friends — —

WORK HABITS

Follows directions —

Neatness — —

Does he give up easily ?

Work independently?

Others — — —

ACADEMIC GROWTH

Language	ave. above below
Arithmetic	ave. above below
Reading	ave. above below
Writing	ave. above below
Music	ave. above below
Others	ave. above below

TEACHER'S COMMENTS

Suggestions:

Figure 11-4. *A parent-teacher conference report form. Devised by F. O. Pappenfuss.*

not be considered models for your teaching situation. Perhaps they do suggest that more than just letter grades can be put on report forms understandably. Profiles and explanations such as those shown in Figure 11-5 may help the school with this aspect of reporting.

Let us state again that we consider it essential that report cards and parent-. teacher conferences be supplemented by careful reporting of standardized-test results. Much information of great value and interest to parents and pupils lies buried in test files. It should be used evaluatively and diagnostically in systematic ways, along with the results of teacher-made tests, to round out the picture of the pupil's progress for his parents. This must be done skillfully and carefully, of course, but we are convinced that it should be done.

Wrinkle's Suggestions

After ten years of experimenting with a number of ways to improve marking and reporting practices, William Wrinkle, a former principal, listed the following twenty-two generalizations that seemed to him to summarize the things he and his staff had learned. You will be amply

---

Metropolitan Achievement Tests
HIGH SCHOOL BATTERY

INDIVIDUAL PROFILE CHART AND REPORT TO PARENTS

Name _____

Grade _____ Age _____
                    years   months

Date of Birth _____

Date of Testing _____

Teacher _____

Norms: National ☐ _____   Am ☐
                       type   Form:
        Local ☐   Bm ☐

This Profile Chart provides information on the student's progress in important areas of the curriculum. Stanine scores in the shaded area on the right represent average achievement; scores 1, 2, and 3, below average achievement; and scores 7, 8, and 9, superior achievement. Information on interpreting the Profile may be found on the reverse side of this sheet.

Tests	1 Reading	2 Spelling	3 Language	4 Language Study Skills	5 Study Skills	6 Vocabulary	7 Information	8 Comp. and Conc.	9 Anal. and Prob. S.	10 Conc. and Und.	11 Information
					Social Studies			Mathematics		Science	
%-ile Ranks											
Stanines											
Above Average	9 8 7	9 8 7	9 8 7	9 8 7	9 8 7	9 8 7	9 8 7	9 8 7	9 8 7	9 8 7	9 8 7
Average	6 5 4	6 5 4	6 5 4	6 5 4	6 5 4	6 5 4	6 5 4	6 5 4	6 5 4	6 5 4	6 5 4
Below Average	3 2 1	3 2 1	3 2 1	3 2 1	3 2 1	3 2 1	3 2 1	3 2 1	3 2 1	3 2 1	3 2 1

To plot the scores: Enter the percentile rank and stanine score for each test in the boxes above the arrows. In each column, below the boxes, circle the number that is the same as the stanine score in the box directly above it. Join the circles with straight lines.

repaid by improved understanding of marking and reporting for the time you spend considering these statements:[3]

1. The statement of any outcome or objective to be evaluated should be analyzed into its specific meanings so that its meaning is clearly stated.
2. The number of different forms should be kept at a minimum. If two or more short forms are to be used at the same time, they should be incorporated into a single form.
3. During a period of experimentation, unless there is plenty of money to spend on printing, forms should be produced by some inexpensive process such as mimeographing. An expensive printed form is less likely to be discarded even if it is known to be inadequate.
4. The basis for an evaluation of the student's achievement should be decided upon. Should the evaluation be in terms of established norms, the class average, or the ability of the student?
5. In the interpretation of a report the likelihood of misunderstanding by parents tends to increase in proportion to the number of details included in the report.
6. Students should have a real part in the development of new forms and practices.
7. The development by students of an understanding of and a favorable attitude toward new practices is a most effective approach to parent education.

[3]W. L. Wrinkle, *Improving marking and reporting practices in elementary and secondary schools* (New York: Rinehart, 1956).

Figure 11-5. *Left, Individual profile chart and report to parents, Metropolitan Achievement Tests, High School Battery. Right, reverse side of chart. (Reproduced with permission of Harcourt, Brace & World, Inc., New York.)*

TO THE PARENTS

Scores on the Metropolitan Achievement Tests, like scores on any other test, are just one form of information about the student. They will be useful to the extent to which they are properly understood by all concerned. By knowing and understanding the strengths and weaknesses of your child, it may be possible for you to provide help and encouragement where it is most needed.

Basically, the eleven Metropolitan tests seek to measure the student's progress in the following areas of learning:

Reading. Understanding main ideas and seeing relationships among them, knowing the literal meaning of words and passages, and reading for retention.

Spelling. Correct spelling of commonly used words.

Language. Proper use of grammar, punctuation and structure.

Language Study Skills. Familiarity with standard references and other sources of information.

Social Studies. Three tests covering (1) understanding and interpretation of various types of social studies information (maps, graphs, etc.); (2) knowledge of words and terms used in social studies; (3) knowledge of facts and information relative to history, government, economics, and sociology.

Mathematics. Two tests—Computation and Concepts, and Analysis and Problem Solving—measure basic computational and problem-solving abilities.

Science. The *Scientific Concepts and Understandings Test* measures understanding of scientific terms and concepts, while the *Science Information Test* covers knowledge and understandings in general science, chemistry, biology, and physics.

How to Understand the Profile Chart. The profile on the other side of this form is a graphic picture of your child's achievement in each of the eleven tests. The scores are recorded as "stanines" based on a STAndard NINE-point scale ranging from very low (1) to very high (9). These scores show the student's standing in comparison with scores earned by a large sample of other students at the same grade level.

Percentile ranks are also given. A percentile rank of 40 means that the student scored as well as or better than 40% of the group on which the percentiles are based. Percentile ranks do *not* represent the per cent of correct answers on a test.

The numbers circled on the Profile indicate the different levels of achievement earned by your child in the tests. Small differences of one or two stanines from one subject to another should not be given too much attention. However, any noticeable differences, or an over-all pattern of high or low scores may suggest the need for consultation among parents, teachers, counselors, and the student. Consultation should also be arranged if you desire further information about these tests or about your child's progress in school.

8. The student's experiences, his successes, difficulties, abilities, and inabilities, should be the subject of frequent conversations between teacher and student. Students should be encouraged to take the initiative in asking for such conferences.

9. The summarization of reports on a student in a departmentalized program by a guidance counselor, a home-room teacher, a core teacher, or the principal involves too big a task and is not a workable plan.

10. Reporting on all students at one time during the school year is chiefly for the purpose of stimulating competitive comparisions; if such stimulation is not a purpose of the reporting, then reports should be made at different times to discourage such invidious comparisons.

11. The scale type evaluation form is unsatisfactory unless each scale item involves only a single outcome, the achievement of which can be expressed in degrees by clearly distinguishable descriptions.

12. The check form is simpler than the scale for use in reporting evaluations and is more economical of space on a printed form.

13. The development of highly detailed, elaborate cumulative record forms is uneconomical; if too detailed and lengthy, they will not be used by most teachers.

14. To ensure an adequate understanding by parents of the status of the student, a conference should be arranged between the parents and the counselor or teacher for the discussion of individual cases.

15. Although it has many real advantages, the conference plan is not a practical solution to the reporting problem, especially at the secondary-school level.

16. Check lists utilizing the best features of the scale-type evaluation, the anecdotal record, and the conference plan should be developed for the evaulation of (a) general outcomes with which the total school program is concerned and (b) more specific outcomes relating to each of the various areas of the curriculum.

17. Parents should be sent a summary form of evaluation focusing attention on desired outcomes of the school program which have been analyzed in detail by the check lists. The evaluation made should involve cooperative activity on the part of students and teachers.

18. Whatever forms for use in reporting are developed, a separate report involving the use of a five-point scale should be maintained for administrative record purposes. Administrative records should not be confused by shifting from A B C D F to H S U to H M L or other sets of symbols.

19. Check forms, unless they are carefully controlled, tend to become increasingly detailed and, therefore, increasingly impractical.

20. The best way to state objectives is in terms of desired behavior outcomes—what the learner should do.

21. Many teachers have difficulty in writing effective comments. A deliberate program for the improvement of the writing of informal comments is essential.

22. The most intelligible way to write supplementary comments in explaining evaluations is to tell what the student did.

TO PROMOTE OR NOT TO PROMOTE

With universal public education in the United States, whose goal now seems to be high-school graduation for all but a tiny percentage of the least-able pupils, non-promotion from one school grade to the next is becoming more and more uncommon, though in some localities it is still appreciable. Quitting school—the "dropout problem"—looms larger on the high-school horizon in most places than does outright failure to get promoted. Emphasis has shifted from non-promotion toward individualizing instruction to match better the varied abilities, interests, and presumed needs of high-school students in our heterogeneous "comprehensive high schools" that enroll virtually the entire age group from the neighborhood served. This often results in very attractive courses for the least able, sometimes so attractive that the "Track 1" students are almost envious, as for example when non-college-preparatory students in their senior year have, in place of fourth-year English, a lively speech-drama course, which the college-bound students are barred from taking. This is a welcome change from the days when a considerable number of students were labeled "dumb-bells" and considered hopeless.

SUMMARY   Thus we see that grading, reporting, and promoting should be related rather intimately to measurement and evaluation. Without adequate measurement, you cannot properly grade the extent of a student's knowledge of a particular unit or course. Without measurement evidence from various tests, including those you yourself construct, to support your conclusions, you cannot report helpfully and convincingly to parents and pupils. Without appropriate measurement and expert evaluation, you cannot help determine which academic "track" (including repeating the grade) is likely to be best for the pupil in the long run. As a teacher, you never outgrow your need for measurement and evaluation.

EPILOGUE   With that paraphrase of a well-known slogan we conclude the body of *Measurement in Today's Schools,* leaving the appendixes and indexes to supplement the knowledge you have acquired in Chapters One through Eleven. We hope that you will continue to learn about measurement. Many colleges and universities offer courses beyond the basic one, such as test construction, individual intelligence testing, personality assessment, projective techniques, factor analysis, scaling techniques, and measurement theory. Also, a number of test publishers offer excellent free articles on measurement principles. Finally, you can keep up-to-date by reading a professional journal such as *Educational and Psychological Measurement* or the *Journal of Educational Measurement.* But most immediately helpful to you may be the many references in *Measurement in Today's Schools,* through which you can extend your grasp of the *MTS* material. We wish you continued growth in knowledge of measurement and evaluation.

RECOMMENDED READINGS

Byrne, R. H., *The school counselor.* Boston: Houghton Mifflin, 1963.

Goodlad, J. I. and Anderson, R. H., *The nongraded elementary school.* New York: Harcourt, Brace, 1959.

Katz, M., Seibel, W. W., and Connolly, J. A., Testing ...testing ...,*Junior Libraries,* 1961, 7, 14-20. Reprinted, with additions, by Educational Testing Service as "Take a reading in measurement."

Kurtz, A. K. and Bertin, M. A., Reappraisal of marking practices, *Educational Research Bulletin,* 1958, 37, 67-74.

Palmer, O., Seven classic ways of grading dishonestly, *English Journal,* 1962, 51, 464-467.

School entrance age—policies and exceptions, *NEA Research Bulletin,* 1963, 41, 77-78.

Wrinkle, W. L., *Improving marking and reporting practices in elementary and secondary schools.* New York: Rinehart, 1956.

APPENDIXES

A SIMPLIFIED
TEST-ANALYSIS PROCEDURE

Preparing the Items

The two characteristics usually determined for a test item are *difficulty* and *discrimination.* How hard is the item for the group tested, and how well does it distinguish between the more able and the less able students? These two aspects of an item are nearly independent of each other, the exception being that a very easy or very hard item cannot discriminate well. If all students mark the item correctly, it has not separated them into two groups, the passers and the failers. Likewise, if all mark it incorrectly (or if only a chance proportion mark it correctly), the item is non-discriminating for the group.

In the following paragraphs, a simple method for analyzing items is presented and illustrated in considerable detail. Preferably, the test or subtest should contain items of only one type (for example, four-option multiple-choice). There should be a considerable number of such items—say, arbitrarily, 50 or more—and they should have been administered to a substantial number of persons. Thus the procedure works best with final examinations prepared cooperatively by several teachers and given to large groups, and less well with daily or weekly tests in a single school class. Even for the latter situation it has some value, however.

Each student should be strongly encouraged to answer *every* item for which he has any information whatsoever, even a vague hunch concerning a single one of the options.[1] Also, time should be available for nearly everyone to try every item.

The items should be arranged as nearly as possible in ascending order of difficulty. This can be done fairly well on a subjective basis, or if the item has been administered previously to a similar group, the original difficulty values may be used. Subjective estimates of relative difficulty based on the average of independent rankings by three qualified persons usually approximate the actual ranks better than an ordering made by only one person.

---

[1] See the discussion on pages 189–193.

Test items should be prepared according to content specifications agreed upon by the teachers who will use them. If possible, each item should be typed on a 5 x 8 card, with the answer *not* indicated on the front of the card. In fact, for purposes of criticism and editing it may be well not to have the answer on the back of the card, either. A separate answer key may be better.

Each item should be constructed with great care, special attention being given to the incorrect options (called distracter, decoys, or foils). It should then be keyed and criticized on a separate sheet *independently* by each person helping to devise the test. This editing is extremely important and should be followed by a detailed conference to reconcile differences, remove ambiguities, and discard items that cannot be revised properly. Though time-consuming, a cooperative approach to test construction pays off by increasing reliability and validity and improving the morale of test-takers.

Statistical item analysis is no substitute for meticulous care in planning, constructing, criticizing, and editing items. It does supplement that intuitive process, however, by revealing unsuspected defects or virtues of the specific items.

A Measure of Discrimination

After the test has been given, score the papers or answer sheets by marking with a red pencil all items *in*correctly answered or omitted. Because of the instructions concerning omissions, they should be few. Each pupil's score will be the sum of his red marks—the smaller the better.

Divide the papers or answer sheets into three piles, as follows:

1. Arrange the N papers by score, beginning on top with the smallest number (best score) and going on down to the largest number (poorest score).

2. Multiply N, the total number of students, by 0.27 and round off the result to the nearest whole number, or look in Table A-5 on pages 353–355 for the appropriate figure, called *n* there.

3. Count off the *n* best papers from the top of the stack. This is the "high" group.

4. Count off the *n* poorest papers from the bottom of the stack. This is the "low" group.

5. Put aside the middle group (approximately 46 per cent of the papers), since it is not used in the item-analysis.

6. Set up a form somewhat like Table A-1, with Item Number, W_L, W_H, $W_L - W_H$, and $W_L + W_H$ headings.

7. W_L is the number of persons in the low group who answered a certain item wrongly, including those who omitted it. It represents the total number of red marks for that item in the low group.

8. W_H is the number of persons in the high group who answered the item wrongly, including those who omitted it. It represents the total number of red marks for that item in the high group.

The larger $W_L - W_H$ is, the more discriminating power the item has. For editing purposes it is well to arrange the items from least discriminating—and therefore in greatest need of scrutiny—to most discriminating. A few items may have negative $W_L - W_H$ values, indicating that more persons in the high than in the low group missed the item. Such items may be mis-keyed, ambiguous, or unrelated in content to the rest of the test.

For convenience, a critical value of $W_L - W_H$ at or above which the item is considered suitably discriminating may be determined from Table A-5 on pages 353–355. Then high-low group data for every option of each unsuitably discriminating item may be secured to aid in the editing process.

A Measure of Difficulty

The larger $W_L + W_H$ is, the harder the item was for the group tested. $W_L + W_H$ may be multiplied by a constant, $\dfrac{100 \times o}{2n(o-1)}$, to obtain an estimate of the difficulty of the item, corrected for chance;[2] here o is the number of options each item has. This approximates the percentage of the students who did not "know" the correct answer. Items in the revised test should be arranged according to $W_L + W_H$, from lowest (easiest) to highest (hardest).

An Illustrative Analysis

Table A-1 shows W_L, W_H, $W_L - W_H$, $W_L + W_H$, and difficulty values for each of the 100 items in a perhaps typical, but hardly excellent, final examination constructed by four college instructors of freshman English and administered with "do-guess" instructions to 243 students at the end of the winter quarter. The item numbers have been rearranged, the least discriminating item now coming first and the most discriminating one last.

When N = 243, 0.27N = n = 66, so there are 66 persons in the low group and 66 in the high group. Therefore, the maximum possible value of $W_L - W_H$ is 66 − 0 = 66, and the minimum possible value is 0 − 66 = −66. These figures would probably never occur except because of mis-keying, however, for even by chance about $\frac{1}{5}$th of the examinees who attempted an item would mark it correctly. Thus the highest expected value for $W_L - W_H$—barring omissions, mis-keying, or extreme misinformation— is [66 − $\frac{1}{5}$(66)] − 0 = 52.8; the lowest is −52.8.

In practice, there will probably be few large negative values, since *most items have at least a little positive discriminating power*. Only three negative $W_L - W_H$ figures occur in Table A-1; the largest of these is −9. The greatest positive $W_L - W_H$ value in the table is 41. It will be instructive to examine these two items (Nos. 30 and 90) carefully in order to infer why they differ radically in discriminating power. Let us take the *least* discriminating item first:

> 30. In preparing a speech the first step is to choose a subject. The speaker should then
>   A. practice.
>   B. collect material.
>   C. choose gestures.
>   D. select main points.
>   E. phrase a thesis.

Responses by the high and low groups (66 students in each) were as shown in Table A-2. The keyed answer was **B**, "collect material," but E, "phrase a thesis," appealed

---

[2]Quite a few test specialists do not favor correcting item difficulty indexes for "chance." For a discussion of this point see F. B. Davis, Item selection techniques, Ch. 9 in E. F. Lindquist, ed., *Educational measurement* (Washington, D. C.: American Council on Education, 1951), pp. 267–285.

TABLE A-1

The 100 Items in a Five-Option Multiple-Choice Teacher-Made Test
Arranged according to Discriminating Power,
from the Least Discriminating to the Most Discriminating

Item Number	Rank Order of Item According to Discriminating Power (1 = Poorest Discrimination)	$W_L = 66$	$W_H = 66$	$W_L - W_H$ (Discrimination)	$W_L + W_H$	Estimated Percentage of Examinees Who Did Not "Know" the Correct Answer to the Item* (Difficulty)
30	1	31	40	−9	71	67
35	2	1	2	−1	3	3
27	3	38	39	−1	77	73
38	4	0	0	0	0	0
31	5	38	37	1	75	71
34	6	28	26	2	54	51
42	7	4	1	3	5	5
72	8	17	14	3	31	29
32	9.5	5	0	5	5	5
60	9.5	5	0	5	5	5
29	11	9	4	5	13	12
39	12	14	9	5	23	22
94	13	6	0	6	6	6
45	14	8	1	7	9	9
28	15	49	42	7	91	86
8	16	58	51	7	109	103**
33	17	31	23	8	54	51
44	19	10	1	9	11	10
51	19	10	1	9	11	10
86	19	10	1	9	11	10
92	21	16	7	9	23	22
81	22	13	2	11	15	14
14	23	16	5	11	21	20
74	24	24	13	11	37	35
57	25	26	15	11	41	39
46	26	12	0	12	12	11
40	27	13	1	12	14	13
48	28	15	3	12	18	17
67	29	15	2	13	17	16
52	30	30	17	13	47	45
20	31	48	35	13	83	79
21	32	54	41	13	95	90
76	33	15	1	14	16	15
68	34	16	2	14	18	17
59	35	17	3	14	20	19
19	36	22	8	14	30	28
62	37	18	3	15	21	20
70	38	21	6	15	27	26
61	39	28	13	15	41	39
43	40.5	37	22	15	59	56

TABLE A-1 (Cont.)

Item Number	Rank Order of Item According to Discriminating Power (1 = Poorest Discrimination)	$W_L = 66$	$W_H = 66$	$W_L - W_H$ (Discrimination)	$W_L + W_H$	Estimated Percentage of Examinees Who Did Not "Know" the Correct Answer to the Item* (Difficulty)
97	40.5	37	22	**15**	59	56
41	42	43	28	**15**	71	67
26	43	57	42	**15**	99	94
49	44	16	0	**16**	16	15
4	45.5	18	2	**16**	20	19
82	45.5	18	2	**16**	20	19
25	47	23	7	**16**	30	28
77	48.5	18	1	**17**	19	18
79	48.5	18	1	**17**	19	18
75	50	19	2	**17**	21	20
66	51	19	1	**18**	20	19
58	52	23	5	**18**	28	27
3	53	29	11	**18**	40	38
18	54	25	6	**19**	31	29
5	55	27	8	**19**	35	33
23	56	39	20	**19**	59	56
100	57	46	27	**19**	73	69
36	58	51	32	**19**	83	79
24	59	23	3	**20**	26	25
37	60	25	5	**20**	30	28
65	61	26	6	**20**	32	30
22	62	45	25	**20**	70	66
9	63	25	4	**21**	29	27
56	64	35	14	**21**	49	46
95	65	59	38	**21**	97	92
7	66	53	31	**22**	84	80
69	67	26	3	**23**	29	27
47	68	31	8	**23**	39	37
17	69	37	14	**23**	51	48
91	70	26	2	**24**	28	27
63	71	51	27	**24**	78	74
1	72	30	5	**25**	35	33
13	73.5	33	8	**25**	41	39
16	73.5	33	8	**25**	41	39
53	75	35	10	**25**	45	43
10	76	38	13	**25**	51	48
54	77	40	15	**25**	55	52
64	78	27	1	**26**	28	27
80	79	37	11	**26**	48	45
55	80	42	16	**26**	58	55
71	81	47	21	**26**	68	64
84	82	30	3	**27**	33	31
89	83	32	5	**27**	37	35
98	84	36	9	**27**	45	43
83	85	37	10	**27**	47	45
11	86	42	15	**27**	57	54
78	87	29	1	**28**	30	28

TABLE A-1 (Cont.)

Item Number	Rank Order of Item According to Discriminating Power (1 = Poorest Discrimination)	$W_L = 66$	$W_H = 66$	$W_L - W_H$ (Discrimination)	$W_L + W_H$	Estimated Percentage of Examinees Who Did Not "Know" the Correct Answer to the Item* (Difficulty)
6	88	39	11	**28**	50	47
96	89	36	7	**29**	43	41
50	90	40	11	**29**	51	48
85	91	52	23	**29**	75	71
73	92	32	2	**30**	34	32
99	93	43	13	**30**	56	53
87	94	38	7	**31**	45	43
93	95	54	23	**31**	77	73
15	96	37	5	**32**	42	40
88	97	37	2	**35**	39	37
2	98	43	8	**35**	51	48
12	99	41	4	**37**	45	43
90	100	49	8	**41**	57	54
Totals				**1762**	**4088**	

$$* \quad \frac{100 \times o}{2n(o - 1)} (W_L + W_H) = \frac{500}{132 \times 4} (W_L + W_H) = 0.947(W_L + W_H),$$ where o represents the number of options per item.

**Slightly fewer persons answered Item No. 8 correctly than would be expected on the basis of chance alone.

more to those students who earned high scores on the test as a whole. Options A and C ("practice" and "choose gestures") were practically useless, since they decoyed only 3 of the 132 persons. Option D, "select main points," discriminated in the proper direction, 8 to 18. The item as a whole was fairly difficult, since 67 per cent of the freshmen did not "know" the correct answer.

By using the above information, the speech teacher may be able to salvage the item without destroying its main point. He would try to determine why Option E attracted the better students. This may indicate the need for additional classroom instruction concerning steps in preparing a speech, or it may highlight a real conflict between **B** and E as the correct answer for the item. If the dilemma can be resolved, new distracters will then be devised to replace ineffective Options A and C.

On the other hand, it may not be feasible to retain the item. Not all poorly discriminating questions can be revised successfully. Sometimes the point tested is not clear or defensible enough to serve as the basis for an item. Therefore, more items for each part of the test outline should be prepared than will be needed in the revised test, so that virtually unrevisable items may be discarded. How many excess items are needed depends on the nature of the test, the purposes for which it will be used, and the care devoted to initial construction and editing. Some items, such as those concerning vocabulary, are much easier to prepare well than are others, such as civics questions.

TABLE A-2

Number of Examinees in High and Low Groups
Who Chose Each Option of Item No. 30 —

Group	Option						Number of Examinees
	A	B	C	D	E	Omit	
High	1	26	0	8	31	0	66
Low	1	35	1	18	11	0	66
Totals	2	61	1	26	42	0	132

Now let us turn to the *most* discriminating item, No. 90:

"Humanity is the mould to break away from, the crust to break through, the coal to break into fire, the atom to be split" is a quotation from
  A. John Dos Passos.
  B. Carl Sandburg.
  C. Robinson Jeffers.
  D. Kenneth Fearing.
  E. Sherwood Anderson.

Numbers of responses to the various options are shown in Table A-3; the keyed answer is **C**, "Robinson Jeffers." Note that all four distracters (A, B, D, E) discriminate in the right direction and reasonably well; each is more attractive to the low group

TABLE A-3

Number of Examinees in High and Low Groups
Who Chose Each Option of Item No. 90

Group	Option						Number of Examinees
	A	B	C	D	E	Omit	
High	2	1	58	3	2	0	66
Low	14	8	17	15	11	1	66
Totals	16	9	75	18	13	1	132

than to the high group. Approximately 54 per cent of the examinees did not "know" the correct answer. This item does not need any editing.

How many of the items should be edited on the basis of option information like that contained in Tables A-2 and A-3? Probably most of them could be improved in this manner, especially by the substitution of better distracters for nonfunctioning ones,[3]

---

[3] Replacing defective options does not raise these items above their excessively rote-knowledge level, of course. Perhaps it would be better to discard these 25 least discriminating items and write 25 items at the comprehension, application, analysis, synthesis, and evaluation levels. See pp. 173–175.

but the labor involved in this process is too great for most teachers unless only a small portion of the items are scrutinized. A rule-of-thumb procedure would be to edit the 25 per cent least discriminating items. For Table A-1, where there are 100 items, this involves taking the first 25 items, whose $W_L - W_H$ values are less than 12. For these 25 items, information like that contained in Table A-4 would be drawn up by two conscientious persons (even high-school students) working together. Then teachers would edit carefully on the basis of the discrimination, difficulty, and option information given in Tables A-1 and A-4.

To provide you material upon which to practice editing, we present the 25 least discriminating items below. They still contain the spelling and typographical errors that appeared on the test itself. Of course, these should have been removed by careful proofing of the stencils before mimeographed copies were run off.

30. [Already appears on page 343.]
35. The subject you choose for a talk should be
    A. one that is wholly new to you.
    B. one that interests you but about which you know nothing.
    C. anything for which you can find material.
    D. anything which will find the required time.
    E. one that interests you and about which you already know something.
27. In a panel discussion the members of the panel
    A. deliver prepared speeches.
    B. ask questions of the audience.
    C. provide informal discussion for audience.
    D. answers questions of the moderator.
    E. speak in rotation from right to left.
38. The best material for a speech
    A. holds interest and develops thesis.
    B. bores audience but develops thesis.
    C. pleases the speaker but annoys the audience.
    D. pleases audience but ignores purpose of speech.
    E. is unreliable but develops thesis.
31. A speaker whose purpose is to instruct should begin by
    A. showing why the information is needed.
    B. telling a funny story.
    C. stating his thesis.
    D. putting a diagram on the board.
    E. stating his qualifications to speak.
34. The fundamental process under which is included methods of organizing a speech is
    A. adjustment to the speaking situation.
    B. articulation.
    C. choice of material.
    D. symbolic formulation and expression.
    E. phonation.
42. Good posture for a speaker should be
    A. rigid and stiff.
    B. oratorical and pompous.
    C. comfortable and natural.
    D. odd and unusual.
    E. lax and undisciplined.
72. In "American Letter" MacLeish expresses
    A. loyalty to a foreign land.

    B. disgust with American industry.

    C. disgust with American tradition.

    D. loyalty to America.

    E. a desire to leave America.

32. In choosing a subject, a speaker should try to find one which

    A. he is or can become enthusiastic about.

    B. he dislikes but which may please the audience.

    C. will annoy his audience.

    D. will require little preparation.

    E. he has seen in a popular magazine.

60. "Roan Stallion" was written by:

    A. Oswald Spengler.

    B. Aldous Huxley.

    C. Robinson Jeffers.

    D. Leonard S. Brown.

    E. George Boas.

29. In public discussion, he makes the best contribution who

    A. argues down all objections to his proposals.

    B. does the most talking.

    C. listens attentively but says nothing.

    D. makes a creative adjustment between conflicting points of view.

    E. refuses to permit the expression of conflicting points of view.

39. The best kind of introduction will

    A. make the audience laugh and feel good.

    B. get favorable attention and lead into subject.

    C. impress the audience with the importance of the speaker.

    D. present major arguments to be developed.

    E. introduce a need step, thesis, and main points of speech.

94. The main idea in the selection in the text from Steinbeck's *The Grapes of Wrath* is to

    A. show the conflict between those who own the land and those who care for it.

    B. tell the story of a farmer who became a day laborer.

    C. describe a family of poverty-stricken children.

    D. explain the importance of rotation of crops.

    E. urge tenants to pay their taxes.

45. In order to avoid stage fright, perhaps the best precaution is

    A. to be thoroughly prepared.

    B. to write your speech and read it.

    C. to display a "don't care anyhow" attitude to the audience.

    D. to display an overconfident, overbearing attitude.

    E. to avoid looking directly at your audience.

28. The round table method of public discussion is suitable for groups of not more than:

    A. 100.

    B. 50.

    C. 25.

    D. 15.

    E. 5.

8. One of the following is a run-on sentence. That sentence is:

    A. Dinner was served, and we ate rapidly.

    B. Some of the people are waiting, others have gone ahead.

    C. This is the problem; the solution is clear.

    D. He paused, adjusted his tie, and rang the bell; the maid refused to open the door.

    E. Whistles, sirens, horns, and firecrackers broke the silence, and the New Year was born.

33. Barnes emphasizes the Four Fundamental Processes of Speech. Of these the first is
   A. phonation.
   B. adjustment to the speaking situation.
   C. choice of material.
   D. control of bodily activity.
   E. projection to the audience.
44. Best advice in developing a lively sense of communication is
   A. be energetic, speak with enthusiasm.
   B. be passive, apathetic.
   C. appear reluctant to meet the assignment.
   D. avoid looking directly at the audience.
   E. speak with an outburst of oratorical display.
51. Steinbeck's *The Grapes of Wrath* pictures primarily:
   A. the shiftlessness of the average American farm worker.
   B. the plight of the Western tenant farmers and migratory workers.
   C. the effect of Communist propaganda on poor tenant farmers.
   D. the immorality of the ignorant migratory workers.
   E. the lack of religious faith among American farmers.
86. A boy whose fascination with a machine later turned to fear was found in
   A. Roan Stallion.
   B. Tractored Off.
   C. R. U. R.
   D. Our Changing Characteristics.
   E. Mr. Mechano.
92. The Wright Brothers' home was
   A. on Albermarle Sound.
   B. at Fort Meyers.
   C. in St. Petersburg, Florida.
   D. on the coast of North Carolina.
   E. on Hawthorne Street in Dayton, Ohio.
81. President Truman in his Fordham Address said the one defense against the atom bomb lies in
   A. bigger and better fighter planes.
   B. an adequate air raid warning system.
   C. aggressive warfare.
   D. making a stronger U. N.
   E. mastering the science of human relationships.
14. Which sentence is best punctuated?
   A. I have no pencil; and I do not want one.
   B. I have no pencil, and I do not want one.
   C. I have no pencil: and I do not want one.
   D. I have no pencil—and I do not want one.
   E. I have no pencil: and I do not want one.
74. Karel Capek, author of "R. U. R." is a
   A. Frenchman.
   B. Czechoslovakian.
   C. American.
   D. Pole.
   E. Italian.
57. Lippman's *Problem of Unbelief* seeks primarily to:
   A. show how peace of mind can be achieved.
   B. denounce the creeds of the leading Protestant denominations.

    C. show that Christianity is a dying religion.
    D. determine the causes of modern man's lack of religious faith.
    E. improve the morals of American youth.

Complete option information for high and low group responses to these 25 poorly discriminating items is provided in Table A-4, where **bold-faced** type indicates the number of persons marking the keyed option.

TABLE A-4

Number of Examinees in High and Low Groups Who Chose Each Option of the 25 Least Discriminating Items

Item Number	Group	A	B	C	D	E	Omit	Number of Examinees (Check Column)
30	H	1	**26**	0	8	31	0	66
	L	1	**35**	1	18	11	0	66
35	H	1	0	1	0	**64**	0	66
	L	0	1	0	0	**65**	0	66
27	H	31	1	**27**	7	0	0	66
	L	26	1	**28**	8	3	0	66
38	H	**66**	0	0	0	0	0	66
	L	**66**	0	0	0	0	0	66
31	H	29	1	28	3	5	0	66
	L	28	2	25	5	6	0	66
34	H	8	0	**40**	18	0	0	66
	L	10	5	**38**	12	0	1	66
42	H	0	0	**65**	1	0	0	66
	L	0	4	**62**	0	0	0	66
72	H	5	0	1	**52**	8	0	66
	L	9	0	4	**49**	3	1	66
32	H	**66**	0	0	0	0	0	66
	L	**61**	3	1	0	0	1	66
60	H	0	0	**66**	0	0	0	66
	L	3	1	**61**	1	0	0	66
29	H	3	1	0	**62**	0	0	66
	L	6	0	1	**57**	2	0	66
39	H	0	**57**	0	2	7	0	66
	L	0	**52**	5	2	7	0	66
94	H	**66**	0	0	0	0	0	66
	L	**60**	3	1	1	0	1	66
45	H	**65**	0	0	0	1	0	66
	L	**58**	1	2	1	4	0	66
28	H	0	2	7	**24**	33	0	66
	L	0	4	11	**17**	32	2	66
8	H	13	**15**	9	21	8	0	66
	L	8	**8**	6	34	10	0	66

TABLE A-4 (Cont.)

Item Number	Group	Option						Number of Examinees (Check Column)
		A	B	C	D	E	Omit	
33	H	1	43	21	0	1	0	66
	L	0	35	25	2	3	1	66
44	H	65	0	1	0	0	0	66
	L	56	1	8	1	0	0	66
51	H	0	65	1	0	0	0	66
	L	2	56	2	5	1	0	66
86	H	0	0	0	0	65	1	66
	L	1	2	2	4	56	1	66
92	H	0	0	1	5	59	1	66
	L	3	0	1	11	50	1	66
81	H	0	0	1	1	64	0	66
	L	0	0	1	12	53	0	66
14	H	1	61	1	3	0	0	66
	L	9	50	2	4	1	0	66
74	H	3	53	2	6	2	0	66
	L	6	42	6	9	2	1	66
57	H	9	0	4	51	2	0	66
	L	11	2	5	40	6	2	66

The 20 speech items (Nos. 26–45) make up only 20 per cent of the entire test, yet 14 of these (70 per cent) appear among the 25 least discriminating items. The first 25 items in the test cover spelling, grammar, and punctuation. Only 2 of these (8 per cent) appear in Table A-4. The last 55 items deal with literature; 9 of these (16 per cent) were poor discriminators. It is obvious, then, that from the percentage standpoint about 5 times as many speech items as non-speech ones seem unsatisfactory (70 versus 14 per cent).

There are several possible explanations for the poor showing of the speech items. First of all, they make up only a fifth of the test and therefore do not have much weight in determining each student's total score. If speech ability is little related to the other components of the test, then no matter how carefully prepared the speech items are, most of them will seem to discriminate poorly.

A second, rather likely, explanation is that good speech items are quite hard to construct, whereas the more standard phases of English are easier to test. Some of the speech items (Nos. 35, 38, 42, 32, 29, 45, and 44) are too easy and cannot discriminate well. Only 2 (Nos. 34 and 33) are near the optimal difficulty level of 50 per cent.

A third possibility, related to the second, is that the speech specialist was a less competent item writer than the other three staff members, or that he exercised less care than they. All four persons were experienced teachers, but novices in constructing objective questions.

A Discrimination Table

The process of item analysis can be simplified by reference to Table A-5. Knowing the number of persons tested, one immediately reads n, the proper number for the high or low group. Then for the number of

TABLE A-5

Determining Whether or Not a Given Test Item Discriminates Significantly between a "High" and a "Low" Group*

Total Number of Persons Tested (N)	Number in Low or High Group (0.27N) ($N_L = N_H = n$)	$(W_L - W_H)$** At or Above Which an Item Can Be Considered Sufficiently Discriminating			
		Number of Options			
		2 (True-False or Two-Option Multiple Choice)	3	4	5
28–31	8	4	5	5	5
32–35	9	5	5	5	5
36–38	10	5	5	5	5
39–42	11	5	5	5	5
43–46	12	5	5	6	6
47–49	13	5	6	6	6
50–53	14	5	6	6	6
54–57	15	6	6	6	6
58–61	16	6	6	6	6
62–64	17	6	6	6	7
65–68	18	6	6	7	7
69–72	19	6	7	7	7
73–75	20	6	7	7	7
76–79	21	6	7	7	7
80–83	22	7	7	7	7
84–86	23	7	7	7	7
87–90	24	7	7	8	8
91–94	25	7	7	8	8
95–98	26	7	8	8	8
99–101	27	7	8	8	8
102–105	28	7	8	8	8
106–109	29	7	8	8	8
110–112	30	7	8	8	8
113–116	31	8	8	8	8
117–120	32	8	8	9	9
121–124	33	8	8	9	9
125–127	34	8	9	9	9
128–131	35	8	9	9	9
132–135	36	8	9	9	9
136–138	37	8	9	9	9
139–142	38	8	9	9	9
143–146	39	8	9	9	9
147–149	40	9	9	9	10

TABLE A-5 (Cont.)

Total Number of Persons Tested (N)	Number in Low or High Group (0.27N) ($N_L = N_H = n$)	$(W_L - W_H)$** At or Above Which an Item Can Be Considered Sufficiently Discriminating			
		Number of Options			
		2 (True-False or Two-Option Multiple Choice)	3	4	5
150–153	41	9	9	10	10
154–157	42	9	9	10	10
158–161	43	9	10	10	10
162–164	44	9	10	10	10
165–168	45	9	10	10	10
169–172	46	9	10	10	10
173–175	47	9	10	10	10
176–179	48	9	10	10	10
180–183	49	9	10	10	10
184–187	50	9	10	10	11
188–190	51	10	10	11	11
191–194	52	10	10	11	11
195–198	53	10	10	11	11
199–201	54	10	11	11	11
202–205	55	10	11	11	11
206–209	56	10	11	11	11
210–212	57	10	11	11	11
213–216	58	10	11	11	11
217–220	59	10	11	11	11
221–224	60	10	11	11	11
225–227	61	10	11	11	12
228–231	62	10	11	12	12
232–235	63	10	11	12	12
236–238	64	11	11	12	12
239–242	65	11	11	12	12
243–246	66	11	12	12	12
247–249	67	11	12	12	12
250–253	68	11	12	12	12
254–257	69	11	12	12	12
258–261	70	11	12	12	12
262–264	71	11	12	12	12
265–268	72	11	12	12	12
269–272	73	11	12	12	13
273–275	74	11	12	13	13
276–279	75	11	12	13	13
280–283	76	11	12	13	13
284–287	77	11	12	13	13
288–290	78	12	12	13	13
291–294	79	12	13	13	13
295–298	80	12	13	13	13
299–301	81	12	13	13	13
302–305	82	12	13	13	13
306–309	83	12	13	13	13
310–312	84	12	13	13	13
313–316	85	12	13	13	13
317–320	86	12	13	13	14

TABLE A-5 (Cont.)

Total Number of Persons Tested (N)	Number in Low or High Group (0.27N) ($N_L = N_H = n$)	$(W_L - W_H)$** At or Above Which an Item Can Be Considered Sufficiently Discriminating			
		Number of Options			
		2 (True-False or Two-Option Multiple Choice)	3	4	5
321–324	87	12	13	13	14
325–327	88	12	13	14	14
328–331	89	12	13	14	14
332–335	90	12	13	14	14
336–338	91	12	13	14	14
339–342	92	12	13	14	14
343–346	93	13	13	14	14
347–349	94	13	14	14	14
350–353	95	13	14	14	14
354–357	96	13	14	14	14
358–361	97	13	14	14	14
362–364	98	13	14	14	14
365–368	99	13	14	14	15
369–372	100	13	14	14	15
406–409	110	14	15	15	15
443–446	120	14	15	16	16
480–483	130	15	16	16	16
517–520	140	15	16	17	17
554–557	150	16	17	17	18
591–594	160	16	18	18	18
628–631	170	17	18	19	19
665–668	180	17	19	19	19
702–705	190	18	19	20	20
739–742	200	18	19	20	20
832–835	225	19	21	21	21
925–927	250	20	22	22	23
1017–1020	275	21	23	23	24
1110–1112	300	22	24	24	25
1480–1483	400	25	27	28	28
1850–1853	500	28	30	31	31
3702–3705	1000	39	43	44	44

*Values for this 2½ per cent level-of-significance table, which is based on the principle of Stanley's ½ per cent-level table (see *American Psychologist*, 1951, 6, 369), were computed by Dr. Ellen V. Piers.

**W_L = number of persons in the low group who answered the item incorrectly or omitted it. W_H = number in the high group who answered the item incorrectly or omitted it.

options each item in the test or subtest has, find the minimum value of $W_L - W_H$ needed in order to conclude that the item has significant discriminating power. In the above example, where N was 243, n is seen to be 66, and the minimum $W_L - W_H$ for acceptable discrimination with five-option items is 12.[4] Purely by accident, this makes the same number of items, 25, eligible for editing as were obtained by the 25 per cent rule of thumb.

If a calculating machine is available, $\dfrac{100 \times o}{2n(o - 1)}$ may be locked in its keyboard and the percentage difficulty value for each item computed very rapidly by using $W_L + W_H$ as the multiplier. By hand, the multiplication is likely to be tedious and inaccurate; therefore, in the absence of a machine, it is recommended that just three points on the difficulty scale be computed in terms of $W_L + W_H$: 16 per cent for the boundary line of a very easy item, 50 per cent for the middle-difficulty item, and 84 per cent for the boundary line of a very hard item. The formulas for obtaining these three "critical" $W_L + W_H$ points are shown in Table A-6.

TABLE A-6

Formulas for Finding $(W_L + W_H)$ Values at Three Difficulty Levels

Percentage of Examinees Who Do Not "Know" the Correct Answer to the Item	Number of Options Each Item Has			
	2	3	4	5
16	$0.160n$*	$0.213n$	$0.240n$	$0.256n$
50	$0.500n$	$0.667n$	$0.750n$	$0.800n$
84	$0.840n$	$1.120n$	$1.260n$	$1.344n$

*n = number of examinees in the low or the high group = 27 per cent of the total number tested, rounded off to the nearest whole number. See Table A-5.

The three $W_L + W_H$ figures may be used to determine roughly whether the item is quite easy, of moderate difficulty, or quite hard. For purposes of arranging the revised items in order of difficulty, the various $W_L + W_H$ values, adjusted subjectively for changes in difficulty brought about by editing, will suffice.

---

[4]This is $12/66 = 18$ per cent of the maximum possible $W_L - W_H$ for an n of 66. If n were 200, a difference of only 20—just 10 per cent of the maximum—would be needed for a five-option item to be significantly discriminating. With an n of 1,000, only 4.4 per cent of the maximum possible difference is required for significance. Therefore, when n is rather small, as it usually is for teacher-made tests, a considerable number of items will be branded improperly as nondiscriminating. As an extreme example, take 31 students (N = 31), for whom the number in the high or the low group (n) is 8. By sheer chance marking 4 out of the 8 persons in the low group would be expected to give the keyed answer to a two-option item, if none of them omitted it. Thus the item could be deemed discriminating according to Table A-5, where a difference of at least 4 is required, only if *every* person in the high group marked it correctly. Table A-5 has some value as a means of determining for how many items in a test complete option information should be tabulated and a thorough scrutiny made, but the basic rule illustrated in Table A-1 on page 344 is to *edit as many items as possible, beginning with the least discriminating ones.*

As shown in the first footnote to Table A-1 on page 000, $\dfrac{100 \times o}{2n(o-1)} = 0.947$ when $o = 5$ and $n = 66$. The last column of that table was obtained by multiplying each $(W_L + W_H)$ by 0.947.

For five options and 66 examinees in each group ($n = 66$), the 16 per cent difficulty point of Table A-1 occurs when $W_L + W_H = 0.256n = (0.256)(66) = 17$. Similarly, the 50 per cent point is $W_L + W_H = (0.800)(66) = 53$. The 84 per cent point occurs when $W_L + W_H = (1.344)(66) = 89$. Therefore, in Table A-1 items will be considered easy if $W_L + W_H$ is 17 or less, of moderate difficulty if $W_L + W_H$ is from 18 to 88, and hard if $W_L + W_H$ equals 89 or more. According to this method, 17 of the 100 items in Table A-1 are easy, while only 5 are hard. Thus the test as a whole is relatively easy.

Obtaining the Mean
and the Standard Deviation
By using the sum of the $W_L + W_H$ column of the item-analysis table, it is rather easy to estimate the average (i.e., mean) "wrongs" score of the N students. To secure this mean wrongs score, *not* corrected for chance, simply sum the $W_L + W_H$ column and divide this sum by $2n$:

$$M_w = \frac{\Sigma(W_L + W_H)}{2n} \text{, where the symbol } \Sigma \text{ means "the sum of."}$$

To correct the mean wrongs score for chance, use the formula

$$M_{w_c} = \frac{o\,\Sigma(W_L + W_H)}{2n(o-1)} \text{ ,}$$

where o is the number of options each item has.

The standard deviation of the wrongs scores is the same as the standard deviation of the rights scores when omits are counted as being wrong, and this statistic, *not* corrected for chance, is easily estimated by means of the formula

$$s = \frac{\Sigma(W_L - W_H)}{2.45n}$$

Note the minus sign in this formula. To secure a standard deviation corrected for chance, multiply the above formula by $\dfrac{o}{o-1}$ to secure

$$s_c = \frac{o\,\Sigma(W_L - W_H)}{2.45n(o-1)} \text{ .}$$

For illustrations, turn back to Table A-1, page 000. There the $W_L + W_H$ column sums to 4,088, and the $W_L - W_H$ column total is 1762. 4,088 divided by $2n$ equals 4088/132, or 31.0, the mean number of incorrect responses, uncorrected for chance, for the 100 items.

$(5 \times 4088) \div (2 \times 66 \times 4) = 38.7$, the mean wrongs corrected for chance. This figure agrees rather well with the mean of the right-hand (difficulty) column of Table A-1, which is 39.0. Thus on the average the correct answer to the 100 items was "known" by about 61 per cent of the examinees and not "known" by about 39 per cent.

The standard deviation not corrected for chance is $1762 \div (2.45 \times 66) = 10.9$, exactly the same for this test as when computed from all 243 total scores. Corrected for chance it becomes $(5)(1762) \div (2.45)(66)(4) = 13.6$.

These approximation formulas based upon only low and high groups are accurate enough for use in most school situations, particularly when the number of students is fairly large, say 100 or more.

A Simplified Procedure for
Obtaining a Reliability Coefficient

Unfortunately, there is no fairly precise method for securing a single-form reliability coefficient ("coefficient of equivalence") without considerable computation. Stanley has devised two shorter procedures yielding results closely approximating those of the conventional methods. His simplified split-half technique has been reported elsewhere[5] in considerable detail and will not be repeated here. Instead, a Kuder-Richardson Formula 20 (KR_{20}) coefficient of equivalence will be obtained from just the low and high group figures in Table A-1, page 344, k being the number of items (100 for our example):

$$KR_{20} = \frac{k}{k-1}\left[1 - \frac{2n\Sigma(W_L + W_H) - \Sigma(W_L + W_H)^2}{0.667[\Sigma(W_L - W_H)]^2}\right]$$

$$= \frac{100}{99}\left[1 - \frac{2(66)(4088) - 227,630}{0.667(1762)^2}\right]$$

$$= \frac{100}{99}\left(1 - \frac{311,986}{2,070,798}\right) = \frac{100}{99}(0.849)$$

$$= .86 .$$

This is the same as the value secured by using the regular KR_{20} formula with all 243 cases.[6] In general, the abbreviated procedure yields slightly lower estimates of KR_{20} than are obtained by using all N cases, but for most practical purposes this negative bias will be negligible.

The only part of the above formula not used in computing either the mean or the standard deviation is $\Sigma(W_L + W_H)^2$. To get it, square each of the 100 ($W_L + W_H$)

---

[5] J. C. Stanley, A simplified method for estimating the split-half reliability coefficient of a test, *Harvard Educational Review*, 1951, 2, 1, 221–224.

[6] From this .86 we can estimate that the average intercorrelation of the 100 items is a little less than .06. This can be done by using the general Spearman-Brown formula to "step down" the 100-item test to estimate the "reliability of a single item—that is, of a test 1/100th as long as this test:

$$\frac{\frac{1}{100}(.86)}{1 + \left(\frac{1}{100} - 1\right)(.86)} = .058 .$$

values in Table A-1 and then sum them: $(71)^2 + (3)^2 + (77)^2 + \cdots + (57)^2 = 227{,}630$. By hand this is a laborious process indeed, but on an electric calculating machine (Friden, Marchant, Monroe) it is simple to secure both $\Sigma(W_L + W_H)$ and $\Sigma(W_L + W_H)^2$ in a single set of operations. In most medium-sized and large school systems there is a machine of this sort and someone who knows how to use it. Getting all *three* needed values for the formula and checking them should take a skilled operator not more than half an hour, if an item analysis table similar to Table A-1 has already been prepared.[7]

This method does not involve splitting the test into halves, a tedious undertaking at best when a test-scoring machine is not available. The split-half odd-even coefficient of equivalence based upon all 243 examinees in .87; it is also .87 when determined from only the high and low groups. KR_{20} coefficients tend to be a little smaller than split-half ones,[8] but again the discrepancy is usually of no practical consequence to the teacher.

The KR_{21} coefficient, which tends to be somewhat smaller than the KR_{20} coefficient for the same data, is easier to compute because it does not require squaring each of the $(W_L + W_H)$'s:

$$KR_{21} = \frac{k}{k-1}\left\{1 - \frac{1.5\{2kn\,\Sigma(W_L + W_H) - [\Sigma(W_L + W_H)]^2\}}{k\,[\Sigma(W_L - W_H)]^2}\right\}$$

$$= \frac{100}{99}\left\{1 - \frac{1.5[2(100)(66)(4088) - (4088)^2]}{100(1762)^2}\right\}$$

$$= \frac{100}{99}\left(1 - \frac{55{,}874{,}784}{310{,}464{,}400}\right)$$

$$= \frac{100}{99}\,(1 - 0.1800)$$

$$= \frac{100}{99}\,(0.8200) = \frac{82}{99}$$

$$= .83\,.$$

---

[7] For further information about this procedure, see J. C. Stanley, Simplified test-analysis statistics, *Journal of Higher Education*, 1956, 27, 498–500. If you plan to work with items scored 0, 1, and 2, see J. C. Stanley, High-low-group statistics for tests composed of items scored trichotomously, *15th Yearbook of the National Council on Measurement in Education*, 1958, pp. 50–56.

[8] L. J. Cronbach, Coefficient alpha and the internal structure of tests, *Psychometrika*, 1951, 16, 297–334.

FIFTY MULTIPLE-CHOICE ITEMS
TO HELP YOU
LEARN STATISTICS

The following multiple-choice questions are designed to help you improve your knowledge of the material in Chapter Three. Each has five options, only *one* of which is meant to be correct. Consult your text freely while answering them. Rather than write in your text, copy the question numbers on a separate sheet of paper and put after each number the letter preceding the correct option (A, B, C, D, or E).

Unless you work on the questions diligently, they will probably not increase your understanding very much. After completing them *all* as well as you possibly can, turn to page 383, where answers and explanations appear. Your score, corrected for chance, equals the number right minus one-fourth of the number wrong. (For an explanation of correction for chance, see page 191.)

1. The arithmetic mean of the scores 4, 5, 7, 6, 4 is
   A. 6.0
   B. 5.5
   C. 5.2
   D. 5.0
   E. 4.8

2. The measure of central tendency to use when reporting data concerning wages in order to avoid the undue influence of a few extreme salaries is the
   A. standard deviation.
   B. quartile deviation.
   C. median.
   D. range.
   E. mean.

3. The median of the scores 4, 6, 7, 5, 4 is
   A. 6.0
   B. 5.5
   C. 5.2
   D. 5.0
   E. 4.8

4. Given seven scores 46, 68, 44, 46, 46, 63, and 68. How many points difference is there between the middle score, 46, and the median when the median is computed from a frequency distribution of these scores where the class interval is 1?
   A. 17.00
   B. 0.67
   C. 0.33
   D. 0.17
   E. 0.00

5. In a frequency distribution, the size of the interval of the class whose lower and upper real limits (i.e., class boundaries) are 9.5 and 19.5 is
   A. 11.0
   B. 10.0
   C. 9.0
   D. 5.0
   E. 4.5

6. In a frequency distribution, the midpoint of the class whose lower and upper real limits are 99.5 and 109.5 is
   A. 107.0
   B. 105.0
   C. 104.5
   D. 102.5
   E. 102.0

7. The *main* reason for grouping data in class intervals as a step toward carrying out calculations of statistical measures by hand (that is, without using a mechanical calculator) is to
   A. reduce the amount of labor involved.
   B. reduce the frequency of clerical errors.
   C. permit the calculation of measures other than the mean.
   D. bring out important trends in the data.
   C. hide the identity of the persons tested.

8. In making a grouped frequency distribution from raw data for *computational* purposes, the *first* step is to
   A. determine the range of scores.
   B. determine the whole-number limits of the classes.
   C. determine the real limits of the classes.
   D. decide upon the number of classes.
   E. select the class interval.

9. What is the *most serious* criticism to be made of the following frequency distribution of test scores, where the "real" class limits are fractional?

Whole-Number

Class Limits	Frequency
44–48	1
40–44	2
36–40	0
32–36	0
28–32	2
24–28	6
20–24	5
16–20	23
12–16	24
8–12	37
4–8	33
0–4	25
−4–0	3
	N = 161

A. Negative scores occur.

B. Thirteen classes are used.

C. There are too many low scores.

D. The class midpoints are not divisible by the range of scores in each interval.

E. The whole-number class limits overlap.

10. The 60th percentile is the point in a distribution

A. where a student has answered 40 per cent of the questions incorrectly.

B. which marks the distance from the median that includes 60 per cent of the cases.

C. below which are 40 per cent of the cases.

D. below which are 60 per cent of the cases.

E. above which are 60 per cent of the cases.

11. What is the arithmetic mean of the following distribution?

Score	f
0–3	7
4–7	3
	N = 10

A. 3.5

B. 3.2

C. 2.7

D. 2.4

E. 2.2

12. $D = P_{90} - P_{10}$. D is a measure of

A. variability.

B. correlation.

C. central tendency.

D. quartileness.

E. modality.

13. The percentage of scores lying between Q_3 and the median is
   A. 25
   B. 34
   C. 50
   D. 68
   E. a variable quantity that depends on the score distribution.

14. What is the standard deviation of the following distribution?

Score	f
2	2
1	4
0	4

   A. $56/10$
   B. $56/100$
   C. $\sqrt{56}/100$
   D. $\sqrt{56/10}$
   E. $\sqrt{56}/10$

15. For the following distribution, where the grouping interval is 1, the quartile deviation or semi-interquartile range, Q, is

Score	f
8	1
6	2
5	4
3	4
2	3
0	2
	N = 16

   A. 2.17
   B. 2.08
   C. 1.79
   D. 1.54
   E. 1.04

16. For the distribution in the preceding item, the median is
   A. 1.75
   B. 3.00
   C. 3.25
   D. 3.62
   E. 4.00

17, 18. On a test with a standard deviation of 20 and an arithmetic mean of 80, an individual with a raw score of 70 will have a z-score of
   A. −10.0
   B. −0.5
   C. −0.1
   D. 0.5
   E. 5.0

and a Z-score $(M = 50, S = 10)$ of
  A. 55
  B. 50
  C. 49
  D. 45
  E. 40

19. What rank should be assigned to a score of 95 in the following distribution, if the rank of the highest score, 97, is 1.5?

Score
97
97
96
95
95
95
94
94
93

  A. 5.5
  B. 6.0
  C. 7.0
  D. 4.0
  E. 5.0

20. How does the mean of N consecutive untied ranks compare with the mean of N ranks in which one or more ties occur?
  A. Former is larger.
  B. No difference.
  C. Latter is larger.
  D. Depends on the number of ties.
  E. Depends on where the ties occur.

21. The Pearson product-moment coefficient of correlation, r_{xy} or r_{12}, may vary between
  A. −2.00 and +2.00
  B. −1.00 and +1.00
  C. −0.92 and +0.92
  D.   0.00 and +1.00
  E.   0.00 and infinity

22. A teacher computed a correlation coefficient between scores on a reading test and scores on a test of current affairs, obtaining a value of .92. He was justified in concluding that, as measured by these two tests,
  A. knowledge of current affairs and reading ability are closely related.
  B. knowledge of current affairs and reading ability are unrelated to each other.
  C. knowledge of current affairs and reading ability are perfectly related.
  D. the coefficient must have been computed incorrectly.
  E. wide knowledge of current affairs is the result of good reading ability.

23. Which one of these r's has the *least* predictive value?
   A.   .91
   B.   .50
   C.   .17
   D. −.23
   E. −1.00

24. A student computed a Pearson product-moment coefficient of correlation, r_{xy}, between 30 paired scores and found it to be 1.05. We are absolutely certain that
   A. he has freakish data.
   B. he should have computed Spearman's rank-difference coefficient of correlation instead.
   C. the means of the two distributions differ.
   D. the correlation between X and Y is high.
   E. the r has been computed incorrectly.

25. If the X distribution is divided into 12 classes and the Y distribution is also divided into 12 classes, the number of tally marks in the scatter diagram will be
   A. N, the number of pairs of scores.
   B. 2N, twice the number of pairs of scores.
   C. 12.
   D. $2 \times 12 = 24$.
   E. $12 \times 12 = 144$.

Multiple-Choice Analogies (26–35)

DIRECTIONS: Each of the following ten items represents an analogy. In every case the first two terms of the item are related to each other in some way, and the third term is related in the same way to *one* of the last five.

Example: Shoe is to foot as hat is to
   A. arm.
   B. hair.
   C. hand.
   D. head.
   E. leg.
Option D, "head," is of course correct.

26. Arithmetic mean is to central tendency as standard deviation is to
   A. average.
   B. variability.
   C. Q.
   D. D.
   E. relationship.

27. Q_3 is to 75th percentile as median is to
   A. 90th percentile.
   B. 75th percentile.
   C. 50th percentile.
   D. 16th percentile.
   E. 10th percentile.

28. Arithmetic mean is to standard deviation as median is to
    A. standard deviation
    B. Q_3
    C. Q_2
    D. Q_1
    E. Q
29. Frequency distribution is to median as ungrouped measures arranged in order of magnitude are to
    A. range.
    B. mode.
    C. class interval.
    D. mean.
    E. middle score.
30. $Q_3 - Q_1$ is to 50% as, for a "normal" distribution, Mean $\pm$ 1SD is to
    A. 32%
    B. 34%
    C. 50%
    D. 68%
    E. 84%
31. Arithmetic mean is to mode as standard deviation is to
    A. range.
    B. median.
    C. midscore.
    D. D.
    E. Q.
32. Median is to point as standard deviation is to
    A. volume.
    B. distance.
    C. square.
    D. score.
    E. area.
33. Positive correlation is to direct relationship as negative correlation is to
    _____ relationship.
    A. incomplete
    B. inconsequential
    C. incorrect
    D. inadequate
    E. inverse
34. Spearman is to rank-difference r_R as Pearson is to
    A. product-moment correlation coefficient.
    B. standard deviation or variance.
    C. quartile deviation.
    D. mean, median, or mode.
    E. D.

35. Rank is to order as score is to
    A. disorder.
    B. magnitude.
    C. median.
    D. rank.
    E. variability.

The remaining questions (36–50) refer to the following test scores:

Grouped Test Scores	f	f × midpoint
310–319	1	314.5
300–309	2	2(304.5)
290–299	4	4(294.5)
280–289	1	284.5
270–279	6	6(274.5)
260–269	12	12(264.5)
250–259	11	11(254.5)
240–249	8	8(244.5)
230–239	2	2(234.5)
220–229	0	
210–219	3	3(214.5)
	N = 50	13,075.0

36. If $\sum$ means "the sum of," then $\sum f =$
    A. -15
    B.   11
    C.   50
    D. 239
    E. 315
37. The size of the interval of each class in the above distribution is
    A. 4.5
    B. 5.0
    C. 9.0
    D. 10.0
    E. 10.5
38. The fractional class limits of the highest class are
    A. 309.50–319.50
    B. 309.50–318.50
    C. 309.95–319.95
    D. 310.50–318.50
    E. 310.50–319.50
39. The midpoint of the middle class (260–269) is
    A. 259.5
    B. 264.5
    C. 265.0
    D. 269.0
    E. 269.5

40. The arithmetic mean is
    A. 260.3
    B. 261.5
    C. 263.0
    D. 264.5
    E. 267.5
41. The median (50th percentile) is
    A. 258.7
    B. 259.5
    C. 260.3
    D. 264.5
    E. 267.3
42. The mode is
    A. 12.0
    B. 259.5
    C. 260.0
    D. 264.5
    E. 265.0
43. The 25th percentile (Q_1) is
    A. 230.1
    B. 240.4
    C. 244.5
    D. 248.9
    E. 249.5
44. The 75th percentile (Q_3) is
    A. 267.0
    B. 269.8
    C. 270.2
    D. 272.0
    E. 274.5
45. Q, the semi-interquartile range, $= \dfrac{Q_3 - Q_1}{2} =$
    A. 8
    B. 12
    C. 17
    D. 20
    E. 23
46. The 10th percentile is
    A. 245.8
    B. 240.0
    C. 239.5
    D. 239.0
    E. 234.5
47. The 90th percentile is
    A. 299.5
    B. 299.0
    C. 294.5

    D. 277.8

    E. 276.1

48. $0.4D = 0.4 \times$ (90th percentile $-$ 10th percentile) $=$

    A. 20

    B. 22

    C. 25

    D. 31

    E. 55

49. Standard deviation $=$

    A. 2

    B. 15

    C. 17

    D. 20

    E. 22

50. The percentile rank of a score of 231 is

    A. 31

    B. 10

    C. 3

    D. 6

    E. 7

THE COMPUTATION
OF SQUARE ROOTS

When determining a standard deviation or an r, one must find the square root of a number. This can be done easily from a table of square roots, such as Barlow's *Tables of Squares, Cubes, Square Roots, Cube Roots and Reciprocals* (London: E. & F. N. Spon, Ltd.). Quite a few statistics texts and other books have shorter tables. If only an occasional square root is needed, it can probably be obtained more easily "by hand" than by searching for a table.

In Chapter 15 of *Mathematics Essential for Elementary Statistics* (New York: Henry Holt, 1951), Helen M. Walker devotes 16 pages to explaining what square roots mean and how they are obtained. The reader who is thoroughly in the dark concerning this topic will want to consult that reference. For others who need merely a little reviewing of material previously learned, the following brief explanation is offered.

1. First take a small three-digit whole number that is a perfect square; **144** is a good illustration. The square root of 144 is a number which, when multiplied by itself, equals 144. To extract the square root of 144, follow these seven steps:

(a)
$$\overset{\textstyle .}{\sqrt{144.}}$$

(b)
$$\overset{\textstyle .}{\sqrt{1_\wedge 44.}}$$

(c)
$$\begin{array}{c} \phantom{\sqrt{}}1 \\ \sqrt{\ 1_\wedge 44.} \\ \underline{-1} \\ 0 \end{array}$$

(d)
$$\begin{array}{c} \phantom{\sqrt{}}1 \\ \sqrt{\ 1_\wedge 44.} \\ \underline{-1} \\ 0\ 44 \end{array}$$

(e)
$$\begin{array}{r} 1 \quad . \\ \sqrt{1_\wedge 44.} \\ -1 \\ \hline 2 \mid 0 \ 44 \end{array}$$

(f)
$$\begin{array}{r} 1 \ 2. \\ \sqrt{1_\wedge 44.} \\ -1 \\ \hline 22 \mid 0 \ 44 \end{array}$$

(g)
$$\begin{array}{r} 1 \ 2. \\ \sqrt{1_\wedge 44.} \\ -1 \\ \hline 22 \mid 0 \ 44 \\ - \ 44 \\ \hline 00 \end{array}$$

(a) Write the 144 with a square root sign and two decimal points, one above the other.

(b) Begin with the decimal point following 144 and move to the left two digits at a time, putting a caret at each stopping place. With 144 only one move and therefore one caret is needed.

(c) Look at the number to the left of the caret. What number *multiplied by itself* is as nearly equal to 1 as possible but not greater than 1? 1, of course, so write this 1 above the 1 and below it. Subtract.

(d) Draw down the next two numbers.

(e) Double the top 1 and write the resulting 2 to the left of 0 44.

(f) Now, how many times does 2 go into 0 4? 2, so write 2 in the answer space above the right-hand 4 and also to the right of the 2.

(g) Multiply the 22 by 2, write this product (44) below the other 44, and subtract. Therefore, the square root of 144 is exactly 12, since 12 × 12 = 144.

2. Take a large decimal fraction, **9342.156**, and find its square root *to the nearest two decimal places.*

(a)
$$\sqrt{93_\wedge 42.15_\wedge 60_\wedge 00}$$

(b)
$$\begin{array}{r} 9 \quad . \\ \sqrt{93_\wedge 42.15_\wedge 60_\wedge 00} \\ -81 \\ \hline 12 \end{array}$$

(c)
$$\begin{array}{r} 9 \\ \sqrt{93_\wedge 42.15_\wedge 60_\wedge 00} \\ -81 \\ \hline 18 \mid 12 \ 42 \end{array}$$

(d)
$$\begin{array}{r} 9 \ 6. \\ \sqrt{93_\wedge 42.15_\wedge 60_\wedge 00} \\ -81 \\ \hline 186 \mid 12 \ 42 \\ -11 \ 16 \\ \hline 1 \ 26 \end{array}$$

(e)
```
              9  6.  6
         √  93ˏ42.15ˏ60ˏ00
            -81
    186  |   12 42
            -11 16
   1926  |    1 26 15
            -1 15 56
                 10 59
```

(f)
```
              9  6.  6  5  4
         √  93ˏ42.15ˏ60ˏ00      = 96.65
            -81
    186  |   12 42
            -11 16
   1926  |    1 26 15
            -1 15 56
  19325  |       10 59 60
               -  9 66 25
 193304  |          93 35 00
                   -77 32 16
                    16 02 84
```

(a) First write down the number with the square root sign, carets, and a decimal point in the answer place. (Notice that this decimal point is always exactly above the decimal point in the number.) Begin at the decimal point in the number and count in both directions by two's, putting a caret between each pair. Zeros are added to the right of the decimal point beyond the last figure in order to have the two numbers to draw down each time. In order to carry out the square root to the nearest two decimal places (rounded off from three places), it is necessary to have six figures to the right of the decimal point.

(b) What number multiplied by itself is as nearly equal to 93 as possible, without exceeding it? 10 × 10 = 100, which is too much. 9 × 9 = 81, so use 9 as the first number in the square root. Multiply it by itself and subtract the 81 from 93.

(c) Draw down the next two numbers (42), double 9, and write 18 to the left of 12 42.

(d) Approximately how many times will 18 go into 124? Not quite 7, for 18 × 7 = 126. Try the next lower number, 6. Write it in the answer space above the 2 and also to the right of the 18. Multiply 6 by 186 and subtract this product, 11 16, from 12 42.

(e) Draw down the next two numbers and double the 96. 19 goes into 126 about 6 times. Repeat the above process.

(f) Double 966, write 1932 in the proper place, and complete the remaining steps.

The square root of 9342.156 is 96.654+, which when rounded off to the nearest two decimal places becomes 96.65. Where test scores are concerned, only one decimal place is usually needed for the standard deviation.

To check the computation of a square root, multiply the value obtained by itself and add to this product the remainder. For example, (96.654 × 96.654) + .160284 = 9342.156000, which agrees exactly with the figure underneath the square root sign in Step (a) on page 372.

A TABLE FOR DETERMINING
SPEARMAN RANK-ORDER
COEFFICIENTS
OF CORRELATION, r_R*

Before using this appendix, please review the material concerning rank correlation on pages 98–100. Table D-1 makes the computation of r_R itself unnecessary when the number of pairs is less than 11. As an illustration we take nine minerals that have a "scratch" order, from 1 (for diamond, which scratches everything else) through 9 (for talc, which scratches none of the other eight but is scratched by each of them). A student is handed the 9 specimens arranged in random order and asked to rearrange them in the "scratch" order. According to the correct order, the arrangement he makes is 1, 5, 4, 3, 2, 7, 9, 8, and 6, so his squared discrepancies are $0^2 + 3^2 + 1^2 + 1^2 + 3^2 + 1^2 + 2^2 + 0^2 + 3^2 = 34$. Go down the right-hand "Sum of Squared Deviations, ΣD^2" column until you find the number 34. Go left in that row until you find the entry, .72, that lies in the 9-things-ranked column. Thus the correlation between the correct order and the student's order is .72. Using the Table E-1 procedure on page 380, he would receive $9(.72)^2 = 5$ points, contrasted with the 2 out of 9 ranks he had exactly correct (Nos. 1 and 8). In order to receive a score of only 2, he would have to obtain an r_R of at least .41; .72 is considerably higher.

---

*For 2 to 10 things ranked.

Table D-1

The Various Values of r_R *for All Possible Sums*
of Squared Deviations (ΣD^2 *) for N's from 2 through 10*

$$r_R = 1 - \frac{6 \Sigma D^2}{N(N^2 - 1)}$$

Sum of Squared Deviations ΣD^2	Number of Things Ranked (N)									Sum of Squared Deviations ΣD^2
	2	3	4	5	6	7	8	9	10	
0	1.00	1.00	1.00	1.00	1.00	1.00	1.00	1.00	1.00	0
2	−1.00	.50	.80	.90	.94	.96	.98	.98	.99	2
4			.60	.80	.89	.93	.95	.97	.98	4
6		−.50	.40	.70	83	.89	.93	.95	.96	6
8		−1.00	.20	.60	.77	.86	.90	.93	.95	8
10			0	.50	.71	.82	.88	.92	.94	10
12			−.20	.40	.66	.79	.86	.90	.93	12
14			−.40	.30	.60	.75	.83	88	.92	14
16			−.60	.20	.54	.71	.81	.87	.90	16
18			−.80	.10	.49	.68	.79	.85	.89	18
20			−1.00	0	.43	.64	.76	.83	.88	20
22				−.10	.37	.61	.74	.82	.87	22
24				−.20	.31	.57	.71	.80	.85	24
26				−.30	.26	.54	.69	.78	.84	26
28				−.40	.20	.50	.67	.77	.83	28
30				−.50	.14	.46	.64	.75	.82	30
32				−.60	.09	.43	.62	.73	.81	32
34				−.70	.03	.39	.60	.72	.79	34
36				−.80	−.03	.36	.57	.70	.78	36
38				−.90	−.09	.32	.55	.68	.77	38
40				−1.00	−.14	.29	.52	.67	.76	40
42					−.20	.25	.50	.65	.75	42
44					−.26	.21	.48	.63	.73	44
46					−.31	.18	.45	.62	.72	46
48					−.37	.14	.43	.60	.71	48
50					−.43	.11	.40	.58	.70	50
52					−.49	.07	.38	.57	.68	52
54					−.54	.04	.36	.55	.67	54
56					−.60	0	.33	.53	.66	56
58					−.66	−.04	.31	.52	.65	58
60					−.71	−.07	.29	.50	.64	60
62					−.77	−.11	.26	.48	.62	62
64					−.83	−.14	.24	.47	.61	64
66					−.89	−.18	.21	.45	.60	66
68					−.94	−.21	.19	.43	.59	68
70					−1.00	−.25	.17	.42	.58	70

TABLE D-1 (cont'd.)

Sum of Squared Deviations, ΣD^2	Number of Things Ranked				Sum of Squared Deviations, ΣD^2	Number of Things Ranked		
	7	8	9	10		8	9	10
72	−.29	.14	.40	.56	122	−.45	−.02	.26
74	−.32	.12	.38	.55	124	−.48	−.03	.25
76	−.36	.10	.37	.54	126	−.50	−.05	.24
78	−.39	.07	.35	.53	128	−.52	−.07	.22
80	−.43	.05	.33	.52	130	−.55	−.08	.21
82	−.46	.02	.32	.50	132	−.57	−.10	.20
84	−.50	0	.30	.49	134	−.60	−.12	.19
86	−.54	−.02	.28	.48	136	−.62	−.13	.18
88	−.57	−.05	.27	.47	138	−.64	−.15	.16
90	−.61	−.07	.25	.45	140	−.67	−.17	.15
92	−.64	−.10	.23	.44	142	−.69	−.18	.14
94	−.68	−.12	.22	.43	144	−.71	−.20	.13
96	−.71	−.14	.20	.42	146	−.74	−.22	.12
98	−.75	−.17	.18	.41	148	−.76	−.23	.10
100	−.79	−.19	.17	.39	150	−.79	−.25	.09
102	−.82	−.21	.15	.38	152	−.81	−.27	.08
104	−.86	−.24	.13	.37	154	−.83	−.28	.07
106	−.89	−.26	.12	.36	156	−.86	−.30	.05
108	−.93	−.29	.10	.35	158	−.88	−.32	.04
110	−.96	−.31	.08	.33	160	−.90	−.33	.03
112	−1.00	−.33	.07	.32	162	−.93	−.35	.02
114		−.36	.05	.31	164	−.95	−.37	.01
116		−.38	.03	.30	166	−.98	−.38	−.01
118		−.40	.02	.28	168	−1.00	−.40	−.02
120		−.43	0	.27				

TABLE D-1 (cont'd.)

Sum of Squared Deviations, ΣD^2	Number of Things Ranked		Sum of Squared Deviations, ΣD^2	Number of Things Ranked		Sum of Squared Deviations, ΣD^2	Number of Things Ranked
	9	10		9	10		10
170	−.42	−.03	224	−.87	−.36	278	−.68
172	−.43	−.04	226	−.88	−.37	280	−.70
174	−.45	−.05	228	−.90	−.38	282	−.71
176	−.47	−.07	230	−.92	−.39	284	−.72
178	−.48	−.08	232	−.93	−.41	286	−.73
180	−.50	−.09	234	−.95	−.42	288	−.75
182	−.52	−.10	236	−.97	−.43	290	−.76
184	−.53	−.12	238	−.98	−.44	292	−.77
186	−.55	−.13	240	−1.00	−.45	294	−.78
188	−.57	−.14	242		−.47	296	−.79
190	−.58	−.15	244		−.48	298	−.81
192	−.60	−.16	246		−.49	300	−.82
194	−.62	−.18	248		−.50	302	−.83
196	−.63	−.19	250		−.52	304	−.84
198	−.65	−.20	252		−.53	306	−.85
200	−.67	−.21	254		−.54	308	−.87
202	−.68	−.22	256		−.55	310	−.88
204	−.70	−.24	258		−.56	312	−.89
206	−.72	−.25	260		−.58	314	−.90
208	−.73	−.26	262		−.59	316	−.92
210	−.75	−.27	264		−.60	318	−.93
212	−.77	−.28	266		−.61	320	−.94
214	−.78	−.30	268		−.62	322	−.95
216	−.80	−.31	270		−.64	324	−.96
218	−.82	−.32	272		−.65	326	−.98
220	−.83	−.33	274		−.66	328	−.99
222	−.85	−.35	276		−.67	330	−1.00

APPENDIX   E

SCORING REARRANGEMENT
(RANKING) TEST ITEMS

In many subjects, especially history, where one of the objectives is to acquire a sense of sequence or chronology, rearrangement questions may be a better testing device than other item forms. Their construction calls for considerable skill in putting together material so that the ranking task will not be too demanding at some points and too easy at others. Comparatively little has been written about the preparation of this type of item, though much has been said about scoring it, but in all likelihood there are potential uses for rearrangement items in many academic fields. Steps in solving a mathematical problem, sequences of equations in chemistry, and relative quality of various literary selections are possible illustrations. An essential condition is that "experts" can agree reasonably well as to how the things should be ranked, since otherwise it will not be possible to devise a satisfactory key. For this reason, independent keying by at least two teachers and reconciliation of differences *before* the items are used are desirable, but of course such precautions should by no means be confined to rearrangement items.

A chronology test item was presented in Table 3-17 on page 99 and scored for two examinees by means of the Spearman rank-difference coefficient of correlation, r_R. A little reflection will make it obvious that the *magnitude* of each discrepancy between the student's response and the keyed rank, not just the fact that they differ, is taken into account. From the historian's point of view, it is far worse to think that the French Revolution occurred before the Roman Empire fell than to place it just prior to the destruction of the Spanish Armada. Similarly, it is "wronger" to rate cork heavier than white oak than to confuse the densities of cork and balsa.

The apparent difficulty of scoring rearrangement items has discouraged most testers from using them. Actually, when a suitable table is available, the task is not formidable. One way to score each item is to compute the r_R between the student's responses and the teacher's key, as shown on page 99, and to multiply this r_R by N, the number of things ranked. Thus the examinee whose rankings on a certain six-option item agree completely with the key secures an r_R of $+1$ and a score of $1 \times 6 = 6$ for the item. If his r_R on another such item is 0, he gets $0 \times 6 = 0$ points credit for that item. By being completely misinformed and securing an r_R of -1, he could earn $(-1) \times 6 = -6$ points. The rearrangement item is just about the only type that takes misinformation explicitly into account.

But using the formula, score = (number of things ranked) $\times r_R$, the various values of r_R are treated as if they constituted an equal-unit scale. As shown in Figure 3-10 on page 90, differences at the high end of the r scale represent greater changes in relationship than do differences of like magnitude between low r's. In an attempt to compensate for these inequalities, the writer prepared Table E-1 by means of the formula $S = $ (number of things ranked) $\times r_R$ *squared* $= Nr_R{}^2$.

TABLE E-1

ΣD^2 *Table for Scoring Rearrangement Items: Score = (Number of Things Ranked)* $\times r_R{}^2$ *(Look up* ΣD^2 *in Appropriate Column)*

Score	Number of Things Ranked (N)					Score
	3	4	5	6	7	
7					0–2	7
6				0	4–6	6
5			0	2–4	8–10	5
4		0	2	6–8	12–16	4
3	0	2	4	10–12	18–22	3
2			6–8	14–16	24–30	2
1	2	4–6	10–12	18–24	32–40	1
0	4	8–12	14–26	26–44	42–70	0
−1	6	14–16	28–30	46–52	72–80	−1
−2			32–34	54–56	82–88	−2
−3	8	18	36	58–60	90–94	−3
−4		20	38	62–64	96–100	−4
−5			40	66–68	102–104	−5
−6				70	106–108	−6
−7					110–112	−7

To score a rearrangement item, simply obtain the $\sum D^2$ (see page 99) "in your head" by comparing the student's responses with a conveniently arranged key. This $\sum D^2$ is used to enter the column of the table for the proper number of things ranked, from which the score is read directly at either the left or the right. All $\sum D^2$ values for $N = 3$ through $N = 7$ are contained in Table E-1.[1] Tables for N's higher than 7 can be prepared rather easily, but it does not seem wise to construct these and thereby encourage teachers to devise more complex and less homogeneous rearrangement items than are usually desirable.

Turn back to Table 3-17 on page 99 for two illustrations of how Table E-1 is used. There Richard's $\sum D^2$ is 40 for 6 events ranked. Looking in the "6" column of Table E-1 we find that 40 lies within the 26–44 $\sum D^2$ range, for which the score is 0. Richard

---

[1] If just 2 things are ranked, the answer will be either right or wrong, so a two-option rearrangement item is essentially a two-option multiple-choice item.

gets no points at all for his inaccurate responses to this item. Had we employed the formula $S = Nr_R$, he would have received $6(-.14) = -.84 = -1$ point.

John, the other examinee for whom ranks are listed in Table 3-17, had a ΣD^2 of 6, which lies within the 6–8 interval of Table E-1 and merits a score of 4. Had he been scored by means of the Nr_R formula, he would have obtained $.83 \times 6 = 4.98 = 5$ points. The $Nr_R{}^2$ scoring method of Table E-1 usually yields scores closer to 0 than the Nr_R procedure. It seems somewhat more defensible on statistical grounds.

ANSWERS TO QUESTIONS
IN APPENDIX B

1. **C.** $(4 + 5 + 7 + 6 + 4)/5 = 26/5 = 5.2$
2. **C.** Only two of the five options (C and E) contain measures of central tendancy; the standard deviation, quartile deviation, and range are measures of variability. Since the arithmetic mean is a function of every score in the distribution, its value would reflect "the undue influence of a few extreme salaries." Whether the highest-paid worker made $5000 or $50,000 is wholly inconsequential so far as the size of the median is concerned.
3. **D.** When arranged in numerical order, these scores are: 4, 4, **5**, 6, 7. The middle score (midscore) is 5.
4. **C.** In numerical order these scores are 44, 46, 46, **46**, 63, 68, 68; their midscore is 46, which has three numbers on each side of it. A frequency distribution of these scores with an interval of 1 is as follows:

Score	f
68	2
63	1
46	3
44	1

The median of this distribution is found by counting half the way up or down the frequency column. The total frequency is 7, and half of 7 is 3.5. Counting up through the 43.5–44.5 class uses only 1 frequency, but counting through the next (45.5–46.5) class involves $1 + 3 = 4$ frequencies, more than the 3.5 required to locate the median. Thus the median is:

$$45.5 + \left(\frac{3.5 - 1}{3}\right)(1) = 45.5 + (2.5)/3 = 45.5 + 0.83 = 46.33.$$

To check:

$$46.5 - \left(\frac{3.5 - 3}{3}\right)(1) = 46.5 - (0.5/3) = 46.5 - 0.17 = 46.33.$$

Therefore, the discrepancy between the median and the midscore in this distribution is $46.33 - 46 = 0.33$, which illustrates the fact that the midscore and the median of a distribution may have different values. Usually the difference is slight, however.

5. **B.** $19.5 - 9.5 = 10$.

6. **C.** $99.5 + \frac{1}{2}(109.5 - 99.5) = 99.5 + \frac{1}{2}(10) = 104.5$.
   To check: $109.5 - \frac{1}{2}(109.5 - 99.5) = 109.5 - 5 = 104.5$.

7. **A.** There are two essentially different reasons for grouping scores: computational (to reduce labor) and graphical (to emphasize important features of the data). One of the best discussions of the latter aspect is contained in Truman L. Kelley, *Fundamentals of Statistics* (Cambridge: Harvard University Press, 1947), Ch. 4, "Graphic Methods."

8. **A.** It is necessary to know the range *before* performing the operations set forth in Options B, C, D, and E.

9. **E.** For instance, into which of the two classes, 44–48 and 40–44, would you put a score of 44?

10. **D.** The 60th percentile is defined as the point in a distribution below which lie 60 per cent of the scores and above which lie 40 per cent of the scores.

11. **C.** $$\dfrac{7\left(\dfrac{0 + 3}{2}\right) + 3\left(\dfrac{4 + 7}{2}\right)}{10} = \dfrac{10.5 + 16.5}{10} = \dfrac{27}{10} = 2.7.$$

12. **A.** It shows the range of the middle 80 per cent of the scores in the distribution.

13. **A.** Q_3 is the 75th percentile, and the median is the 50th percentile. Twenty-five per cent of the scores lie between these two points, since $75 - 50 = 25$.

14. **E.** $$\dfrac{\sqrt{(2 + 4 + 4)\,[2(2^2) + 4(1^2) + 4(0^2)] - [2(2) + 4(1) + 4(0)]^2}}{10}$$

$$= \dfrac{\sqrt{10(12) - 8^2}}{10} = \dfrac{\sqrt{56}}{10}.$$

15. **D.** $Q = \dfrac{\text{75th percentile} - \text{25th percentile}}{2}$

$$= \dfrac{\left[5.5 - \left(\dfrac{4 - 3}{4}\right)(1)\right] - \left[1.5 + \left(\dfrac{4 - 2}{3}\right)(1)\right]}{2}$$

$$= \dfrac{(5.5 - 0.25) - (1.5 + 0.67)}{2} = \dfrac{5.25 - 2.17}{2}$$

$$= \dfrac{3.08}{2} = 1.54.$$

16. **C.** $2.5 + \left(\dfrac{8-5}{4}\right)(1) = 2.5 + 0.75 = 3.25.$

To check: $3.5 - \left(\dfrac{8-7}{4}\right)(1) = 3.5 - 0.25 = 3.25.$

17. **B.** $z = \dfrac{\text{Score} - \text{Mean}}{\text{SD}} = \dfrac{70 - 80}{20} = \dfrac{-10}{20} = -0.5.$

Therefore, this individual is half a standard deviation below the mean of the group with which he was tested.

18. **D.** $50 + 10(-0.5) = 50 - 5 = 45.$ See page 139.

19. **E.** Three tied scores of 95 occur. If there were no ties, these three places would have ranks of 4, 5, 6. Since one score of 95 is as good as another, we assign the average of 4, 5, and 6 (which is 5) to each of the three scores. Note that $4 + 5 + 6 = 15$, the same as the sum of the new ranks: $5 + 5 + 5 = 15$. Whether or not ties occur, the sum of a certain number (N) of consecutive ranks beginning with 1 will always be $[N(N + 1)]/2$. If there are 9 ranks, as in this question, their sum will be $(9 \times 10)/2 = 45$.

20. **B.** As noted above with reference to Question 19, the method of assigning to tied scores the average rank that would have occurred without ties keeps the sum of untied and tied sets of ranks of the same length identical. Since the sum is unchanged, the mean, which is the sum divided by N, the number of ranks, is also unchanged. It will always be $\dfrac{N + 1}{2}.$

21. **B.** See page 87.

22. **A.**

23. **C.** An r of 0 has the least possible predictive value. The closer to 0 r gets, *regardless of sign,* the poorer prediction becomes.

24. **E.** The r discussed in Chapter Three simply cannot be greater than $+1.00$ or -1.00, except when computational errors are made.

25. **A.** Each tally mark represents a pair of scores. There are N pairs of scores in all. The number of cells in a 12×12 scatter diagram is 144, but some of these will probably be blank, while others will have more than one tally. See Table 3-13 on page 89, which has $13 \times 13 = 169$ cells, 17 of which contain the 20 tallies. $169 - 17 = 152$ of the cells are empty.

26. **B.** The arithmetic mean is a measure of central tendency; the standard deviation is a measure of variability.

27. **C.** Q_3 is the 75th percentile; the median (Q_2) is the 50th percentile.

28. **E.** Both the mean and the standard deviation are based upon all scores in the distribution; the median and Q are both percentile measures. Also, the mean is used with the SD, while the median is used with Q. The analogy is: A certain kind of measure of central tendency is to a similar sort of measure of variability as another kind of measure of central tendency is to a similar sort of measure of variability.

29. **E.** A grouped frequency distribution has a median, whereas ungrouped measures have a midscore (the middle score, if the number of scores is odd, or the average of the two middle scores, if the number is even).

30. **D.** 50 per cent of all the measures in a distribution always lie between Q_3 and Q_1. In a normal (so-called "bell-shaped") distribution, 68 per cent of all cases lie within one standard deviation of the mean.

31. **A.** The arithmetic mean is the most reliable measure of central tendency, the mode the least reliable; the standard deviation is the most reliable measure of variability, the range the least reliable.

32. **B.** The standard deviation is a linear distance along the base line of a frequency distribution.

33. **E.** When correlation is positive, high scores on one test tend to go with high scores on the other test, while low scores tend to go with low scores. This is a direct relationship. When correlation is negative, high scores on one test go with low scores on the other, and vice versa. This is an inverse relationship.

34. **A.** Spearman derived the formula for the rank-difference coefficient of correlation; somewhat earlier Pearson had derived the basic formula for *r*.

35. **B.** Ranks denote order only. We do not know how high or low a score the person who obtained a certain rank may have had. Scores tell how many points the examinee earned—that is, the *magnitude* of his achievement.

36. **C.** "The sum of f" is the total frequency, N.

37. **D.** For example, 310–319 means 310, 311, 312, 313, 314, 315, 316, 317, 318, and 319—a total of 10 numbers. Likewise, the difference between the upper and lower "real" class limits $= (319 + 0.5) - (310 - 0.5) = 319.5 - 309.5 = 10$.

38. **A.** See above.

39. **B.** $(260 + 269)/2 = 529/2 = 264.5$. Likewise, $259.5 + (10/2) = 269.5 - (10/2) = 264.5$.

40. **B.** $13,075.0/50 = 261.5$.

41. **C.** $50/2 = 25$. $259.5 + \left(\dfrac{25 - 24}{12}\right)(10) = 259.5 + (10/12) = 260.3$. Similarly, counting from the top down as a check, $269.5 - \left(\dfrac{25 - 14}{12}\right)(10) = 269.5 - (110/12) = 269.5 - 9.2 = 260.3$.

42. **D.** The mode is the midpoint of the class having the greatest f. 12 is the largest figure in the f column, and the midpoint of its class is $(260 + 269)/2 = 264.5$.

43. **D.** $\frac{1}{4}$ of 50 is 12.5. Count up 12.5 frequencies. $239.5 + \left(\dfrac{12.5 - 5}{8}\right)(10) = 239.5 + (75/8) = 239.5 + 9.4 = 248.9$. Or, $\frac{3}{4}$ of $50 = 150/4 = 37.5$. Counting down, $249.5 - \left(\dfrac{37.5 - 37}{8}\right)(10) = 249.5 - (5/8) = 249.5 - 0.6 = 248.9$.

44. **D.** The 75th percentile is $\frac{3}{4}$ of the way from the bottom of the distribution and $\frac{1}{4}$ of the way from the top. $\frac{1}{4}$ of 50 is 12.5. Count down 12.5 frequencies. $279.5 - \left(\dfrac{12.5 - 8}{6}\right)(10) = 279.5 - (45/6) = 279.5 - 7.5 = 272.0$. To check, count up 37.5 frequencies. $269.5 + \left(\dfrac{37.5 - 36}{6}\right)(10) = 269.5 + (15/6) = 269.5 + 2.5 = 272.0$.

45. **B.** Q_3 is the 75th percentile, found to be 272.0 in Question 44, above, and Q_1 is the 25th percentile, 248.9 in Question 43. $(272.0 - 248.9)/2 = (23.1)/2 = 11.55 = 12$.

46. **C.** $\frac{1}{10}$ of 50 is 5. $239.5 + \left(\dfrac{5-5}{8}\right)(10) = 239.5$. Counting down, $\frac{9}{10}$ of 50 is 45.

$239.5 - \left(\dfrac{45-45}{2}\right)(10) = 239.5$.

47. **C.** $50 - 0.9(50) = 5$. Count down 5, or count up 45. Obviously, it is easier to count down 5. Counting up is useful as a check, though. $299.5 - \left(\dfrac{5-3}{4}\right)(10)$

$= 299.5 - (20/4) = 294.5$. Thus the 90th percentile is the midpoint of the 290–299 class: it lies exactly halfway within that class, 5 units below the upper real limit and 5 units above the lower real limit. Check by counting up: 289.5

$+ \left(\dfrac{45-43}{4}\right)(10) = 289.5 + 5 = 294.5$.

48. **B.** Use the answers to Questions 46 and 47 in solving this. $0.4(294.5 - 239.5)$
$= 0.4(55) = 22.0$.

49. **E.** $\dfrac{\sqrt{50[1(314.5)^2 + 2(304.5)^2 + \ldots + 3(214.5)^2] - (13{,}075.0)^2}}{50} = 22$.

50. **E.** $100 \left[\dfrac{3 + \left(\dfrac{231.0 - 229.5}{239.5 - 229.5}\right)(2)}{50}\right] = 100 \left[\dfrac{3 + \left(\dfrac{1.5}{10}\right)(2)}{50}\right] = 100 \left(\dfrac{3 + 0.3}{50}\right)$

$= 2(3.3) = 6.6 = 7$.

OBJECTIVES
FOR AN INTRODUCTORY UNIT
IN BEGINNING ALGEBRA,
"USING LETTERS FOR NUMBERS"[1]

Classifi-cation in Bloom's Taxonomy	Percentage weight of objective			Number of items testing this objective	Per cent of total items
k^2	20%	1. To learn the meaning of some of the important words used in algebra:		10	22
		algebraic expression	literal number		
		base	parentheses		
		coefficient	power		
		difference	product		
		equation	quotient		
		exponent	substitution		
		factor	symbol		
		formula	sum		
		inverse	term		
		like terms	unlike terms		
k	10%	2. To gain knowledge of the order of operation in evaluating expressions and of the rules for operating with zero, with parentheses, with exponents, and with like and unlike terms.		6	14

[1]This preliminary formulation of objectives for a 2–3 week introductory unit was prepared as a class exercise in a test construction course by Sister M. Jacinta Mann and Mr. Edward Sasse, experienced teachers of mathematics.

Classification in Bloom's Taxonomy	Percentage weight of objective		Number of items testing this objective	Per cent of total items
k	5%	3. To be able to recognize illustrations of the commutative principle.	1	2
k	5%	4. To comprehend the notion of using letters to stand for numbers.	1	2
c^2	20%	5. To translate mathematical symbolism into verbal statements and vice versa.	6	14
ap^2	25%	6. To learn how to add, subtract, multiply, divide, and find powers of literal numbers.	14	31
ap	10%	7. To develop facility and accuracy in substitution in and evaluation of algebraic expressions and formulas.	5	11
an^2	5%	8. To gain skill in comprehending the interrelationships among these basic algebraic ideas.	2	4
Affective domain		9. To develop a realization of the importance of algebra in the modern world. (Perhaps best evaluated by observation.)	—	—
Affective domain		10. To create a friendly attitude toward mathematics.	—	—
Totals	100%		45	100

[2] In the cognitive domain, *k*nowledge, *c*omprehension, *ap*plication, and *an*alysis.

Definitions, Instructional Procedures, and Evaluation

1. TO LEARN THE MEANING OF SOME OF THE IMPORTANT WORDS USED IN ALGEBRA.

How Taught: A vocabulary list is compiled day by day (left on front board) as the new words arise. The student is, therefore, conscious of what new words he is expected to know and what their correct spelling and syllabication are. Continual review is interspersed with class work where the words arise.

Evaluation: 1. unit test
2. quizzes
3. oral questioning in continual review discussions mentioned above
4. observing the student's actual use of these words, i.e., when the student asks about "the sign of the second term" instead of pointing to it and asking "what's the sign supposed to be?"

2. TO GAIN KNOWLEDGE OF THE ORDER OF OPERATION IN EVALUATING EXPRESSIONS AND OF THE RULES FOR OPERATING WITH ZERO, WITH PARENTHESES, AND WITH LIKE AND UNLIKE TERMS.

How Taught: As these rules arise and are explained and illustrated, the students add the names of the rules next to their vocabulary list. They are required then to study them so that in oral drill they can repeat the various rules *in their own words.* This all takes place, of course, simultaneously with learning to apply the rules in problems.

Evaluation: 1. unit test
2. quizzes
3. oral drill in class

3. TO BE ABLE TO RECOGNIZE ILLUSTRATIONS OF THE COMMUTATIVE PRINCIPLE.

How Taught: As are the vocabulary words. It could be added to that list.

Evaluation: 1. unit test
2. quizzes
3. class discussion with oral questioning

4. TO COMPREHEND THE NOTION OF USING LETTERS FOR NUMBERS.

How Taught: A class discussion of symbolization in general should precede the particular use of it in algebra. Then the idea must permeate all future discussions until it is felt that every child is familiar and friendly with the xyz's. There are available some excellent audio-visual aids in this area.

Evaluation: 1. unit test (difficult to form questions)
2. oral discussion

5. TO TRANSLATE MATHEMATICAL SYMBOLISM INTO VERBAL STATEMENTS AND VICE VERSA.

How Taught: There is no substitute for oral and written drill in this matter. The drill material can be composed of quite interesting and meaningful examples.

Evaluation: 1. unit test
2. quizzes
3. oral and board drill

6. TO LEARN HOW TO ADD, SUBTRACT, MULTIPLY, DIVIDE, AND FIND POWERS OF LITERAL NUMBERS.

How Taught: These skills are taught simultaneously with the rules mentioned in Objective 2. There needs to be much drill on the various skills and the combinations of them. This drill is achieved by way of blackboard work, oral work, and written homework assignments. The "spelling bee" type of game may be useful to employ here. Ninth graders usually still have sufficient simplicity to enjoy them.

Evaluation: 1. unit test
2. quizzes
3. oral drill and homework assignments

7. TO DEVELOP FACILITY AND ACCURACY IN SUBSTITUTION IN AND EVALUATION OF ALGEBRAIC EXPRESSIONS AND FORMULAS.

How Taught: Same as 6; in this case the type of problem lends itself to composition of interesting drill material.

8. TO GAIN SKILL IN COMPREHENDING THE INTERRELATIONSHIPS AMONG THESE BASIC ALGEBRAIC IDEAS.

How Taught: As each new term is taught, it should be related to the others in the list, always encouraging the pupil to *discover* the relationship himself.

Evaluation: Same as Objective 2

9. TO DEVELOP A REALIZATION OF THE IMPORTANCE OF ALGEBRA IN THE MODERN WORLD.

10. TO CREATE A FRIENDLY ATTITUDE TOWARD MATHEMATICS.

How Taught: These two objectives cannot be taught for *directly* (i.e., effectively so) but must be kept in mind through every activity. The teacher must have achieved these objectives in his own "self," so that they will "rub off" on the students. Many little surprise opportunities will arise for the alert teacher to utilize.

Bulletin boards planned by students and teacher together, films on the subject, and field trips to local industries can aid in the achievement of these objectives.

Evaluation: 1. observation of individuals in class and out of class
2. discussion with the study hall teacher and parents

At the end of the unit, attainment of Objectives 1–8 was tested by items at appropriate levels of Bloom's *Taxonomy*.

ALGEBRA APTITUDE TEST
RAW SCORES
OF 211 EIGHTH GRADERS,
CONVERTED
TO STA-ELEVEN SCORES[1]

Raw-Score Interval	Raw-Score Frequencies	Sta-Eleven Score	Actual Sta-Eleven Frequencies	Theoretical Sta-Eleven Frequencies	$\dfrac{(Actual - Theoretical)^2}{Theoretical}$
59	4	10	4	2.57	0.80
58	2				
57	4	9	6	5.89	0.002
56	5				
55	11	8	16	13.82	0.34
54	8				
53	10				
52	12	7	30	25.53	0.78
51	15				
50	9				
49	9	6	33	36.86	0.40
48	12				
47	10				
46	8				
45	9	5	39	41.65	0.17
44	6				
43	9				
42	4				
41	4				
40	5				
39	6	4	34	36.86	0.22

[1] Mr. Neal R. Gamsky furnished these raw scores, which he had converted to sta-eleven scores by the procedure on pages 81–84.

Raw-Score Interval	Raw-Score Frequencies	Sta-Eleven Score	Actual Sta-Eleven Frequencies	Theoretical Sta-Eleven Frequencies	$\dfrac{(Actual - Theoretical)^2}{Theoretical}$
38	5				
37	4				
36	1				
35	1				
34	5				
33	4				
32	2				
31	2				
30	1	3	25	25.53	0.01
29	3				
28	4				
27	–				
26					
25	1				
24	–				
23	1				
22	3				
21	2				
20	1	2	15	13.82	0.10
19	3				
18	3	1	6	5.89	0.002
17	2				
16	–				
15	–				
14	–				
13	1	0	3	2.57	0.07
Sums	211		211	210.99	

The mean of these 211 sta-eleven scores is $[4(10) + 6(9) + \cdots + 3(0)]/211 = 1072/211 = 5.08$, fairly close to the expected value, 5.

The variance of the sta-elevens is $\{211[4(10^2) + 6(9^2) + \cdots + 3(0^2)] - 1072^2\}/211^2 = [211(6378) - (1072)(1072)]/211^2 = 196,574/44,521 = 4.4153$. $\sqrt{4.4153} = 2.1$, fairly close to the expected value for the standard deviation, 2.

Notice that the 211 *raw* scores are skewed negatively—that is, the test was too easy (had too little ceiling) for these eighth graders. The sta-eleven scores are more symmetrical (i.e., less skewed) than the raw scores. In the right-hand column of the table you will note that the "fit" of the actual sta-eleven scores to the desired ones is best for Sta-elevens 9 and 1 (squared discrepancy divided by desired frequency is only 0.002) and worst for Sta-elevens 10 and 7 (0.80 and 0.78, respectively). Even then, however, the actual frequency for Sta-eleven 10 is only 1 more than the best possible actual value, 2.57 rounded off to 3, that it could have, and for Sta-eleven 7 the actual frequency, 30, is only 4 more than its best possible actual value, 26. We have succeeded rather well in "unskewing" the initially skewed scores by "squeezing" them at the top and "stretching" them at the bottom.

CONVERTING PERCENTILE RANKS TO z-SCORES, OR z-SCORES TO PERCENTILE RANKS, IN A NORMAL DISTRIBUTION

Percentile Rank	z	Percentile Rank	z
99	2.3263	73	.6128
98	2.0537	72	.5828
97	1.8808	71	.5534
96	1.7507	70	.5244
95	1.6449	69	.4959
94	1.5548	68	.4677
93	1.4758	67	.4399
92	1.4051	66	.4125
91	1.3408	65	.3853
90	1.2816	64	.3585
89	1.2265	63	.3319
88	1.1750	62	.3055
87	1.1264	61	.2793
86	1.0803	60	.2533
85	1.0364	59	.2275
84	.9945	58	.2019
83	.9542	57	.1764
82	.9154	56	.1510
81	.8779	55	.1257
80	.8416	54	.1004
79	.8064	53	.0753
78	.7722	52	.0502
77	.7388	51	.0251
76	.7063	50	.0000
75	.6745	49	−.0251
74	.6433		etc.

PUBLISHERS
OF STANDARDIZED TESTS

The following list includes every test company for whom five or more entries are indexed on pages 1215–1221 of Oscar K. Buros, ed., *The Fifth Mental Measurements Yearbook*. Highland Park, New Jersey: Gryphon Press, 1959.

Acorn Publishing Co., Inc., Rockville Centre, Long Island, New York

Australian Council for Educational Research, 369 Lonsdale Street, Melbourne C.1, Victoria, Australia

Bureau of Educational Measurements, Kansas State Teachers College, Emporia, Kansas

Bureau of Publications, Teachers College, Columbia University, New York 27, New York

California Test Bureau, Del Monte Research Park, Monterey, California

College Entrance Examination Board, 475 Riverside Drive, New York 27, New York

Consulting Psychologists Press, Inc., 270 Town and Country Village, Palo Alto, California

Educational Records Bureau, 21 Audubon Avenue, New York 32, New York

Educational Test Bureau, 720 Washington Avenue, S.E., Minneapolis, Minnesota

Educational Testing Service, Princeton, New Jersey

Robert Gibson and Sons, Ltd., 45 Queen St., Glasgow, Scotland

C. A. Gregory Co., 345 Calhoun St., Cincinnati 19, Ohio

Grune and Stratton, Inc., 381 Fourth Ave., New York 16, New York

Guidance Centre, Ontario College of Education, University of Toronto, 371 Bloor St., W., Toronto 5, Ontario, Canada

Harcourt, Brace and World, Inc., 757 Third Ave., New York 17, New York

George G. Harrap and Co., Ltd., 182 High Holborn, London W. C. 1, England

Houghton Mifflin Co., 2 Park St., Boston 7, Massachusetts

Institute for Personality and Ability Testing, 1602 Coronado Dr., Champaign, Illinois

National Bureau of Educational and Social Research, Department of Education, Arts, and Science, Pretoria, Union of South Africa

National Foundation for Educational Research in England and Wales, 79 Wimpole St., London W. 1, England
National League of Nursing Education, Inc., 2 Park Avenue, New York 16, New York
Newnes Educational Publishing Company, Ltd., Tower House, 8–11 Southampton St., Strand, London W. C. 2, England
Ohio Scholarship Tests, Department of Education, State of Ohio, Columbus 15, Ohio
Oliver and Boyd, Ltd., Tweeddale Court, High Street, Edinburgh 1, Scotland
Psychological Corporation, 304 East 45th St., New York 17, New York
Psychometric Affiliates, Box 1625, Chicago 90, Illinois
Public Personnel Association, 1313 East 60th St., Chicago 37, Illinois
Public School Publishing Company, 345 Calhoun St., Cincinnati 19, Ohio
Scholastic Testing Service, Inc., 3774 West Devon Ave., Chicago 45, Illinois
Science Research Associates, Inc., 259 East Erie St., Chicago 11, Illinois
Sheridan Supply Co., P. O. Box 837, Beverly Hills, California
Steck Co., Austin 1, Texas
C. H. Stoelting Co., 424 North Homan Ave., Chicago 24, Illinois
University Book Store, 360 State St., West Lafayette, Indiana
University of London Press, Ltd., Little Paul's House, Warwick Square, London E. C. 4, England
University of Minnesota Press, Minneapolis 14, Minnesota
Veterans' Testing Service, American Council on Education, 6018 Ingleside Ave., Chicago 37, Illinois
Western Psychological Services, 10655 Santa Monica Blvd., Los Angeles 25, California

NAME INDEX

SUBJECT INDEX